Trout Streams
and Hatches
of Pennsylvania

OTHER BOOKS BY CHARLES R. MECK

Fishing Small Streams with a Fly Rod

Great Rivers, Great Hatches *(with Greg Hoover)*

Meeting and Fishing the Hatches

Patterns, Hatches, Tactics, and Trout

Mid-Atlantic Trout Streams and Their Hatches

Arizona Trout Streams and Their Hatches
(with John Rohmer)

Trout Streams and Hatches of Pennsylvania

Charles R. Meck

A Complete Fly-Fishing
Guide to 140 Streams

3RD EDITION
A Backcountry Guide
Woodstock, Vermont

An Invitation to the Reader

With time, access points may change, and road numbers, signs, and landmarks referred to in this book may be altered. If you find that such changes have occurred near the streams described in this book, please let the author and publisher know, so that corrections may be made in future editions. Other comments and suggestions are also welcome. Address all correspondence to:

Fishing Editor, The Countryman Press, P.O. Box 748, Woodstock, VT 05091

Library of Congress Cataloging-in-Publication Data
Meck, Charles R.
    Trout Streams and Hatches of Pennsylvania / Charles R. Meck. —3rd ed.
        p.   cm.
    Rev. ed. of: Pennsylvania trout streams and their hatches. 2nd ed., rev. and expanded. © 1993.
    ISBN 0-88150-453-X
    1. Trout fishing—Pennsylvania—Guidebooks. 2. Fly fishing—Pennsylvania—Guidebooks. 3. Aquatic insects—Pennsylvania. 4. Pennsylvania—Guidebooks. I. Meck, Charles R. Pennsylvania trout streams and their hatches. II. Title.
SH688.U6M43 1999
799.1'757'09748—dc21   98-53006
                                                            CIP

Published by Backcountry Guides, a division of
The Countryman Press, P.O. Box 748, Woodstock, VT 05091

Distributed by W. W. Norton & Company, Inc., 500 Fifth Avenue, New York, NY 10110

Text and cover design by Joanna Bodenweber
Cover photo by George Robinson/f-STOP Pictures, Honesdale, PA
Interior photos by the author unless credited otherwise
Maps by Dick Widhu and Paul Woodward,
© 1999 The Countryman Press

Printed in the United States of America

10 9 8 7 6 5 4 3 2 1

I have dedicated this third edition of *Trout Streams of Pennsylvania* to **Russ Mowry** of Latrobe, Pennsylvania. Once in a lifetime you come across a man like Russ. In my 50 years of fly-fishing I have never met a more generous person, nor a more gifted fly-tier. It was indeed my great pleasure to have fished with Russ for more than 20 years. Russ recently passed away and as a tribute to him, I asked some of his friends to write a few paragraphs about him.

"I knew Russ Mowry for almost 40 years. I wish it could have been longer. Russ was a fly-fishing and -tying mentor; always willing to share his ideas and his famous parachute dry flies with friends and strangers alike. He was one of those people you just enjoyed sharing time with—on and off the water. He always had a joke to tell and commented positively about everyone. People like Russ all end up on that blue-ribbon trout stream in the sky."

—Mike O'Brien, editor, *Mid Atlantic Fly Fishing Guide* magazine

"There probably aren't too many readers of this book who don't know already that Russ was one heck of a fly-tier—though a few might not know how generous he was with the wonderful flies that he tied. Often I watched him open his truck, dig his big red duffel bag out—the one with the two zillion flies—and tell perfect strangers, 'There you go, help yourself to anything that looks good to you,' then walk away and let them have what they wanted. Offering the contents of that bag to fly-fishers always seemed to me like setting out an open jar of honey before a bear. But old Russ sincerely meant 'help yourself,' and always seemed a little hurt at the polite guys who really couldn't."

—Chuck Robbins, author of *Odyssey at Limestone Creek*

"Russ had sort of an easygoing demeanor, and a laid-back sense of humor. Several years ago, on a trip to New Zealand, Russ was rigging up for his first day on the stream. He was tying on his 'signature fly,' a parachute Adams. (Few people could tie them as well, and nobody could tie them better.) Teasingly, the guide said, 'I don't think that pattern will work down here.' Russ replied, 'Well, I'm going to give it a go anyway on this trout that is sipping below the riffle.' Of course in short order Russ caught and released a plump 18-inch rainbow, whereupon he wryly said, 'I knew I could catch fish on these flies down here, because I tied them special for the trip.' 'What did you do that was different?' the guide asked. 'I wound the hackle counterclockwise to compensate for being south of the equator,' Russ replied. Tight lines, Russ. You are missed."

—Dale Johnson, friend

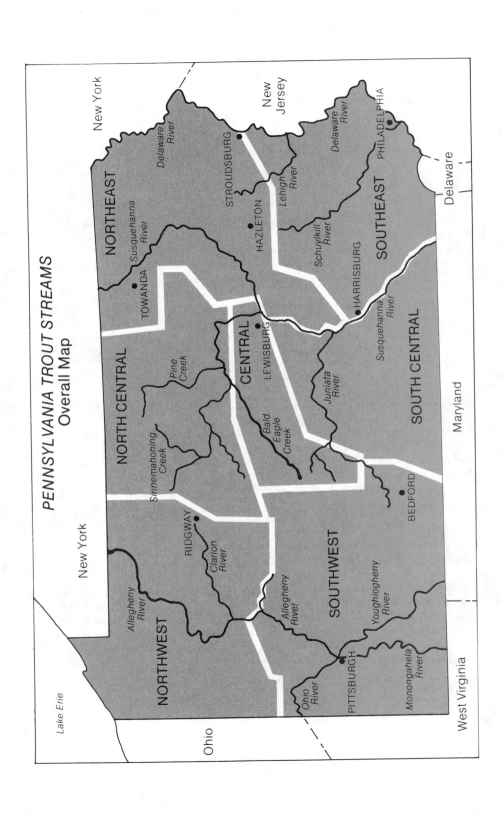

PENNSYLVANIA TROUT STREAMS
Overall Map

Contents

Acknowledgments   9

I | Introduction to Pennsylvania Streams and Rivers   13

2 | Introduction to the Hatches of Pennsylvania   17

3 | Streams of Northeastern Pennsylvania   49
TOMS CREEK **49** • LACKAWANNA RIVER **52** • TOBYHANNA CREEK **57** • FISHING CREEK (COLUMBIA COUNTY) **59** • BOWMAN CREEK **63** • DELAWARE RIVER **66** CLARKS CREEK **70** • LACKAWAXEN RIVER **73** • HAYES CREEK **74** • HICKORY RUN **75** • LEHIGH RIVER **76** • MEHOOPANY CREEK **78** • TOWANDA CREEK **79** MUD RUN **80** • POHOPOCO CREEK **81** • BRODHEAD CREEK **83**   BIG BUSHKILL CREEK **85** • DYBERRY CREEK **87**

4 | Streams of Southeastern Pennsylvania   89
EAST BRANCH, BRANDYWINE CREEK **90** • PICKERING CREEK **94** • SAUCON CREEK **96** • LITTLE SCHUYLKILL RIVER **98** • BUSHKILL CREEK **102** • WEST VALLEY CREEK **104** • QUITTAPAHILLA CREEK **105** • VALLEY CREEK **107** • TULPEHOCKEN CREEK **110** • RIDLEY CREEK **114** • FRENCH CREEK **115** • OCTORARO CREEK **117** DONEGAL CREEK **119** • CEDAR CREEK **120** • LITTLE LEHIGH CREEK **120** MONOCACY CREEK **123**

5 | Streams of North-Central Pennsylvania   127
SINNEMAHONING PORTAGE CREEK **127** • LYMAN RUN **129** • MILL CREEK **130** GRAYS RUN **132** • LARRYS CREEK **133** • FIRST FORK, SINNEMAHONING CREEK **134** EAST FORK, SINNEMAHONING CREEK **137** • LOYALSOCK CREEK **138** • HOAGLAND BRANCH **142** • ELK CREEK (SULLIVAN COUNTY) **144** • MUNCY CREEK **145** CEDAR RUN **146** • LITTLE PINE CREEK **148** • PINE CREEK **151** • WEST BRANCH, PINE CREEK **158** • LYCOMING CREEK **159** • SLATE RUN **161** • KETTLE CREEK **165** CROSS FORK CREEK **169** • HAMMERSLEY RUN (FORK) **171** • YOUNG WOMANS CREEK **172** • STONY FORK **174** • OSWAYO CREEK **175** • ALLEGHENY RIVER **177** GENESEE FORKS **180** • NINEMILE RUN **181** • DRIFTWOOD BRANCH, SINNEMA-HONING CREEK **182**

6 | Streams of Central Pennsylvania 185
PINE CREEK 185 • LITTLE JUNIATA RIVER 189 • ELK CREEK 193 • SPRING
CREEK 195 • PENNS CREEK 199 • BALD EAGLE CREEK (JULIAN) 204 • LOWER
BALD EAGLE CREEK (BELOW MILESBURG) 208 • BALD EAGLE CREEK (TYRONE) 210
BIG FILL RUN 212 • VANSCOYOC RUN 214 • WHITE DEER CREEK 214 • FISHING
CREEK 216 • PINEY CREEK 220 • CLOVER CREEK 221 • SPRUCE CREEK 222
SIXMILE RUN 226 • LOGAN BRANCH 228 • TIPTON RUN 229 • BELL GAP
RUN 229 • CANOE CREEK 231

7 | Streams of South-Central Pennsylvania 235
LAUREL RUN 235 • GREEN SPRING CREEK 237 • MIDDLE SPRING CREEK 240
LOST CREEK 241 • LITTLE TONOLOWAY CREEK 242 • WILLOW RUN 244 • LETORT
SPRING RUN 245 • BIG SPRING RUN (CREEK) 247 • YELLOW BREECHES CREEK 249
FALLING SPRING BRANCH 252 • MUDDY CREEK 256 • CODORUS CREEK 257
KISHACOQUILLAS CREEK 261 • HONEY CREEK 263 • TEA CREEK 265 • EAST
LICKING CREEK 266 • BIG COVE CREEK 267 • BLACKLOG CREEK 270 • STANDING
STONE CREEK 272

8 | Streams of Northwestern Pennsylvania 273
WEST BRANCH, TUNUNGWANT CREEK 273 • EAST BRANCH, TUNUNGWANT
CREEK 276 • THOMPSON CREEK 277 • CALDWELL CREEK 279 • SUGAR CREEK 281
PINE CREEK 283 • OIL CREEK 283 • SLIPPERY ROCK CREEK 287 • NESHANNOCK
CREEK 289 • COOL SPRING CREEK 291 • LITTLE SANDY CREEK 291 • ALLEGHENY
RIVER (BELOW KINZUA DAM) 293 • NORTH FORK, RED BANK CREEK 295 • CLARION
RIVER 297 • SPRING CREEK 301 • EAST BRANCH, CLARION RIVER 302 • WEST
BRANCH, CLARION RIVER 303 • BROKENSTRAW CREEK 304 • KINZUA CREEK 305
EAST BRANCH, MAHONING CREEK 306 • TIONESTA CREEK 309 • EAST HICKORY
CREEK 310

9 | Streams of Southwestern Pennsylvania 313
BUFFALO CREEK 314 • YELLOW CREEK (INDIANA COUNTY) 318 • SOUTH BRANCH,
TWO LICK CREEK 319 • CHEST CREEK 322 • BOBS CREEK 325 • COXES CREEK 327
CASSELMAN RIVER 328 • STONYCREEK RIVER 331 • LOYALHANNA CREEK 334
LAUREL HILL CREEK 336 • YOUGHIOGHENY RIVER 338 • LITTLE MAHONING
CREEK 342 • YELLOW CREEK (BEDFORD COUNTY) 344 • COVE CREEK 347 • WILLS
CREEK 348 • RAYSTOWN BRANCH, JUNIATA RIVER 350 • BRUSH CREEK 351

10 | Tying Patterns for Pennsylvania's Hatches 353

11 | Some Proposals for Better Fishing on Pennsylvania Streams 375

Appendix: Hatch Charts 384
Index 403

ACKNOWLEDGMENTS

How do you get an idea for a book? Often the beginning is a combination
of sources culminating in a manuscript. *Trout Streams and Hatches of
Pennsylvania* (which was titled *Pennsylvania Trout Streams* in its first two
editions) is a direct result of a request by John Randolph, editor and publisher of the highly regarded *Fly Fisherman* magazine. Several years ago
John asked me to develop a story about Pennsylvania's top 10 streams for
a special edition of his magazine. As a result of that article, and subse-
quent requests by the Pennsylvania Trout Unlimited Council to present a
talk on the streams of the Commonwealth, I developed the present manuscript. Thanks to John for giving me the opportunity to write for his magazine, and to the state TU Council.

Many others have assisted in the project. In southwestern
Pennsylvania Russ Mowry, Ken Igo, and Tim Shaffer helped with the
hatches and took time to reacquaint me with trout streams I hadn't fished
for 20 years. Ken furnished the hatches for Loyalhanna Creek. Bob Foor of
Everett, Carl Dodson of Martinsburg, and Nelson Hamel of Altoona aided
on the hatches of Yellow Creek. The late Bob Davis of Big Run supplied
some of the hatches on Little Mahoning Creek. Nate Rascona and Ken
Sarver of Somerset, John Sanner of Rockwood, and Tim Shaffer of Latrobe
helped with the hatches on Laurel Hill. Art Gusbar of Friedens and Pat
Docherty of the US Army Corps of Engineers supplied data on the
Youghiogheny; Bob Beck of Altoona helped with Canoe Creek; Danny
Deters and Ed Gunnett, both of Williamsburg, assisted with Piney and
Clover Creeks. Tony Stair and Bob Bryant of Hyndman guided me on
Brush Creek and Wills Creek. Thanks also to Howard Bach of the Western
Pennsylvania Conservancy for helping me locate fly-fishermen in the
southwestern area.

In north-central Pennsylvania Jack Mickievicz helped tremendously
with the hatches and background information on Genesee Forks, Ninemile
Run, and the upper end of Pine Creek. Pete Ryan and Vic Howard of
Coudersport assisted with the hatches and background on the Allegheny
River, and Stewart Dickerson of Shinglehouse assisted with the hatches on

Oswayo Creek. Tom Finkbiner and Mike O'Brien helped with the hatches on Pine Creek, Slate Run, and Cedar Run. Dennis Renninger of Hillsgrove and John Plowman of Mechanicsburg helped with the history and hatches on Elk Creek, Hoagland Branch, and Loyalsock Creek. Curt Thompson of Wharton assisted with First Fork and East Fork. Rich Meyers of Pottstown helped with the hatches on Young Womans Creek and Phil Baldacchino with the hatches and history on Kettle Creek, Cross Fork Creek, and Hammersley Fork. Jack Busch of Erie, Don Foltz of Lincolnville, Marshall Young of Union City, Tony Palumbo of Hermitage, Ted Fauceglia of Sharpsville, the late Bob Davis of Big Run, and Tom Greenlee of Tionesta assisted with hatch information and stream background for northwestern streams. John Salandra of Brockway enlisted some of the better-known fly-fishermen in the Brockway area, including Mike Veltri, Hank and John Foradora, Brent Rearick, Dick Koval, and Blackie Veltri.

In the southeast Joe Petrella of Downingtown, Wayne Poppich of King of Prussia, Barry Staats of Media, and Mary Kuss of Haverford assisted in the suburban streams around Philadelphia. Dick Henry and Ellwood Gettle of Lebanon, and Larry Gasser of Fleetwood helped with orientation and the hatches on the Tulpehocken. Thanks to Frank Plucinsky of the Tulpehocken Trout Unlimited chapter for use of his emergence chart. Desmond Kahn, Jim Leonard, Ken Depoe, and Don Whitesel helped on Lancaster County streams. Joe Kohler of Allentown assisted with the hatches on Little Lehigh, Cedar, and Monocacy Creeks.

In the south-central region Jim Gilson of Port Royal, Reed Gray and Dennis Sieber of Lewistown, and Steve Bullich of Reedsville helped tremendously with Honey, Tea, Kishacoquillas, and East Licking Creeks. Gene Macri gave me hatches and other data for Falling Spring Branch, Big Spring Run, and Yellow Breeches Creek. Dan Meckley, John Taylor, and Brian Berger assisted with York County streams. Ed Lehman, Steve Frey, and John Fetterhoff aided in the Fulton County area. Phil Stewart helped with Blacklog and Standing Stone Creeks.

In the northeast Bob Dibble of Wyalusing helped on the Mehoopany, and Don Baylor on the Brodhead and Big Bushkill. Mike Marinelli and Jay Kapolka assisted with the Pohopoco and Mud Run. Bob Sentiwany of White Haven helped in identifying hatches on Hickory Run, Hayes Creek, the Lehigh River, and the Delaware River. Rick Eck of Honesdale helped with the hatches on the Dyberry. Barry and Cathy Beck of Berwick helped with Fishing Creek. John Churnetski and Lee Eckert of the Wyoming Valley area helped with the hatches on the Lackawaxen.

Many additional people assisted me on the second edition. On south-western streams like Coxes Creek and the Casselman River, Chuck Furimsky of Rockwood spent several days with me showing me the waters. Len Lichvar of Stoystown and Randy Buchanan of Johnstown helped me with the Stonycreek River. Tom Wolfe of Portage spent a day fly-fishing with me on Bobs Creek.

In the northeast Don Baylor of Stroudsburg and Bob Stevens of Bartonsville assisted on the Tobyhanna Creek. Jim Misuira of Blakely and Mike Stevens of Dalton helped with the Lackawanna River near Scranton.

On north-central streams Jack Mickievicz of Quiggleville helped with the West Branch, Pine Creek, and Lyman Run, Tom Dewey of Coudersport assisted with Mill Creek, and Don Bastian of Cogan Station with Larrys Creek.

In the southeast Jim Leonard of Claymont, Delaware, and Des Kahn of Newark, Delaware, helped with West Valley Creek. Dick Henry fished with me on the Quittapahilla, and Rich Keesler of Easton on the Bushkill.

For this third edition Jan Witwer of Coburn spent time with me on Pine Creek in central Pennsylvania. Jim Gilson of Port Royal and Bob Lynn of McConnellsburg spent time with me on Willow Run and Little Tonoloway Creek, respectively. Thanks also to Bill Hubler of Port Royal, who gave me information on Lost Creek. Al Gretz gave me names of Trout Unlimited members throughout the state who might help with some of the hatches. Alvin Grove of State College also furnished some names.

In the third edition Robert Budd of Hollidaysburg rewrote the section on the Little Juniata River. Kurt Thomas helped tremendously sorting out the pros and cons of the Clarion River. Thanks also to my wife, Shirley, for typing many of the changes. Thanks to the Cortland Line Company and Lora Hall for their fine cooperation in supplying high-quality fly-line.

Thanks also to Ralph Frankenberger for developing photographs for the book; to Albert Nakpil of Penn State University, who aided me countless times with word processing; to Rod Bond of Harrisburg, who made sketches of the maps; and to the Pennsylvania Fish Commission for its help. Edward Miller, Edward Manhart, and Richard Snyder of the commission gave considerable assistance. Finally, thanks to Carol Kersavage for her untiring effort in editing the manuscript.

Introduction to Pennsylvania Streams and Rivers

Pennsylvania has much to offer fly-fishermen, whether they are experts or novices. Picturesque mountain streams; scenic, uncluttered, secluded valleys; limestone springs teeming with brook, brown, and rainbow trout—Pennsylvania has them all.

You don't have to travel far to enjoy excellent trout fishing in our state. There are fantastic streams near some of Pennsylvania's major cities. Little Lehigh and Cedar Creeks flow through Allentown; the Tulpehocken is near Reading, French Creek near Phoenixville, and Valley Creek near Philadelphia; Clark, Stony, and Fishing Creeks are found just north of Harrisburg; Clover Creek and the Little Juniata River are near Altoona; the Loyalhanna is not far from Pittsburgh; and on and on.

Pennsylvania boasts 10,000 miles of trout streams classified as either wild-trout or stocked waters. They range from 2- or 3-foot-wide streams to large rivers like the Delaware, Youghiogheny, and Clarion. Many display a diversity both in the insect life and the number of trout they contain. Many of the more fertile waters are the highly alkaline limestone streams common in central Pennsylvania near State College, Altoona, and Lewistown. But other streams with a high degree of alkalinity can be found in the Lock Haven area, around Allentown, Chambersburg, Lebanon, Carlisle, and McConnellsburg. And don't exclude Pennsylvania's north-central streams from your fly-fishing plans. Many of these large streams, most flowing from north to south, contain plenty of early and midseason hatches and teem with trout eager to take the proper imitation.

You'll find special regulations on more than 100 miles of the streams and rivers in Pennsylvania. The Pennsylvania Fish Commission has enhanced dozens of streams by earmarking specific areas of them with these special rules. You'll see these special regulations, where they apply, highlighted at the beginning of the stream descriptions in chapters 3 through 9. Special regulations include catch-and-release, fly-fishing only, trophy trout, and delayed harvest. All are designed to maintain an optimum trout population in the regulated area. A delayed-harvest area, for example, by setting a late opening date for trout season, assures the angler that the section will hold a good supply of trout until the middle of June. In trophy-trout waters, only fish over 14 inches may be taken—and in very limited numbers. Regulations constantly change; make certain you check the latest regulations in the *Summary of Fishing Regulations and Laws* booklet you receive when you buy your fishing license.

The streams and rivers of Pennsylvania have an abundance of insect activity; hatches appear on the waters throughout much of the fishing season. Some years you can begin the season with a hatch like the quill gordon, blue quill, or Hendrickson in April, and end the season in October with a slate drake or blue dun hatch. Between the beginning and ending days appear many abundant, spectacular hatches of mayflies, stoneflies, caddisflies, crane flies, midges, as well as ants and other assorted insects straying too near the water. Hatches appear and many trout rise even in July and August on streams abandoned by fishermen who thought the waters to be void of fish.

In the upcoming chapters we'll explore much of the aquatic life and the streams and rivers of Pennsylvania. For it is with precise knowledge of the hatches on specific waters that novice and expert anglers can enjoy the rewards of a more complete sport—fishing on streams when a hatch of insects appears and being adequately prepared with the proper imitation. We'll examine suitable patterns—whether they are wet flies, dry flies, or nymphs—for the major hatches on Pennsylvania streams.

For all its riches in water, fish, and insects, however, Pennsylvania has problems. An immediate concern for all the Commonwealth's citizens is the number of miles of posted trout waters here. Just 20 years ago Penns Creek was open anywhere below PA 45. Now much of the property below Spring Mills and above Coburn is posted. Once the state declared some of its waters wild-trout zones some property owners closed fishing on their land. Big Fill in Blair County was open to public fishing over its entire length just 10 years ago. Now some of the property just above Centre County's Bald Eagle is posted against trespassing.

There's much you can do to prevent further reductions in the number of stream miles available to you. Enjoy your stay on the stream, but also respect the property owner's rights. Take everything home that you brought to the stream. Patrol the stream, and keep it clean. Several years ago a friend brought his son along on a trip with me to the Falling Springs near Chambersburg. When we went back to the car to grab a sandwich, the boy tossed his bag near the stream. I asked him to pick it up and place it in a nearby container.

How many streams have you seen with scars of recent fishermen? Vince Gigliotti and Terry Carlsen regularly take garbage bags with them so they can collect debris left behind by careless sportsmen. We all should be prepared to do the same. Annually, just before Christmas, I take gifts to some of the farmers and landowners who have allowed me to hunt on their land and fish on their water. You'd be surprised how much goodwill these small gifts create.

Let's look at the chapters in the book and how they're organized. Chapter 2 examines many of the mayflies, caddisflies, and stoneflies found on the streams of the Commonwealth. Unless and until you become familiar with these insects, when they appear, and on what streams, you probably won't be prepared to fish the great hatches of Pennsylvania. Chapters 3 through 9 explore in detail some of the better streams and rivers of Pennsylvania, arranged by region. Some of these regions overlap, but the index will help direct you to specific waters.

Maybe I've omitted some of your favorite streams from the book. It's impossible to know all the hatches and sections of all the streams and rivers of the Commonwealth. To include them all would require several volumes, and several decades. I hope that those streams I have included will provide you with many hours of good fly-fishing and many hatches successfully matched. If you're looking for some of the lesser-known streams, read *Mid Atlantic Trout Streams and Their Hatches*.

Some of the streams and rivers I describe may have declined or improved in trout or insect populations since this book was completed. A few years ago Spruce Creek received a shot of liquid manure that killed thousands of trout in the stream for miles. Almost annually someone or something deposits contaminants in the Little Juniata River. On some occasions contamination follows a train spill, on others a truck accident, and too often it's intentional. As Pennsylvanians and as avid fishermen we must guard our natural resources jealously so that not only we, but also future generations, can enjoy the solitude and rewards of pure water.

Chapter 10 suggests some tying descriptions to help you match many of the hatches and spinner falls found on Pennsylvania streams. Whether you tie or buy your imitations, this part of the book will be useful.

Chapter 11 includes a wish list of suggestions that can make Pennsylvania streams and Pennsylvania trout fishing even better. Why not reduce the limit of trout killed per day? Chapter 11 examines this question. Why should you join a local chapter of Trout Unlimited, Federation of Fly Fishermen, or the Izaak Walton League? Chapter 11 tells you why.

You'll find new streams and rivers included in this third edition. These include Chest Creek in Cambria County, East and West Branches of

Tunungwant Creek in McKean County, Sinnemahoning Portage Creek in Cameron County, Yellow and Two Lick Creeks in Indiana County, Middle Spring and Green Spring Creeks in Cumberland County, Toms Creek in Pike County, Saucon Creek in Northampton County, Pickering Creek in Chester County, and Laurel Run in Huntingdon County.

In addition, I have made changes to 16 waters previously listed. In many of these I have added or deleted hatches for streams, or recognized new regulations, new local people, or new concerns.

Ratings of Pennsylvania Trout Streams

How does one stream rate against another? Which are Pennsylvania's finest streams? What makes a trout stream one of the best? In the RATING heading at the beginning of each stream, I have assigned one, two, three, or four stars to each stream. Those with four stars are the very best in the state; they, and most of the three-star streams, hold some spectacular hatches, as well as good populations of streambred and/or holdover trout. What about the setting—is it along a busy highway? How about fishing pressure—will you see a lot of anglers? These factors and more also go into the rating system. Here is how I've defined the four categories:

> ✴ Not great, but worth getting your feet wet
> ✴✴ Holds some good hatches, stocked trout, and possibly some holdover trout
> ✴✴✴ Holds several great hatches and lots of native trout
> ✴✴✴✴ The best there is

2 | Introduction to the Hatches of Pennsylvania

It's the opening of another trout season in Pennsylvania. If you already fly-fish, are you prepared for the great hatches on many of our state's streams? Do you know where and when these hatches appear? Do you know what imitations match what hatches? How about those of you who are just starting—does the complex know-how of fly-fishing seem too much to learn? Perhaps you're wondering if it's worthwhile fishing the hatches—if you are prepared with the proper pattern and appear on a stream when the hatch starts, will that really improve your chances of success? You bet it will! Let me give as an example an incident that occurred just two years ago to a newcomer to fly-fishing.

Dave Butt, of State College, had never been fly-fishing, but he was eager to learn and pleaded with me for almost a year to take him out. During a January blizzard we planned a trip to the Little Juniata River for the upcoming May. Every time Dave saw me after that, he reminded me of our approaching fishing excursion. Dave had no fishing tackle, so I suggested he use mine. Then he could decide whether he liked the new sport before he spent money on waders, a rod, reel, line, and other fly-fishing necessities. Dave had never cast a fly prior to our May trip.

The long-awaited evening finally arrived. Dave donned a pair of over-sized waders and one of my old Orvis fishing vests. Like a child anticipating Christmas morning, he anxiously headed for the river, hoping to witness the hatches I promised would appear that evening. We hiked upriver a half mile, over a railroad track, up a hill, then down to the water. Almost as soon as we saw the river clearly through the brush, Dave saw trout rising. Before we could even tie a fly on the tippet, brown trout rose to a good supply of light cahills.

Less than five minutes after he entered the river Dave was thrashing the surface with his Light Cahill pattern—but he encountered immediate problems. First, he had difficulty casting any distance with that confounded fly on the end of his line. Second, the dry fly mimicked a wet fly and sank for him every time. Third, he couldn't seem to cover a rising fish.

Soon, however, the dry fly began to behave properly and floated. Next Dave covered rising trout, casting a few feet upriver from the surface-feeders. I turned away from Dave for a short time to watch a dozen or so trout feeding below at the tail of the pool. Soon I heard a yell, looked up toward Dave, and saw a slack line.

"Missed that one," Dave shouted.

The cahill hatch peaked, and dozens of the duns remained on the water. Trout rose all around Dave—upstream and downstream. Possibly two dozen trout filled the pool with splashing rises. Dave's casting techniques had improved considerably, and he successfully covered a constant riser just a few feet above him on the second cast. Another strike, and another slack line.

"Missed another one," Dave bellowed as he cast to another fish within his limited casting range. On the next cast Dave dropped his Cahill just a foot above and in line with a third riser.

Another yell. When I looked up I saw the ultimate reward—a tight line. I knew my novice had hooked his first trout on a fly. If you want to know the joy that such an event produces, accompany a beginner on his first successful fly-fishing trip.

By 8:00 PM Dave had landed three cahill-eating browns. Only sporadic light cahills remained as any evidence of the fantastic hatch that had appeared just an hour before. Then, almost as a signal that the last hatch had waned, it was time for the next one: Sulphur duns made their highly predictable appearance. I quickly tied a size-16 Sulphur on Dave's line, and he cast to possibly 20 trout now rising in the pool. Thousands of sulphurs filled the air, with more on the surface. What a fantastic hatch! It continued for more than half an hour that evening, then ended as quickly as it had begun.

But the Little Juniata had one other event for us before hatching activity ended that evening. Around 8:30 the spinners of the sulphurs that had emerged as duns the evening before returned to the stream with their bright orange egg sacs to deposit the next generation of that mayfly species. For another half hour the river was alive with trout rising everywhere—in the pool, in the riffle above, and at the tail. We hastily tied a Sulphur Spinner onto Dave's leader, fumbling with the clinch knot in the half-light near dusk. Almost every cast brought a strike to Dave's spent-wing imitation.

It was now near 9:00, and still some trout rose to the diminishing supply of adult naturals. Dave pleaded with me to stay for a few more casts, but I reminded him that we had to head back to the car about a half mile away and I didn't want to stumble through the undergrowth in total darkness. That evening—the first evening Dave ever fly-fished—he caught and released a half-dozen trout. Granted, for an accomplished fly-fisherman, to catch a half-dozen trout under the conditions Dave and I found that evening would have made for just an average outing. But for someone who had never cast or caught a trout on a fly, that night's fishing was quite an accomplishment.

As we headed back to the car, Dave kept asking when we could return for another exciting night of fishing. This is what success produces—not a dying interest in the sport, but an everlasting devotion to fly-fishing.

Why did Dave experience immediate success on the Little Juniata that night? First, he fly-fished over trout actively feeding on a plentiful supply of naturals. Second, I knew which mayflies would appear and at about what time, and I had prepared for the occasion with an adequate supply of imitations to copy the hatches and spinner fall. Third, we didn't elect to fly-fish over a natural that was too small; instead we fished fairly large mayflies that could be copied with sizes 14 and 16. And finally, we selected hatches like the sulphur and the light cahill, which are surprisingly predictable in their appearance. With a little knowledge of the hatches of Pennsylvania you too will experience this type of success, whether or not you are an accomplished fly-fisherman. Dozens of the state's other great trout streams have equally superb hatches; you're likely to have success similar to what Dave and I experienced. That is, if you take some time to learn a little about the hatches.

Mayflies, Caddisflies, and Stoneflies

Many words may be foreign to the beginning fly-fisherman: *hatch, spinner, dun, spinner fall, nymph, natural,* and so on. To understand why trout take wet flies, dry flies, and nymphs, it's essential to have a basic understanding of the biology of the aquatic insects on which they feed and so come to understand these terms. Let's first look at the typical life cycle of a mayfly.

Mayflies of different genera lay their eggs in different ways. Some sit on the water to deposit the fertilized eggs; others drop the eggs while flying above the water; others sit on the water for a short period, deposit their eggs, and then take flight again. Some (like most of the genus *Ephemerella*) carry their eggs in a ball or sac under the female's abdomen and drop them into the water. After depositing eggs the female mayfly *spinner* (the adult capable of mating) usually dies, often on the surface of a stream.

In the stream the eggs take several weeks to hatch into *nymphs* (the

A slate drake on Sixmile Run.

larval form of the mayfly). These nymphs usually have specific habitats. Some closely related mayflies live in loose gravel (*Ephemera* spp.); some live in mud or silt (*Hexagenia* spp.); others live under rocks (*Stenonema* and *Epeorus* spp.); some species live on or in aquatic weeds (some *Ephemerella* spp.); and others swim freely about the bottom of the stream (*Isonychia* spp.). Not only are scores of nymphs specific to their habitat, but many kinds are also particular about the velocity of the water where they live. Slate drakes (*Isonychia* spp.) usually inhabit fast-water sections of a stream. Hendricksons *(Ephemerella subvaria)* are found in all types of water, but yellow drakes *(Ephemera varia)* customarily occupy slower areas, usually pools of a stream. Other nymphs, like the speckle-winged dun (*Callibaetis* spp.), regularly inhabit ponds and lakes.

Most mayfly species live under water for about 340 days as nymphs, although there are numerous exceptions. As the nymph feeds and grows, it regularly sheds its skin or exoskeleton and develops a new one. Some species, depending on size and length of time they live as nymphs, go through 5 or 10 of these transformations, called *instars*.

A year after the eggs were fertilized the nymph begins to move toward the surface. At or near the water's surface the nymph splits its skin dorsally and appears on the surface as a mayfly *dun*, or subimago (an immature, nonmating adult). (There are exceptions here, however, like *Epeorus* spp.) The mayfly dun rests on the water for a split second to several minutes, depending again on the species and on the weather, before flying away. Abnormally cold weather, especially in spring and fall, delays or prevents the dun from taking flight. These conditions are of special importance to the fly-fisherman.

If and when the dun or subimago escapes, it flies toward a branch to rest. On extremely cold, miserable days many duns struggle to rocks or debris on the shoreline and remain there. In a couple of hours to a day or more the dun again goes through a transformation, losing its outer skin (pellicle) and becoming a *spinner* (also called an adult or imago) with glassy, clear wings. This spinner is a mating adult. Often, in the evening, male spinners form a swarm over the water, waiting for females to join them. When the females enter the swarm, they are impregnated by the males. Females then move toward the water's surface and deposit their fertilized eggs, and the cycle begins again. Mayflies live out of the water as air-breathing duns and spinners usually for less than five days. Thus the name for the order of insects that contains the mayflies is Ephemeroptera, which comes from the Greek for "short lived."

This is a very generalized description, and there are many exceptions. For example, some mayflies—like the female white mayfly (*Ephoron* spp.)— never change into spinners, but mate as duns. A few species remain as nymphs for two years (some *Ephemera* spp.), and many life cycles last only a few months (some *Baetis, Pseudocloeon,* and others). This latter type, with multiple broods, may appear as many as three times a year.

When the term *hatch* is used in this book, it usually refers to duns emerging on the surface. When the nymph splits its pellicle or skin near the surface and changes into a dun, it is referred to as an *emerger. Spinner fall* is that time when females (and in some instances males) return to the water to deposit eggs and fall onto the surface *spent,* or with wings outstretched. *Natural* refers to the nymph, dun, or spinner of a species.

Caddisflies (order Trichoptera) and stoneflies (order Plecoptera) are similar to the mayfly in their development. Stoneflies and mayflies, however, lack one stage of the complete insect life cycle and are therefore considered to have incomplete metamorphoses. Caddisflies do experience this stage, called the *pupa* or resting phase (diapause). This period usually lasts several weeks. Caddisfly larvae, like mayfly nymphs, are specific in their habitat. Unlike stonefly and mayfly nymphs, however, caddis larvae lack the tough outer shell called the exoskeleton. Therefore, some caddis (but not all) construct a protective shelter or case. Caddisflies can be grouped according to the type of case they build. Some, like the green caddis (*Rhyacophila* spp.), are free swimmers on the bottom and construct no shelter. Other important Pennsylvania caddis, like the grannoms

(*Brachycentrus* spp.), build a case of twigs. Still others build a cover in the form of a net (the little black caddis), and the dark blue sedge (*Psilotreta* spp.), common on many Pennsylvania waters, makes a case of coarse stone fragments. The nymph turns into a pupa inside its case.

Stonefly nymphs take one to three years to develop, depending on the species. When they do emerge, mating usually takes place when the male and female are resting on some surface rather than while they are in flight.

You can see by this brief description of the life cycles of mayflies, stoneflies, and caddisflies that the nymph or larva of a species is available to trout almost every day of the year, whereas the adult is available for only about a week. A skilled angler nymph-fishing will usually outperform one who is dry-fly fishing—when there is no hatch. During a hatch the dry fly reigns supreme, except when few trout rise to the supply of naturals on the surface.

The Hatches on Pennsylvania Streams

Several years ago a fly-fisherman called me from Massachusetts and asked if he could fish with me and see some of those hatches I had written about in *Meeting and Fishing the Hatches*. John and I met on a central-Pennsylvania stream, Spruce Creek, in mid-May. We were on the upper section of the creek near the town of Baileyville. In this area Spruce is extremely small—only about 10 feet wide. Within an hour of our initial meeting a concentrated sulphur hatch appeared on the surface. Streambred browns almost anticipated the hatch and began rising just as the hatch began. After 10 years of fly-fishing this was the first hatch that John had ever seen. Many people tell me similar things—that they have never experienced the great hatches and spinner falls that writers describe.

Why don't more fisherman fish the hatches and spinner falls? Are such occurrences rare? Are hatches found on only a few, select Pennsylvania streams?

Much of the general neglect of hatches by fishermen comes from a lack of information. Many anglers are amazed at how predictable the mayflies' appearance can be. Fish the Little Juniata, Spruce, Spring, Falling Springs, and many other streams on an evening in late May and you'll see a sulphur hatch. Fish Spring Creek, West Valley Creek, or one of hundreds of other streams on a mid-July morning and you can be certain that there will be a trico hatch. A knowledge of the hatches—on what days they might appear, at what time of day, on what stream or river, and what to use to copy the insects—can transform a frustrating fishing experience into a successful trip.

This book includes three charts that list the major hatches on

Pennsylvania streams according to the time of year that they appear; these begin on page 384. In any such hatch discussion there are a few disclaimers to remember. These concern the life cycles of mayflies, caddisflies, and stoneflies. Some species have more than one brood a year; that is, eggs are laid, and nymphs develop and hatch, two or more times a season. Some mayflies have more than two broods. Although hatches are generally predictable, emergence dates vary from year to year by as much as a few weeks. Dates shown in this book's charts are approximate average dates of the first appearances of the insect in central Pennsylvania. Hatches occur earlier in the southern part of the state and later in the north.

The time of day a species will probably appear is also given. This often varies because of weather. For example, under normal April weather conditions, the Hendrickson hatch on Bald Eagle Creek in central Pennsylvania appears on the surface from 2:00 to 4:00 PM. Two years ago, in a particularly warm April, hendricksons appeared on the first day of the season, April 19, almost a week ahead of schedule for that stream. Not only did the Hendrickson appear prematurely in the year, but also it emerged earlier in the day than is customary. On that opening day with an 80-degree air temperature, the Hendrickson arrived on the surface a good three or four hours ahead of schedule. By 10:00 AM the surface was filled with duns. Some years earlier, on the same stream, the Hendrickson hatch appeared after 6:00 PM.

A blue quill male dun. You find this species (*Paraleptophlebia adoptiva*) on many Commonwealth streams in mid-April.

In chapter 10 I suggest possible body colors for imitating various duns and spinners. Body color often varies considerably from stream to stream. Look at the green drake on Penns Creek and compare it with the same species found on Kettle Creek or Cedar Run. On Cedar the green drake's underbelly is white, whereas on Penns and Kettle it is a dark cream. Body size also differs from stream to stream. The green drake on Penns Creek is a good 2 to 3 hook sizes larger than the same insect found on Cedar and Kettle.

Finally, if you've fished the hatches for any length of time, you already know that not all insects are found on all streams. Maybe your favorite stream has only one, two, or three major hatches all season. That's true for the lower end of Bald Eagle Creek. Yet it's a terrific trout stream—if you fish when one of the three species appears.

Let's look more closely at Pennsylvania hatches through the season. Combine this information with a careful reading of the appendix's hatch charts and you should be ready to meet the hatches all year.

The April Grays

Another trout season has begun in Pennsylvania. Is this the year you devote entirely to fly-fishing? But wait, you say, productive fly-fishing doesn't begin until late in May. Ask those frustrated anglers on several opening days when blue quills, quill gordons, or hendricksons appeared. Ask them if they would have exchanged their spinning rods for fly-rods.

If they wouldn't, they're in error. As soon as the water temperature approaches 50 degrees insect activity begins, and trout can be caught. Usually this occurs first in the southeastern part of the state. On hundreds of occasions I've witnessed not just one hatch the third or fourth week in April, but rather two, and often three hatches appearing concurrently. Dozens of streams, especially those in the north-central region like the Loyalsock, Cedar Run, Slate Run, Cross Fork, and Kettle Creek, contain all three April hatches.

Fishing often is extremely variable on these first days of the fishing year, however. Early spring produces cold water, which in turn might delay the predicted hatches. But fly-fish on your favorite stream when it does host the early hatches and you can experience an early bonus.

I like to fish Loyalsock or Lycoming Creek from April 20 to 25, especially after the water temperature has had time to moderate. When the water is above 50 degrees (preferably above 52 degrees) the three gray hatches of April emerge rapidly. Fly-fish when the air temperature is below 60 degrees and the sky is cloudy, and you have all the ingredients for a successful trip. On several trips to the Loyalsock in Lycoming County I have experienced just those favorable conditions.

When I checked the water temperature on the upper end of the Loyalsock's fly-fishing-only section around 10:00 AM it registered 52 degrees. It was April 22, and I felt confident that a hatch would occur. Little did I realize that three separate species would appear. By 11:00 AM blue quills, struggling desperately to become airborne, rode the surface from the pool to the riffle below. Few if any of the duns took flight, but only an occasional trout rose to the first surface food of the year.

Shortly after 12:30 PM the first quill gordon appeared. Several trout, awakened by this larger food supply, started to rise for the stunned duns. Not one of these duns appeared to escape the combined misfortunes of cold air and high water to take flight. Trout went on a feeding frenzy, with dozens of fish feeding. Cast after cast I hooked trout on my size-14 imitation. The hatch seemed to last for hours. Stunned duns from miles above still drifted past me at 2:00 PM, and trout still rose to the bonanza from upstream. A third species, the Hendrickson, then complicated matters by appearing on the surface. This last species didn't emerge in the numbers the other two had, probably because this was just the beginning of the Hendrickson hatch. The next few days might produce more insects.

Little Pine Creek in north-central Pennsylvania also contains the three April grays. Often, from April 20 to April 25, the three emerge simultaneously. Fred Templin and I have had countless memorable trips to Pine and Little Pine Creeks. Once we hit Little Pine on the third week in April and fly-fished over all three hatches. As is often the case in April, the water level was high on Little Pine, and it seemed almost impossible to fish with anything smaller than a Muddler or Woolly Bugger. About 11:00 AM, though, a sporadic hatch of miniature blue quills appeared in the eddy of a swollen pool in the Carson Flat section. Even with the runoff from a recent late-spring snowstorm, trout began to feed on these small, dark gray naturals. Not only did they rise in the back eddy protected by a huge fallen hemlock, but they also began rising in the riffle above and throughout the pool. Blue quills appeared on the surface by the hundreds, not by the tens as they had before. Shortly after noon a second, larger, gray fly appeared in among the smaller mayflies. Some trout still fed on the smaller blue quill, while others switched abruptly to the quill gordon. Which trout was taking which fly? Have you ever felt that you should have prepared for fishing with two fly rods complete with two imitations?

By 2:00 PM surface action subsided and Fred and I moved upstream to the next fairly slow pool—and just in time. The Hendrickson had already begun to emerge. It seemed that the trout captured any natural that rested before struggling to become airborne. Almost all of the surface-feeders readily took the imitation, with isolated refusals.

What a day! Three hatches, rising trout, few refusals, and not one other fly-fisherman to enjoy the event. Maybe the cold weather or the high water kept them away.

I prefer dry-fly fishing, but many early-season excursions depend on the proper weather and water conditions; poor conditions limit dry-fly fishing. How many of these early trips with high water have been saved with a wet fly or nymph that copies one of the April grays? Just before and during hatches in April a Hendrickson Nymph has rescued me from many a barren day. On other days and other streams, like the Mehoopany in northeastern Pennsylvania, a Quill Gordon wet fly has worked.

More than it affects any other mayflies, weather affects the hatching activity of the April grays. A few days of extremely cold weather when the quill gordons or hendricksons appear can produce a sparse hatch the next year. Even though one or all of these April mayflies inhabits a stream, the density of the species varies significantly because of the hazards of early-spring weather.

It's April and the season has just begun. Will you be ready for the April grays with plenty of size-18 Blue Quills, size-14 Quill Gordons, size-14 Hendricksons and Red Quills, and some size-14 Black Quills? Or will you, like so many other fishermen, become frustrated at the first hatch of the season because you're ill prepared?

Caddis Time

April has ended, and the first spring hatches are a thing of the past. Annually there's a dearth of hatches during the first two weeks in May. Usually the last mayfly species of the early season to appear is the black quill around the end of April. The next species, the sulphur, doesn't emerge for about two weeks. What do you do now? Those early-May days are prime times to fly-fish for caddis. Look at the Little Juniata River, Spring Creek, or the lower Bald Eagle—all three have excellent green caddis hatches appearing around May 5. Visit Pine Creek around May 1 and you'll likely encounter the concentrated but often frustrating cream caddis hatch. Thousands of these caddisflies appear in the air throughout the day on Pine Creek. Or visit Penns Creek or Fishing Creek in the latter part of April—you'll probably encounter a black caddis or a grannom hatch. All of these heavy caddis hatches appear in a relatively short time, from late April through mid-May.

Maybe you've become frustrated with caddis hatches. Often when caddis are in the air, I cast about violently with a dry-fly imitation, like the Fluttering Caddis, trying to tempt a trout to the surface. More often, however, trout are feeding on the emerging pupae as they try to escape to the surface. Look, for example, at the splashing rises so evident during caddis hatches. These rises are a certain sign that trout are chasing emerging pupae, not the adults.

A series of events on the Little Juniata River changed my thinking on fishing a caddis hatch. As usual I tied on a Green Caddis dry fly, while thousands of the naturals fluttered past me. Few trout rose, but I continued to cast. Suddenly my dry fly sank and became a wet fly submerged just a few inches beneath the surface. As my Green Caddis made its first swing or arc as a wet fly, I noticed a swirl at it. On my next cast I deliberately fished the pattern wet and twitched it slightly as it made its swing. This time there was another swirl at the fly, and then a strike. I fished the rest of the afternoon and evening with that dry fly converted to a wet fly, caught dozens of trout, and missed countless others. On many casts with the Green Caddis I had multiple strikes.

I went home that evening to my fly-tying vise and tied a few dozen emerging Green Caddis Pupae patterns that have changed little since that initial success. I tied the pattern on a size-18 hook with a body made of gray-green ultratranslucent nymph dubbing and a couple of turns of a dark brown grouse hackle to imitate the legs and wings of the emerger. The pattern continues to be one of the most effective on Pennsylvania streams in early May.

Caddisflies aren't limited to the north-central streams of the state. They appear in considerable numbers on many others. Bowman Creek has a fishable grannom hatch in May and a spotted sedge later in the same month. Valley Creek in the southeastern part of the state near Valley Forge has an excellent green caddis hatch early in March and April. And Oil Creek in northwestern Pennsylvania has a tremendous caddis population.

If it's May it's prime caddis time. Caddis patterns are effective through most of the season, however. In July and August when you see splashing rises and some caddis on the water, switch to a pupa imitation. Possibly the best time to fly-fish on the lower Bald Eagle is on a July or August morning. Riffles that the night before seemed to be void of any remaining trout come alive for half an hour or so when the green caddis makes its appearance. Although a number of caddis species select the early part of May to appear, don't forget your caddis patterns for the entire season—caddis time is almost anytime during the fishing season in Pennsylvania.

If you had to select just one week of the entire fishing season in which you could fly-fish, which week would it be? For me, in central Pennsylvania it would be May 25 to June 1. Why? Within that span of a week you'll witness sulphur, light cahill, green drake, brown drake, slate drake, March brown, blue-winged olive dun, and gray fox hatches—and many others—on Pennsylvania streams. Don't expect all these hatches on all your favorite streams; in fact, fly-fishing is often easier if the water is not congested with multiple hatches. When it is, selecting the proper imitation is often arduous. Look at Penns Creek. Droves of enthusiastic fly-fishermen head there for the acclaimed green drake hatch and coffin fly spinner fall. The majority of these avid anglers come away from their experience disappointed. Often, at the end of May when these hatches are in their prime on Penns, so too are several other hatches. Sulphur duns and spinners, ginger quills, light cahills—all these appear at the same time as the drake.

In late May many Pennsylvania streams display at least two or three hatches—the sulphur, light cahill, and green drake. The north-central and northeastern streams exhibit blue-winged olives, March browns, and gray foxes during the day, and brown drakes, gray foxes, slate drakes, and green drakes in the evening.

Let's examine in some detail two of the largest mayflies to appear at this time of the year, the green drake and the brown drake.

It's Brown Drake Time

The brown drake is alive and well on at least 19 Pennsylvania streams. It has been 15 years since I first witnessed this superb hatch on Pine Creek. At the time I was totally unprepared for the hatch and the events that followed.

On June 3 several of us decided to try our luck on the lower end of Cedar Run in Lycoming County. About 7:00 PM large male spinners began appearing overhead in the undulating flight so common for some species. This impressive but unfamiliar spinner dumbfounded all of us with its unexpected appearance that evening. What was it? Could it be an enlarged version of the March brown adult—the great red spinner? Within half an hour the gorge on the lower end of Cedar filled with layers of male and female spinners. We moved down to the mouth of Cedar where it enters Pine Creek.

The water on Pine above Cedar Run felt warm to the touch and was, in fact, in the low 70s. Just below Cedar, Pine registered 68 degrees, its temperature evidently reduced by the cooling effects of this moderate-sized tributary—perfect for the massive spinner fall that was about to unfold. This was to be the greatest spinner fall that any of us had ever seen. By 8:00 PM thousands of fertilized females, laden with eggs, moved upstream past us in unison, just a few feet above Pine's surface. The females were so profuse that all of us could hear a humming from the movement of their wings. We were still perplexed. What was this hatch? We all agreed that it had to be an abnormally large great red spinner.

The spinners touched the water. We tied on Great Red Spinners with spent wings and started casting to more than 50 trout rising in the eddy just below Cedar Run. Trout nearby gorged themselves on this huge supply of food, sucking in three and four spinners at a time. By this time

The March brown appears on streams throughout the Commonwealth in mid-May.

thousands of spinners had descended to the surface. I captured a spent spinner nearby and examined it. It definitely was not a great red spinner; it was, in fact, a species I had seen only once before, on the Beaverkill in New York State. Three of us fished in total confusion that evening—we had hundreds of trout rising around us but could catch only a few of them on the Great Red Spinner and later on an Early Brown Spinner pattern.

I collected a few male spinners to take home with me to identify later. The wings looked heavily spotted or barred under my stereomicroscope. This suggested that the species was member of the genus *Ephemera*, closely related to the green drake and yellow drake. It was, in fact, the brown drake *(Ephemera simulans)*. I vowed never again to visit Pine Creek without a good supply of brown drake imitations, so I tied a dozen to resemble both the dun and spinner.

It wasn't until two seasons later that I next encountered the brown drake. I had told Greg Hoover stories about the tremendous hatch on Pine Creek and he was anxious to see it. Greg wrote a graduate paper on the green drake on Penns Creek and is one of the most knowledgeable entomologists in the East. We arrived on Pine Creek, 2 miles below Cedar Run. Dana and Dave Poust of Tombs Run, and Tom Finkbiner of Slate Run, told us that the hatch had begun just two days before. We started fly-fishing early in the morning on May 28 over the heavy blue-winged olive dun hatch so common on Pine. Olive duns appeared on the water until well after 10:00 AM. Shortly after the hatch both Greg and I noticed a small number of female brown drakes appearing over the water. The few turned into hundreds by 11:00 AM, and trout fed on them under an overcast sky. Both of us were surprised at this freak appearance, since the normal time for the spinner fall is near dusk. We quickly tied on appropriate patterns and cast toward a dozen or so trout feeding on this larger mayfly. The pattern worked. No disappointment like the last encounter with this species—the trout freely took the imitation.

Near dusk thousands of the brown drakes appeared over the water in their egg-laying ritual. One problem developed, though—the water temperature had risen above 70 degrees that hot late-May day. Spinners fell, but only a dozen or so trout rose to them, and those that did rise seemed to do so lethargically. Greg complained about the few trout that rose to the tremendous spinner fall.

Water temperature, however, is only one of the obstacles to successfully fishing the brown drake. At best the brown drake appears on Pine for four days; at worst it appears for as few as three. On numerous occasions I have missed the hatch and spinner fall completely because of their brief appearance. Before you travel to Pine Creek for the brown drake, check with someone near the stream on the status of the hatch.

Another impediment to making the brown drake the prime hatch of Pennsylvania is the temperamental nature of the species. Even when duns have emerged, I have waited in vain a day or two later at dusk for the spinners to return to the water. They never did one spectacular evening on Pine Creek. Male spinners formed a swarm around 8:00 PM, and females entered the swarm to mate. These females normally would have flown back to the stream and deposited their eggs. On this occasion these females flew back to the trees and not to the stream, canceling any chance for a great evening of matching the spinner fall.

A final barrier to fishing the brown drake hatch successfully is its limited distribution. Brown drakes appear on First Fork, East Fork, and Cross Fork, and on Kettle and Pine Creeks. I have heard reports that some brown drakes exist on Thompson Creek in Crawford County, Neshannock Creek in southern Mercer County, and the upper part of the Delaware River above Equinunk in Wayne County.

The extensive green drake hatch on Penns Creek is fairly predictable. Once the species begins appearing on the lower end near Weikert, hatching activity moves upstream 4 to 6 miles each night until it reaches Coburn. Not so with the brown drake, although there is some evidence to substantiate the claim that the spinner fall extends a day longer in the Cedar Run area than near Slate Run, 6 miles downstream.

The past few years the brown drake hasn't emerged in the numbers it once did on Pine Creek. Tom Finkbiner at Slate Run bemoans the loss of this great hatch on the stretch from Blackwell downstream to Waterville. Tom feels that acid water from nearby mines, entering from Babb Creek at Blackwell, has caused the decline of the drake.

With all of its shortcomings, the brown drake has the potential to be the most sensational hatch you'll encounter in your life. In a short period of time you'll witness an explosive hatch or spinner fall and large trout, some over 20 inches long, gorging themselves on the large mayfly. At the same time you'll find few competing fly-fishermen, and best of all, if you've prepared for the hatch and spinner fall, you'll probably experience a productive, rewarding evening on a spectacular stream.

Even though the hatch on Pine Creek has declined, there are at least 19 other Commonwealth streams that harbor the brown drake. Pick your stream from chart V in the appendix, and be prepared for the hatch of a lifetime.

Three Weeks with the Green Drake

Mayflies catch but a fleeting glimpse at an above-water environment. That's why they're called ephemeral. Many live as adults only two to five days. Some mayfly species emerge just a few days on a stream and then are gone for another year; others appear on a stream for a week or more. A scant few, like the trico, emerge for two or three months, and some species emerge several times every year. The green drake often exists above water on a particular stream for less than a week. Wouldn't you like to stretch the length of the green drake hatch from less than a week to two or three weeks?

Twenty years ago Dick Mills and I began fishing the great green drake hatch on Penns Creek. We had a friend in Millheim near the stream who called us every time the hatch appeared. Tom Taylor and Lloyd Williams joined Dick and me fishing that hatch for some years, but we always returned home to the Wilkes-Barre area disillusioned. Why? Normally we'd encounter a tremendous hatch of duns or an impressive coffin fly spinner fall, but rarely did we do well during the excitement. Certainly trout rose for the surface food, but they routinely refused our imitations.

Many anglers contend that the only really heavy green drake hatch exists on Penns Creek. The green drake is part of the mystique of that stream. The species, however, is abundant on a surprisingly large number of Pennsylvania streams. It is so common that you can start in south-central Pennsylvania the third week in May and continue to fish over the same species a couple of weeks later on some of the northeastern and north-central streams.

For several years Ed Gunnett of Williamsburg recounted stories about a fantastic green drake hatch on a local stream. He promised to alert me when the hatch next appeared. We met on Canoe Creek at 6:00 PM on May 23 to witness this impressive hatch. When we arrived we scanned the water at a pool just a few miles upstream from Canoe Creek Dam. Already hundreds of green drake duns were in flight, and trout cruised the pool catching laggards.

Canoe Creek is a small, unimpressive trout stream. With its brush-covered banks and narrow pools, even skilled fly-casters find it difficult to cover rising trout. Further, by the third week in May the water level was a mere trickle compared to its spring flow. Small pools and shallow riffles produced difficult fly-fishing.

But by 7:00 that evening dozens of green drakes, as large as the Penns Creek version, thrashed on the surface in an attempt to get their heavy bodies airborne. In each miniature pool trout rose to these massive mayflies. The green drake that evening had the stage all to itself; only a handful of sulphurs appeared. There was no confusion about what the fish were taking, so my son, Bryan, and Ed tied on Green Drake dry flies. Just about every trout that rose to a natural that evening took the copy.

The olive sulphur.

Canoe's green drake hatch is different from the same hatch on Penns. The number of drakes on the water that evening was sufficient to bring trout to the surface, but it wasn't excessive, as it often is on Penns Creek. After a trout captured a green drake, it might be a minute before another dun passed overhead, giving a fisherman plenty of time to cover the trout with an imitation. There were few other mayflies on the surface that evening, a second advantage to fishing the hatch. In pool after pool Bryan and Ed caught trout on the Green Drake dry fly, some exceeding 15 inches on this small, heavily fished stream near Altoona. Duns emerged for more than two hours that evening, while trout rose in concert with the hatch.

Four days later, on May 27, Bryan and I headed to three small but extremely productive streams vacated by most of the early-spring anglers. These three—the Vanscoyoc, Big Fill, and Bald Eagle—have some incredible hatches in late May, and one of these is the green drake.

Afternoon fishing in late May is frequently unrewarding if no hatch appears, but green drakes typically emerge on these heavily canopied streams during the afternoon. We selected a slow, man-made pool about 200 feet long and 10 feet wide on Vanscoyoc Run to watch for the drakes. By the time we arrived at the pool, drakes were already in the air. Bryan tied on a Green Drake fly, and I captured some of the escaping duns, a few of which were much larger than the others. The smaller dun was the green drake. The larger mayfly was a good 2 hook sizes bigger—it was a dark green drake *(Litobrancha recurvata)*. Green drakes and the dark green drakes appeared to emerge in equal numbers for the next hour—in the middle of a hot late-May day. Trout after rising trout in that small pool took Bryan's imitation. Some of the trout measured over 15 inches long— from this heavily fished but fertile stream.

On May 29 of the same year I arrived on Pine Creek below Cedar Run just in time for a combined hatch of brown and green drakes. For every four or five brown drakes emerging there was one green drake. That same evening the green drake emerged on Penns just below Coburn.

A week later, on June 5, I fished the same hatch on the Narrows of Fishing Creek above Lamar. Although Fishing Creek is just 20 miles north of Penns, the drake appears a good week or two later, because the water on Fishing Creek is much cooler than on Penns. The hatch on Fishing Creek is not as concentrated as it is on Penns; therefore you don't have to contend with as many naturals on the water, and fishing the drake seems to be more rewarding.

What a great year! Fly-fishing continued to be good over green drake hatches for longer than two weeks on several different streams in central Pennsylvania. On May 23 the hatch appeared on Canoe Creek, later on the Vanscoyoc, Pine, and Big Fill. A week later it appeared on Fishing Creek. Until 10 years ago I was one of those anglers who thought you had to fish Penns Creek to meet a decent hatch of drakes. Not anymore.

With a reasonable awareness of which streams harbor this large burrower and when the mayfly normally appears on each stream, you can extend your green drake season, as I did. I began fly-fishing over the drake on May 23 and concluded it on June 8—17 days devoted to fishing over the giant of the East. How can you extend the time you fly-fish over the green drake hatch? Select a couple of the Commonwealth streams listed in chart V on page 395. Check with local fly-fishermen to see when the hatch appears on those streams, and carry a good selection of nymph, dun, and spinner imitations.

Olive Bodies

If you've ever hit a hatch of blue-winged olives you know how explosive it can be. For many years, in late May and early June, I hit fantastic hatches of these mayflies on Mehoopany, Bowman, and Pocono Creeks as well as the Delaware River in northeastern Pennsylvania. The hatch on central Pennsylvania's Bald Eagle Creek near the end of May lasts for only a few days, but the intensity brings trout to the surface in a feeding frenzy. Kettle Creek and many of the well-known north-central streams hold the same or similar hatches in late May and early June. Even limestone streams like Big Fishing Creek, Logan Branch, and the Little Juniata River boast good hatches. And the beauty of it all is that the hatch occurs in broad daylight—usually in late morning with a burst around 11:00 AM. I have seen these and other Keystone streams come alive with feeding trout for an hour or more.

Anglers call at least four mayfly species "blue-winged olive duns." Probably the most important on many streams is one of the largest, *Drunella cornuta*. This blue-winged olive is also one of the first to appear; I've witnessed many hatches as early as May 20. I usually use a size-14 Blue-Winged Olive Dun to copy the hatches, which appear daily for about a week or two. On the Bald Eagle the hatch usually lasts less than an hour, but creates some great matching-the-hatch opportunities. Even freestone streams like Kettle and Pine hold great hatches. The *D. cornuta* hatch generally ends in early June.

But the activity doesn't end there—a second, somewhat smaller, almost overlooked hatch often occurs just when the first one wanes. Just ask Dennis Hiltunen and J. P. Thornton, both of State College, if this second, smaller hatch is important. Recently they contacted me about a hatch they encountered on Penns Creek in late June and early July. Trout refused anything but almost an exact copy of the dark olive-black spinner of this species, *Drunella cornutella*.

Just recently I had calls from across the state from frustrated anglers. In 1998 many Delaware River, Brodhead Creek, and Spruce Creek fishermen saw a hatch they hadn't encountered before. Don Baylor, a skilled entomologist from Stroudsburg, heard about the hatch on Brodhead Creek. I encountered the hatch myself on Spruce Creek in early June. For almost an hour at dusk thousands of these mayflies dotted the water, and trout fed eagerly on the duns. For two evenings I tied on a size-16 Sulphur to match this hatch, with little success. On the third evening I captured a female "sulphur" and examined it. This mayfly had the same color as a sulphur on its legs, wings, and tail: cream to creamish yellow. But the body of the female was a bright olive color. The male has a dark brown body, and all the fishing literature describes this sex, not the female. Now I know why I had only limited success with my regular Sulphur pattern.

That evening I went home and tied up a dozen new patterns to copy the olive sulphur I had just seen. Onto a size-16 hook I tied creamish yellow legs and wings, then added a medium olive extended body made of the finest vernille I could find. The very next evening I took those dozen Olive Sulphurs with me to Spruce Creek. I arrived at the stream about 8:15 PM and didn't have to wait long to see if my new pattern would catch trout. Within 15 minutes the riffle in front of me held hundreds of these olive duns and trout began picking off many of the laggards.

By the way, the male dun of this species has a dark brown body with legs, wings, and tail very similar to the female's. The species is *Ephemerella needhami.*

Quill Gordons

I've fished over many spectacular quill gordon hatches in my life. I'll never forget the one I saw in mid-April on Bobs Creek in southwestern Pennsylvania. Nor will I forget the quill gordon hatch I met on Baker Run just north of Lock Haven, nor the one on Bald Eagle Creek near Julian on opening day. But probably the greatest hatch of quill gordons I ever fished over occurred on the Loyalsock just north of Williamsport. Thousands and thousands of dazed duns rode the water on that mid-April afternoon, and trout surface-fed for two hours. All of these momentous events occurred around the middle of April. That's the best time to fish this hatch—or at least that's what I thought until this past year. Let me explain.

I fly-fished one of my all-time-favorite streams, Sixmile Run, in mid-June. This stream holds an unbelievable variety of mayflies. I even found a new gray drake species *(Siphlonurus mirus)* on the stream in early June. In mid-June you can expect to see some blue-winged olives and slate drakes. I came prepared with plenty of Blue-Winged Olive patterns in sizes 14 to 20. I sat by this small central-Pennsylvania freestone stream watching little blue-winged olives and slate drakes emerge that afternoon. A fine drizzle fell, and hundreds of insects covered some of the eddies. Trout fed on these laggards for hours. About 4:00 PM another hatch appeared and I captured one of the duns so I could see which pattern to use. It looked like a quill gordon, though maybe a tad smaller. Besides, this was June 14, and quill gordons had long since ended their annual appearance. Anyway, I tied on a size-14 Quill Gordon—and trout hit that pattern with reckless abandon for the next hour.

I decided to wait around until dark to see what spinner falls I encountered on this prolific stream. About 8:00 PM a hundred or more spinners met over a small, deep riffle. These also looked like the adult of the quill gordon dun that anglers often call the red quill spinner. Spinners mated that evening and fell onto the surface just before dusk. Trout fed freely on

the spent spinners in the riffle and the pool below. I tied on a Rusty Spinner pattern that more closely represented the naturals and caught a half-dozen trout while the spinners fell.

What a hatch! What a spinner fall! I captured a few of the male spinners in the air and sent them off to a friend of mine who's a skilled entomologist. He later identified the spinners as

Quill gordons emerge as late as mid-June.

Epeorus plerualis—the quill gordon. What? The quill gordon emerges as late as mid-June? That really surprised me. I came back several times that mid-June and saw quill gordons emerging each time; there were spinner falls each evening. The insects continued to emerge until late June.

I noted several differences between the June and April hatches. In April the hatch usually appears around 1:00 PM and lasts for an hour or two. The duns from the previous day or two (depending on the air temperatures, it can take two or three days for a dun to change to a spinner) appear back over the stream as spinners at about the same time that the duns emerge. In June the duns appear in late afternoon—around 4:00 PM. Spinners appear over the stream around 8:00 PM.

So the next time you fly-fish on a cool mountain steam that holds a good quill gordon hatch, look for some to appear as late as mid-June.

Late-Season Hatches

The angling crowds of spring have gone. The waters of most of Pennsylvania's trout streams are low. Many of these waters have become marginal habitat with temperatures too high for any trout population. On the bright side, most of the anglers who crowded the streams and rivers in spring have gone, and the waters are clear. The fact is that there are hatches in these weeks, too, and many trout remain in some of Pennsylvania's better streams.

By and large late hatches are meager. With the addition of the trico on scores of waters, however, you will find a small but dependable hatch that continues daily for a few months. Other hatches continue to appear into the late season. Hatches like the cream cahill, light cahill *(Heptagenia marginalis)*, yellow drake, and at least two blue-winged olive dun species *(Drunella [Ephemerella] lata* and *D. [E.] cornuta)* persist throughout much of late summer and into autumn.

This is also the time to use patterns mimicking some of the common terrestrials. Ants, beetles, grasshoppers, and crickets make up much of a trout's diet in July, August, and September. And many Commonwealth streams experience a hatchlike influx of winged ants in late August.

Recovering Rivers of Pennsylvania and Their Hatches

For the past couple of decades many anglers have witnessed an alarming increase in the number of posted streams in the Commonwealth. Parts of the Little Juniata River, Spring Creek, Penns Creek, and others have seen NO TRESPASSING signs posted on various sections. Anglers often condemn this loss. But have you thought about the great number of state trout streams and rivers that until recently had been polluted but now hold good populations of trout? Consider how many Keystone waters have recently returned from bouts with pollution. Rivers like the Lackawanna, Youghiogheny, Casselman, and Stonycreek now hold good populations of trout. Streams like the Quittapahilla and Coxes now hold trout populations where just a few years ago there were none. Just 10 to 30 years ago all these streams and rivers were polluted. Some of these once-filthy waters now hold great streambred brown trout populations, and most of them have holdover trout.

What has given impetus to the increase in the number of fishable streams and rivers in the state? First, the Clean Streams Law of 1937, along with later amendments, was designed to clean up pollution from most sources. Second, the reduced volume of coal production in the state and more stringent regulations have helped.

Hatches You Can Expect to See

Even though many of these recovering rivers still see slugs of mine-acid drainage sent down their waters, some boast decent hatches. Downwings seem to appear on most of the contaminated waters, so you'll find stoneflies and caddisflies fairly common. Some waters, like the Casselman River and Coxes Creek, have only meager hatches. But three rivers hold fishable trico hatches, one boasts a heavy green drake, and all hold light cahills.

I'll never forget the first time I checked the bottom of a rock on the Lackawanna River just northeast of Scranton. I found a half-dozen black cahill nymphs crawling on it. I checked five other rocks in the same riffle and found more of the same. The light cahill *(Stenacron interpunctatum)* seems to return to these rivers first. Rivers like the Lackawanna and Stonycreek boast respectable light cahill hatches. If you want to fly-fish over trout rising to a hatch on these waters, then the time to do it is in late May when the light cahill appears.

A second important mayfly hatch to appear on these rivers is the sulphur. Many of them support a good hatch around the third week in May. Carry sizes 16 and 18 to match this hatch.

Some of these once-polluted rivers also hold the multibrooded little blue-winged olive dun. Hatches appear in late March and April and again in September and October.

All returning waters hold good downwing hatches. The Little Schuylkill holds a dozen species of caddisflies in numbers large enough to create a hatch. Stoneflies can withstand a more highly acidic environment than can mayflies, and they are common in many of these recovering rivers. The Lackawanna and Stonycreek Rivers hold respectable hatches of the sister species to the western salmon fly. You'll find this large *Pteronarcys* on these rivers in June and July.

If you plan to fly-fish one of these recovering rivers your best match-a-hatch opportunity comes in late May and early June. Try arriving on the water in the evening and fishing until dusk. You might expect to witness a light cahill or sulphur hatch. And remember, the next time somebody complains about all the streams and rivers being posted, remind him how many rivers have recently returned from pollution.

Little Blue-Wings

Art Michaels edits the *Pennsylvania Angler,* one of the most outstanding state fishing publications in the United States. He recently asked me to do a story on one of the most common, but least-respected, hatches on Keystone State streams and rivers. We decided that story would center on the little blue-winged olive dun. Why feature a size-20 mayfly? You'll find this extremely common hatch on state streams twice a year—early spring and again in September and October, with the fall hatch often much more rewarding. Let me explain.

Andy Leitzinger plans an annual late-fall fishing trip to central Pennsylvania. One recent trip took place on a cool, overcast late-October day. As we approached the Little Juniata River that morning, a heavy fog enveloped the entire valley. By 1:00 PM the temperature had barely reached the 50s, and the protracted morning fog had given way to an overcast, leaden sky. I wore a heavy shooting jacket that constantly reminded me that I should have been hunting for grouse that day, not fly-fishing for trout.

By early afternoon we headed upriver to a section that held some heavy trout. As soon as we arrived we noticed several trout feeding on the surface. I doubted that any hatch would appear this late in the season, but I stopped and scanned the pool to discover what was bringing these trout to the surface. I saw dozens of little blue-winged olive duns struggling to free themselves of their nymphal shucks. Few of them succeeded and trout fed freely in a last binge before the onset of winter. Andy and I simulta-neously tied on size-20 Blue-Wing patterns. In the hour that the hatch lasted—one of the last mayfly hatches of the season—we landed a half-dozen fish.

The spring emergence of this mayfly seldom seems to cause the feed-ing frenzy that the fall one does. However, I've seen good hatches appear as early as March 5 on Spring Creek and March 18 on the Little Juniata River. In spring it's especially important to select a long, slow pool where you can follow the duns and see surfacing trout.

Whether you fish the spring or fall hatch, try to arrive at the stream by noon and be prepared with a size-20 imitation. Don't overlook the nymph and emerger. A Pheasant Tail or Hare's Ear Nymph works well fished in the riffle when the hatch appears. Use the new technique for tying emerger patterns found in chapter 10.

Where can you find a hatch of little blue-wings? It's easier to say where you *won't* find one. This species frequents many more streams and rivers than any other hatch of which I'm aware. (See chart V in the appendix for a list.) Add the fact that it appears in March and April and again in September and October and you can see why, even given its diminutive size, it tends to be an important hatch on Keystone waters.

A Fly for All Summer

I remember the first time I saw a hatch of slate drakes on Bowman Creek; it was 1967. I spotted nymphal shucks attached to many of the rocks at the lower end of the stream in early June. Shortly after that first encounter I wrote an article for a northeastern-Pennsylvania outdoors magazine. I entitled it "A Fly for All Summer." Little did I realize how prophetic that title would become.

Since that first encounter I have seen annual hatches, concentrated and sporadic, for more than 30 years. I've witnessed good hatches and spinner falls in late May, June, and July and again in September and October. Like most fly-fishers I became convinced that these appearances meant two or three separate species. Backing up this premise I noted that the fall slate drake could be copied with a size-14 imitation, whereas I used a size 12 to imitate the June species.

About 10 years ago two entomologists, Boris Kondratieff and J. Reese Voshell Jr., clumped many of the familiar species of slate drakes or *Isonychia,* such as *I. harperi, I. sadleri, I albomanicata, I. matilda,* and others, into one species: *I. bicolor.*

But why the difference in size between those appearing in early summer and those emerging in early fall? Adults of the same genus appearing in spring have a longer period to develop (seven months—although much of that time is during winter, when little development occurs), whereas the fall brood or generation must develop in just three months.

In their study Kondratieff and Voshell found that *Isonychia* nymphs emerging in May crawled farther away from the water to emerge than did those emerging in summer or fall. In streams where few exposed in-stream rocks or debris occur, the species emerges in the stream. In those places where duns appear on the surface, dry-fly fishing should be much more successful. The two investigators also found abdominal color differences among different members of the same species.

Several streams I fly-fish hold great slate drake hatches. Almost without exception the fast-flowing north-central streams in the state hold respectable hatches from late May to late September. On streams like the Loyalsock, Lycoming, and First Fork you'll see respectable hatches on many summer evenings. On one great Keystone stream I've witnessed a superb hatch of slate drakes in early June—and all the duns emerged on the water's surface, not on exposed rocks. On that stream I experienced wonderful dry-fly fishing with a size-12 imitation for more than a week after the duns first appeared. I hit the same species again in mid-to-late September and matched it with a smaller Slate Drake.

When this species hatches, don't ignore the emerger. Read chapter 10 and you'll learn how to tie an immensely productive *Isonychia* emerger pattern. I often fish this pattern when I see a good number of slate drakes emerging and no rising trout. If you add the bi-cycle technique as I suggest in chapter 10 you'll find it an effective way to cope with trout feeding on and under the surface.

Once you find a sizable population of slate drakes on one of your favorite Commonwealth streams you will have some good matching-the-hatch opportunities from late May through October. Truly this species is a "fly for all summer." Streams with slate drakes are listed in chart V in the appendix.

The Trico on Freestones

Fifteen years ago I had the great pleasure of fly-fishing with Barry Beck and Vince Marinaro. Barry has an excellent fly-fishing shop near Benton and is one of the finest fly-fishermen I have ever known. Vince had written several books, including the classic *A Modern Dry-Fly Code.* Vince was visiting Barry at his country home, next to Fishing Creek in northern Columbia County. It was a muggy July evening, and Vince reminisced about the great trico hatch present this time of year on Falling Spring Branch.

"I wish we could fish over a trico hatch tomorrow," Vince remarked, "but I doubt that there are tricos on any of these freestone streams nearby."

Dick Mills and I indicated that Bowman Creek in Wyoming County, just 25 miles away, had a respectable trico hatch that we had been fishing for the past few years. Although Bowman Creek is quite productive, it is considered a typical freestone stream with few or no dissolved substances (such as calcium) and a pH (a measure of acidity and alkalinity) near or just below 7—neutral to slightly acidic. Vince pleaded with us to go to Bowman the next morning so he could witness his first trico hatch on a Pennsylvania free-stone stream. Vince and countless others had associated trico hatches with lime-stone water.

A female trico dun.

We arrived at the fly-fishing-only stretch of Bowman the next morning before 8:00. Trico duns had already emerged, and a swarm of male spinners began to form above the riffle at the head of the so-called Barn Pool. Vince waded across the stream so he could get in a good position to view the hatch and spinner fall and to wait for rising trout. His wait was brief, for in 10 minutes several browns began feeding on the first female spinners to fall spent. It wasn't long before

Vince caught his first trout on a freestone trico fall. The spinner fall often doesn't last very long on those hot, humid mornings so common in late July. By the time the fall had ended about half an hour later, Vince had hooked a handful of trout on his size-24 imitation. He was elated at his success and at the surprisingly heavy trico spinner fall on this freestone water.

If you plan to fish the trico on one of the more than 50 streams in Pennsylvania that harbor this species, there are a few important points to remember. Since males and females are dissimilar in body color and tail structure, carry imitations of both sexes. And keep in mind that this is one of a handful of species in which both sexes fall to the surface spent. The female, after entering the swarm of males, drops to the surface, lays her eggs, and dies on the water, usually spent—that is, with wings out-stretched. The male spinner also dies over the water.

It seems that the longer the trico fall continues, the more difficult the trout are to deceive. Use the same Trico Spinner pattern in September that you employed in July and you'll likely catch fewer fish. Trout seem to become unusually capable of distinguishing the natural from the copy as the season progresses. I have had innumerable encounters with trico spinner falls on dozens of Pennsylvania streams over the past 20 years. I've encountered them on northwestern waters like Thompson Creek; on north-central waters like the Loyalsock, Pine, and Kettle; and on southeastern streams like West Valley Creek, just outside Philadelphia. Heavy trico hatches also develop on central-Pennsylvania streams like Spring Creek, in Centre County, and the upper end of Clover Creek, near Martinsburg in Blair County.

Yes, tricos are abundant throughout Pennsylvania. If you want to determine whether or not your favorite stream possesses a trico spinner fall, examine it on a late-July or August morning, preferably between 7:30 and 9:00. Look 10 to 20 feet above fast water at the head of a pool for small, undulating mayflies moving in a swarm. On streams like Elk in the central part of the state, some anglers mistake the spinner of the blue quill *(Paraleptophlebia guttata)* for the trico. The trico, however, is much smaller (size 24, compared to size 18 for the spinner of the blue quill). In addition tricos eventually move to the surface of the stream, whereas the larger mayfly undulates for hours.

If you haven't found the trico on your favorite stream, don't give up your search. Check another part of the stream. The hatch may occur far-ther up- or downstream. Elk Creek, Clover Creek, and the Little Juniata River are good examples. All three have trico hatches, but only in selected areas. Explore the entire stream thoroughly before you conclude that the hatch is missing from it.

Elk Creek in Sullivan County contains plenty of holdover trout and a good native brown trout population. The stream joins the Loyalsock just above Hillsgrove. On a recent August morning I witnessed an excellent trico spinner fall on the lower 3 miles of this freestone stream. A major tributary to the Elk, Hoagland Branch, also has the trico on its lower mile.

Spend some summer mornings on your favorite freestone stream in Pennsylvania—it might just contain a terrific trico hatch and spinner fall. After all, the trico is more abundant on Commonwealth streams than most anglers realize. Chart V in the appendix might help you get started.

White Mayflies in August

Hatches appear early and abundantly on the Little Juniata River. As early as May 1 I've seen yellow and green caddis bring brown trout to the surface. By mid-May sulphurs dot the evening surface of this productive river. The last week in May light cahills blend with the emerging sulphurs. The river has a dozen popular and productive mayfly and caddisfly hatches. By the time August appears, you're certain the Little Juniata holds no more surprises. But wait!

John Randolph, Bob Panuska, and I met Allan Bright and Terry Moore at Spruce Creek Outfitters one late-August evening a while ago. The five of us decided on the spur of the moment to fish the Little Juniata. We proposed to hit a lower section of the river just above Petersburg. John is the editor of *Fly Fisherman* and just a year before had asked me to write a story on the return of this river. Now he had a chance to experience this rejuvenated trout stream and some of its late-season hatches for himself.

The past summer had been unmerciful to the Little Juniata, and to all Pennsylvania streams. Extreme heat and drought brought trouble to many of them. Trout kills were common throughout the state. The Little Juniata, however, survived—no, more than that, it thrived. Water temperatures on this large stream rarely exceeded 75 even while air temperatures rose above 100.

The five of us arrived on the water at 6:45 PM. Already a good number of slate drakes had emerged near the edges. Eddies carried dozens of *Isonychia* nymphal shucks upstream past us. Before I decided what fly I'd try, Allan Bright had already caught several trout on a Slate Drake pattern.

But we hadn't come to see the slate drake appear. I was hoping that John and Bob would get a true impression of the diversity of this stream and see some of its white mayflies. That mayfly already had appeared for more than a week—but spottily and with very mediocre results.

By 7:45 PM we noticed a few *Ephoron* moving in their characteristic flight a foot above the riffle. Within half an hour thousands of these white mayflies had emerged and begun their mating ritual. They seemed to tantalize the trout by flying just a few inches above the surface. Trout up to 15 inches long lost their timidity and leaped into the air to capture an errant dun or spinner. Dozens of trout in the pool below and upstream in the riffle tried to capture mayflies. Bob Panuska had more than 10 trout feeding in front of him, and 3 of these appeared to be near 15 inches long. Many of the rises occurred over the riffle at the head of the pool.

The action continued well past dusk. Thousands of mating duns and spinners still darted just inches above the surface, and trout still rose to the food. What a fitting end to a match-the-hatch season on the Little Juniata River!

Few anglers realize that the Little Juniata holds this late-season hatch. When anyone mentions the white mayfly, most fishermen immediately think of the great hatch on the Yellow Breeches in south-central Pennsylvania.

The Yellow Breeches holds dozens of hatches that emerge throughout the fishing year, but it is best known for a single species—the white mayfly. Many anglers who fly-fish the Breeches do so only in late August, when this water is teeming, both with these pale insects and with fly-fishermen.

Park near the Allenberry Inn in late August after 5:00 PM and you'll witness a carnival atmosphere similar to the festival that occurs on Penns Creek when the green drake appears. Fishermen discuss their strategies, including what flies they're using, all the time trying to work their way onto the stream where they have room to cast freely. It's like opening day on a well-stocked stream. Fly-fishermen, elbow to elbow, try casting to rising trout.

But there are several other trout streams in the state that host white mayfly hatches in late summer. The Bald Eagle near Julian has a respectable hatch, but the water temperature of this marginal stream often doesn't cooperate when the hatch appears. Several times I've found 75-degree water in late August and quit before the hatch appeared. The lower—and cooler—end of the Bald Eagle at Curtin contains a few white mayflies. One August 22 I fished over enough spinners to catch three trout on my imitation. The hatch is not heavy, however.

Spruce has a sparse hatch of white mayflies on its lower reaches. Credit Joe McMullen for the presence of the late-August mayfly on that stream. For years Joe has driven to the Yellow Breeches during the hatch, brought back fertilized eggs, and deposited them in his section of Spruce Creek. The hatch isn't heavy there either, though.

The greatest white mayfly hatch of all is on the smallmouth hot spot of the East, the North Branch of the Susquehanna River and the main stem around Harrisburg. I had my first encounter with the white mayfly over 20 years ago on this northeastern-Pennsylvania river. Hatches of pale mayflies are so heavy and concentrated here around August 1 that some of the steel bridges between Wilkes-Barre and Scranton must be closed— the masses of crushed insects make the roadways slippery. Smallmouths gorge themselves for about a week on these mayflies, and a size-14 White Wulff takes plenty of bass. The hatch begins in early July around Harrisburg and toward the end of July near Tunkhannock. The hatch is earlier on the river because of the warmer river temperatures, which cause the nymphs to mature a bit faster than they do in the cooler trout waters of the Commonwealth.

There are other trout streams that contain the white mayfly. Start checking some of your fishing spots around August 15—even earlier if the stream you're checking has warmer summer temperatures or is located in the southern half of the state. Look for the hatch on moderate to large trout streams that contain some slow water.

Keep exploring the Commonwealth's waters in late August and you might meet a bonus end-of-the-season white mayfly hatch. In chart V in the appendix I've listed 14 streams and rivers that contain good numbers of white mayflies. Bob Panuska of Miami, Florida, recently wrote a note thanking me for the great fishing weekend when the white mayfly appeared. He ended his letter: "I'll never forget that night on the Little Juniata River. It seems to me that's what fishing's all about."

Terrestrials on Pennsylvania Streams

Clayt Dovey's an experienced angler, a great fly-fisherman, and the pro- ducer of outdoors programs for WJAC-TV in Johnstown, Pennsylvania. He and his wife, Adelle, have roamed the world for unusual fish-and-game stories. Clayt comes back to Pennsylvania each year to do some fly-fishing. Recently he and Dick Mayer of Johnstown invited me to join them on Wayne Harpster's property on Spruce Creek. Trico spinners fall in good enough numbers in early September on this productive limestone stream to bring big browns to the surface.

Fishing over a trico spinner fall this late in the season can bring mixed results, and most of the large trout refused our lifelike imitations. The trico spinner fall lingers later into each day in September than in July and August, and we fished over rising trout until early afternoon without much success.

Clayt had some success with a beetle, so I tied one on, too. I fished the beetle in the home pool where Jimmy Carter fly-fishes frequently. This stretch, although it has large browns, is difficult to fly-fish because of the overhanging hemlocks on the far shore. Besides, it's close to the cabin, so it's fished regularly by all the guests. On one of my first half-dozen casts I plopped the beetle just inches from the far bank under the cover of a heavy evergreen branch. The beetle floated a foot or two before a large shadow followed, then sucked in the small terrestrial. The lunker thrashed, shook from side to side, went deep, then seemed to sulk under the under-cut bank. After a gentle nudge from my 9-foot Orvis Western graphite rod, the heavy brown headed toward me away from the rooted bank. Fifteen minutes later I netted it and removed the beetle pattern from its mouth. With the release of that trout all three of us quit fishing for the day. What a way to end the day—releasing a 22-inch brown on a size-16 beetle imitation!

Sparse hatches are the order of the day in July, August, and September. Don't fish on those days without a good supply of ants and beetles. These and other terrestrials, like the grasshopper, have saved numerous late-summer trips. The Poly Beetle is a must for hatchless sum-mer days. It is extremely easy to tie, taking less than a minute per pattern even when tied by a relative beginner. Chapter 10 gives a quick but simple tying description.

Some New Mayflies on Pennsylvania Waters

Many of the mayflies present on Pennsylvania streams have been thor-oughly described by Schwiebert, Marinaro, Wetzel, Caucci and Nastasi, or any of the many other writers. Some species, however, remain out there yet to be identified.

When Will Flowers worked at Florida State University and later at Clemson, he identified many mayflies for me. In 1975 and 1976 I sent Will more than 30 male spinners that I was unable to identify. One of these was a dark brown mayfly that appeared on Fishing Creek in Clinton County. It looked somewhat like a Hendrickson, but it was darker and emerged around the middle of April. Will tentatively identified it as a sub-species of *Ephemerella subvaria*, the true Hendrickson. In *Hatches II* (Winchester Press, 1986) Caucci and Nastasi confirm that observation, indicating that they have discovered several Hendrickson subspecies.

Another hatch appeared that same year on Bowman and the Mehoopany in Wyoming County, on the Bald Eagle in Centre County, and on dozens of other Pennsylvania streams. This hatch, a blue-winged olive dun tentatively identified as a subspecies or a new species, resembles *Drunella (Ephemerella) cornuta*. There's so much confusion about blue-winged olives. Most anglers put any olive-colored mayfly into this cate-gory. But dozens of these mayflies have unusual body colors ranging from pale to dark olive, and they may vary in size from 14 to 20. The majority of these blue-winged olives belong to the genus *Drunella*.

Many of the so-called blue-winged olives of Pennsylvania remain to be identified. One such unidentified species emerges in abundance on Pine Creek in Lycoming County. Fish this great stream in mid-June around 11:00 AM and you'll meet this hatch. Of course, fishing for trout at this time of the season can be unrewarding because the water temperature rises rapidly. But on one occasion several years ago the water temperature registered a respectable 68 degrees in mid-June. At the section several of us refer to as the Cemetery Pool, I was surprised to see a number of trout rising. Tiny three-tailed olive mayflies emerged in heavy numbers and seemed to be in no hurry to take flight. In a small section of slow water with a riffle above, probably two dozen trout fed on these small, lethargic olive duns.

I collected a half-dozen male duns, put them in Styrofoam cups with some vegetation in each, and placed the cups under the shade of several sycamores on the bank. I then tied on a Little Blue-Winged Olive often used to copy many of the *Baetis* spp. hatches. The pattern has the same proportions as the emerging mayfly but is a much darker olive than the natural. The trout had a seemingly inexhaustible supply of real mayflies, and they refused my pattern time after time—until the hatch diminished in intensity. Then for about half an hour trout took the pattern infrequently.

The captured male duns metamorphosed into male spinners within a day. The species *(Dannella simplex)* had not been mentioned in fishing literature before. It may, however, be widespread on diverse streams and rivers of the Commonwealth.

A light cahill, *Heptagenia marginalis,* begins appearing in early June and continues throughout summer into September. The hatch and spinner fall are predictable. The hatch is very sporadic, and duns escape rapidly from the surface, leaving scant time for rising trout. The spinner presents a different story. Mating adult females appear over fast water about 8:00 PM and remain there, sometimes almost motionless, for half an hour or more. These spinners sometimes seem suspended just a few inches above the surface. Because of their habitual flight pattern they are inconspicuous. I hadn't noticed them until I saw trout coming completely out of the water in a series of riffles on the Bald Eagle near Julian. There trout fed actively on these hovering egg-laden adults. Oddly, trout refused my Light Cahill pattern completely on this occasion. The natural had a pale olive cast to its cream underbelly, but that shouldn't have made a big difference.

I finally lay down on the bank parallel to some fast water to see how the trout were feeding on these insects. The mayflies were at first motionless, but after a while they would move rapidly up- or downstream. I tied on a spider pattern with a long hackle and a cream body. The longer hackle kept the dry fly floating higher on the water. That's all the trout needed.

Most of the state's waters contain at least one species imitated by the Slate Drake. There are about a half-dozen closely related species that use this same common name. The duns are very similar, and most of them have dark gray bodies, slate-colored wings, pale gray tails, and dark brown front legs with the rear pair cream. It's not difficult to identify this group of slate drakes. The group has not been given the credit and importance it deserves, however. Other than the blue-winged olive, blue quill, and trico, no mayfly appears for as long or in the same numbers as the slate drake. Hatches appear as early as late May, and species continue to emerge well into October on Commonwealth streams and rivers. These late hatches often become the last hatch before winter approaches.

Occasionally autumn slate drakes share the spotlight with another tardy species, the blue dun (an *Acentrella* species). When you meet a hatch of slate drakes in early fall you can experience some great fly-fishing, because your choice of patterns is simplified. The rewards of matching a late slate drake are many. Often the mayflies that emerge do so in a cool above-water environment, slowing down their escape considerably.

Greg Hoover identified the great speckled olive *(Siphloplecton basale)* on Clarks Creek, and recently Rich Meyers identified a fall of great red spinners *(Stenonema pudicum)* on Young Womans Creek.

During the 1998 fishing season I found two species on Pennsylvania streams that I had never encountered before. The first, a gray drake *(Siphlonurus mirus)*, I found on Sixmile Run in central Pennsylvania in early June. The male spinner is extremely easy to identify: It has a brownish black hind wing. Look for spinner falls around 7:00 PM during the first two weeks of June. The second species was *Ephemerella needhami* on the Delaware River and Spruce Creek.

These are just some of the hatches you'll encounter on your fishing trips throughout Pennsylvania's streams and rivers. Be sure to look out for others as well.

3 | Streams of Northeastern Pennsylvania

The streams of northeastern Pennsylvania are found in a diverse area. Fly-fish on the Pocono streams in late summer and you'll experience coffee-colored, often marginal waters. Look at Brodhead Creek and the Lehigh or the Lackawaxen River. These and many more waters have suffered from the ravages of population growth and natural disasters. Hurricanes Diane in 1955 and Agnes in 1972 devastated the area. The flooding and result-ing channelization destroyed much of the habitat for natural reproduction of trout and aquatic insects. In particular the Brodhead, Lehigh, and Lackawaxen lost the great green drake hatches they had prior to 1955.

But time and the efforts of many dedicated environmentalists have assisted in the recovery of some streams. The Brodhead Chapter of Trout Unlimited has made habitat improvement an important goal on local streams. The Lehigh River has regained its once-dominant green drake, along with a healthy population of streambred brown trout.

TOMS CREEK

Access Toms Creek is on US 209 about 20 miles north of Stroudsburg. The only easy way to reach the stream is from the picnic area at its lower end. Lower Egypt Road parallels the stream, but it's a steep descent to reach it. Your best bet is to park at the picnic area and hike upstream to fish. There's about 2 miles of open, regulated water.

Special Regulations 2.1 miles from Delaware Water Gap National Recreation Area boundary downstream to the mouth.

Rating ✳✳

Patterns to Match the Hatches Early Brown Stonefly (#12), Blue Quill (#18), Hendrickson (#14), Quill Gordon (#14), March Brown (#12), Sulphur (#16

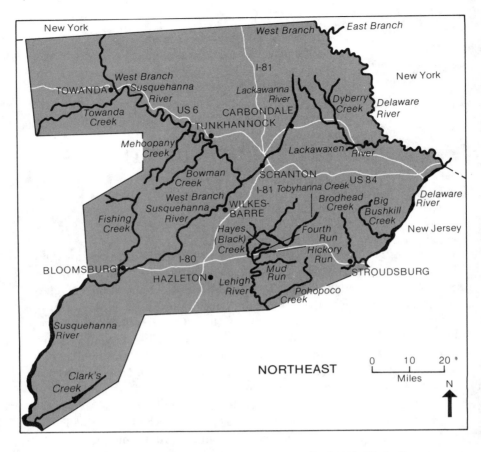

and #18), Green Drake (#12), Little Yellow Stonefly (#16), Little Green Stonefly (#18), Light Cahill (#14), Little Blue-Winged Olive Dun (#20)

Where the heck is Toms Creek? I didn't have the slightest idea—I had never fished it. But when a photo by John Randolph, editor of *Fly Fisherman* magazine, appeared on the cover of the second edition of *Trout Streams of Pennsylvania* anglers began to ask. Finally, after several attempts over a two-year period, I arrived at Toms Creek on a hot mid-August day. If I were to select the poorest time to fish Pennsylvania waters—that is, those streams without a trico hatch—it would be a mid-August afternoon. When I arrived at the Toms Creek Picnic Area and looked at the low stream I almost turned around and headed south. But I had traveled more than 100 miles out of my way to fish this stream so I was determined to give it a try—for a couple of minutes.

I entered the stream and placed a thermometer in the middle of a

small riffle. I scanned the stream in the picnic area and saw plenty of
stream improvement devices that had been placed there several years ago
by a dedicated youth group. Some of these devices formed 3-foot-deep
pools, even in these low-water conditions. I checked the thermometer,
which gave me a 62-degree reading—not bad for a hot August afternoon. I
made a long-distance cast in an attempt not to disturb any spooky trout.
As my Patriot dry fly landed on the surface I saw several trout scatter and
move upstream quickly. I headed upstream and fished just below the next
stream improvement device. Here two logs formed a deep, well-oxygenated
pool. I cast the Patriot into the foamy water and it immediately disappeared. I set the hook and fought a heavy trout, moving near shore where
I wouldn't get tangled in a tree. I finally landed a 14-inch brown trout.
What a beautiful fish! I headed upstream to the next fairly deep pool and
made another cast. Here I landed a 6-inch streambred brown.

In two hours on that heavily canopied stream I caught a dozen trout—
in mid-August. Some of the credit goes to the character of the stream and
to the stream improvement devices. Toms Creek has a heavy canopy,
which keeps the temperature cool; the deep pools and riffles, with plenty
of rocks, boulders, and stream improvement devices, protect the trout.

Whom can we credit for this small gem? The Delaware Water Gap
National Recreation Area owns the land. That means that these 2 miles of
catch-and-release water will forever be ours to use. The Pocono area has
developed phenomenally over the past few decades, but the Toms Creek

One of the many stream improvement devices installed on Toms Creek.

area should remain pristine.

Toms holds some great early-season hatches. You should find trout rising to a variety of early-season insects like the quill gordon, blue quill, and Hendrickson. Don't overlook this stream in late April. Dave Baker of Oreland frequently fishes Toms Creek. He's an expert fly-tier who has developed a pattern called the Black Flymph. It has a black body and a brown hackle, and that's all there is to this simple but extremely productive pattern. Dave says that the quill gordon hatch on Toms Creek is outstanding. Get there about noon or a little before to experience this tremendous hatch firsthand.

If you like small-stream fly-fishing in scenic, well-canopied water, with plenty of wild brown trout, then you've got to try Toms Creek.

LACKAWANNA RIVER

Access To reach the Lackawanna River exit I-80 in Dunmore and take PA 347 north, then turn left on SR 1016 (North Valley Avenue) to the river.

Special Regulations Trophy-trout project—5.2 miles from the Gilmartin Street bridge in Archbald downstream to the Lackawanna Avenue (PA 347) bridge in Olyphant. Excepted is a midsection area extending 0.7 mile from the Depot Street bridge in Jessup downstream to the footbridge in Robert Mellow Park.

Rating ✳✳✳

Patterns to Match the Hatches Little Blue-Winged Olive Dun (#20), Quill Gordon (#14), Hendrickson (#14), Sulphur (#16), Light Cahill (#14), Gray Fox (#12), Tan Caddis (#16), Green Drake (#10), Slate Drake (#12), Pteronarcys Stonefly (#8), Gray Sedge (#14), Dark Brown Dun (#16), Dark Gray Caddis (#16 and #18), Slate Drake (#12), Trico (#24), Blue Quill (#18), Brown Caddis (#16 and #18), Little Black Caddis (#18)

Mike Stevens and Stan Sowa cohost an outstanding program, *Pennsylvania Outdoor Life,* on WNEP-TV in Moosic, produced by Don Jacobs. Mike wanted to get some footage on the Lackawanna River for an upcoming program. He invited me to fly-fish this recovering river and share my thoughts on its future as a trout stream. I waded into the Lackawanna River near the ball field in Archbald. When I first entered the water I thought Mike and his cameraman Larry Lavelle had played a cruel hoax on me. Surely this silt-filled pool held no trout. After a quick glance up- and downriver I questioned whether or not *any* of this water held trout.

As I slowly walked through ankle-deep silt thoughts came to my mind of how badly this river had been polluted just 20 years ago from coal silt,

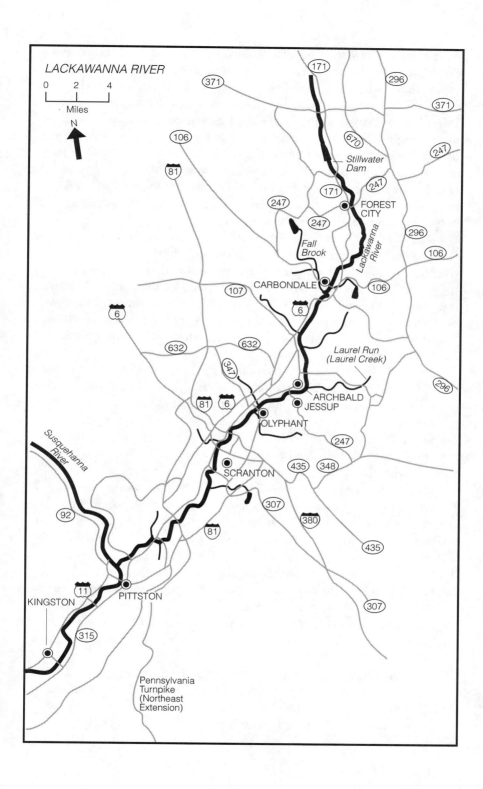

LACKAWANNA RIVER

0   2   4
Miles

N

mine acid, and raw sewage. Mike had assured me that the Lackawanna River had recovered sufficiently to contain a good supply of streambred brown trout. When I glanced downriver again, I noticed several riseforms on the surface—probably chubs or minnows. I cast just above the first fish—no take. Six casts later I gave up. I moved upriver to another rising fish, changing from an attractor to a Little Blue-Winged Olive Dun. My first cast landed just 2 feet above the rising trash fish. I saw a form move toward the dry fly, break the surface, and the struggle began. Five minutes later I netted a foot-long streambred brown trout. I looked up at Mike in utter amazement; now I was a believer in one of the Lackawanna River's best-kept secrets—streambred brown trout.

After I caught three of these beautiful Lackawanna trout I began checking for insect life in the river. On every rock in this section of the river in Olyphant I found many rock clingers (family Heptageniiadae). Light cahill nymphs *(Stenacron interpunctatum)* by the thousands inhabit this river. Evidently the sewage-treatment plants and elimination of much of the mine-acid drainage have done wonders for the Lackawanna River.

I revisited the river six months later to fish it once more. This time I fished with Jim Misiura of Blakely. Jim has caught trout in this river for more than 17 years. He has landed many golden streambred brown trout over 18 inches long. He's had a hold of several in the 24-inch-plus category. Jim guides out-of-area anglers on the Lackawanna.

Recently Jim and I took a tour of the river from Olyphant to Archbald. Even though the river flows through the area called Mid-Valley and more than a half-dozen towns, Jim pointed out many access points where anglers can readily enter the water.

We first stopped at an access point in the Philip Candella Sports Complex in Olyphant. "See that manhole cover?" Jim said as he pointed to the near bank upriver. "Paul Robertson, a local angler, recently caught an 18-inch brown trout there. Paul has fly-fished the river for 29 days without being skunked." Jim and I decided to fly-fish off Laurel Street in Jessup. As we entered the river Jim showed me a pool that held a trout over 30 inches long. In two hours of fly-fishing the Lackawanna River the two of us caught more than 20 trout. Jim caught two over 15 inches long—unbelievably bright golden-and-red streambred trout from the Lackawanna River. He also caught five heavy brown trout in a small area of pocket water.

Jim isn't the only one who can substantiate reports of huge trout in the river. Just ask Alesia Grabowski and her father, Anthony Grabowski. Together they operate a taxidermy business in Archbald. Alesia can tell you of dozens of trout over 20 inches long taken from the Lackawanna River.

Bryan Meck landing a brown trout during a Trico spinner fall.

Mayfly hatches on the river are sparse. Jim Misiura has seen a few green drakes emerge in late May. Light cahills in late May present the best mayfly hatch to fly-fish. The river also holds a good number of down-wings, including a gray sedge in June and even some of the large *Pteronarcys* and *Acroneuria* spp. stoneflies. If you like to fish the hatches then fish this river in late May.

You will find a surprisingly respectable hatch of tricos on the river near the ball field in Archbald in July, August, and September. At that time of the year you'll also find some blue quills on the water, and a good hatch of brown caddis.

In July and August you'll find Jim casting a hopper, beetle, cricket, or ant over some of the lunkers on the Lackawanna River. Jim says that these terrestrials produce plenty of trout for him in late September.

What about water temperatures—how does the river hold up in summer? Jim says that even after a week of 90-degree days the water will remain near 70 degrees. Plenty of springs and cold tributaries keep the river cold much of the summer. What a valuable resource!

There's a total of 39.5 miles of trout fishing on the Lackawanna, from Susquehanna County to where it enters the Susquehanna River in Pittston. You'll find impoundments on the river, including Stillwater Lake just north of Forest City. The best fishing and the most streambred brown trout can be found from Carbondale to Olyphant. The river holds many deep holes, productive riffles and pockets, and some long glides. In most places it flows about 50 to 60 feet wide. Even in the heavily populated Mid-Valley region you can find isolated well-canopied areas.

Jerry Palko, an excellent outdoor writer for the *Scranton Times,* recently wrote an article about the recovering Lackawanna. Jerry indicated that the Pennsylvania Fish Commission has recognized the value of this impressive stretch of the Lackawanna. The commission reclassified the river as class A water, the top classification a stream or river can receive. In addition the commission has designated a section between Archbald and Jessup as a trophy-trout section. Preliminary indications suggest that anglers will be able to keep two trout a day over 14 inches. The commission must discard the trophy-trout idea for a no-kill section. Can you imagine how much revenue a well-run no-kill trout project could generate? All the river needs is some cleaning and a no-kill section, and anglers from miles around will flock there to catch its large streambred browns.

Jim Misiura and Frank Lukasewicz of Justus are two proponents of the no-kill section. Frank related to me a story about several anglers who had just killed several trout over 20 inches long taken from the river. They told Frank they planned to use them for fertilizer in their garden.

If authorities play their cards correctly, anglers will come in droves to fly-fish the Lackawanna River. The National Park Service is working with individuals, local governments, the Lackawanna Heritage Valley Authority, the Lackawanna River Corridor Association, the Lackawanna County Regional Planning Commission, and the Army Corps of Engineers on the Lackawanna Heritage Valley River, Trail, and Greenway Study. The group has developed a 40-mile greenway along the Lackawanna River from the Stillwater Dam to Pittston. This group will help provide access to the river for all to enjoy.

All of us should support the large umbrella organization, the Lackawanna Heritage Valley Authority. It can be reached through Harry Linsay at 717-963-6400. You should also support people like Bernie McGurl, executive director of the Lackawanna River Corridor Association (LRCA), in further enhancing the river as a natural resource. The group developed a Lackawanna River Citizens Master Plan. The goals of this plan are "to restore the Lackawanna River, improve its habitat for fish and wildlife, and improve its recreational opportunities."

"The greenway study will look at the environmental problems such as mine acid, sewage overflows, flood protection, and enhancement of fish and wildlife," says Bernie McGurl, executive director of the LRCA. If you want more information on this worthwhile organization you can call 717-347-6311.

Yes, the Lackawanna has returned from years of neglect and down-right abuse. A river once filled with coal silt, mine acid, and raw sewage is now a fairly clean, cool stream teeming with heavy streambred brown trout. Pollution problems persist, but organizations like the Lackawanna River Corridor Association should mitigate these.

Another problem is that many anglers feel they have to kill the trout they catch. Killing streambred brown trout for fertilizer? The Lackawanna River is too valuable a resource to waste. Killing trout in this productive river benefits no one. Keeping the river teeming with streambred trout, however, will benefit the valley, the state, the Pennsylvania Fish Commission, and, most of all, the angler.

TOBYHANNA CREEK

Access You'll find Tobyhanna Creek in northwestern Monroe County. Much of the public section of the Tobyhanna flows through State Game Lands 127. To access the delayed-harvest section take PA 423 about 3 miles north of PA 940. You'll find several parking areas. From here you have to walk a half mile or more to the stream. You can access the upper end of the stream off PA 611.

Special Regulations Delayed harvest, artificial lures only—from the confluence of Still Swamp Run 1 mile downstream to the Pennsylvania Power and Light service bridge.

Rating ✷✷

Patterns to Match the Hatches Little Blue-Winged Olive Dun (#20), Early Brown Stonefly (#14), Blue Quill (#18), Little Black Caddis (#16), Hendrickson (#14), Tan Caddis (#14), Dark Green Drake (#10), Slate Drake (#12), March Brown (#12), Light Cahill (#14), Trico (#24), Brown Caddis (#16)

❝I like to fish Tobyhanna Creek because I like to get frustrated. Often you find trout rising all over the surface and you can't see what they're taking," said Bob Stevens of nearby Bartonsville. Bob should know—he has been on this stream frequently in May and June for the past five years. He is often baffled while trying to move trout on some of the slower sections into taking any pattern he presents.

One late-August day Don Baylor, Bob Stevens, and I hiked down a game trail to a bridge marking the lower end of the delayed-harvest water on Tobyhanna Creek. I looked upstream and downstream and saw a 50-foot-wide pool with very slow-moving water and some weed beds. As the three of us scanned the regulated area we saw a half-dozen trout surface-

The delayed-harvest Area on Tobyhanna Creek.

feeding. We fished over these trout for more than two hours and had two strikes, but no trout. I soon realized that what Bob Stevens had told me—how he often gets frustrated on the Tobyhanna—had some merit. When, then, is the best time to fish this water?

The Tobyhanna does hold a good supply of hatches. Just ask Don Baylor of Stroudsburg. Don recently inventoried the insects on this stream for the Tobyhanna Conservation Association. He runs Aquatic Resource Consulting out of Stroudsburg. Besides being knowledgeable about the insects, he is an accomplished fly-fisher. The number of Hendrickson nymphs on the Tobyhanna surprised even Don. He feels a good time to hit the Tobyhanna is mid-to-late April, when you'll find blue quills and Hendricksons on the surface.

Don also found three *Baetis* spp. on the Tobyhanna. Make certain you carry plenty of Little Blue-Winged Olive Duns anytime you plan to fish this stream. If you enjoy nymph-fishing, then a Hare's Ear to copy the *Baetis* should work well. Slate drakes also abound, emerging throughout summer and fall.

Don has also found a good number of downwings on the Tobyhanna. "I found a lot of early brown stoneflies in the stream, but I didn't bother to fish this hatch because it usually appeared before the season began. Now with the delayed-harvest area being open all year, I'll be back here to fish that stonefly hatch," he told me.

Don't overlook damselfly nymphs. When Don and I checked the rocks in slower sections we saw quite a few of these.

The Tobyhanna has the characteristic Pocono brownish tint to its water, caused when a stream flows through bogs and picks up tannic acid. There are some faster sections, but also many slow sections on this 50- to 60-foot-wide stream. The current barely moves on some of these slower areas.

Much of the lower end of this stream flows through private property. Just before it flows into the Lehigh River at the upper end of the Francis E. Walter Dam there's a 3.5-mile private section called the Dream Mile Club, then another called the Lower Toby Club. John Churnetski, a great fly-fisher, is president of the Dream Mile Club.

Will you too become frustrated when you fly-fish the Tobyhanna? Try fly-fishing the stream when it produces one of its great hatches like the Hendrickson. If you successfully match the hatch you'll keep coming back.

FISHING CREEK (COLUMBIA COUNTY)

Access T 700 gets you to the upper end from Grassmere to Coles Creek. PA 487 parallels the creek from Coles Creek to Bloomsburg.

Rating ✳✳

Patterns to Match the Hatches Blue Quill (#18), Quill Gordon (#14), Hendrickson (#14), March Brown (#12), Sulphur (#16), Blue-Winged Olive Dun (#14), Light Cahill (#14), Little Green Stonefly (#16), Slate Drake (#12 and #14), Pink Lady (#14), Gray Caddis (#16), Trico (#24), Yellow Drake (#12)

Wow! Thirty years had passed by so quickly since I had last fly-fished the area around Moms Pool on Fishing Creek. Three decades ago Barry Beck, Dick Mills, and I fly-fished that stretch two or three times a week. Now Dave Colley and I parked at the Boy Scout campgrounds at Camp Lavigne and hiked down a well-worn path almost a mile to that memorable place. Until recently, Dave owned Fishing Creek Outfitters just a couple of miles from where we fished. He's one of that growing number of fly-shop owners who have become expert fly-fishers. Dave has created a fly he swears by, the Stack Shuck Parachute. He says that this pattern works especially well on Fishing Creek.

We finally arrived at the riffle just above Moms Pool. I was remembering vividly those dozens of evenings I had spent in late June and much of July waiting for the yellow drake to appear at dusk. Talk about cold water—I always wore long underwear, even in the middle of summer, to

Dave Colley fishes Fishing Creek in Columbia County.

stave off the extremely cold water on Fishing Creek. Thirty years ago there were no neoprene waders. What memories this latest trip revived!

We fished several riffles above the pool without any success. Just two days before, high winds and thunderstorms had devastated the area. Even now, two days later, the stream ran almost a foot higher than normal. Dave said that it had been totally unfishable just the day before. For old times' sake I just had to check that water temperature. As I dipped my thermometer in the stream I could tell the water was cool. Dave and I both came up with 59-degree readings—on a hot afternoon in early July. As I looked skyward Dave pointed out plenty of jenny spinners undulating in the afternoon sun.

We retraced our steps and drove downstream a short distance below Benton. Dave suggests that a good day's fly-fishing would consist of fishing from PA 254 upstream to Benton. In this stretch you'll find plenty of 3- to 10-foot-deep pools and ample productive riffles.

When we arrived at the stream it looked like a small tornado had hit the area. We had to climb over numerous fallen trees to reach the water. Once we did, we saw huge trees blocking old, favorite pools. We spent a couple of hours fishing this stretch. An occasional trout fed in the tail of several of the pools. Because the water was high the trout seemed to be turned off that afternoon, although we did manage to land a few. We talked to a spin-fisherman who also lamented his lack of success. He said

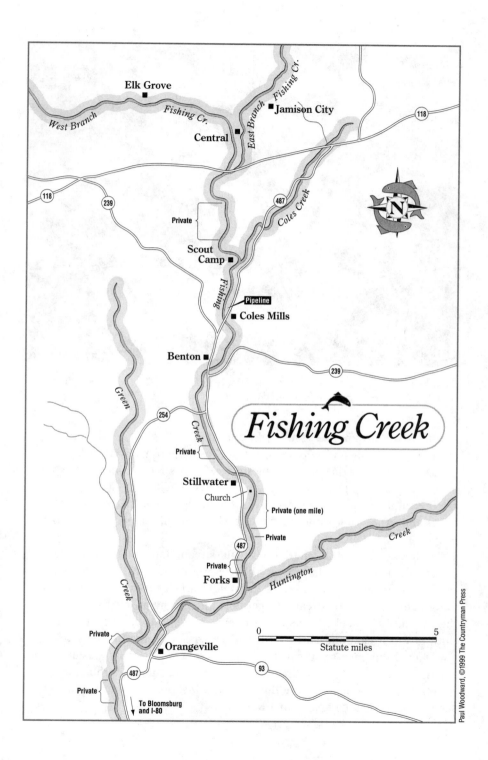

Elk Grove

Jamison City

West Branch

Fishing Cr.

East Branch Fishing Cr.

Central

118

118

239

Coles Creek

487

Private

Scout
Camp

Fishing

Pipeline

Coles Mills

Benton

239

Green

254

Fishing Creek

Creek

Private

Stillwater

Church

Private (one mile)

Private

487

Creek

Private

Forks

Huntington

Creek

0 _____ 5
Statute miles

Private

Orangeville

487

93

Private

To Bloomsburg
and I-80

Paul Woodward, ©1999 The Countryman Press

PHOTO BY BARRY BECK

Cathy Beck with a record brown trout caught on a fly on Fishing Creek. The lunker measured 28 inches long and weighed 8¼ pounds.

that just two days before trout had been on a feeding binge. He and a friend had caught—and released—18 trout in the pool we were fishing.

Dave says that the stream comes alive when a hatch appears or spinners fall. Probably two of the most productive hatches on Fishing Creek are the sulphur and the March brown. You'll also see some tricos on its lower end. And don't forget that the creek still holds some yellow drakes in late June.

Cold water, great hatches, a beautiful stream, large water, deep pools—Fishing Creek seems to have everything going for it. But that's not the case. There're some critical issues that might affect the future of this potentially great trout stream. Uppermost among the problems that haunt this stream is its acidity. This has become so bad, especially on the upper third of the stream and particularly on the East Branch, that the state has abandoned the once-great catch-and-release section it had set aside in the Grassmere section. Fishing Creek isn't alone in this acidity problem. Several other streams, like the Bowman and Mehoopany, that begin in the same general area have similar troubles.

What can interested groups do to combat the acidity in the stream? Recently local anglers formed an organization called the Fishing Creek Watershed Association. This group plans to install limestone diversion wells on some of the tributaries of the East Branch of Fishing Creek. If you fish this stream then you owe it to yourself to join this organization. You can contact it c/o Columbia County Conservation District, 702 Sawmill Road, Bloomsburg 17815.

Some local anglers also complain about the private waters cropping up along Fishing Creek. Although there are four or five private areas (see map), much of the stream still remains open.

Fishing Creek holds good cold water downstream to Orangeville, where the warmer Huntington Creek enters. Fishing Creek is a crystal-clear freestone stream ranging from 30 to 50 feet wide. Some of its riffles and most of its pools hold good numbers of trout. You'll find streambred and stocked browns, planted rainbows, and native brookies in the stream. Fishing Creek begins in Sullivan County. The West and East Branches join near PA 115. The stream then flows south for 20 miles before it enters the Susquehanna River at Bloomsburg. Little Fishing Creek, another stocked trout stream, also enters near Bloomsburg.

For stream conditions and latest hatches stop in at Fishing Creek Outfitters. It's located a few miles north of Benton just off PA 487.

What does the future hold for Fishing Creek? With the help of the Fishing Creek Watershed Association, it could easily become a viable trout stream again.

BOWMAN CREEK

Access It's easy to access the lower half of Bowman. PA 309 gets you to the lower half of the stream, and PA 29 accesses the section around Noxen. LR 3002 and T 313 reach some of the stream above Noxen.

Special Regulations Delayed harvest, fly-fishing only—1 mile, from near PA 292 downstream to near the confluence with Marsh Creek.

Rating ✳✳✳

Patterns to Match the Hatches Little Blue-Winged Olive Dun (#20), Blue Quill (#18), Quill Gordon (#14), Hendrickson and Red Quill Spinner (#14), Early Brown Stonefly (#12), Grannom (#12), Light Stonefly (#12), Spotted Sedge (#14), March Brown (#12), Gray Fox (#14), Light Cahill (#14), Little Green Stonefly (#16), Little Yellow Stonefly (#16), Green Drake (#12), Blue-Winged Olive Dun (#14), Pale Evening Dun (#16 and #18), Dark Blue Sedge (#12), Slate Drake (#12 and #14), Yellow Drake (#12), Trico (#24)

A lot of years had passed since I called Bowman Creek my home stream—26, to be exact. Now I had an opportunity to spend a morning on the stream with George Smith and Ron Payne. I had scheduled a book signing event at Ron's fly shop, Backmountain Outfitters, in the afternoon. George, the outdoors editor for the *Wilkes-Barre Times Leader,* wanted to fish with us and write a column about the experience.

We decided to spend a couple of hours on the stream just above and below the spot where Roaring Run enters. Locals call this area Root Hollow. As I entered Bowman Creek I quickly realized the water was too deep and swift to cross where I had planned. I grabbed a stick and tried to wade to the other side, to no avail—recent thunderstorms had pushed Bowman more than a foot above its normal late-June flow. I decided not to endanger my life and hiked downstream on the PA 309 side. Still, even with the additional flow, Bowman looked great—clear and cool. When I checked my thermometer I couldn't believe the 59-degree reading for June 20.

As we fished hundreds of blue-winged olives emerged. Because of air temperatures in the low 80s these mayflies escaped the surface quickly; no trout fed on the surface. I'm convinced that you should fish these blue-winged olives (*Drunella* spp.) when the weather deteriorates. On a cool, cloudy day the duns tend to rest longer on the surface. Add a bit of drizzle and it might be one of the best matching-the-hatches episodes you've ever experienced.

We had little success where Roaring Run enters so we hiked downstream to a nondescript glide just above Evans Falls. Ron was the first to catch a trout—on a nymph. I hooked a brookie on my Patriot dry fly. Just below, George Smith caught and released a trout on a Dark Olive Bead Head tied on a tandem.

In that rather commonplace glide we picked up a half-dozen trout in the next hour on an assortment of dry flies and nymphs. Remember, this stretch was a foot above normal, in late June, and on a catch-and-kill section. Some of the brook trout and a couple of the rainbows seemed to be wild fish. We also caught browns that morning. Bowman is one of the few streams that hold some streambred browns, native brookies, and, in the Roaring Run tributary, wild rainbows.

Bowman Creek begins in the far northeastern corner of Luzerne County on North Mountain. It flows in a northeasterly direction for more than 30 miles before it enters the Susquehanna River near Tunkhannock in Wyoming County. In its upper reaches the stream runs through bogs and swamps and picks up tannic acid. In the upper end—above the town of Stull—you'll find plenty of native brookies. You have to hike in to reach the upper end of this stream, but if you enjoy catching brook trout, it's well worth your effort.

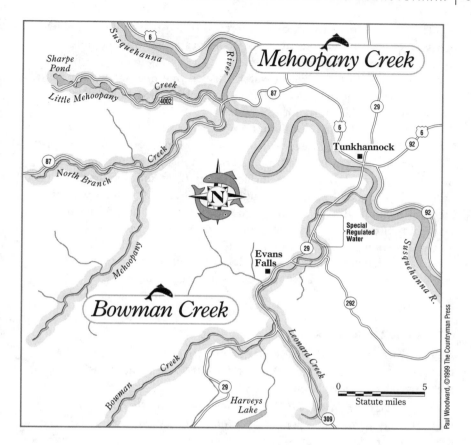

But Bowman has some problems. Two of them—urban encroachment and lingering acid problems—might decrease the fishing value of this tremendous resource. The entire Back Mountain section, including Dallas and Shavertown, has grown steadily in the past few years. The Endless Mountain section near Tunkhannock has also seen an increase in population with a boom in the local economies. All of this adds up to additional angling pressure on this top-notch stream. Toss in some problems with acidity and you might wonder what the future has in store for this highly touted trout stream.

Several years ago some of the anglers who claim Bowman as their favorite stream complained that as soon as the Pennsylvania Fish Commission planted trout in it they vanished. Some, like Ron Payne, claim that many of the trout move downstream to the Susquehanna River. When the river warms these trout move back up Bowman Creek. Others assert that trout leave the main stem for some of the less acidic tributaries. Who knows?

Three miles downstream from where we fished that morning Bowman boasts a delayed-harvest section. For many years that was the only water I fished. I'll never forget the first time I saw a trico hatch appear on the Barn Pool section of the project water. I fished that one hatch on at least 10 occasions. You'll find trico hatches on much of the lower half of the stream from late July through September.

But Bowman holds a lot more than a trico hatch and spinner fall. Probably the first hatch I ever saw there was a Hendrickson in late April. That year the hatch was of enormous proportions; on an inclement day the insects literally covered the surface in the Barn Pool section. You'll find an abundance of hatches throughout April and May; blue-winged olives and yellow drakes in June; and tricos just about every morning from mid-July through much of September. I've even see a smattering of green drakes on the project water in late May. Bowman also holds some great caddis hatches—and a good variety of them. Early in the season you'll find grannoms and spotted sedges. In early June some sections around Noxen boast rising trout and a heavy dark blue sedge hatch.

DELAWARE RIVER

Access You can reach the West Branch and the main Delaware on PA 191 from Hancock downriver for 10 miles. SR 4014 takes you to the upper West Branch in Pennsylvania.

Special Regulations Artificial-lures-only season from October 1 to midnight the day before the opening of trout season—West Branch, Delaware River, from the Pennsylvania–New York border downstream to the confluence with the East Branch of the Delaware River.

Rating ✳✳✳✳

Patterns to Match the Hatches Little Black Stonefly (#16 and #18), Early Brown Stonefly (#14), Little Blue-Winged Olive Dun (#20), Blue Quill (#18), Quill Gordon (#14), Hendrickson and Red Quill (#14), Grannom (#12), Olive Caddis (#13 and #16), Gray Caddis (#14 and #16), Tan Caddis (#14), Sulphur Dun and Spinner (#16 and #18), Gray Fox and Ginger Quill (#12 and #14), March Brown (#14), Green Drake and Coffin Fly (#10), Light Cahill (#14), Brown Drake Dun and Spinner (#12), Chocolate Dun and Spinner (#16), Pink Lady (#14), Slate Drake (#12 and #14), Blue-Winged Olive Dun (#14 and #16), Cream Cahill (#14 and #16), Olive Sulphur (*Ephemerella needhami* female) (#16), Dark Brown Dun (*Ephemerella needhami* male) (#16), Golden Drake (#12), Trico (#24), White Mayfly (#14), Blue Dun (#24)

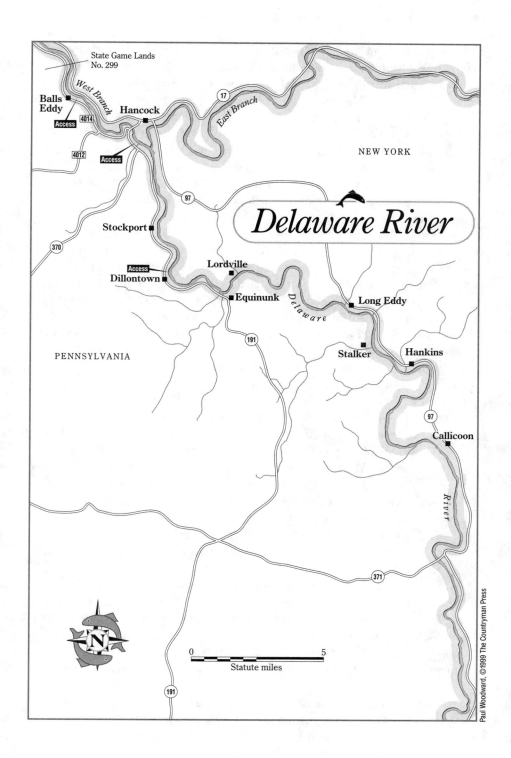

State Game Lands
No. 299

West Branch

Balls
Eddy

Access

4014

Hancock

East Branch

17

NEW YORK

Delaware River

97

4012

Access

Stockport

370

Access

Lordville

Dillontown

Equinunk

Delaware

Long Eddy

PENNSYLVANIA

191

Stalker

Hankins

97

Callicoon

River

371

N

0   5
Statute miles

191

Paul Woodward, ©1999 The Countryman Press

"Watch out for frostbite!" Rick Eck yelled back to me as we waded in thigh-deep water on the West Branch of the Delaware River. Rick owns River Essentials, an Orvis shop at the intersection of PA 191 and PA 370. For August 6 it was a downright eerie feeling. From my waist down I froze—from my waist up I was hot. That's what a 300-foot-deep tailwater will do to you, even in the dog days of summer. Rick and I bent over simultaneously with our thermometers to check the cool—no, cold— temperature. Both of us recorded 46 degrees at 9:00 AM. Rick said that the stretch we planned to fly-fish, just upstream from Balls Eddy, had produced a great trico hatch and spinner fall the past couple of days. Would it have one today? As we headed upriver next to the shore we counted a dozen or more trout feeding on cream midges that hatched while we waded. We cast over each riser a couple of times, then moved on to the next. For more than an hour we cast to trout, some of them heavy, rising to midges.

But we were looking for the famed Delaware trico hatch. By 10 AM only a few appeared in the glide where Rick had seen thousands the day before. Only a handful of trout rose in the section we had planned to fly-fish. So Rick headed to the lower end of this long eddy while I fished the upper end. I heard a groan from downstream and saw Rick lose a heavy trout on a Trico pattern. I continued to use a tandem with a size-16 Bead Head Pheasant Tail. I cast over a riser and my Patriot dry fly sank. I set the hook and landed a heavy 14-inch Delaware River brown trout. We saw no further action so we headed upriver to a productive riffle. We didn't do much better in this area either—just a couple of trout on a Bead Head.

That same afternoon I renewed an acquaintance with Fred Drake and his son Gary at Al Caucci's Delaware River Club. Fred's fly-fished the river since 1975. He is on the West Branch daily either in the no-kill area upriver in New York or just behind his trailer. All afternoon long we fished over a heavy *Baetis* spp. hatch. Thousands of duns rested on the water, but few trout rose to feed on them. Fred, Gary, and I managed to catch a dozen trout on an assortment of Green Midges and Pheasant Tails.

If you fly-fish the Delaware River look for Sam Vigorita of Warminster and some of his friends from the Main Line Fly Tyers. Sam's one of the top fly-fishers on the river. He can cast a fly 90 feet almost perfectly. What would Sam have considered an excellent day of fishing on the Delaware 10 years ago? He experienced some 100-trout days. What's a good day now? Sam considers a 35- to 50-trout day excellent. He blames some of the reduction in productivity in the increase in angling pressure on the river.

Sam's friends tell me that he outfishes just about everyone on the river. Besides his expert casting ability, what sets him apart from the angling crowd? Sam often uses oversized dry flies, along with huge

Woolly Buggers and leech patterns, on the river. Even when there's a hatch Sam often uses large dry-fly patterns. His favorites? He ties Dun Variants, Cahills, March Browns, and Brown Spinners in sizes 6, 8, and 10. He use a Mustad 94840 in sizes 6 and 8, and a Mustad 79580 to tie the size 10s. Sam often uses three—yes, three—hackles to keep these patterns floating. He ties some with a blue dun, a grizzly dun, and a light ginger hackle.

How does he fish his patterns? On occasion Sam will impart movement to the large dry flies, especially when few trout rise to any hatch. He often catches trout with this tactic—many of them big. Sam weights his leech and Woolly Bugger patterns, sometimes adding weight to the body, sometimes a lead shot just in front of the fly. Then he lifts the fly up—and then lets it sink. This tactic really works with Delaware lunkers.

Try Sam's methods and patterns if you're on the Delaware. He's found them successful for many years.

The West Branch flows out of the Cannonsville Reservoir at Deposit, New York, and the East Branch out of the Pepacton Reservoir at Downsville, New York; they join near Hancock. There's about 10 miles of fishing in Pennsylvania on the West Branch. In New York you'll find a specially regulated area on the West Branch. The West Branch is usually much colder than the East Branch; if you find the West Branch too cold you can go downriver to Hancock and fish the Junction Pool. You'll find good fishing on the Pennsylvania side all the way down to Calicoon. That's about 30 miles of excellent fly-fishing.

Access to the Delaware is extremely limited; if you hike over private land to reach the river, get permission first. The Pennsylvania Fish and Boat Commission recently added another access area, but many more are needed. You can access the river at the state game lands north of Balls Eddy, the Balls Eddy Access, Shehawken Access, and Buckingham Access. You will find a couple of access points on the New York side. Pennsylvania anglers can fish from the New York side. Once in the river you can wade up- and downstream.

Both New York and Pennsylvania ceased stocking fingerlings in the Delaware quite a few years ago. Studies indicate that there's excellent reproduction. You'll find browns dominating rainbows in the West Branch by 3 or 4 to 1. Still, in recent trips to this great river I've seen several things that have disturbed me. First, I have not caught the number of large rainbows that I did several years back. This can be attributed to the increase in fishing pressure. Second, some of the hatches on the river don't seem as heavy as they were a few years back. Some anglers who fly-fish this river regularly tell me that it sometimes flows muddy with high water; they think that this has something to do with the decrease in the insect population. Third, when I first wrote about the river in 1988 I found few guides on the river. Presently there are over 70 guides on the upper Delaware River. Just think of the increase in fishing pressure with all those guides on the river!

There are other problems. Rick Eck has seen the river's temperatures fluctuate tremendously. He's seen water as warm as 75 degrees one day; the next day, when dam authorities released water, the temperature might cool to 46 degrees. This temperature roller coaster affects the hatches and the quality of the fishing. Some anglers have heard reports of striped bass in the upper reaches. These predators will certainly do a number on many of the smaller trout.

Despite these problems the Delaware River is still a tremendous trout fishery. Many locals who fish here will tell you that the river has the finest wild rainbows in the East. Rick Eck tells it like it is: "You don't fish for trout on the upper Delaware—you hunt for them." Once in a while you can fish for trout blind but on most occasions you'll be fishing over risers. If trout aren't feeding the river can be extremely unforgiving. I've had hatchless days on which I struggled to catch one trout.

What's the best time to fish the river? Bob Sentiwaney and I fished the river for an entire day almost a decade ago. We had little success until evening, when the stream came alive with rising trout. Duns and plenty of spinners bring trout to the surface around sunset.

The river has hatches throughout the year. When you don't see mayflies use a cream or green midge pattern. Fred Drake uses midge patterns throughout the summer with great success. The midge he ties has a cream or green body, a thin brown Z-Lon shuck for a tail and CDC for the wings and tied downwing. Hatches begin in April, when you'll see blue quill, quill gordon, and great Hendrickson emergences. But probably the best time to match the hatch on the Delaware is late May and early June. Then you'll see the green and brown drakes, slate drake, sulphur, pink lady, blue-winged olives, and many more. The brown drake is especially heavy on the West Branch.

Stop in at West Branch Anglers or at River Essentials, where you'll be greeted by Brendan Curry or guides Chuck Swartz, Sherrie Anderson, or Steve Vogt. Remember, there are 70 guides on the river; if it's your first time fishing here, it might be a good idea to use one. They can show you where the trout are and what they're feeding on.

CLARKS CREEK

Access Clarks Creek flows just 10 miles north of Harrisburg. PA 325 follows its entire length.

Special Regulations Delayed harvest, fly-fishing only—1.9 miles, from the

Pennsylvania Game Commission parking area on PA 325 downstream to the PGC access road at Iron Furnace.

Rating ✱✱

Patterns to Match the Hatches Early Brown Stonefly (#12), Little Blue-Winged Olive Dun (#20), Blue Quill (#18), Black Quill (#14), Great Speckled Olive Dun (#12), Hendrickson (#14), Sulphur Dun and Spinner (#16), March Brown (#12), Blue-Winged Olive Dun (#14), Light Cahill (#14), Slate Drake (#12 and #14), Dark Green Drake (#10), Little Green Stonefly (#16), Yellow Stonefly (#14), Yellow Drake (#12)

G reg Hoover lives in Halifax, just a half-hour drive from Clarks Creek. He recently made a study of the green drake on Penns Creek. Greg is an entomologist working for Pennsylvania State University, and a past president of the Pennsylvania Entomological Society. He fishes Clarks Creek about 20 times a year. Several years ago, in late April, Greg recognized a new hatch on the stream. He identified it as the great speckled olive dun *(Siphloplecton basale)*.

I visited with Greg a year later and we fly-fished over a decent hatch and spinner fall of this species. The hatch and fall bring Clarks Creek trout to the surface for this early-season mayfly. Fishing over this new species, we both caught trout. Greg feels that many of the fly-fishermen who see the hatch believe it's a quill gordon. The body of the quill gordon, however, is much darker than that of the great speckled olive.

Greg fishes Clarks Creek frequently from mid-March through August. From July on he feels the stream gets extremely difficult to fish with its typically low, gin-clear water. The largest trout he has caught on Clarks was a 22-inch brown trout.

Clarks holds a fair number of early hatches, including some black quills. Greg feels that three of the best early-season hatches are the early brown stonefly, Hendrickson, and March brown. Don't expect the intensity of these hatches to measure up to those on the Loyalsock or the upper Allegheny, but be assured that they can provide residents of the Harrisburg area with ample opportunities to match the hatch.

Dick Henry of Lebanon fly-fishes on Clarks from early April until September. He's seen decent hatches of blue-winged olive duns on occasion, and a few sulphurs on the water. Dick cautions that neither insect hatches in large numbers. He suggests that the two most important mayfly hatches on Clarks are the Hendrickson and the March brown. Dick feels terrestrials work well on this stream. "When leaf rollers are on the water," he says, "the trout often go wild, and nothing but a leaf roller imitation will take them."

Clarks Creek reminds me of so many other isolated valley streams, like

Greg Hoover spends several weeks on Clarks Creek each year. Greg first identified the *Siphloplecton* hatch on the stream.

East Licking Creek and Blacklog Creek. It begins near Tower City and flows southwest for 20 miles before entering the Susquehanna River near Dauphin. The city of Harrisburg maintains the DeHart Reservoir about 10 miles upstream from its mouth. Above the dam Clarks is a small stream running from 10 to 30 feet wide. The state stocks the area above the dam with plenty of trout. Fly-fishing in this upper stretch presents plenty of problems, with dense bushes and brush on the banks. Below the dam the stream widens to 30 to 40 feet. Water released from the bottom of the reservoir keeps Clarks fairly cool downstream throughout much of the summer. The flow is slow, and the bottom contains a mixture of sand, gravel, and rocks.

But containing a reservoir on Clarks Creek is also a curse. DeHart Reservoir supplies much of the water for the city of Harrisburg and it is constantly under pressure to supply more. If authorities draw more water from the reservoir the stream below suffers immensely. The Pennsylvania

Environmental Defense Fund is fighting this increased allotment, suggesting that authorities get additional water from the Susquehanna River below. If you fish the water below the reservoir, you should support this organization.

Clarks contains a 2-mile delayed-harvest fly-fishing-only section. Even after the middle of June you can find trout in this section. The stream contains a good supply of stocked trout, some holdovers, and possibly a few native trout.

LACKAWAXEN RIVER

Access US 6 follows the Lackawaxen from Honesdale to Hawley, and PA 590 and a paved secondary road parallel the river below.

Rating ✳✳

Patterns to Match the Hatches Blue Quill (#18), Hendrickson and Red Quill (#14), Early Brown Stonefly (#12), Quill Gordon (#14), Blue-Winged Olive Dun (#14 and #16), Gray Fox (#14), March Brown (#12), Green Drake and Coffin Fly (#10), Sulphur Dun and Spinner (#16), Yellow Drake (#12), Trico (#24)

Jerry Lewis has lived on the Lackawaxen River since 1929. He remembers well how productive this great river was prior to 1955 and Hurricane Diane. He tells stories of enormous green drake hatches and coffin fly spinner falls that occurred in back of his house in late May and early June. "That's when the lunker browns surface-fed," Jerry says. "In one evening fly-fishing over the green drake, I caught a half-dozen trout—all over 20 inches long."

Those memorable days have vanished. Many of the once-deep, once-productive pools and gravel stretches essential to green drake nymphs have been buried by silt and debris from several floods. Now only a few drakes appear. Will the hatch ever regain its prominence?

Annually John Churnetski and Lee Eckert, of the Wyoming Valley, and Carl Laurer, of Emerson, New Jersey, meet at Jerry Lewis's home near Rowland for the opening of the trout season in Pennsylvania. Some of these mid-April days have been cold and blustery with flurry-filled, leaden skies. Even on days when the temperature barely rises to 47 degrees, however, hendricksons often appear. For those early days of the season John, Lee, and Carl select patterns like the Quill Gordon (wet and dry), Hendrickson (wet, dry, and nymph), and Little Black Caddis (wet and dry).

The Lackawaxen begins in northwestern Wayne County near Pleasant Mount. It travels southeast about 20 miles to the town of Honesdale, where it picks up additional volume from another trout stream, Dyberry Creek. The Lackawaxen then flows south-southeast for 8 miles to Hawley, where Middle Creek enters the main stem. Just downriver the Lackawaxen adds water from Lake Wallenpaupack, then flows east for 15 miles in Pike County to the town of Lackawaxen, where it enters the Delaware River. There's about 40 miles of good trout-fishing water on the Lackawaxen, some excellent hatches, and a good supply of trout—even some holdovers.

If you enjoy fishing large water and don't mind plenty of anglers nearby, try the Lackawaxen, especially when the enormous Hendrickson hatch appears around April 23.

HAYES CREEK

Access Most of the upper part of Hayes flows through private land. The lower 2 miles remain open only because the stream flows through state game lands. There are 1.5 miles of open water above PA 534, and 0.5 mile below. Get on the stream on PA 534, then hike up- or downstream.

Rating ✳✳

Patterns to Match the Hatches Early Brown Stonefly (#14), Blue Quill (#18), Quill Gordon (#14), Hendrickson and Red Quill (#14), Gray Fox and Ginger Quill (#12 and #14), March Brown (#12), Light Cahill (#14), Slate Drake (#12 and #14), Little Green Stonefly (#16), Yellow Stonefly (#14)

Bob Sentiwany and I stopped at Hayes Creek (also called Black Creek) where it crosses PA 534. We hiked upstream along a path that follows the creek. As we walked under a heavy canopy of evergreens, Bob boasted about the excellent trout the water contained. The upper end held plenty of brook trout, and the lower end, a good supply of streambred browns. We saw several pools over 5 feet deep, and each held several native trout.

Yellow and green stoneflies emerged from many of the pools, and trout rose to a few that didn't become airborne immediately. Hayes, however, contains much more than just two stonefly species. March browns emerge in good numbers the last week of May. Earlier, in April, you can fish to rising trout when blue quills, quill gordons, and Hendricksons appear.

Hayes begins at Pocono Mountain Lakes. Discharge from the top of the lake plus effluent from sewage-treatment facilities below warm the stream unnaturally in June, July, and August. Temperatures then approach and exceed 70 degrees. The stream flows southwest under the Pennsylvania Turnpike and I-80 and then into state game lands for 2 miles before it joins the Lehigh River. Halfway between I-80 and PA 534,

Fourth Run enters the main stem. This branch adds plenty of cool water but also some tannic acid to the main stem.

If you enjoy small-stream fly-fishing on water that contains some good hatches and high-quality streambred trout, then you'll enjoy fishing Hayes Creek. This stream could be made even better if the state placed a catch-and-release policy on it.

HICKORY RUN

Access PA 534 gives access to Hickory Run.

Special Regulations Catch-and-release—1.5 miles, from Sand Spring Run downstream to the mouth.

Rating ✳✳

Patterns to Match the Hatches Early Brown Stonefly (#14), Blue Quill (#18), Quill Gordon (#14), Hendrickson and Red Quill (#14), Gray Fox and Ginger Quill (#12 and #14), March Brown (#12), Light Cahill (#14), Little Green Stonefly (#16), Yellow Stonefly (#14)

Hickory Run lies halfway between Hayes Creek and Mud Run. Below the highway are 3 miles of top-notch small-stream catch-and-release water. Hickory ranges from 15 to 20 feet wide, with plenty of narrow riffles and small pools teeming with streambred browns and brookies. It holds some hefty trout. Bob and Mary Lou Sentiwany operate the AA Pro Shop just a few miles away. Bob's largest trout on Hickory Run measured 19 inches long and weighed about 3 pounds.

Bob's concerned about the number of poachers on Hickory Run. In some areas there are only a few posters noting that the lower end contains a catch-and-release area.

Like Hayes Creek and Mud Run, Hickory contains a good supply of aquatic insects. Plenty of March browns appear, albeit sporadically, the last week in May. The Hendrickson presents some decent fly-fishing in late April, especially if Hickory's temperature rises above 50 degrees. If you meet these or any of the hatches listed you'll experience some fantastic fly-fishing to rising trout.

Hickory begins just east of the Pennsylvania Turnpike and flows southwest through Saylorsville then into Hickory Run State Park. From PA 534 downstream to the Lehigh River the stream contains a catch-and-release area. Bob Sentiwany says the best fly-fishing on the stream is located just before it enters the Lehigh. Hickory warms above 70 degrees in the summer; a dam on a branch, Sand Spring Run, causes the thermal problem. The state stocks both the main stem and Sand Spring Run upstream from PA 534.

LEHIGH RIVER

Access Access to areas of the Lehigh just above the dam is difficult. You'll also see some private water in this area. If you plan to fish any section of the river, it's a good idea to check with Bob Sentiwany at Lehigh Tannery. He can tell you what's hatching and where to fly-fish. Access becomes relatively easy from Gouldsboro to Thornhurst, via a parallel secondary road. Much of the water in this area is open to fishing. When the Lehigh reaches White Haven, about 30 miles downriver from Gouldsboro, it becomes an impressive river. You'll encounter many white-water rafters in this section, especially on weekends. PA 940 follows the Lehigh on its lower end and crosses the river at White Haven. From White Haven to Lehigh Tannery a secondary road and PA 534 approach the water.

Rating ✳✳

Patterns to Match the Hatches Early Brown Stonefly (#12), Blue Quill (#18), Quill Gordon (#14), Hendrickson and Red Quill (#14), Sulphur Dun and Spinner (#16), Gray Fox and Ginger Quill (#12 and #14), March Brown (#12), Blue-Winged Olive Dun (#14), Light Cahill (#14), Slate Drake (#12 and #14), Green Drake and Coffin Fly (#10), Tan Caddis (#16), Black Caddis (#14), Pink Lady (#14), Chocolate Dun (#16), White Mayfly (#14), Blue Dun (#20 and #22)

The Lehigh River was a great trout fishery. In the 1930s, 1940s, and 1950s the river teemed with trout and hatches, especially the great green drake hatch. This hatch and many more disappeared after 1955, though, because of indiscriminate spraying and because of damage from floods caused by Hurricanes Agnes and Diane. Later the hardy Hendrickson reappeared, but mainly to lethargic, nursery-reared trout.

Guess what? The Lehigh has returned with gusto. Just a year ago the green drake reappeared in a hatch abundant enough to bring heavy trout to the surface. They continue to appear in good numbers. The drake at present emerges upstream from the Francis E. Walter Dam. A few years ago the Hendrickson hatch proved to be one of the heaviest hatches in memory.

Recently I revisited the stream with Bob Sentiwany. We headed behind Bob's fly shop in the Lehigh Tannery area. The lower end of the stocked area, from the Francis E. Walter Dam to just below Lehigh Tannery, presents large-water problems similar to those on some big western rivers. In this section footing is treacherous, and wading even a few feet is an experience. Here the river ranges from 100 to 150 feet wide. Tobyhanna and Bear Creeks enter just above the dam and add considerable volume to the river. As we cautiously waded into some deep pocket water we noticed a half-dozen trout surface-feeding on a variety of cahill spinners and microcaddis. The last time I had fly-fished the Lehigh, 20 years before, I saw few insects and fewer trout.

Bob and I headed upriver to a section just below the dam to look for feeding trout. Here the Lehigh contains deep pools and mile-long riffles. The locals call this section Devils Elbow. Although most of this water remains open to fly-fishing, access is difficult. In color the water below the dam resembles weak tea, because of the infusion of tannic acid, mainly from the Tobyhanna.

As Bob fished I collected dozens of March brown duns. This species appears on the Lehigh in massive numbers.

Around 5:00 PM Bob and I headed for our final fishing destination— the Lehigh River Falls Club. (*Note:* The Lehigh River Falls Club has temporarily ceased operation because of a court case over navigable waters. The ruling is under appeal.) The club leases a mile of water just below Lehigh Falls and PA 115. Here we met Mike Zavacky and Glenn Hooper of Pen Argyl and William Williams of Easton. "Hoop" raved about the Hendrickson hatch he had witnessed the past April and the fabulous green drake hatch that occurred just a week before. We headed upriver to the top of the private stretch to get away from the club's stocked trout. Above the dam the Lehigh ranges from 30 to 60 feet wide.

At the upper end of the club's posted water (1 mile below Lehigh Falls and PA 115), there's some excellent pocket water. When we arrived there we saw a dozen trout feeding on caddis. The splashing rises to these insects indicated the fish were taking the downwing naturals. I captured a couple of caddis, examined the tan body and size, and selected a size-16 Tan Caddis pattern. Bob tied on the same pattern. For the next hour the frenzied feeding continued. Bob's first trout proved to be a 7-inch stream-bred brown. The next trout that sucked in his caddis was a 6-inch native brookie.

In another few minutes Bob took a hefty brown trout that looked like a native. In a little more than an hour the two of us caught some small and medium-sized trout up to 15 inches long. Most were holdover or streambred trout. By 8:00 PM the Lehigh had proved it has returned as a prime trout stream. A smorgasbord of insects appeared in the air: several coffin flies, thousands of ginger quills, March browns, light cahills, and assorted other mayflies and caddisflies hovered in the air above us.

The Lehigh begins in southwestern Pike County, then flows southwest to White Haven to form the boundary between Luzerne and Monroe Counties. A few miles upstream from White Haven is a relatively new flood-control project, the Francis E. Walter Dam. It's a shame that the dam, which possesses a bottom release, is not more accommodating to the fantastic cold-water fishery it could provide downstream. If releases were planned in summer, the lower end of the Lehigh would become a productive trout stream and bring in thousands of fishermen to boost the local economy.

The Lehigh has many long, deep pools with riffles above. It picks up volume from numerous small creeks, and many flow through bogs and open ponds. Some side streams contain brook trout, but many are posted against trespassing. Streams like Lehigh, Ash, Buckey, Wolf, and Trout Runs—as well as Choke Creek, a larger tributary that flows into the main stem around Thornhurst—flow into the Lehigh. Two major tributaries, Tobyhanna and Bear Creeks, enter the main stem at or near the dam.

The Lehigh has regained some of its hatches. Sections of the river now hold plenty of holdover trout, and above the dam there's good evidence of a healthy streambred population of brook and brown trout. The Lehigh has returned.

MEHOOPANY CREEK

Access PA 87 parallels the lower end of the Mehoopany and most of the North Branch. A secondary road from Forkston to Lopez takes you to the upper half of the stream. You have to hike in to enjoy the fishing on the upper Mehoopany and its tributaries.

Rating ✳✳

Patterns to Match the Hatches Blue Quill (#18), Quill Gordon (#14), Hendrickson and Red Quill (#14), Green Caddis (#16), Tan Caddis (#16), Brown Caddis (#16), Light Stonefly (#12), March Brown (#12), Blue-Winged Olive Dun (#14), Light Cahill (#14), Slate Drake (#12 and #14), Little Green Stonefly (#16), Trico (#24)

Bob Dibble of Wyalusing will tell you that Mehoopany Creek is full of contradictions. It is a productive stream at times and barren at others. It exemplifies what fly-fishermen think of as pristine water, yet it sometimes has problems with acidity in its headwaters. At times it displays fantastic hatches, like the blue-winged olive dun around the end of May. At other times it's void of any hatches whatsoever. Still, hit the Mehoopany on one of its better days with a fantastic hatch appearing and you're in for a memorable day of fly-fishing.

The Mehoopany begins in the southwestern end of Wyoming County and flows northeast 15 miles before it enters the Susquehanna River. Above Forkston the Mehoopany picks up several fine small tributaries loaded with brook trout up to 10 inches long. Opossum, Somers, Henry Lott, South, Stony, and Kasson Brooks flow into the main stem within a few miles of one another. All of them, until recently, held trout over a foot long. Bill Wilson and Doc Ayers have fly-fished the Mehoopany and its tributaries for many years. They contend that given the recent onslaught of angling pressure, along with summers with little precipitation and high temperatures, fly-fishers will now find fewer and smaller native trout. Some of these tributaries are difficult to reach but can be rewarding to fish with their plentiful supply of native trout. The main stem above Kasson Brook holds plenty of native brookies also.

The upper end of the Mehoopany above Forkston usually contains cool water all season. From Forkston to the Susquehanna, however, the water temperature often rises above 70 degrees during June, July, and August, reserving fishing for the cooler hours. The North Branch flows into the main stem just downstream from Forkston. The pool formed at this junction holds trout throughout much of the season. A hundred yards below this junction lies another deep pool with a good trout population.

The Mehoopany contains plenty of small-to-medium-sized boulders throughout. You'll also find pools spaced 100 or more yards apart between many unproductive riffles.

The Mehoopany has several heavy mayfly hatches and plenty of stoneflies and caddisflies. Probably the heaviest hatch is the blue-winged olive dun, which appears for a week in late May or early June. The duns emerge anywhere from 8:00 to 11:00 AM, depending on the weather. The adults of these mayflies, the dark olive spinners, mate in the evening. Add to this hatch some sulphurs, light cahills, and March browns, and you'll see that you can meet some exciting hatches on the Mehoopany.

The best hatches and largest trout extend from Forkston downstream about 5 miles. On that stretch in early May you can see light stoneflies and the tan caddis. In early June, in addition to blue-winged olives during the day, you can see light cahills, olive spinners, dark blue sedges, and slate drakes in the evening.

TOWANDA CREEK

Access PA 414 parallels the stream all the way from the town of Towanda west to Canton.

Special Regulations Delayed harvest, artificial lures only—1.7 miles, from SR 3007 downstream to T 350.

Rating ✳

Patterns to Match the Hatches Tan Caddis (#14), Hendrickson (#14), March Brown (#12), Green Drake and Coffin Fly (#10), Brown Drake (#12), Trico (#24)

In June 1972 Hurricane Agnes devastated much of northeastern Pennsylvania. In its wake it left many flooded towns and cities, and trout streams left desolate by scouring of the streambeds. Towanda Creek exemplifies the destruction caused by this violent storm and its aftermath. Before the catastrophe Towanda contained a decent hatch of green drakes—now the hatch appears sporadically. Many local fly-fishermen in the Canton area avoid the creek today. Harry Jenkins lives next to the stream but rarely fishes it. Larry Thoren's home also borders the water, but he seldom enters it. Both fly-fishermen and many others in the Canton area travel 40 to 50 miles to fly-fish on Pine or Kettle Creeks rather than stay at home and fish the Towanda.

But Towanda Creek has some good hatches and an adequate supply of trout for the early season. Try this stream after the first couple of weeks of the season; you'll encounter few anglers and even fewer fly-fishermen.

MUD RUN

Access Access to Mud Run is extremely limited; only three or four hiking paths take you to the stream. The upper section lies in an organized camping area of Hickory Run State Park off PA 534. The state stocks only this upper section by using a private dirt road to the stream. Pools and riffles in this upper end don't compare with the lower end. The middle section lies just west of where the Northeast Extension of the Pennsylvania Turnpike crosses PA 534. There's a FLY-FISHING ONLY sign to show you the way to the stream.

Special Regulations Delayed harvest, artificial lures only—2.5 miles in Hickory Run State Park.

Rating ✳✳

Patterns to Match the Hatches Quill Gordon (#14), Hendrickson and Red Quill (#14), Grannom (#16), Green Caddis (#16), March Brown (#12), Sulphur Dun and Spinner (#16), Light Cahill (#14), Green Drake and Coffin Fly (#10), Slate Drake (#12 and #14), Little Green Stonefly (#16)

What a name for a stream! You'd expect to see a slow, meandering, mud-filled creek flowing through intensively farmed land. The name doesn't appropriately describe Mud Run. Located in the eastern end of the scenic Poconos, Mud Run almost defies you to reach it. A trip to the stream is both rewarding and frustrating.

Mike Marinelli, Jay Kapolka, and I gathered our fishing gear and headed toward the lower end of the section open to public fishing on Mud Run. Jay had prepared us by saying that we had to hike some distance—maybe a mile. We headed down an old path made by fishermen next to a private section owned by the Jervis Corporation. We crossed several small swamps and walked directly into a thick stand of 10-foot-high rhododendrons. After almost a mile of hiking we still heard no stream. Finally, about 15 minutes later, we headed down a steep, boulder-filled decline by crawling on our hands and knees until we finally reached Mud Run.

What a fantastic, spectacular sight—Mud Run in all its magnificent, hurrying splendor! A high, roaring waterfall above us fell into a deep, rock-filled pool below. This was the true Mud Run. Even when you're in the stream, Mud Run defies you to walk up- or downstream. High cliffs and huge boulders prevent you from any easy approach to the tan-colored pools. On this section of Mud Run wading is truly hazardous.

Mike, Jay, and I leapfrogged upstream, each of us casting in a pool or two. Only a few hendricksons appeared while we fished, but all three of us elected to use Red Quills. In each sizable pool we caught several trout. All of them appeared to be streambred browns and brook trout ranging in size from 6 inches to a foot. Obviously the state doesn't stock these trout. How would anybody reach this lower section to stock it? After fighting rapids, rocky cliffs, boulders, and deep water for three hours, we headed back to the car. To reach the car we again had to climb the steep mountain of boulders and cross through the rhododendrons.

Mud Run flows northeast in Carbon County, entering the Lehigh River near Lehigh Tannery, where Bob and Mary Lou Sentiwany run the AA Pro Shop. Bob knows all of the hatches on Pocono streams well, and Mary Lou ties outstanding fly patterns. Bob says the abundant March brown hatch on Mud Run brings up some heavy trout.

There's more to fly-fishing than casting and catching trout. You'll enjoy spectacular scenery on this stream, and if you don't mind hiking in, you'll love Mud Run.

POHOPOCO CREEK

Access US 209 parallels much of the Pohopoco east of Lehighton.

Rating ✳✳

Patterns to Match the Hatches Little Blue-Winged Olive Dun (#20), Dark Brown Caddis (#16), Quill Gordon (#14), Hendrickson and Red Quill (#14), Blue Dun (#20), Green Caddis (#14 and #16), Grannom (#16), Blue Quill (#18), Blue-Winged Olive Dun (#14), Green Drake and Coffin Fly (#10), Slate Drake (#12 and #14), Light Cahill (#14), Yellow Drake (#12), Rusty Brown Caddis (#14 and #16)

Many people call Pohopoco Creek "Big Creek." Others attempt to call it by its proper name, although no two fishermen seem to pronounce it the same. The Pohopoco doesn't currently resemble the stream I first fly-fished 30 years ago. At that time no reservoir interrupted Pohopoco's upper and lower sections. Also, 30 years ago all of the stream was open to fishing.

The Army Corps of Engineers created a dam about 3 miles upstream from the Pohopoco's confluence with the Lehigh River. The Beltzville Reservoir, with some sections over 100 feet deep, contains a bottom release. Because of the foresight of the Corps of Engineers this release keeps the 2 miles of open water below the dam cool all summer. Water temperatures below the dam remain in the 60s in July and August. This lower section contains some heavy trout, many holdovers, and plenty of trout planted by the state. The stream here ranges from 50 to 70 feet wide.

The reservoir contains some large brown trout. Jack Reichelderfer, of Pocono Gateway Sporting Outfitters, said that trout up to 30 inches long have been caught near the dam.

Above the dam the stream narrows to about 30 feet. From the upper end of the dam to Kresgeville much of the stream remains open to fishing but receives no state stocking. This section depends on streambred trout. From Kresgeville upstream, however, there's about 8 miles of stocked water. The stream is open and stocked above Effort. Middle and Dotters Creeks, two main tributaries to the Pohopoco, also receive stocked trout.

Mike Marinelli and Jay Kapolka of Levittown and I fly-fished the unstocked water of Pohopoco Creek in early May two years ago. In this section of the stream the southern bank harbors a heavy canopy of rhodo-dendrons, while the northern bank has alders and hemlocks. Our dry flies seemed to attach to an alder, hemlock, or rhododendron as often as they rested on the surface.

When we approached the stream shortly after noon, we saw several quill gordons fly toward the far bank. Smaller, size-22 blue duns (*Baetis* spp.) emerged frequently as we waded upstream. All of us tied on patterns to match the afternoon's hatch of the blue dun. As we approached the first sizable pool, possibly six trout rose to blue dun naturals on the surface. Both Mike and Jay caught trout on their Blue Duns and later on a size-16 Tan Caddis. Well after the blue dun hatch ended, the tan caddis continued to emerge, but trout rose only sporadically to the hatch. Trout refused to rise because the water temperature that afternoon only reached 48 degrees. Mike and Jay caught several streambred brown trout from 6 to 10 inches long. They seldom catch trout in this section much larger.

The Pohopoco contains many good hatches throughout the season. The blue duns and quill gordons of April give way to tan caddis and grannoms in early May. Later in May, slate drakes, light cahills, and blue-winged olive duns appear. If you plan to be on this stream in late May or June, make certain you carry a good supply of Blue-Winged Olive Duns in sizes 14 and 16.

The Pohopoco presents some difficult wading because of its rocks and boulders. It has some deep debris-filled pools with productive riffles above. Jack Reichelderfer knows the stream and its hatches. Stop in at his store in Lehighton and check conditions with him before you fish the "Big Creek."

BRODHEAD CREEK

Access PA 447 parallels the upper part of the Brodhead, and a paved secondary road the lower half.

Rating ✳✳✳

Patterns to Match the Hatches Little Blue-Winged Olive Dun (#20), Quill Gordon (#14), Hendrickson and Red Quill (#14), Tan Sedge (#14 and #16), Sulphur Dun and Spinner (#16 and #18), Gray Fox and Ginger Quill (#12 and #14), March Brown (#12), Blue-Winged Olive Dun (#14), Slate Drake (#12 and #14), Light Cahill (#14), Pink Lady (#14), Cream Cahill (#14 and #16), Yellow Stonefly (#14), Trico (#24), Olive Sedge (#14 and #16)

Monroe County in northeastern Pennsylvania contains some fantastic trout streams. Within a few miles of Stroudsburg you can fish on Pocono, McMichael, Big Bushkill, and Brodhead Creeks. All present great fly-fishing, with many hatches and plenty of stocked, holdover, and streambred trout. Fly-fish on any of these in late April and you'll likely fish over a tremendous Hendrickson hatch that lasts for a couple of hours in the afternoon. Fish these same waters on a late-May morning and you'll probably fish over a super blue-winged olive hatch.

Progress and immigration from New York and New Jersey have caught up with Monroe County. Land prices are rising. The quantity of posted waters increases annually as more private fishing clubs develop. More and more anglers fish on less and less water, putting undue pressure on the remaining precious public-access streams.

In addition to being subject to all the problems associated with a booming local economy, the Monroe County streams have been slow to recover from a calamitous flood caused by Hurricane Diane in 1955. After that flood the Corps of Engineers channelized much of the Brodhead just above and below the PA 191 bridge. Later studies by the Pennsylvania Fish Commission in cooperation with the Brodhead Chapter of Trout Unlimited showed an alarming decrease in the wild-trout population in the channelized area. In an effort to improve habitat on the Brodhead, the chapter has placed more than 400 tons of boulders in the stream. This effort has had results—a recent survey shows that the trout population increased tenfold after installation of the boulders. But there's more work to do, and the chapter plans additional workdays to further improve the stream through its Restore the Brodhead project.

Don Baylor met me on the Brodhead recently. Don lives in Stroudsburg and works with fishing clubs as an entomologist. He's given many talks on mayflies to fly-fishing organizations throughout the United States. We fished the upper end of the open water near Analomink. The Brodhead reminds me of a small Beaverkill. The streambed contains many huge boulders, small rocks, gravel, and sand. The siltation problems so common on our southeastern streams appear minimal here. The Brodhead contains an abundance of productive pocket water with stocked, holdover,

Don Baylor conducts many studies of aquatic life on Brodhead Creek.

and streambred trout. The upper ends of many of the pools contain productive deep riffles.

Don and I fished the Brodhead on a hot June evening after the air temperature had topped out at 91 degrees. The water temperature at 7:00 PM was 71 degrees. Nothing much happened until dusk. This often typifies activity on hot summer evenings. At dusk hundreds of sulphur duns emerged. Still more sulphur spinners returned to the water to deposit fertilized eggs. In a productive area ahead of us only two trout occasionally rose to this feast. Don hooked a heavy 14-inch holdover brown, while I looked for rising trout. None showed. We left the stream well after dusk. I've experienced many instances like this one, where a tremendous hatch or spinner fall occurs and few or no trout rise.

From Analomink downstream to the Delaware the Brodhead presents 6 miles of open water. Just below Stroudsburg the stream enters an inaccessible gorge. Effluent from two plants pushes a heavy load of treated sewage into the lower 3 miles of stream. Two other excellent trout streams, McMichael and Pocono Creeks, join the Brodhead in Stroudsburg. Both waters contain hatches similar to those found on the Brodhead.

Local fishermen have labeled certain areas on the stream. Going downstream you'll find PA 191 (High Bridge), the area channelized after the flood; Whirlpool; Stokes Avenue; Stokes Mill; and Moose Lodge. Above Analomink the water is posted. A mile above that town you'll see the Paradise Branch enter the main stem. The Brodhead Forest and Stream Club posts this lower part of the branch and the main stem in that area. The Henryville Conservation Club controls the Paradise Branch upstream, and Parkside Anglers the main stem upstream. Were it not for these private clubs, the Brodhead in that area would be more highly developed, and fishing in the open section below would suffer.

The Brodhead contains an enormous supply of Hendricksons that appear from mid- to late April. Recently Don Baylor has seen tricos on the Brodhead in August. Add to these a dozen or more other heavy hatches and you see why fishing the Brodhead can be rewarding.

BIG BUSHKILL CREEK

Access PA 402 crosses the stream at Ressica Falls.

Special Regulations Delayed-harvest, fly-fishing-only project—6.1 miles, on the Ressica Falls Scout Reservation property except 200 yards on each side of the falls.

Rating ✳✳✳

Patterns to Match the Hatches Blue Quill (#18), Quill Gordon (#14), Hendrickson and Red Quill (#14), Grannom (#14), Tan Caddis (#14), Gray Fox and Ginger Quill (#12 and #14), March Brown (#12), Light Cahill (#14), Slate Drake (#12 and #14), Gray Caddis (#14), Yellow Stonefly (#14), Little Green Stonefly (#16), Cream Cahill (#14 and #16)

As early as 8:00 AM the temperature approached 70 degrees. Don Baylor and I registered at the Boy Scout headquarters at Ressica Falls before fishing on the Big Bushkill. We parked our car at the designated lot and hiked downstream 2 miles to fly-fish a section below Piano Pool.

Don prefers fishing the Big Bushkill early in the morning. He's had a lot of success using Stonefly Nymphs on this boulder-strewn stream, which is filled with several stonefly species. These nymphs remain active in the morning.

We entered the stream where a heavy riffle flowed into a 6-foot-deep, 50-foot-long pool. I checked the water temperature on this late-June morning, and at 9:00 AM it registered 69 degrees. Any productive fly-fishing on this hot summer morning would be short lived. Don hooked a couple of browns and a brook trout at the tail of the pool, and missed two at the head.

Above the pool lay a half mile of deep pocket water. Don picked up several more trout on a caddis pattern. A few blue quills emerged rapidly from the surface, along with a hodgepodge of stoneflies. In the backwater, cream cahill spinners lay spent from their final egg-laying ritual the night before. Both Don and I picked up trout in that stretch before the heat and humidity got to us and we quit.

Don often fishes the Big Bushkill earlier in the season. The stream holds an exceptionally heavy blue quill hatch the third week in April. If the water has warmed sufficiently, the blue quill and the Hendrickson hatches can last for hours, with plenty of rising trout. At about the same time Don fishes, grannoms appear on the surface. Don says that grannoms vary in color on the Big Bushkill and that there are light and dark phases of the species. The stream also holds abundant March browns and blue-winged olive duns.

Like the brown-stained Tobyhanna, the Big Bushkill flows from the Pocono Plateau. The Bushkill warms rapidly in summer. Upstream it contains more than a half-dozen impoundments with top-water releases that considerably warm the water below.

The Bushkill's streambed has every kind of rock, from huge boulders to small stones. Wading this uneven surface can be hazardous. There's about 6 miles of fly-fishing water on the Scout reservation. The farther downstream you hike, the less likely you are to meet other fly-fishermen.

Some of the stretches have been named: the Firestone, Little Falls, Piano Pool (shaped like a piano), and Chapel Pool (the Boy Scouts hold worship services nearby). If you don't mind hiking, you can fly-fish in an isolated area with plenty of stocked and some holdover trout.

DYBERRY CREEK

Access You reach the Dyberry from PA 191 north out of Honesdale, where it enters the Lackawaxen River. The section above the fairgrounds contains productive water for early-season fly-fishing, with plenty of quill gordons in mid-April. Upstream a blacktop road off PA 191 crosses the Dyberry at Day Bridge. The pool at Day Bridge is deep and productive. Just across the bridge another paved road to the right parallels the upper part of the main stem. Two miles above Day Bridge you'll cross the Mary Wilcox Bridge. The delayed-harvest, fly-fishing-only section begins at the bridge and goes upstream 0.8 mile.

Travel another mile upstream, and you'll see the East Branch on your right and the West Branch on your left. You can park in state game lands to fish either branch. Tanners Falls lies 1 mile up the larger West Branch. This area contains spectacular scenery, deep pools, and a good early trout population. The East Branch begins in Upper Woods Pond. This impoundment holds the only kokanee salmon in the Commonwealth.

Special Regulations Delayed harvest, fly-fishing only—0.8 mile, from the Widmer property line about 1 mile below Tanners Falls downstream to the Mary Wilcox Bridge.

Rating ✳✳

Patterns to Match the Hatches Blue Quill (#18), Quill Gordon (#14), Hendrickson and Red Quill (#14), Grannom (#14), Sulphur Dun and Spinner (#16), Gray Fox and Ginger Quill (#12 and #14), March Brown (#12), Slate Drake (#12 and #14), Yellow Stonefly (#14), Dark Blue Sedge (#12), Little Black Caddis (#16), Little Blue Dun (#22)

Recently hot weather, droughtlike conditions, and urban development have taken their toll on the Dyberry. Stream temperatures now often rise well into the 70s and stay there too long. Trout search out small spring-fed tributaries to survive. If these fish find a cool spring, and if a gray heron or raccoon doesn't find them, they might live through the season. A few trout do hold over in some of the deeper pools on the main stem. The 20-foot-deep pool just below the dry General Edgar Jadwin Dam holds trout all year long. Another pool just above the delayed-harvest stretch that Rick Eck of Honesdale tagged the Five Pounder Hole holds trout through the summer. But much of the main stem of the Dyberry contains little cover and slow, shallow water; it warms quickly in summer.

The Dyberry needs a host of stream improvements the way a seedling needs water. This once-great trout stream contains many sections with long, shallow pools with some riffles and pocket water between. Devices like logjams, rocks, and gabions would help rejuvenate the stream. In 1984 several fly-fishermen in the area formed a Pike-Wayne Chapter of Trout Unlimited. This group has constructed stream improvement devices under the Adopt-a-Stream arm of the Pennsylvania Fish Commission.

Another hazard to trout in the stream comes in late May when lamprey eels by the thousands move up the Delaware, into the Lackawaxen River, then into the Dyberry. These parasites latch onto any trout or pickerel they can find.

Hatches begin early on the Dyberry and continue through much of the fishing season. Rick Eck says the blue quill *(Paraleptophlebia adoptiva)* and quill gordon often appear before the season begins. You can take advantage of these early hatches on the delayed-harvest area.

Mid-April and late May hold the most productive hatches. After the blue quills and quill gordons, you'll see a good hatch of hendricksons on the Dyberry. In mid- to late May, March browns and gray foxes emerge by day and sulphurs in the evening. In early June two downwings, the yellow stonefly and dark blue sedge, bring trout to the surface. Even as late as September you'll see blue quills, slate drakes, and a size-22 blue dun on the water.

If Honesdale native Rick Eck and other members of the Pike-Wayne Trout Unlimited Chapter have a choice, they invariably choose to fish the Delaware or Lackawaxen Rivers over the Dyberry. Therein lies part of the problem: Why place stream improvement devices on the Dyberry when the fantastic Delaware is only 10 miles away?

4 | Streams of Southeastern Pennsylvania

Southeastern Pennsylvania—who would think that fly-fishermen could catch healthy, heavy, native brown trout only a few miles from the Philadelphia city limits? Who would believe, in this urbanized area, that some great mayfly hatches like the sulphur appear? Who but the anglers who fish these streams regularly would believe that caddisflies still appear on southeastern streams in excellent numbers?

Despite their unexpected excellence, however, the streams of the southeast have encountered a number of serious problems—some of which will determine whether these waters will continue to hold trout and provide anglers hours of recreation. Problems of growth will decide whether man and his environment can coexist in any sort of harmony in this region. Housing developments, industrial parks, road construction, and farming near headwaters produce enormous siltation problems on local streams. Look at Ridley, Darby, and Valley Creeks as examples. Ridley and Darby become coffee colored after a moderate rain. This siltation problem affects the hatches on these streams drastically. Take a walk along Darby Creek. In one pool you'll notice a car's fender, in the riffle above maybe a discarded barrel, farther upstream a shopping cart—all dumped into the stream. Valley Creek exemplifies the hazards of chemical pollution. What have we done to our precious environment?

Wayne Poppich of King of Prussia says that the trout streams of southeastern Pennsylvania are on the brink of disaster. Moreover, conditions in the southeast have implications for the rest of the state. How we deal with the problems of pollution and population in this area will determine how streams in the rest of the state survive in the future. If these hard-pressed waters in the southeast survive our onslaught, then the future for trout fishing for the entire state appears bright. If these streams finally succumb to so-called progress, however, can others be far behind?

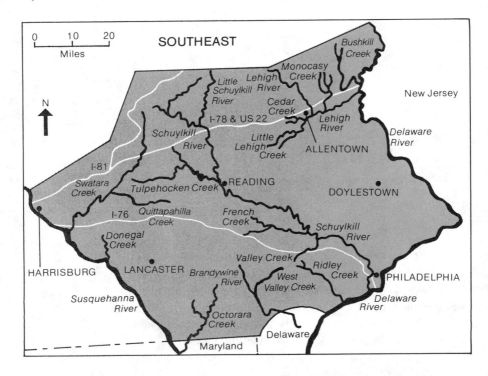

Regional, county, state, and national parks have become the salvation of many of the southeastern streams, a number of which lie within or have their headwaters in these protected areas. Some of Valley Creek's best fishing is contained within Valley Forge National Park; Ridley Creek holds a state park and an arboretum in its headwaters; and the Little Lehigh and Tulpehocken run through extensive park systems. Interested sportsmen's and nature groups in the southeast provide another important ingredient to the stability of these streams. The Delco Manning and Valley Forge Chapters of Trout Unlimited have undertaken many environmental projects dedicated to the protection and preservation of streams in their vicinity. They need your help to protect the future of these waters.

With all of its problems, however, southeastern Pennsylvania indeed boasts some exceptional trout fishing and some great opportunities for matching the hatch.

EAST BRANCH, BRANDYWINE CREEK

Access PA 282 closely parallels the East Branch, especially its upper end.

Special Regulations A delayed-harvest, artificial-lures-only section is in effect as of January 1, 1999, for 1.2 miles from Dorlans Mill Road downstream to Dowlin Forge Road.

Rating ✳✳

Patterns to Match the Hatches Little Black Stonefly (#16), Blue Quill (#18), Green Caddis (#16), Tan Caddis (#16), Little Blue-Winged Olive Dun (#20), Sulphur (#16), Light Cahill (#14), Slate Drake (#12 and #14), Trico (#24), Little Yellow Dun (#20), Big Slate Drake *(Hexagenia atrocaudata)* (#6)

In many of my Pennsylvania stream descriptions I've sung the praises of local Trout Unlimited chapters. They've made stream improvements, adopted streams, and enhanced waters in many ways, all to further trout fishing in the Commonwealth. On Kettle Creek the Kettle Creek Watershed Association deserves the credit for working to preserve that great stream. The East Branch of Brandywine Creek owes its very existence, but especially its future as a viable trout stream, to the Brandywine Trout and Conservation Club (BTCC) in Downingtown. This group has worked closely with local government, landowners, and the Pennsylvania Fish and Boat Commission to develop the full potential of this great urban stream located just 40 air miles west of Philadelphia.

What has it done to merit this recognition? First, it is this club, through three area trout nurseries, that raises trout for the stream. In a year it raises 10,000 trout for the East Branch and one of its tributaries, Beaver Creek. Its annual bill to feed the trout runs about $3,000. It's one of the oldest cooperatives in the state, organized in 1963. At its Devereux Nursery the club also raises and stocks 800 holdovers 14 to 20 inches long.

Second, BTCC members have been active in developing a delayed-harvest section for the stream. Recently I had an opportunity to fly-fish on the middle section of the East Branch with Dave Riggio of Exton and John Diak of Downingtown. Both are active members of the BTCC and both were eager to show me where the proposed delayed-harvest section would go on this stream. We headed north on PA 282 out of Downingtown to Dowlin Forge Road, turned right, and went upstream less than a mile to the point where Shamona Creek enters the East Branch. This small tributary was cloudy from a thundershower the evening before, but the main stem of the East Branch ran clear.

As we entered the water we saw several tricos already in the air. The trico hatch here is rather sparse because of the heavy canopy. Dave and John assured me that the hatch appeared in larger numbers 3 miles downstream in Kerr Park in Downingtown. We checked the water temperature: 62 degrees. We fished for an hour in this middle section of the proposed delayed-harvest area, then hiked up Struble Trail to fish an upper section of the regulated water.

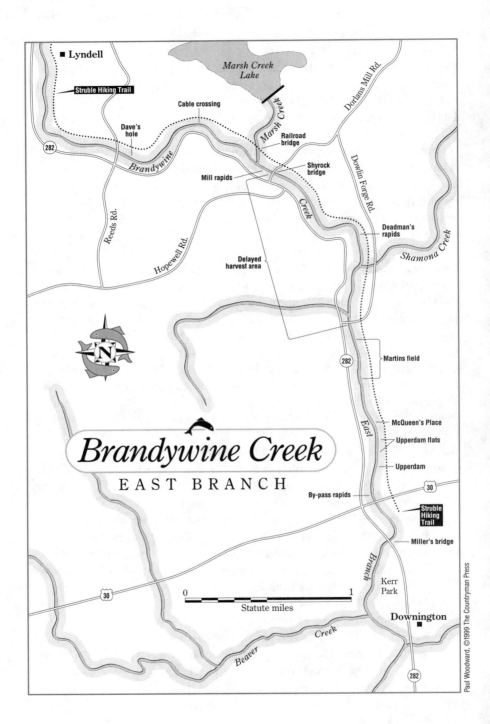

Lyndell

Struble Hiking Trail

Marsh Creek Lake

Dorlans Mill Rd.

Cable crossing

Dave's hole

282

Brandywine

Railroad bridge

Marsh Creek

Shyrock bridge

Mill rapids

Dowlin Forge Rd.

Reeds Rd.

Hopewell Rd.

Creek

Deadman's rapids

Shamona Creek

Delayed harvest area

282

Martins field

East

McQueen's Place

Upperdam flats

Brandywine Creek

EAST BRANCH

Upperdam

30

By-pass rapids

Struble Hiking Trail

Miller's bridge

Branch

Kerr Park

30

0   1
Statute miles

Downington

Beaver

Creek

282

Paul Woodward, ©1999 The Countryman Press

Here John saw a trout in a deep riffle. He fished the same section for more than an hour and finally caught an 8-inch rainbow. Dave and I headed downstream and had a half-dozen chubs of assorted sizes to claim for a morning of fishing. Still, now that this stream has an officially approved delayed-harvest area, I'm sure you'll find trout the entire year. Why? Recently when the Fish and Boat Commission electroshocked a portion of the proposed regulated water it found some streambred brown trout—in addition to a few planted trout—in mid-July.

The delayed-harvest section extends for 1.2 miles, from the bridge on Dowlin Forge Road upstream to the Dorlans Mill bridge. The club will add stream improvement devices similar to those already installed on its Reeds Road and Kerr Park projects. And the BTCC already has additional plans for stream improvements. If you live in the southeast and you believe in what this active club has done and will do, you've got to support its efforts. Contact the membership chairman, Jim Gilpin, at 322 Highland Avenue, Downingtown 19335; or you can write the club directly at P.O. Box 32, Downingtown 19335.

There's about 10 miles of stocked water on the East Branch of the Brandywine. You'll find about 6 miles of stocked water above the delayed-harvest area, and 3 miles below. And you'll find planted trout from Glenmoore downstream to the lower end of Kerr Park in Downingtown. You'll find some streambred trout in the upper half of the stream.

John Diak and Dave Riggio most often use caddis imitations. They both feel that these downwings produce some good hatches on the stream. But you'll also find some stoneflies and mayflies on the East Branch. In addition to some tricos you'll see little blue-winged olives, slate drakes, blue quills, and sulphurs.

The stated goals of the Brandywine Trout and Conservation Club are simple yet tremendously important to the future of the stream. Dave said, "We keep a close relationship with the state, maintain open relationships with streamside landowners, and educate the public on the benefits of our local natural resource through club meetings, kids' clinics, and slide show presentations to community groups."

If you fish this surprisingly good urban trout stream and you see one of the members of the Brandywine Trout and Conservation Club, make certain you thank him for his untiring work in making the East Branch of the Brandywine a great place to fly-fish. Were it not for this tremendously active conservation group I am certain that the East Branch would not be the stream that it is today.

PICKERING CREEK

Access You'll find Pickering Creek on PA 29 just a few miles southwest of Phoenixville. You can reach the stream by taking the Phoenixville Pike to PA 29.

Special Regulations Delayed harvest, artificial lures only—1.5 miles, from SR 1019 (Charlestown Road) downstream to 330 yards upstream from the railroad bridge.

Rating ✱✱

Patterns to Match the Hatches Little Black Stonefly (#18), Little Blue-Winged Olive Dun (#20), Tan Caddis (#14), Black Caddis (#14), Slate Drake (#12 and #14), Sulphur (#16), Pale Evening Dun (#16), Little Yellow Stonefly (#16)

Question: What's probably the poorest time of the year to test the merits of a trout stream?

Answer: To me, it's an afternoon in the middle of August. Why? You'll probably see no hatch, hot air temperatures, low- and warm-water conditions—you've got everything going against an eventful trip.

So guess when I selected to fish Pickering Creek? You got it—mid-August. Paul Raubertas, Ray Young, Jim Law, and I arrived at the stream on a busy Friday afternoon. Here the Pickering flows through a heavily forested area. Were it not for the heavy traffic on PA 29 you'd never realize that you were only a few miles northwest of Philadelphia.

Paul and Jim have fished the Pickering for the past couple of years and feel it's one of the better streams in the area. Paul, Jim, and Ray are members of the Southeast Montgomery Chapter of Trout Unlimited. All three are highly involved in that

A late season trout from Pickering Creek.

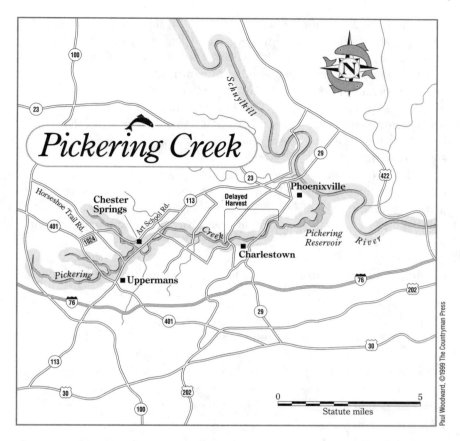

Paul Woodward, ©1999 The Countryman Press

chapter and its important activities. Ray is the current president, with a goal of increasing chapter membership. The club is also planning Adopt-a Stream projects to turn Wissahicken and Pennypack Creeks into viable trout streams. You can read about the club's progress through its Web site, run by Paul Raubertas (http://www.SKLARNET.com/trout/index.htm); or you can contact Paul via e-mail (prks@worldnet.att.net). Jim is youth chairman for Pennsylvania Trout; his e-mail address is jim.law@synergis.com.

Once we'd all suited up we decided to head upstream and fish a few pools. Ray and I checked the water temperature: 70 degrees. Not bad for a hot mid-August afternoon. As we waded upstream we saw several small trout scatter from some pocket water. Paul, Ray, and I used a variety of patterns through the next few pools without any success. Finally, I decided to give the tandem a try in a productive-looking riffle-pool section. I tied on a Patriot dry fly with a size-16 Bead Head Pheasant Tail Nymph behind it. On probably my second cast I had a strike and landed a heavy fallfish. Two more casts and I had another strike. This one fought for several minutes before I was able to get it into the net: a 14-inch brown trout. Paul and Jim made a few comments about the tandem as I began casting it again into the same water. Several casts later the Patriot sank, I set the hook, and had another heavy fish on the line, this time a rainbow. A few casts more and I netted another brown trout.

This was too much for Ray Young. He tied on the same tandem combination, a Patriot and a Bead Head Pheasant Tail. We now worked our way downstream toward our cars. In the next pool downstream Ray missed his first strike, but set the hook on the second one, and it immediately broke him off.

While we fished we saw a few slate drakes and yellow stoneflies emerge. Scattered on the rocks in faster sections of the streams we saw many nymphal shucks of recently emerged slate drakes. The stream also holds some tan and black caddis hatches earlier in the season, along with some sulphurs.

Does Pickering Creek hold trout on a hot mid-August afternoon and evening? You bet it does. Does it hold trout year-round? You bet it does.

SAUCON CREEK

Access You can reach the Saucon via several streets. In Hellertown you can take High Street (SR 3004), which turns into Seidersville Road. Fire Road parallels the stream in the park; Ravena Street, above the park.

Special Regulations Selective-harvest program—2.1 miles, from the upstream boundary of the city of Bethlehem property downstream to the SR 0412 bridge.

Rating ✳✳✳

Patterns to Match the Hatches Little Blue-Winged Olive Dun (#20), Sulphur (#16), Tan Caddis (#14), Yellow Drake (#12), Blue Quill (#18), Trico (#24), Hex Mayfly (#6)

"Charlie, you've got to fly-fish this stream some day!" That's what Rod Rohrbach kept telling me about a productive limestone stream that flowed near Bethlehem. Rod should know about this stream. He and Pat Cuskey own the Little Lehigh Fly Shop in Allentown, just a few miles away. Now I was finally going to find out whether this creek, the Saucon, deserved the praise he gave it.

Rod arranged for me to meet Rich Heiserman at the Little Lehigh Fly Shop. Rich fishes Saucon Creek dozens of times each year. Rich and I talked a bit about the stream and then decided to give it a try. With I-78 nearby it took us only 20 minutes to reach this urban stream. We drove to Saucon Park just north of I-78, parked in the large lot next to the swim-

Saucon Creek near Bethlehem holds a good trico hatch.

ming pools, assembled our gear, and headed for the stream quickly. It was already 9:30 AM, but maybe, just maybe, some of Saucon's streambred browns were still feeding on trico spinners. As we arrived at our destination in the park Rich warned me to avoid fishing on weekends here because of the huge crowds.

Rich has fly-fished for no more than five or six years, but you couldn't prove that by fishing with him. He ties great caddis patterns, casts a fly flawlessly, and knows area streams well. As soon as we entered the limestone stream we saw a half-dozen trout feeding on an assortment of caddisflies and tricos. Rich tried a Trico pattern for half an hour but few trout looked at it. He then switched over to a size-18 Tan Caddis and the complexion of the morning changed completely. On his second or third cast he picked up his first Saucon wild trout of the day. In the next couple of hours Rich picked up a half-dozen more trout on that pattern. Not bad in a heavily used park, on a hot July day. We left the stream after two hours of fishing. Was I impressed? You better believe I was!

If you plan to fish the park area, do so during the week. On summer weekends it's impossible to fish this stretch of water. Even on this Monday in midsummer we found many kids playing in the stream. To avoid the crowds you can head upstream to the Seidersville Road bridge a mile above the park.

For many years Rich practically had the Saucon to himself—until part of the stream was designated a selective-harvest area. That special designation, by the way, means that anglers can't kill many of the wild trout in this precious stream. After the Pennsylvania Fish and Boat Commission gave the stream special regulations Rich saw a noticeable increase in the number of anglers.

The Saucon boasts some good hatches. You'll see tricos throughout the summer months and sulphurs in May and June. Emerging with the tricos you'll find plenty of blue quills every summer morning. Tan caddis make up an important part of the trout's diet in this stream. They usually appear in late May.

In the park Saucon Creek averages about 30 to 40 feet wide with a few 3-foot pools and many productive 1- to 2-foot-deep riffles and glides. You'll see a lot of springs entering the main stem in the park, assuring a good supply of cold water throughout the summer.

You'll find plenty of streambred browns and some faster water above the regulated area. Rich has fly-fished much of the 8 miles of stream. Saucon enters the Lehigh River just north of the park. If you want a day of great fishing over streambred browns in an urban area then you've got to try Saucon Creek. Was Rod Rohrbach correct in his appraisal of Saucon Creek? You bet he was! Will I return to this productive limestone stream in southeastern Pennsylvania? What do you think?

LITTLE SCHUYLKILL RIVER

Access To reach the Little Schuylkill take PA 61 north of Hamburg to PA 895, then turn right (east) on Township Route 745 near McKeansburg.

Special Regulations Delayed harvest, artificial lures only—1.7 miles, from PA 895 (New Ringgold Bridge) in New Ringgold downstream to T 848 at Rausches Bridge.

Rating ✳✳

Patterns to Match the Hatches Little Black Stonefly (#16), Little Blue-Winged Olive Dun (#20), Hendrickson (#14), Dark Gray Caddis (#14 to #18), Olive Green Caddis (#16), Gray Fox (#12), Light Cahill (#14), Sulphur (#16 and #18), Green Caddis (#16), Black Caddis (#12 and #20), Yellow Stonefly (#14), Tan Caddis (#16), Brown Caddis (#16 to #20), Dark Brown Dun *(Ephemerella needhami)* (#16), Olive Caddis (#20)

I've recalled in an article for *Fly Fisherman* magazine and in a previous edition of this book the walks along several tributaries of the Schuylkill River that I made as a child. Just about every day I hiked along one of

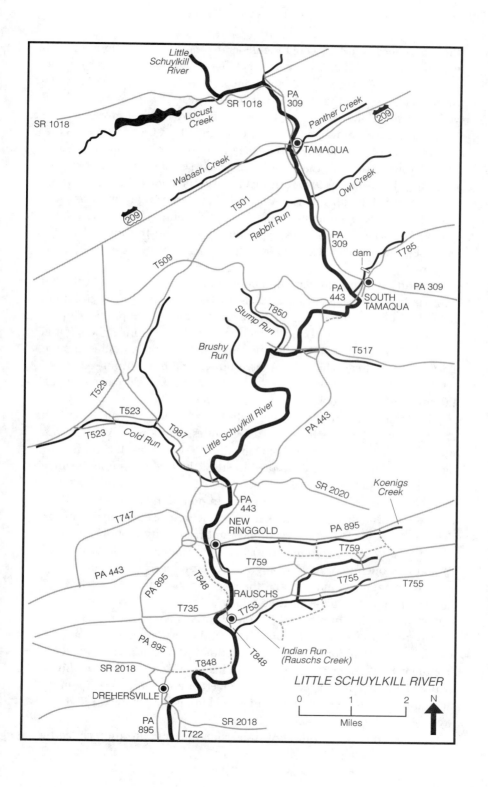

Little
Schuylkill
River

Locust
Creek

SR 1018

SR 1018

PA
309

Panther Creek

209

TAMAQUA

Wabash Creek

209

T501

Owl Creek

Rabbit Run

PA
309

dam

T785

PA 309

PA
443

SOUTH
TAMAQUA

T509

T850

T517

Stump Run

Brushy
Run

Little Schuylkill River

T529

T523

T987

Cold Run

PA 443

T523

SR 2020

Koenigs
Creek

PA
443

NEW
RINGGOLD

PA 895

T747

T759

T759

PA 443

PA 895

T848

T759

T755

T755

T735

RAUSCHS

T753

PA 895

Indian Run
(Rauschs Creek)

SR 2018

T848

T848

LITTLE SCHUYLKILL RIVER

DREHERSVILLE

PA
895

T722

SR 2018

0   1   2   N

Miles

these branches, and I accepted the general condition and coloration of the water as normal. I didn't know any better—and I certainly didn't believe it could be reclaimed. Each and every one of these tributaries—like the West Branch in Cressona and the Little Schuylkill near Tamaqua—flowed black with coal silt in the 1940s and 1950s. As kids we referred to these streams with one general term—we called all of them "Black Creek." When these waters flowed black no one cared—they had no friends. In my wildest dreams I never thought that 40 years later these waters would hold fish—or that I'd be fishing for trout in them. Yet tremendous changes have occurred in Schuylkill County. Anthracite or hard coal mining was king here for decades. No one questioned what this mining had done to our streams—as long as the money kept pouring in. With the advent of stricter mine-sewage disposal laws, though, the branches of the Schuylkill began clearing.

Reports starting cropping up about anglers catching trout in the Little Schuylkill near Tamaqua in the 1970s. In 1976 the newly formed Little Schuylkill Conservation Club in Tamaqua recognized the progress the river had made and began stocking trout. The next year, club members found not only that many of the tributaries, like Rausch Creek, Cold Run, and Locust Creek, already held streambred brown and brook trout—some of which had found their way into the main stream—but also that some of the trout the clubs stocked had wintered over.

The revitalization of this river didn't just happen. Concerned citizens and local organizations have worked countless hours to make this a productive trout fishery. The Little Schuylkill Conservation Club continues to be a leader. The club has continued to stock the river, monitors it to identify pollution sources, has placed 500 tons of limestone in the tributaries, and recently built a cattail marsh to aid in pollution control.

Eugene Dougherty feels that some of the best fishing outside of the delayed-harvest section can be found right in the city of Tamaqua. He recalls a story about a young fly-fisher who fished a section of the river in that city one morning and caught 35 trout on a fly. The club stocks trout from Tamaqua upriver, and the state plants trout in the delayed-harvest area just below New Ringgold.

What does the future hold for the Little Schuylkill River and other nearby tributaries? Recently a new group, the Eastern Pennsylvania Coalition for Abandoned Mine Reclamation (EPACAMR), has emerged. President Ed Wytovich of Ashland and his organization have combined with federal and state agencies in a concerted effort to attack the mine-acid drainage problem in 16 counties, including the Schuylkill River watershed.

Cooperating fully with EPACAMR is another organization called the

Schuylkill Headwaters. Dave Derbes of Pottsville is president of this group, whose goal is to revitalize the entire Schuylkill River. Has progress been made in other tributaries like it has in the Little Schuylkill? Dave proudly tells of the wild brook trout now found in sections of the West Branch of the Schuylkill just above Cressona. With these organizations at work the future certainly looks bright for the entire Schuylkill watershed.

The Little Schuylkill still has its share of water-quality problems, though. The 50- to 80-foot-wide river drains a large basin and with heavy rains it can experience a silt flow turning the river black. Most of this silt emanates from Panther Creek at the south end of Tamaqua. An upriver desilting dam near South Tamaqua has helped control the problem, but the impoundment has to be dredged frequently. In most pools, rocks and the bottom in general still hold a covering of silt. Fish generally use the pools as resting areas and move into the more insect-abundant silt-free riffles to feed. Look for most of the feeding trout in these riffles.

Caddisflies abound in this recovering river. Get here in mid-May and you're in for a treat fishing over trout rising to the olive caddis. You'll find other downwings on the water. As early as March little black stoneflies can create feeding situations. In June and July you'll find yellow stoneflies and tan caddis emerging.

Typical of many revitalized rivers, the Little Schuylkill's mayfly hatches remain sparse. It does hold fairly good sulphur and little blue-winged olive dun hatches. The latter appears in September and produces some great autumn fishing opportunities. Other hatches like the gray fox, brown dun (Ephemerella needhami), and light cahill emerge in limited numbers. As the river continues its recovery mayfly hatches should improve in numbers.

You'll find a delayed-harvest area on a 1.7-mile section just down-river from New Ringgold. T 848 off PA 443 parallels the river in this section. There's plenty of parking along the delayed-harvest area thanks to the dedication of people and clubs like the Schuylkill Chapter of Trout Unlimited, the Orwigsburg Business and Professional Association, and Koch's Lawn and Garden Equipment.

The river holds trout from South Tamaqua to its junction with the Schuylkill River near Port Clinton. The most productive section on the river, however, is from New Ringgold downriver to Drehersville. You'll find limited access on some sections above New Ringgold. Don't neglect the excellent fishing opportunities from Tamaqua upriver to Pine Creek at PA 54; this section, part of which flows through State Game Lands 227, is one of the most picturesque, with its towering cliffs and huge boulders.

Water temperatures hold up well during the summer, rising into the mid-70s. Tributaries hold a generous supply of cold water and streambred trout. Part of the river flows from the Still Creek Reservoir, whose water flow has held up well even in droughts.

Because the river is only 60 miles from Philadelphia and 30 miles from Allentown you'll find a lot of anglers from these two areas traveling to the Little Schuylkill to enjoy the fishing and the idyllic setting. Throughout the summer fishing pressure on the delayed-harvest area remains high.

BUSHKILL CREEK

Access Bushkill Drive just north of Tatamy follows the lower Bushkill, PA 191 part of the Little Bushkill, and T 626 the upper end of the Bushkill.

Special Regulations Catch-and-release—1.1 miles, from the dam at Binney and Smith downstream to the 13th Street bridge.

Rating ✳✳

Patterns to Match the Hatches Little Black Stonefly (#16), Little Blue-Winged Olive Dun (#20), Hendrickson (#14), Green Caddis (#16), Sulphur (#16), Light Cahill (#14), Slate Drake (#12), Blue-Winged Olive Dun (#14), Tan Sedge (#16 and #18), Trico (#24), Blue Quill (#18), *Acroneuria* (Brown) Stonefly (#10), Little Sulphur (#24), White Mayfly (#14), Tiny Blue-Winged Olive (*Pseudocloeon* spp.) (#20 to #24)

It's one of the 10 largest limestone streams in the Keystone State. It holds plenty of streambred brown and a few rainbow and brook trout. If you fly-fish here in late February, March, May, July, or September you'll encounter great hatches on this 50- to 60-foot-wide stream. From mid-July through much of October you can expect to see trout rising every morning to a good supply of tricos. The stream often gets little respect from in-state residents, but you'll find plenty of nonresidents fly-fishing here. Many New Jersey fly-fishers visit this productive limestone creek flowing only a couple of miles from the border. New York City residents also fly-fish on this stream, which flows through Northampton County in southeastern Pennsylvania, only 70 miles from New York City. Bushkill Creek in Easton, Pennsylvania, has everything a fly-fisher could ever want.

In late July I met Rich Keesler of Easton to fish the diminutive, early-morning trico hatch and spinner fall. Rich has fly-fished the Bushkill for the past 20 years. He ties dozens of flies commercially and builds top-notch fly-rods for anglers fishing the stream. Rich has fished most of the hatches this stream holds. He especially enjoys fishing to trout rising over little blue-winged olive duns and tricos in August, September, and

October. Rich has even seen some white mayflies on the lower end of this stream in late August.

In late July, especially on warm days, you can expect to meet the trico hatch before 8:00 AM. The morning Rich and I hit the stream the hatch appeared before 7:00, and the spinner fall ended before 9:00. At every access point we saw heavy swarms of mating spinners and trout rising to spent spinners. We caught only a couple of brown trout because of off-color water created by a heavy storm the night before. Still, Rich fished the trico hatch again the next morning. In the midst of a heavy spinner fall and less turbid water he caught 16 streambred trout—some in the 14-inch class.

Many concerned people and organizations have contributed to the betterment of Bushkill Creek. Rich says that much of the credit for the excellent access to the stream goes to two organizations, the Forks of the Delaware Trout Unlimited Chapter in Easton and the Bushkill Conservancy. The 80 members of Trout Unlimited have devoted many hours to stream restoration projects and, with the help of the conservancy, planted many trees along its banks. The conservancy has purchased some land along the stream and turned it over to the Northampton County Park System. Almost a mile of stream is now in public hands thanks to the efforts of the conservancy.

Two major companies with plants along the stream have also contributed to the enhancement of the stream. Binney and Smith, the maker of Crayola crayons, and Pfizer, a major drug firm, allow access to more than a mile of catch-and-release water. You'll find good, productive, fast-water sections in this regulated area.

Lafayette College in Easton, in cooperation with the Bushkill Conservancy, monitors the entire watershed. By checking the stream regularly, all concerned can make certain nothing happens to this vital resource.

Rich Keesler feels that the Bushkill's largest numbers of trout and coolest water are found from Stockertown downstream. A good number of springs keep this lower section cool throughout the summer. In July and August you'll find water temperatures in the mid-60s. The pH of this limestone stream ranges from 7.6 to 8—well on the alkaline side of a neutral pH, 7.

Just below Stockertown the Little Bushkill joins the Bushkill. The main stem and the Little Bushkill hold trout above Stockertown. Here you'll see higher water temperatures and fewer wild trout. The stream begins above Jacobsburg State Park and flows for about 11 miles before it enters the Delaware River at Easton. There's an additional 7 miles of fishing on the Little Bushkill above Stockertown. You'll find plenty of slow water with some riffles and productive pocket water throughout. Near Tatamy you'll find some fast, deep pockets flowing through heavy boulders and over limestone ledges. Rich says a Pheasant Tail works well in this section. The catch-and-release area is just north of Easton.

Several years ago one of the landowners along the lower end posted his land to fishermen. The Delaware Forks Chapter of Trout Unlimited asked that particular landowner if members of the club could take trash out of his section of water. This action so impressed the landowner that he allowed fishing on his property again. Thanks to the chapter for a job well done!

WEST VALLEY CREEK

Access West Valley Creek begins a few miles northeast of Exton and flows southwest toward Downingtown. You'll find the best fly-fishing from Whitford Road downstream to US 322. Clover Mill Road parallels much of the upper delayed-harvest area, and Valley Creek Road follows the lower end of the stream. On the lower end near US 322 you'll find a meadow open to fishing. Jim Leonard says that this area holds good trico and sulphur hatches. Here too you'll see a small cool tributary, Broad Run, enter the main stem.

Special Regulations Delayed harvest, artificial lures only—from the mouth of Colebrook Run downstream 1.2 miles to just below the railroad tunnel.

Rating ✳✳

Patterns to Match the Hatches Hendrickson (#14), Little Black Caddis (#16), Tan Caddis (#16), Sulphur (#16), Light Cahill (#14), Yellow Drake (#10), Trico (#24), Big Slate Drake (#8), Cream Cahill (#14)

I traveled to West Valley Creek with Jim Leonard of Claymont, Delaware, and Des Kahn of Newark, Delaware, in August 1992 to fish the trico hatch. Jim had recently severely sprained his ankle and walked with the aid of a cane. Des and I descended a steep, slippery hill to the stream just below the railroad tunnel. Jim stayed behind, walking feebly on his ankle. Once we arrived at the 20- to 30-foot-wide stream we saw thousands of tricos above the water and some floating in the eddy of a big pool below.

Although West Valley flows through a highly urbanized area, the canopy and cover along it convey thoughts of being many miles away from the Philadelphia area rather than just a few. The creek has a good number of deep runs and pools and some good riffles, but because of the canopy and narrow stream you'll find accurate fly-casting an extreme challenge in some parts.

Since West Valley flows within miles of one of the highest populated areas in the East you'd expect it to have some problems—problems that threaten its very existence as a viable trout fishery. First and foremost the stream suffers from urban sprawl. New housing projects, companies, roads, and all the complications that accompany the exodus are present. Sedimentation from expansion projects is bound to have an effect on future hatches on the stream. Along with urbanization come the problems of overfishing and posted lands. Much of the stream below the project water is posted. Of the 4.6 miles from Whitford Road to US 322, only about 2.5 miles are open to fishing.

The creek above Whitford Road is marginal and gets warm in the summer. Cool springs in the quarry area keep West Valley relatively cool throughout the summer. The Fish Commission has recently electroshocked the stream in fall and found a good number of holdover trout. The Valley Forge Chapter of Trout Unlimited has worked with vibert boxes in the stream in hopes of getting some wild trout. The chapter has completed many stream improvement projects here in recent years. If you believe in saving trout fishing for future generations on this Chester County stream you should join the Valley Forge Chapter of Trout Unlimited in its efforts to keep the stream open and clean.

Thanks are also due to the Clark family, who own a stretch just below the railroad tunnel. They have kept their water open to fishing. West Chester Fish and Game operates a trout hatchery on a feeder stream and supplements the trout planted by the state. Jim Leonard says the club also has been active in landowner relations, stream cleanups, and stream improvements.

With all its problems West Valley Creek still presents matching-the-hatch opportunities. In mid-May you can fly-fish over trout rising to a good hatch of sulphurs. From July right through September, if you arrive on the stream early in the morning you can fish daily over a trico hatch.

Be sure to stop in at the Brandywine Outfitters on US 30 in Exton for the latest information on the stream conditions and hatches. Peter Cooper and Ken Schwam can help make your fishing trip an enjoyable one.

QUITTAPAHILLA CREEK

Access US 422 parallels much of the Quitty's upper end downstream to Annville, and Syner Road much of the lower end.

Special Regulations Delayed harvest, artificial lures only—0.6 mile, from the Spruce Street bridge on T 398 downstream to the lower boundary of Quitty Nature Park.

Rating ✳✳

Patterns to Match the Hatches Little Blue-Winged Olive Dun (#20), Sulphur (#16), Trico (#24)

As a kid, Dick Henry, a longtime fly-fisher from Lebanon, remembers disparaging remarks people made about the stream. "It was always a joke—a sick joke about how area companies polluted this limestone stream," Dick comments.

For years the Quittapahilla, or "Quitty," contained chemicals that prevented any trout from living in it. Dick remembers that even in the late 1940s, someone stocked the upper end of the Quitty with fingerlings. A year later he found 12-inch trout living in the water. But by 1950 the upper spring had dried up completely from nearby quarry operations. Now the upper spring only flows intermittently, and authorities have constrained this upper end that flows through Lebanon into a 50-foot-wide concrete channel. Summer heat warms this "ditch" considerably.

"Without the many limestone springs found on the stream below the ditch the Quitty would be unsuitable for trout," Dick claims. He should know; he performed extensive temperature studies on the stream over the course of two years. On July 20, 1991, with an air temperature of 95 to 97 degrees, Dick found the following water temperatures on the Quitty: Annville Park, 71; first bridge below Annville, 72; upper stone-arch bridge, 72; cement bridge, 72; old mill, 74; second stone-arch bridge, 75; a quarter mile from the mouth, 75; and the mouth (where it joins with the Swatara Creek), 75 degrees. Not only has the temperature remained relatively cool, but the stream now holds several good hatches and a good population of planted and holdover trout. Not bad for waters that have been ravaged by chemical and limestone pollution and spills over the past 50 years.

In fact, the Quitty remained a joke until a steel company in Lebanon ceased operations in 1985. Since that time it has made a gallant comeback. Just recently, in recognition of its improvement, the Fish Commission instituted a delayed-harvest area on the Quitty. Bryan Meck, Dick Henry, and I recently visited that area in Annville. As Bryan entered the stream he sank into mud along the shore up to his knees. Be careful when wading this stream—especially in slower areas, you too will sink into the silt.

Since no hatch appeared on the special-project water Bryan tied on a combination of fly patterns. He used a dry-fly Patriot as a strike indicator, then tied a 2-foot section of tippet material onto the Patriot at the bend of the hook to which he tied a Green Weenie. In an hour of fishing Bryan picked up 10 trout in the delayed-harvest section—excellent for early September, and a reflection of the catch-and-release philosophy of most of the project anglers.

You'll find trout on the Quitty from Snitz Creek, entering between Lebanon and Cleona, downstream to its mouth. On its lower end you'll find a classic open limestone stream with a sluggish flow and plenty of aquatic plants.

Hatches remain a mystery on the Quitty. At present you'll only find a few fishable ones on the stream. Probably the most numerous is the trico, which appears daily from late July through late September. You'll find this morning hatch on the lower half of the stream—where the Quitty flows through open meadows. On a good day Dick Henry picks up 10 to 12 trout during a trico hatch. Dick has also seen some little blue-winged olive duns and sulphurs on the stream, but not in large numbers. Check the abundant aquatic weeds on the lower half of this stream and you'll find a good supply of freshwater shrimp.

When hatches don't appear Dick Henry relies on terrestrials—especially in midsummer. In an afternoon on the stream Dick might take as many as 30 trout on a size-22 or -24 ant.

With so much going for the Quitty you'd think concerned environmentalists have rescued it forever. Not so! Area development of shopping centers and housing threatens to cut short the recovery of this Lebanon County limestone stream. As a result siltation remains a serious problem. The stream begins near Lebanon and flows 11 miles west through Cleona and Annville until it enters Swatara Creek. Much of this area has been or will be heavily developed.

Thanks must go to Joe Waybright for his efforts. Joe worked with landowners making certain anglers had access to the Quitty, and he led the effort for a delayed-harvest area.

Has the Quitty returned from a long period of benign neglect? You bet it has! All of us must now guard the future of this extremely valuable, but fragile resource.

VALLEY CREEK

Access To reach Valley Creek take US 202 to New Centerville. Find Valley Forge Road and drive north to the stream.

Special Regulations No-kill zone—Valley Creek and its tributaries.

Rating ✳✳

Patterns to Match the Hatches Dark Olive Caddis (#16), Little Blue-Winged Olive Dun (#22), Pale Gray Crane Fly (#20), Pale Yellow Crane Fly (#20),

Blue-Winged Olive Dun (#16), Green Caddis (#16), Sulphur Dun and Spinner (#16), Light Cahill (#14), Trico (#24), Light Olive Caddis (#16)

What great history this stream holds! Just a little over 200 years ago the lower end of Valley Creek sheltered Washington's discouraged, desperate Continental army. Some of the most productive pockets and pools on the stream lie within a few feet of Lafayette's headquarters during the Revolutionary War. The very spot you're fishing could be a spot where Washington, Lafayette, or one of their soldiers crossed. Three miles of the lower end of Valley Creek lie within the boundaries of Valley Forge National Historic Park.

But all is not well with this fantastically productive brown trout stream. Wayne Poppich, who has a deep, sincere affection for Valley, has seen it receive two doses of cyanide over the past 20 years. Fifteen years ago the stream received another shot of pollution; this time Conrail spilled PCBs into the stream. When the pollution occurred the state stopped stocking the stream. However, as with Spring Creek in central Pennsylvania—which also became polluted—the halt to stocking Valley was a blessing in disguise. Hordes of early-season anglers looking for recently stocked trout have vanished.

Joe DeMarkis releases a trout caught on the Little Schuykill River.

Yes, thousands of streambred browns inhabit this limestone stream located only minutes from Philadelphia. But as with Spring Creek, entirely too many trout die after swallowing an angler's live bait and hook. Why doesn't someone in authority protect this valuable resource by allowing only artificial lures on Valley Creek?

Poppich has said that if Valley Creek were located in central

Pennsylvania, environmentalists would be more aware of its value; because it's located in a sprawling metropolitan area, it doesn't get the respect it deserves. "Only because of its limestone aquifer has Valley Creek been able to withstand the ravages of man," says Poppich. "If the same exploitation happened to Ridley, French, or Darby they'd be dead streams."

The Valley Forge Chapter of Trout Unlimited of West Chester has devoted thousands of man-hours to the preservation of the fishery on this stream. Members have built channeling devices on one of Valley's tributaries, Little Crabby Creek. A system of baffles allows spawning trout to migrate upstream. The local Trout Unlimited chapter also filed suit in one of the recent pollution incidents and works with the Pennsylvania Department of Environmental Resources to remedy calcium sedimentation and warm-water discharge into Valley from a quarry site.

Trout Unlimited, the Green Valley Association, and the Open Land Conservancy also received cooperation recently from the Trammell Crow Company when the latter planned to divert Little Crabby Creek. After Trout Unlimited talked with Trammell Crow, the company hired the architectural firm Curtis, Cox, Kennerly, and Weston to design a new stream channel that would accommodate trout. This shows what can happen when companies and environmentalists cooperate on a worthwhile project.

This limestone stream has summer water temperatures that rarely exceed 70 degrees. Valley Creek is 20 to 30 feet wide, and many anglers on it catch streambred brown trout over 15 inches long.

Joe Petrella Jr. of Downingtown, Frank Swarner and his son Chip of Glenmoore, and Wayne Poppich fly-fish regularly on Valley in the park. Joe's office is only 10 minutes from the stream, and he regularly spends his lunch hour fishing. I met Joe, Frank, Chip, and Wayne on Valley one evening not long ago. Hundreds of little blue-winged olives emerged off the riffles from 6:00 PM until dark. At least six heavy trout rose in the pool Joe selected to fish. Joe often fishes when the dark olive caddis emerges, and he lands and releases heavy 16-inch browns during this hatch. Wayne landed a 20-inch brown on Valley last year. Chip Swarner, then 12 years old, was an excellent caster and fisherman. Chip hooked one trout that evening that broke his hook, and landed another streambred brown over a foot long.

There's a total of 13 miles of fishing on Valley and 2 miles on its tributary, Little Valley Creek. Valley Creek enters the Schuylkill River near the national park.

Valley Creek is presently in the middle of a controversy that will most definitely determine its future as a viable productive trout stream. The Environmental Quality Board—composed of members of the governor's cabinet, directors of fish and game commissions, and others—will eventually decide the future of the stream. Joe Armstrong and the Valley Forge Chapter of Trout Unlimited have worked diligently to have Valley Creek classified as an exceptional-value stream. Other folks want the stream designated high-quality—lower than exceptional value. On exceptional-value waters, authorities allow no discharges that would reduce existing water quality. A high-quality designation for Valley Creek, on the other hand, would allow some degradation to the stream. In 1993 authorities designated Valley Creek as exceptional value. Because of urbanization and development, Valley Creek continues to have a storm run-off problem.

Will Valley continue to be a proud stream with some great streambred browns? Will the state or the federal agencies change the regulations on this fine stream to prohibit bait-fishing? Only time and demands from interested groups will tell.

TULPEHOCKEN CREEK

Access Take SR 3055 (Van Reed Road) north out of West Lawn to the stream.

Special Regulations Delayed harvest, artificial lures only—3.8 miles, from the first deflector below the Blue Marsh Dam downstream to the covered bridge.

Rating ✳✳✳✳

Patterns to Match the Hatches Little Blue-Winged Olive Dun (#20), Little Black Stonefly (#18), Pale Olive Caddis (#16 and #18), Tan Caddis (#16 and #18), Yellow Crane Fly (#16), Brown Gray Caddis (#14 and #16), Black Caddis (#12 and #16), Sulphur Dun and Spinner (#16), Green Caddis (#16 and #18), Yellow Drake (#12), Trico (#24), Cream Midge (#26), Big Slate Drake (#8)

In my 50 years of fly-fishing I've witnessed every possible thing that can occur on a stream. Yes, everything! I'll never forget that trip to Henry's Fork in Idaho about 15 years ago, when I saw a man in a prone position float past me. He begged me to grab him and hold him upright. I did and probably saved him from drowning. I also remember that night on Fishing Creek in Columbia County when a flycatcher grabbed my fly and fluttered 20 feet above the surface; only after I gave a yank on the line did it let go. On one trip to Washington's Yakima River I hooked famous fly-fisher Dave Engerbrettson in the ear. We had to take him to the hospital to get the hook removed. So I really have seen everything that can possibly happen on a stream. But wait—on my recent trip to the Tulpehocken I experienced something new.

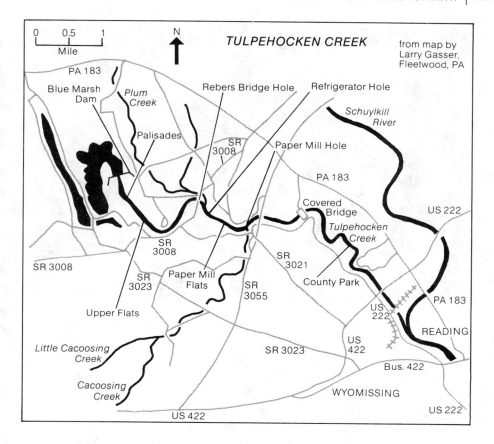

Tony Gehman and Dave Eshenower own Tulpehocken Creek Outfitters in West Lawn. As I've said many times, I find that fly-shop owners are some of the best fishers in the state. Tony and Dave are no exceptions. I asked them to take me on a morning trip to see the trico hatch on Tulpehocken Creek. We met at the Rebers Bridge at 8:00 AM and waded upstream a half mile to get away from some of the anglers. Wading on this stream is relatively easy in most places, so we headed upstream where we couldn't hear the roar of engines or cars crossing the open iron bridge. Dave and I decided to fish a 3-foot-deep riffle, while Tony headed to a faster section upstream where he saw some rising trout. As I cast toward a rising trout, I heard a phone ring—yes, a phone. I looked over at Dave and saw him answer his cellular phone. In 50 years, that was a first for me.

The Tulpehocken means great trout fishing to many anglers. Fly-fishers travel from all parts of the state to fish the Tully. On that recent trip, for instance, I saw Joe Frumento from Philadelphia. Every day he gets free Joe travels to this stream to fly-fish.

A Tulpehocken trout caught during a trico hatch.

Many anglers who fish the tailwater on a regular basis can identify two specific noises that are common on the stream. One of those is a clicking noise and the other a series of "ohs." What do they mean? Trout on the stream get fished over constantly and have become highly selective—to the point of frustrating many of the fly-fishers trying to catch them. You'll hear the click of anglers looking through fly boxes for a fly that might change their luck. Other anglers are checking through their boxes for a finer tippet material to catch the trout. What about the "ohs"? Those are responses to the dozens of trout each angler misses each time he fishes.

Dave, Tony, and I finished our morning of fly-fishing just a short walk upstream from the Rebers Bridge in a nondescript 3-foot-deep glide. In front of us we had more than a dozen trout sporadically rising to caddis, tricos, and midges. All three of us had many, many strikes, but few hook-ups. Why? These trout have become so adept at quickly grabbing, then spitting out, the fly that few of them get hooked. It's just plain luck when sometimes you do hook up. And sometimes when you feel a strike you've been conditioned to set the hook so quickly and you're using such a light tippet that you break the fly off.

We ended the morning landing a dozen trout and missing three times that many. The rainbows in this stream fight tremendously. They're extremely acrobatic and often take you into your backing. Tony and Dave used a caddis pattern while I fished the tandem with a Patriot and a Tan

Caddis Bead Head. Four trout struck my size-12 Patriot dry fly, which I was using as a strike indicator. A dozen trout among us—not bad for a hot July morning.

The secret to a successful day on the Tulpehocken is a fine tippet, the right pattern, and a drag-free drift (wet) or float (dry fly). And Dave and Tony have developed some great patterns to free you from frustration on this stream. They call them CDC Pop Emergers. They tie them for the very common caddis hatches on the stream and the sulphur mayfly. They also tie and sell a CDC Almost Adult Caddis in an emerald green color. They find that this color is extremely effective for caddis. Don't attempt to fly-fish this stream without a good supply of caddis patterns, from pupae to emergers to adults. Common body colors on the stream are tan and green.

But the Tulpehocken has more than just downwings. Fish here in late May and you'll see sulphurs appearing nightly for three weeks. If you plan to fly-fish any summer evening make certain you have plenty of Cream Midge patterns in sizes 24 and 26. You'll also see some yellow drakes in June and July, but always—and I mean *always*—carry plenty of caddis patterns. Possibly the trico brings out the most anglers. You'll see them getting ready for the hatch as early as 6:00 AM.

The stream is easy to wade and ranges from 60 to 80 feet wide. There's a bottom release on the Blue Marsh Dam upstream 1.5 miles from the Rebers Bridge. Because the dam is fairly shallow (about 40 feet) and has become silted, the effects of a bottom release have been lessened somewhat. Water temperatures rise well into the 70s on hot summer afternoons. A few of the feeder streams do add a cool shot of water to the main stem. Usually Cacoosing Creek stays in the 60s throughout the summer months. The water volume on the Tully can vary from 100 to 2,000 cubic feet per second. Such great variation must affect the trout and the hatches on the stream. The Corps of Engineers has got to cooperate more closely with anglers to preserve this important trout fishery. Although this section is a delayed-harvest area, most anglers return their trout to fight another day.

You'll find great fishing on this stream from the section anglers call the Pallisades downstream almost 4 miles to the covered bridge. Be aware that there's presently a lot of road construction on US 222 and US 422. Watch for detours to the stream.

If you want more information on this top-notch urban fishery contact Tulpehocken Creek Outfitters. You can visit their Web site at http:// www.tcoflyfishing.com. Dave Eshenower, Tony Gehman, or Mike Brunner will let you know what's hatching.

Each October the stream receives equal numbers of brown and rainbow fingerlings. Area groups and interested individuals float-stock the stream. The Tulpehocken Chapter of Trout Unlimited is one of these groups and has worked hard to preserve this trout fishery. It has installed many stream improvement devices. If you plan to fish this stream it's imperative that you join this club and sponsor its activities.

Do you want to get frustrated trout fishing—but enjoy it? Then spend a day on Tulpehocken Creek. It's well worth the trip.

RIDLEY CREEK

Access Ridley Creek begins in Chester County and flows southeast into Delaware County. It's located just west of Media off US 1. Ridley Creek Road and Knowlton Road parallel much of the stream. A bicycle path gives access to 3 miles of stocked water in the state park.

Special Regulations Delayed harvest, fly-fishing only—0.6 mile, from the falls in Ridley Creek State Park downstream to the mouth of Dismal Run.

Rating ✷✷

Patterns to Match the Hatches Little Black Stonefly (#14 and #16), Early Brown Stonefly (#12), Tan Caddis (#14 and #16), Brown Caddis (#14 and #16), Little Black Caddis (#16 and #18), Little Blue-Winged Olive Dun (#20), Hendrickson and Red Quill (#14), Quill Gordon (#14), Light Olive Caddis (#16), Sulphur Dun and Spinner (#16), Gray Fox (#12 and #14), March Brown (#12), Blue-Winged Olive Dun (#14), Light Cahill (#14 and #16), Slate Drake (#12 and #14)

Barry Staats, Mary Kuss, and I planned a day of fly-fishing on one of the better suburban fly streams near Philadelphia, Ridley Creek. Barry has often boasted about the quality of fly-fishing on this stream so close to his Sporting Gentleman store, in Media. He's confirmed that the stream often contains rising trout and several decent mayfly, stonefly, and caddisfly hatches. Mary teaches fly-fishing classes at Barry's store. She's an expert caster, and she's familiar with the aquatic life of southeastern streams. Mary has been a fly-fisher since her 16th birthday and an accomplished caster for the past 10 years. The *Philadelphia Inquirer* recently ran a pictorial story on her fishing ability. Mary believes that the three heaviest hatches on Ridley are the little black stonefly in March, the light olive caddis near the end of April, and the sulphur in mid- and late May. Watching Mary cast on the fly-fishing section of Ridley proved her expertise for me.

Mary expressed concern that the put-and-take mentality of many area anglers is really strong. "Fishing pressure remains high on Ridley for a couple of days after opening day and in-season stockings, then falls off dramatically," she explained.

Ridley Creek, despite the urban sprawl surrounding it, contains some holdover trout and acceptable water quality. Its main salvation lies with the 2,600-acre Ridley Creek State Park and the 700-acre Tyler Arboretum in its upper end. Dismal Run houses a trout nursery run by the Delco Anglers and Conservationists. This private stream flows through the arboretum's property. Barry claims that this small, cold tributary harbors some streambred browns. Upstream from the arboretum and state park are a golf course and farmland.

Ridley is topped by a heavy canopy of beech and sycamore through much of its 7 miles of stocked water. At the lower end of the state park there's a 0.6-mile delayed-harvest section that runs downstream to Dismal Run.

Ridley Creek ranges from 20 to 40 feet wide and contains many pools 3 to 6 feet deep, with some deep, productive riffles between. Water temperatures in July and August rise into the high 70s. Trout look for springs or cool tributaries like Dismal Run or Jeffers Run during these hot spells. The state stocks the stream from the Colonial Plantation in the state park downstream to Rose Valley.

FRENCH CREEK

Access French begins with water from Scott Run and Hopewell Lakes in French Creek State Park. The creek flows from Berks County southeast into Chester County, picking up tributaries like Pine Creek, Rock Run, South Branch, Beaver Run, and Birch Run before flowing through Phoenixville and emptying into the Schuylkill River. Its course is within 40 minutes of Philadelphia. A blacktop road follows the stream to Kimberton.

Special Regulations Fly-fishing only, delayed harvest—0.9 mile, from the dam at Camp Sleepy Hollow downstream to Hollow Road.

Rating ✳✳

Patterns to Match the Hatches Little Black Caddis (#18), Little Tan Caddis (#18), Brown Caddis (#16), Olive Caddis (#16), Sulphur Dun and Spinner (#16), Gray Fox (#14), March Brown (#12), Light Cahill (#14), Slate Drake (#12 and #14), Little Blue-Winged Olive Dun (#20), Cream Cahill (#14), Trico (#24), Big Slate Drake (#8), Perla Stonefly (#12)

Leon Rosenthal, a dentist from Abington, has fly-fished on French Creek for more than 40 years. Many changes have occurred in those years to this heavily fished yet productive trout stream just 40 minutes from Philadelphia. Leon tells how development in the headwaters has greatly diminished this once-proud stream.

Mary Kuss, Barry Staats, and I arrived at the fly-fishing-only area at Sheeder Mill Road one day recently. I saw Steve Reifsneider of Pottstown checking the rocks for aquatic insects and went over to see what he'd found. There's an unusual diversity of mayfly, caddisfly, and stonefly hatches on French. Looking at several submerged rocks proved it. Examining two rocks Steve lifted in a riffle showed several mayfly species. As we checked the rocks a heavy downpour began. Surely there'd be no fly-fishing today. As quickly as it had begun, however, the rain ended, and French Creek appeared no more discolored than before.

We glanced to the flat section below the bridge and saw trout feeding occasionally on size-16 olive caddis. Barry and Mary headed down toward the rising trout. Barry tied on an appropriate imitation to match the emerging caddis, while Mary tied on a size-16 caddis pupa. Both Barry and Mary coaxed rainbows and browns to the surface for their patterns. The two landed a half-dozen trout on caddis imitations in an hour. Trout rose all morning, and most took a caddis pattern freely. Occasional sulphur duns also appeared on this morning—May 6, a good week ahead of schedule.

French ranges from 30 to 60 feet wide and contains lots of deep runs, productive riffles, and pocket water. The state stocks approximately 15 miles of the stream, from St. Peters downstream to the village of Kimberton. The fly-fishing area runs from 100 yards above Sheeder Run Road upstream to Hollow Road, almost 0.9 miles. Much of the stream contains a canopy of sycamores.

French Creek remains productive until early June. Temperatures after that time often rise into the mid- to upper 70s, and you'll find smallmouth bass where trout resided earlier. Steve Reifsneider has occasionally caught holdover trout.

Even with its shortcomings French maintains its stature as a good southeastern trout stream. Jack Mickievicz of Douglasville says the stream contains an unusual diversity of mayflies but few spectacular hatches. If you're on the stream at the right time, however, matching the hatch can be rewarding. Hendricksons, blue quills, March browns, gray foxes, slate drakes, and many more mayflies appear throughout the season. Caddis hatches become the fly-fisherman's salvation on French Creek. Even before the season begins tan and brown caddis appear. Carry plenty of size 16 and 18 caddis patterns with you if you're fishing this stream.

OCTORARO CREEK

Access PA 472 crosses the West Branch, and paved roads off that route parallel the stream. PA 896 crosses the East Branch, and secondary roads approach much of that branch.

Special Regulations West Branch Octoraro Creek—delayed harvest, fly-fishing only—1.9 miles, from about 220 yards below PA 472 downstream to near the second unnamed tributary below SR 2010.

Rating ✳✳

Patterns to Match the Hatches Early Brown Stonefly (#14), Blue Quill (#18), Hendrickson and Red Quill (#14), Black Quill (#14), Little Black Caddis (#18), Cream Caddis (#16), Green Caddis (#14), Sulphur Dun and Spinner (#16), March Brown (#12), Blue-Winged Olive Dun (#14), Gray Drake *(Siphlonurus quebecensis) (#*14), Light Cahill (#14), Slate Drake (#12), Brown Caddis (#16), Cream Cahill (#14), Yellow Drake (#12), Trico (#24), Big Slate Drake (#6)

Quaint Amish buggies plodded along the country road as we headed south from Lancaster. Pennsylvania Dutch country holds some exciting trout streams in this scenic section of Lancaster County. We first crossed the West Branch of the Octoraro on PA 472. At that point Black Rock Gorge begins. This unusual, spectacular gorge with huge rocks has been classified an outstanding geological site by the state. Just below that point a delayed-harvest section begins and continues downstream for almost 2 miles. A heavy canopy shades much of the upper end of the West Branch. Pennsylvania also includes the Octoraro in its scenic-river system. Just being on this stream evokes contentment.

At the lower end of the fly-fishing project I recently met Don Whitesel of Millersville, Desmond Kahn of Newark, Delaware, and Jim Leonard of Claymont, Delaware. It's only a 45-minute drive from Newark to the Octoraro. All three fly-fish the Octoraro frequently. Jim and Des know the hatches well. Desmond recently received his degree from the University of Delaware in insect ecology.

At first glance the Octoraro reminds you of a central-Pennsylvania limestone stream, especially in the meadow where we chose to fish. It was a cool mid-June evening, and the Octoraro water registered 60 degrees. Desmond assured me that the temperature often rises into the high 70s on hot summer days. All three have caught holdover trout here.

By the time we arrived on the stream a few cream cahill spinners were in the air. Jim said these spinners had appeared in fair numbers the past couple of evenings. Jim and I selected Light Cahill patterns, while Desmond chose a Sulphur Comparadun, and Don fished a Light Cahill wet fly. Just at dusk a few remaining sulphur duns emerged. In two hours on this tranquil stretch of the Octoraro the four of us caught 18 trout—trout hooked in the middle of June in southern Lancaster County.

Indeed, the delayed-harvest area of this stream means a good supply of trout until mid-June.

This area contains some good holding water with deep riffles and small pools. The stream here ranges from 15 to 20 feet wide, but some long, flat sections widen to 25 to 30 feet. The Southern Lancaster County Sportsmen's Association and the Donegal Chapter of Trout Unlimited have placed many valuable improvement devices throughout the stream.

The Octoraro has been hit with two floods within the past 30 years. These floods, plus intensive upstream farming, cause a serious siltation problem on the drainage system.

At the West Branch of the Octoraro near Quarryville in Lancaster County, Des Kahn picks up a trout during a sulphur hatch.

The West Branch begins near Nickle Mines. As it flows south it adds Meetinghouse Creek, Bowery Run (stocked), and Stewart Run (stocked) before it enters Octoraro Lake. The East Branch ranges from 20 to 30 feet wide and contains some deep pools. It begins near Christiana, adding Williams, Buck, Valley, and Officers Runs, along with Valley Creek. Farther downstream the East Branch picks up additional volume with Knott, Ball, Knights, Bells, Coppers, and Muddy Runs before it joins the West Branch in Octoraro Lake. If you're in the Lancaster area don't miss this small, scenic, productive trout stream.

DONEGAL CREEK

Access To reach the stream from the Lancaster area, drive out of town on PA 230 and turn left at Mt. Joy onto PA 772 (Mt. Joy Road).

Special Regulations Delayed harvest, fly-fishing only—2.4 miles, from 275 yards below PA 772 downstream to T 334.

Rating ✳✳

Patterns to Match the Hatches Little Blue-Winged Olive Dun (#20), Sulphur Dun and Spinner (#16), Gray Fox and Ginger Quill (#12 and #14), March Brown (#12), Trico (#24)

Between Elizabethtown and Mount Joy in western Lancaster County lies a terrific limestone trout stream called Donegal Creek. The Donegal Fish and Conservation Association has worked for the preservation and upgrading of this stream. For years this group has had the good fortune to be headed by Ken Depoe. Through Ken's efforts the group has established a nursery on the stream and made hundreds of improvements on the water. Without these improvements Donegal Creek would be a shallow limestone stream with a few deep holding pools. Given the dozens of man-made devices put in place by the association, the stream contains plenty of long, flat sections and small pools holding a good supply of trout. Ken says that before they installed the devices the stream ranged up to 30 feet wide and averaged 6 inches deep. Now the stream only extends 15 feet across, but it averages 2 to 3 feet deep.

Donegal's water remains relatively cool through much of summer. The upper end lacks any significant canopy to protect the stream, however. Ken says that after a few days of 90-degree weather the water temperature might rise into the low 70s, but by morning it's often back into the high 50s. When Don and Kathy Whitesel and I visited the stream on a June morning I checked the water temperature. Would you expect to see a 53-degree reading in the middle of June on a Lancaster County stream?

Much of the delayed-harvest area has a good canopy that shades the 20-foot-wide stream all day. The upper end of the water flows through meadowland. Ken Depoe transported fertilized trico eggs from Falling Springs near Chambersburg and placed them in Donegal Creek. The upper meadow now has a fantastic trico hatch from early July through September.

The Donegal watershed causes dilemmas for the stream, however. The two major problems that keep this from being a top-quality trout stream are siltation and the high nitrogen content of the water—both caused by upstream farming. The stream devices have helped with the first concern, settling out much of the particulates. The water's high nitrogen content, however, affects natural reproduction of trout. Ken recently placed fertilized eggs in the stream, but all died shortly after they came in contact with the nitrites.

Even though Donegal Creek has some problems, it's a great stream to fly-fish. Add a trico or sulphur hatch and you'll experience a productive day.

CEDAR CREEK

Access You can reach Cedar Creek by turning off PA 29 onto Parkway Boulevard.

Rating ✳✳

Patterns to Match the Hatches Little Blue-Winged Olive Dun (#20), Sulphur Dun and Spinner (#16), Light Cahill (#14), Tan Caddis (#16), Trico (#24)

What a fantastic, cool limestone stream! Cedar Creek flows through the Allentown park system—and it's open to fishing. Farsighted officials acquired the stream bottom of Cedar and the Little Lehigh in Allentown for the public to enjoy forever. The quality of life for all in the Allentown area is enhanced by their park system, the finest I've seen in Pennsylvania.

The state classifies 1.6 miles of Cedar as wild-trout water, and the creek holds an excellent population of streambred browns. Fish one of the productive pools, riffles, or flats near dusk on any summer evening and the stream comes alive with rising trout. In late May these trout feed freely on sulphur duns and spinners in the evening. From July 1 to October 1 you can fly-fish over fish rising to spent tricos every morning. At almost any time you'll catch wary browns 5 to 15 inches long. Like any resource these fish should be immediately returned so other fishermen can enjoy the same quality of fly-fishing.

In the park Cedar ranges from 20 to 30 feet wide. Its willow-lined, undercut banks provide plenty of cover for the wild-trout population. The stream contains many pools, some long, flat sections, and productive riffles. About 2 miles of Cedar Creek run within the city park and some open water above PA 29 is in a county park. Little Cedar enters the main stem in the city park. This tributary flows through Trexler Park and is closed to fishing. Below the park the state stocks a short section of Cedar Run.

LITTLE LEHIGH CREEK

Access SR 3001 accesses the upper end of the Little Lehigh near Ancient Oaks, and Country Club Road gets you to the lower end.

Special Regulations Delayed harvest, fly-fishing only—1.4 miles, from Laudenslagers Mill Dam upstream to T 508. Heritage-trout angling—1 mile, from the upstream face of Fish Hatchery Road bridge downstream to near the 24th Street bridge.

Rating ✳✳✳✳

Patterns to Match the Hatches Little Black Stonefly (#16), Little Blue-Winged Olive Dun (#20), Blue Quill (#18), Hendrickson (#14), Sulphur (#16 and #18), Early Brown Stonefly (#14), Tan Sedge (#14), Yellow Drake (#12), Spotted Sedge (#14), Cream Cahill (#14), Light Cahill (#14), Trico (#24), Hex Mayfly (#6), Little Black Caddis (#18 and #20)

It's a happening—an experience you don't want to miss. John Balliet of Allentown does it every day off. Dozens of others do the same thing. What do all of these people do? Exactly what is it that you should experience? It's the trico hatch on the Little Lehigh. It's well worth an early-morning trip to the stream from July through September to see dozens of anglers anxiously preparing for this hatch. Seated by a bench there's an angler cleaning his line. At picnic tables along the creek you'll find other anglers changing leaders, adding finer tippets, or tying on their favorite minute pattern to copy the mayfly of the day, the trico.

As the duns still emerge and the first spinners begin falling, anglers take their place along the stream and wait for rising trout. Posted every 100 feet or so along the stream you can find an eager fly-fisher scanning the surface for signs of feeding trout. This scene continues every summer morning well past the day the first heavy frost appears, in late September or October.

If you want to see and fish the hatch on this fertile limestone stream but prefer to avoid this sometimes circuslike atmosphere, then plan to fish the trico outside the regulated area. Yes, out of the heritage-trout-angling and delayed-harvest areas of the stream. In total there's about 2.5 miles of regulated water. The Little Lehigh has a total of more than 12 miles of fishable water. Rod Rohrbach and Pat Cuskey own the Little Lehigh Fly Shop. Rod confirms that some of the best fly-fishing on the stream can be found outside the regulated areas. Seven miles of the stream flow through a city park. Thanks to the foresight of the city of Allentown this stream will be open for all to enjoy forever.

Rod Rohrbach has kept temperature records on the Little Lehigh since he opened his shop. He's never seen a temperature higher than 61 degrees in the morning nor lower than 38 in winter.

The Little Lehigh begins near Alburtis. This cool limestone stream adds flow from Toad Creek, Iron Run, and Spring Creek. By the time the

stream enters the city park it ranges from 40 to 60 feet wide. Even in the park you'll find plenty of cool water entering the stream through a number of springs. Walk into the Little Lehigh Fly Shop and you'll see what I mean. The shop is an old springhouse on Hatchery Road. Inside you'll see a spring that enters the creek running through the shop. Seated around a picnic table just outside the shop will probably be some of the Little Lehigh Fly Fishers, a very informal club, chatting about the morning they just experienced, the trout they caught or missed, the patterns that worked or failed. Two or three of these regulars will be tying a new or improved fly to catch a trout tomorrow that refused their pattern today. Members include the likes of Jack Mullaneaux, Rick Heiserman, Paul Grant, Bill Hicks, John Coxey, Dick Jones, Al Miller, John Sniscak, Dave Masters, John Ruland, Stan Malina, Rod Rohrbach, and anybody else who can take the fun and frivolity that occur daily at the shop. The shop runs several seminars on fly-fishing annually with well-known speakers like Gary Borger, Lefty Kreh, Bob Miller, and others.

The Little Lehigh boasts some great hatches other than the trico. Sulphurs bring plenty of trout to the surface in May and early June. Just like the trico, however, after a week or two of heavy pressure trout become highly selective, and even the best copy of the natural is often refused. Early and late in the season, and also on most overcast drizzly days, little blue-winged olives take precedence on the stream. Add good yellow drakes in June and a big hex hatch in August and you can see why this stream boasts a large population of trout.

You'll find angling pressure extremely high on this stream much of the year. Why? First, the Little Lehigh is a productive limestone stream in its own right. Second, this great creek is situated in a heavily populated area and only an hour from Philadelphia. Third, most of the stream is open to anglers. As I stated before, 7 miles of the stream flow through a city park system.

Given this heavy pressure, it's important to use the right pattern on the Little Lehigh. Rod Rohrbach and his regulars have narrowed the thousands of possible patterns to a manageable few that will save the day for you if you plan to fish here. Here are the top six patterns—that is, when no hatch appears:

- **Al's Rat.** Developed by Al Miller, this is one of the most popular patterns for the stream. It's a simple pattern tied on a size-20 hook. A thin body is made with brown monocord and a wind of muskrat fur at the thorax. That's it—it's simple, but extremely productive.
- **Griffith's Gnat** in sizes 20–24.
- **Ants** in sizes 12, 14, and 18–24.
- **Henryville Special.** Use sizes 18–24 and bodies of peacock, muskrat, or green or red floss.
- **Little Lehigh Cranefly.** Tie this with rusty brown thread, fine muskrat dubbing, and one turn of an andulusian hackle on a size-18 hook.
- **Philadelphia Lawyer.** Paul Grant ties this with a white quill body in the front and muskrat dubbing, palmered with two turns of grizzly hackle, in the rear on a size-24 hook.

Stop in at the Little Lehigh Fly Shop and sit down at the table just outside. You'll learn more in an hour of two of watching and listening than you will fishing the stream for an entire week. The regulars there have seen and experienced it all.

MONOCACY CREEK

Access Illicks Mill Road east of Schoenersville Road.

Special Regulations Trophy-trout project—1.9 miles, beginning at the dam

Tricos on the Little Lehigh.

at Illicks Mill and running upstream to and including the Gertrude Fox Conservation Area.

Rating ✳✳✳

Patterns to Match the Hatches Little Blue-Winged Olive Dun (#20), Little Black Caddis (#16), Sulphur Dun and Spinner (#16), Light Cahill (#14), Trico (#24)

The Monocacy, Little Bushkill, Cedar Run, and Little Lehigh flow through highly developed areas of Pennsylvania. The Allentown-Bethlehem-Easton area is in the midst of an economic boom. With the increased development, people fear that one of the prized streams in the Lehigh Valley will be affected. The kind of incident we fear occurred on the Monocacy in June 1985. A chemical spill at the intersection of PA 512 and US 22 killed more than 30,000 fish in the Monocacy. Native brown trout made up a high percentage of the dead fish. Joe Kohler of Allentown feels that the spill did not affect the insect life on the stream, however. After the spill the Fish Commission decided not to stock the most affected area, from the Illicks Mill Dam upstream, although it recently posted the area as trophy-trout water.

Dr. John Hampsey, of Bethlehem, fly-fishes on the Monocacy weekly during the season. He's a member of the Monocacy Chapter of Trout Unlimited and the Monocacy Watershed Association. Both organizations have been active in preserving the stream. Their major concerns are development along the bank and storm-runoff control. Their goal is to control development along the stream and monitor developers during the building phase of projects. Recently the local Trout Unlimited chapter installed deflectors in the stream, the first of many planned improvements. The Bethlehem Parks Department cooperates fully with the chapter in its projects.

As with the Little Bushkill (near Easton), Cedar Creek, and the Little Lehigh, the Monocacy contains good hatches of sulphurs and tricos. Joe Kohler and John Hampsey look forward to mornings from early July well into October, when tricos appear in massive numbers on the Monocacy. On summer afternoons John relies on terrestrials such as ants and beetles. These, plus the green inchworm, work well all summer long.

There's about 9 miles of fishable water on the Monocacy. The upper 5 miles are considered wild-trout water, with 1.9 miles of trophy-trout water. The lower 4 miles, including the part that flows through the city of Bethlehem, are stocked. The stream ranges from 40 to 60 feet wide, has a good flow of limestone water, and remains fairly cool all summer.

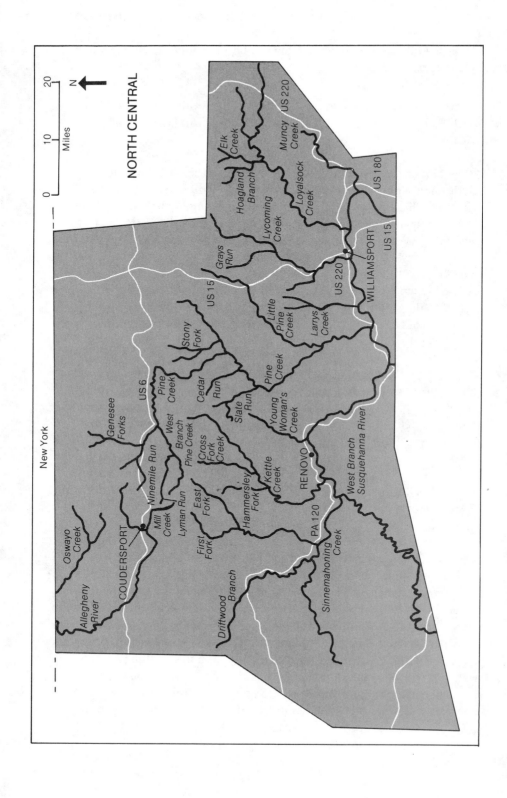

NORTH CENTRAL

5 | Streams of North-Central Pennsylvania

The home of the brown drake, the green drake, and the fabulous April trio—that's what the north-central streams mean to many Pennsylvania fly-fishermen. Travel to any one of dozens of streams in Lycoming, Potter, McKean, Tioga, Clinton, and Cameron Counties in April and you'll meet prolific hatches like the blue quill, Hendrickson, and quill gordon. Travel to many of these same streams in late May and most will exhibit the dynamic duo of brown and green drakes—and also toss in some additional hatches like the blue-winged olive and the slate drake.

But the north-central Pennsylvania streams hold much more than just a few hatches. Many of them contain yellow drakes and tricos all summer. If only the water on these freestones remained cooler in July and August. Hatches like the yellow drake, trico, slate drake, sulphur, and others often emerge in 70-plus-degree water void of trout. Nevertheless, the headwaters of some of these streams contain cool water throughout the summer. The upper end of Kettle, Young Womans Creek, Lick Run, the First Fork above Wharton, and the East Fork hold hatches and trout through August.

There's more to the north-central streams than just fly-fishing. They afford idyllic scenery with few other fishermen and towering mountains as a backdrop to crystal-clear trout streams. Travel up Pine Creek Valley or the valleys that embrace First Fork or Kettle, and you'll witness splendor and breathtaking beauty reserved for few other places in the East. If you haven't yet fly-fished on these streams, what are you waiting for?

SINNEMAHONING PORTAGE CREEK

Access PA 155 parallels Sinnemahoning Portage Creek up to the town of Sizerville. Above this town the stream holds a good number of streambred brown trout, but also has some posted property. Gardeau Road (T 470) reaches the upper end.

Rating ✳✳

Patterns to Match the Hatches Little Blue-Winged Olive Dun (#20), Blue Quill (#18), Quill Gordon (#14), Hendrickson (#14), Green Drake (#12), Brown Drake (#12), Slate Drake (#14), Blue-Winged Olive Dun (#14), Light Cahill (#14), Yellow Stonefly (#16), Little Green Stonefly (#18)

How in the world did a stream in Pennsylvania get a name like this? And would you believe that this stream flows just a short distance from Allegheny Portage Creek? In years gone by Native Americans traveled from the Susquehanna River to the Allegheny River by canoe. They traveled up the Sinnemahoning to Emporium, then up Sinnemahoning Portage Creek (SPC) to what is now Keating Summit. Just north of that town they picked up Allegheny Portage Creek (APC), which took them to the Allegheny River at Port Allegany. Both "Portage" streams, in their upper reaches, hold good populations of streambred brown trout. Of the two the state plants trout only in Sinnemahoning Portage Creek.

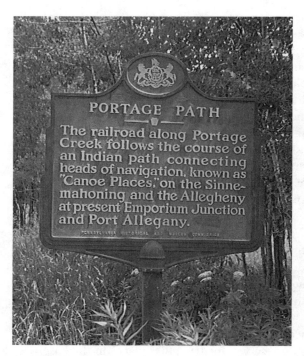

A sign near Sinnemahoning Portage Creek telling all how the stream got its unusual name.

SPC holds some great hatches in the early and midseason. You get good emergences of blue quills, Hendricksons, and quill gordons in April; in late May the lower end of the stream holds green and brown drakes. Fish one of these prolific hatches and you'll often see plenty of streambred and planted trout rising.

Even in summer SPC holds some hatches and trout. As the air temperatures rise and the pools and riffles lower, look for trout in some of the deeper, spring-fed pools. Recently Dan Brehm of nearby Emporium showed me some of his favorite stretches of this productive stream. Dan just began fly-fishing but he already enjoys matching one of the hatches on the stream.

LYMAN RUN

Access You can reach Lyman Run from Galeton off US 6 on SR 2002. Take Lyman Run Road, which parallels the stream.

Special Regulations Selective-harvest program—4 miles, from Lyman Lake upstream to Splash Dam Hollow.

Rating ✳✳✳

Patterns to Match the Hatches Little Blue-Winged Olive Dun (#20), Blue Quill (#18), Quill Gordon (#14), Hendrickson (#14), Early Brown Stonefly (#14), Little Black Caddis (#16), Brown Caddis (#14), Sulphur (#16 and #18), March Brown (#12), Light Cahill (#14), Green Drake (#10), Slate Drake (#12), Blue-Winged Olive Dun (#14), Dark Green Drake (#8), Golden Stonefly (#8 and #10)

❝ If you want to experience wild-trout fishing in a situation as close to nature as it comes, this is it," Jack Mickievicz said as we eagerly headed toward Lyman Run to fish for a couple of hours. "My best day on this stream occurred several years ago, when I caught 53 brook trout— some of them over 12 inches long, and many of them streambred," Jack continued. Jack hits this highly productive small stream all season long— he lives only 10 miles away in Douglasville.

This 15- to 20-foot-wide, Potter County freestone runs through a hemlock bottom. It holds plenty of brookies, some holdover browns, and a few rainbows that move upstream from an impoundment below, Lyman Lake. In every section above the dam you'll find springs entering the main stem that provide plenty of cool water throughout the summer. Watch your step as you walk along this small gem—the streambanks are uneven, with holes hidden by high wisps of swamp grass. It's often easier to wade in the stream, but make certain you keep a low profile: These are wary trout.

Lyman Run holds a fly-fishing-only stretch beginning just above the dam and running upstream for 4 miles. Avoid the first half mile just above the lake. Here the stream separates into five or six channels each only a foot or two wide.

There are about 3 miles of stream below the lake, but the water temperature here runs as high as 80 degrees on many summer afternoons. The state forgot one thing when it designed this lake—a release from the bottom to cool Lyman Run below. The warm water from Lyman also affects the quality of trout water in the West Branch into which it empties. Above the lake it's a different matter. Here you'll find equal numbers of productive runs, pools, and riffles. Watch your cast—you'll find some sections lined nearly bank to bank with overhanging alders.

Recently, in an hour of leisurely fly-fishing in early August, Jack Mickievicz and I caught 20 trout in a 200-foot section of Lyman Run. Some of these beautifully colored brook trout ran as large as 8 inches long. In one heavy run I picked up a half-dozen trout in a few minutes.

Usually trout on Lyman are receptive to almost any pattern. Attractors and terrestrials work well in midsummer. However, hit Lyman when a hatch appears and you're in for some great matching-the-hatch fun. You'll find enough green drakes on the surface in late May and early June to bring up some of the heavy trout the stream hides.

Lyman Run flows miles from any occupied dwelling, much of it through state forest land. With all this going for it you'd think you'd never find any type of pollution problem. Not so. Thompson Run flows into Lyman about 3 miles upstream from the lake. There's an abandoned Potter County landfill located up that run. In spring, when waters fill the old landfill, contaminates leach into Thompson Run and then into Lyman. This could eventually lead to the ruination of Lyman Run. Travel along Thompson Run and you'll see DANGER signs now posted, cautioning you about the water.

Don't miss this fine stream if you're in the area. If you enjoy catching plenty of native brookies with an occasional holdover brown and plenty of unspoiled scenery, then you'll enjoy Lyman Run.

MILL CREEK

Access The lower end of Mill Creek parallels US 6 to Sweden Valley. Upstream from this point PA 44 takes you to the stream.

Rating ✳✳✳

Patterns to Match the Hatches Little Blue-Winged Olive Dun (#20), Blue Quill (#18), Quill Gordon (#14), Hendrickson (#14), Black Quill (#12 and #14), Sulphur (#16), March Brown (#12), Light Cahill (#14), Green Drake (#10), Dark Blue Sedge (#12), Yellow Drake (#10), Needle Fly (Slate Stonefly) (#16)

Tom Dewey, Joe Selvage, and I headed down Cartee Street in Coudersport. The two anglers wanted to show me what remained of the

"Goodsell Hole." Both Tom and Joe live in Coudersport and fish the area streams extensively. The three of us stood in a backyard where Mill Creek enters the Allegheny River. Of course, calling it the Allegheny "River" here is a bit of an overstatement: Almost as much water enters from Mill Creek as does from the river. Prior to 1954, at the spot where Mill Creek entered the river the two streams formed a huge pool called the Goodsell Hole. In 1954 authorities channeled both the Allegheny River and Mill Creek to prevent further flooding in Coudersport. You'll find Mill Creek flowing now in a deep concrete channel for several blocks from the library to its confluence with the river. Where Mill Creek enters the Allegheny you'll find a 10-foot falls. "There's no way for the trout to come up Mill Creek from the river," said Tom Dewey. "This ramp in effect isolates Mill Creek trout from the rest of the watershed." That's not such a bad idea—Mill Creek has a respectable supply of streambred browns.

Tom Dewey and Joe Selvage know Mill Creek well. The two have developed an exciting new software program for fly-fishermen called FLYbase. This enables the fly-fisher to use his PC to forecast a hatch and to conduct research on aquatic insects that previously took several books and hours of reading. The software operates on any IBM-compatible computer and can be ordered from P.O. Box 872, Coudersport 16915. Within a few years all informed anglers will be equipped with software like this.

Mill Creek is a truly productive wild-trout stream. As with most of the others so designated, Mill Creek cannot withstand the taking of a great number of its trout. When you fly-fish this gem you must practice voluntary catch-and-release. Unless you do, it will go the way of many of our other good wild-trout streams. Also ask landowners for permission before you fish.

You'll find more brook trout in Mill Creek above Sweden Valley. From Sweden Valley downstream you'll catch more streambred brown trout. Trout Run enters Mill Creek in Sweden Valley. You can even catch some good-sized brown trout right in Coudersport before Mill becomes channeled.

Fly-fishing on parts of Mill Creek is difficult but well worth the effort. You'll find alders growing on both banks and these bushes seem determined to grab almost every cast you make over this 15- to 20-foot-wide stream.

Penn State entomologist Greg Hoover calls Mill Creek a miniature Penns Creek due to its many hatches. The most notable hatch on Mill occurs in late May, when the green drake appears. This is the time to catch (and release) some of the lunkers in this stream. Dependable sulphur hatches appear on Mill for more than two weeks in late May. Be prepared to match both the dun and spinner. You'll also find several little blue-winged olive dun hatches on the stream. If you enjoy fishing nymphs, try a Hare's Ear.

Do Tom Dewey and Joe Selvage enjoy fly-fishing on their home stream, Mill Creek? In one year you might find Tom on the water 25 to 30 times and Joe 15 to 20 times. During many of those trips Tom and Joe will catch and release several golden streambred brown trout over 15 inches long.

GRAYS RUN

Access Take Grays Run Road off PA 14 to reach the stream.

Special Regulations Selective-harvest program—2.2 miles, from the Grays Run Hunting Club property line downstream to the bridge (T 842) on Grays Run Road.

Rating ✶✶

Patterns to Match the Hatches Early Brown Stonefly (#14), Blue Quill (#18), Quill Gordon (#14), Hendrickson (#14), Black Quill (#12 and #14), Red Quill Stonefly (#14), Light Stonefly (#14), Sulphur (#16), Light Cahill (#14), Green Drake (#10), Slate Drake (#12), Dark Blue Sedge (#12), Blue-Winged Olive Dun (#14), Little Green Stonefly (#16), Little Yellow Stonefly (#16), Little Blue-Winged Olive Dun (#20)

❝It's a wild-trout stream of high quality." That's what longtime fly-fisher Bob McCullough of Williamsport thinks about Grays Run. He's correct—but there's more. What an idyllic setting for a stream! Crystal-clear water flows through a deep forest of hardwoods and conifers, every once in a while interrupted by a huge fallen tree bearing evidence of a past violent storm. Many of these toppled trees block this 15- to 20-foot-wide mountain stream. Here you'll find small pools, undercut banks, and small productive riffles. Grays Run is a great place to spend a day fly-fishing among spectacular scenery and wild trout.

But Grays Run has much more than scenery going for it. You'll have some good matching-the-hatch episodes on this stream just 15 miles north of Williamsport via PA 14. As the season begins in mid-April you'll find hatches like the blue quill, quill gordon, and Hendrickson. By late April you'll find an unusual mayfly appearing on Grays Run: the black quill. Using a Black Quill to copy the dun or an Early Brown Spinner to match the spinner can produce good results. Some of the best fly-fishing on Grays Run occurs near the end of May when this rather small mountain stream holds its annual green drake hatch. This is the time to get some of the heavy streambred brown trout or native brook trout here. Into June,

July, August, and September you'll often do well using a size-14 Adams to copy the slate drake that appears most of the summer.

Try to fly-fish on Grays Run near the end of May or early June for the green drake it hosts. This big mayfly brings some of Grays Run's lunkers to the surface. Bob McCullough likes to fish terrestrials. He says that early June is the time to fish the green inchworm imitation on this freestone stream. Inchworms by the thousands fall off the trees along the streambank.

There's a 2.2-mile, fly-fishing-only stretch at the upper end of the open water. You'll find fishing pressure rather high on this project water. After the hordes of anglers have left the stream you might want to try the area below the regulated water. Here you'll find some streambred brown trout up to 15 inches long and some native brookies nearly a foot long. From the Grays Run Camp downstream to where the stream enters Lycoming Creek, there's 4 miles of water, only briefly interrupted by a private section. Just above the fly-fishing-only project you'll find private water owned by the Grays Run Club.

LARRYS CREEK

Access PA 287 parallels the lower 5 miles of Larrys Creek, PA 973 gets you to the middle section of the river above Salladasburg, and the Water Company Road (T 374) takes you to the upper end. You have to hike in to reach much of the upper water.

Rating ✶✶

Patterns to Match the Hatches Little Blue-Winged Olive Dun (#20), Blue Quill (#18), Quill Gordon (#14), Hendrickson (#14), Black Quill (#12 and (#14), Grannom (#16), Sulphur (#16), Gray Fox (#12), Light Cahill (#14), Green Drake (#10), Little Yellow Stonefly (#16), Little Green Stonefly (#16), *Pteronarcys* Stonefly (#8), Blue-Winged Olive Dun (#14), Slate Drake (#12), Blue Dun (Western Olive) (#20 and #22), Tiny Blue-Winged Olive (*Acentrella* spp.) (#20 to #24), Dark Gray Stonefly (#16), Tiny Blue-Winged Olive (*Pseudocloeon* spp.) (#20 to #24)

A couple of days a week Don Bastian guides for Fishing Creek Outfitters, and works with Cathy Beck as assistant fly-fishing-school instructor. Don ties commercially for Fishing Creek Outfitters. I've never seen better comparaduns than those tied by Don. In the 1970s and 1980s Don frequently fly-fished on one of his favorite small nearby streams, Larrys Creek.

Don lives in Quiggleville only 5 miles from this small but productive freestone stream, and vividly recalls the first time he fly-fished Larrys Creek for the green drake. He saw coffin fly spinners appear and went back to his car for his fly-fishing gear. For the next week Don had the green drake and the coffin fly and the stream to himself. He caught dozens of trout on that initial introduction to this sometimes frustrating hatch.

I met Don on the stream recently in the middle of June. The two of us fished for the better part of an afternoon and saw a good number of slate drakes and blue-winged olive duns emerge. Few trout rose to either sparse hatch. The two of us, however, did manage to catch and release a dozen streambred brown and brook trout.

Larrys Creek gets little attention from the fly-fishing fraternity. Yet it has some great hatches and plenty of streambred trout. Above Salladasburg water temperatures average in the low 60s all summer long. Rarely a day goes by from April to late June that you don't see a generous number of mayflies, stoneflies, and caddisflies appearing on the stream.

The 4.5 miles of stream below Salladasburg on the main stem range from 30 to 50 feet wide. Above Salladasburg you'll see a much smaller stream ranging from 15 to 30 feet wide. From Salladasburg to the Susquehanna River the river has some deep pools and big trout. The farther you head downstream, the more marginal the water becomes. Although anglers catch some heavy trout down to the river, the best fishing is above the bridge at Larryville. Dave Rothrock fishes Larrys Creek frequently and finds a good concentration of streambred brown trout between the two bridges in Salladasburg.

The First Fork enters the main stem just below Salladasburg and the Second Fork in the town. Both forks contain mainly private water. The Larrys Creek Fish and Game Club and the Elbow Bend Club post large sections of the Second Fork.

Roaring Run, a tributary above Salladasburg, does pour in some mine acid, reducing the productivity of the main stem.

If you're looking for a small stream with streambred brown trout and some good hatches like the green drake, slate drake, Hendrickson, and blue quill, why not give Larrys Creek a try? You'll see few anglers and a surprisingly generous supply of hatches.

FIRST FORK, SINNEMAHONING CREEK

Access Take PA 872 north from Jericho.

Special Regulations Delayed harvest, artificial lures only—from the mouth of Bailey Run downstream for 2.1 miles.

Rating ✸✸

Patterns to Match the Hatches Little Blue-Winged Olive Dun (#20), Blue Quill (#18), Black Caddis (#16), Quill Gordon (#14), Hendrickson (#14), Tan Caddis (#14), Blue Dun (#20), Sulphur Dun and Spinner (#16 and #18), Gray Fox (#12), March Brown (#12), Green Drake and Coffin Fly (#10), Brown Drake (#12), Blue-Winged Olive Dun (#14), Slate Drake (#14), Light Cahill (#14), Green Caddis (#14), Rusty Caddis (#14), Yellow Drake (#12), Pale Evening Dun (#18), Trico (#24), Big Slate and Rusty Spinner (#8)

Visit the First Fork just below Wharton, where Bailey Run enters, and look downstream. If you didn't know better you'd think you were fishing on a Montana stream. The scenery on this Potter County freestone is magnificent, and the early-season fly-fishing is often outstanding.

A typical Pennsylvania freestone stream, the First Fork warms quickly after the first of June. On that occasional year, however, when air temperatures average below normal, First Fork can be productive into July. Typically First Fork, especially below Wharton, is a marginal stream, while above Wharton cool water and a good supply of native browns produce excellent fly-fishing into June and July. There are 5 miles of high-quality water from Costello, where Freeman Run enters, downstream to Wharton. The East Fork of the Sinnemahoning is a major tributary to the First Fork, entering at the town of Wharton.

The First Fork above Wharton is a cold-water stream with plenty of pools and miles of fishable water. First Fork begins about 8 miles northeast of Costello, where Borie Branch and Prouty Run join. This small stream flows southwest to Costello, where it picks up an equal volume in Freeman Run, doubling the size of the main stem. Skip Gibson and I have witnessed tremendous green drake and blue-winged olive dun hatches 2 miles above Costello on the First Fork. Halfway downstream to Wharton, Big Nelson Run enters, and at Wharton the East Fork combines with the main stem to produce a much larger stream. In 13 miles, from its headwaters to Wharton, First Fork increases in size threefold. Three miles below Wharton, Bailey Run links with First Fork, adding a shot of cool water in summer. Two other tributaries that add volume to First Fork— Brooks and Lushbaugh Runs—enter near the George Stevenson Dam. Below the dam the stream warms early, providing habitat for many smallmouth bass. The First Fork below Wharton is a typical large freestone stream with plenty of riffles, pocket water, and deep pools.

Hatches on the First Fork can be unusually spectacular, especially in April, May, and early June. Curt Thompson operates the Hemlock Acres campground near Wharton. He's written outdoors columns for the *Coudersport Leader Enterprise* on the hatches on the First Fork watershed. The Hendrickson remains his favorite hatch on the First Fork. It's not unusual for Curt to catch 30 to 40 trout during a Hendrickson emergence. The First Fork also has all the typical April hatches, and in generous supply. Hatches imitated by the Blue Quill, the Quill Gordon, and the Hendrickson emerge from the middle of April until early May. Curt has fly-fished over April blue quills each afternoon for more than two weeks on First Fork.

Hatch intensity declines from early May until the third or fourth week of that month and then resumes with unbelievable diversity. With this resumption of hatches you'll witness the true character of First Fork. In quick succession hatches like the brown drake, green drake, sulphur, and slate drake fill the air in the evening, while the blue-winged olive, gray fox, and March brown become air-breathing adults during the day. The problem here isn't whether there'll be a hatch, but rather which hatch or spinner fall the trout will favor. Often the dun or spinner you're prepared to copy doesn't develop into the dominant hatch of the day or evening.

The slate drake emerges in midevening, just when the green and brown drakes subside. On the First Fork, Slate Drake patterns are particularly important. Here they copy at least three similar *Isonychia* species prevalent on the water from late May through October. Most of these are large-sized mayflies (10 to 14) that appear in the early evening. Don't fly-fish the First Fork from late May on without a generous supply of Slate Drake patterns and White-Gloved Howdys. You can be certain duns have emerged if you see nymphal shucks on exposed rocks in the stream. At this time of year always examine the rocks for large brown-black nymphal shucks of recently emerged slate drakes. Inspect them carefully, and you'll be prepared for an evening hatch or spinner fall.

A healthy brown drake population lives in the First Fork. This species is truly an ephemeral mayfly. The dun and spinner appear above water for three to five days out of a year. Although it is a difficult hatch to meet, once you have succeeded you'll never want to miss it. The green drake often appears a few days before the brown drake. Above Wharton the green drake often appears throughout the daylight hours, making an entire day of matching this large mayfly a delightful challenge.

First Fork, East Fork, Little Pine, and Oswayo Creek are four of the few freestone streams in the north-central area that contain abundant sulphur hatches. To match this hatch appropriately you need a size-18 Sulphur rather than the standard size-16. The sulphur reigns supreme at the junction pool in Wharton, where East Fork enters. The sulphur begins the third week in May and continues into early June, usually appearing just before dusk.

First Fork contains plenty of productive pocket water and riffles. That combination just below Bailey Run makes this section perfect for fishing the brown and green drakes. Wading this big water can be treacherous, however, because of the huge boulders scattered pell-mell throughout much of the stream.

If scenery is important to you, and fishing over hatches is a bonus, try the First Fork of the Sinnemahoning or one of its productive tributaries. Ted Kulik of the First Fork Lodge in Costello, and Curt Thompson of Hemlock Acres near Wharton, know the hatches and stream well. They'll gladly share fishing stories about the stream. The First Fork is especially productive from the opening of the season until early June. Still, this stream contains a generous share of hatches and plenty of hefty trout almost from the beginning of the year.

The Fish Commission designated a delayed-harvest area on the First Fork in 1992. This area, just below Bailey Run, holds good hatches in April and May.

EAST FORK, SINNEMAHONING CREEK

Access There's about 10 miles of top-notch water on East Fork up to Conrad. A blacktop road from Wharton to Cherry Mills parallels the stream. Above Conrad the road becomes dirt. Upstream from Wharton, East Fork contains a heavy canopy for the first 2 miles. Above that you'll see fields and grown-over farmland interspersed.

Rating ✻✻

Patterns to Match the Hatches Blue Quill (#18), Quill Gordon (#14), Hendrickson and Red Quill (#14), Great Stonefly *(Phasganophora capitata)* *(*#10), Tan Caddis (#14), Sulphur Dun and Spinner (#16), March Brown (#12), Light Cahill (#14), Green Drake and Coffin Fly (#10), Brown Drake (#12), Slate Drake (#12 and #14), *Pteronarcys* Stonefly (#6), Green Caddis (#14), Rusty Caddis (#14)

A very Ripple lives in Costello 5 miles from the East Fork. He's fly-fished on the stream since World War II began. Avery has experienced good years on the stream, but recently he's seen some poor ones. The past few years have been unkind to East Fork and other north-central streams, bringing acute drought and devastating summer heat. For the past few years Avery has quit fishing the branch before the Fourth of July. Will the stream return to its prior renown? Time and nature will tell. I remember the stream when the elements were kinder to it.

Skip Gibson and I first fished the East Fork 15 years ago. Trout activity ended near noon that day on First Fork, so we headed up this major tributary for some afternoon fishing. Native brown trout abounded on this fertile mountain stream. All afternoon we caught these streambred fish. The native-trout population in East Fork is so good that the Fish Commission has designated its middle part as wild-trout water. Because of that classification, and because some of this section is posted, the middle East Fork is not stocked. However, above and below the wild-trout water East Fork annually receives trout.

East Fork contains many rock-filled pools, pockets, and riffles. Pools tend to be separated by 200 to 300 feet of fast water above and below. The stream averages 30 to 40 feet wide.

If you're fortunate enough to fly-fish on this stream in late April, you're in for a treat with some of the hatches. Blue quills, quill gordons, and Hendricksons abound. Even into May you'll see sulphurs in the evening and March browns during the day. Check with Curt Thompson at the Hemlock Campground near Wharton on what's emerging on East Fork. Curt's fly-fished this stream when green drakes and brown drakes emerged. He says the lower 3 miles hold the most brown drakes.

During years in which the East Fork receives plentiful rains this stream can be spectacular. Don't miss it!

LOYALSOCK CREEK

Access PA 87 parallels the Loyalsock from Montoursville to Forksville and the Little Loyalsock to Dushore. PA 154 follows the upper Loyalsock from Forksville to Laporte.

Special Regulations Delayed harvest, artificial lures only—1.4 miles, from the Lycoming County line downstream to Sandy Bottom.

Rating ✳✳

Patterns to Match the Hatches Blue Quill (#18), Quill Gordon (#14), Hendrickson (#14), Early Brown Stonefly (#14), Great Brown Stonefly (#12), Light Stonefly (#12), Sulphur Dun and Spinner (#16), Gray Fox (#14), March Brown (#12), Green Drake and Coffin Fly (#10), Slate Drake (#12 and #14), Chocolate Dun (#16), Great Stonefly *(Phasganophora capitata)* (#10), Yellow Drake (#12), Cream Cahill (#14 and #16), Trico (#24), Dark Slate Drake and Rusty Spinner (#8)

The Loyalsock. What history this area contains! Look at the Whistle Pigs, a club devoted to fly-fishing that has existed for more than a century. It's probably the oldest such organization in Pennsylvania—possibly in

The Whistle Pigs line up at Ludys Riffle on Loyalsock Creek.

North America. The Whistle Pigs now claim the Loyalsock as their home stream.

In years gone by, however, the club fished in western Clinton County, on Young Womans Creek. In 1887 a small group of trout-fishing devotees took a train from Harrisburg and then a horse and buggy to their final destination, Young Womans. These hardy souls camped in tents, caught a good supply of brook trout, and became the nucleus of the century-old trout club. They first called themselves the Pioneers of Fort Necessity.

On February 2, 1910, the group formally organized into a club. At that time they changed their name to Whistle Pigs. Why not? They first met, and continue to meet, on Groundhog Day.

In 1911 the Whistle Pigs relocated their "bivouac area" to the Hillsgrove section of the Loyalsock. They continued to pitch tents near the creek until 1945. Finally, in that year, they struck a deal with the Ogdonia Fish and Game Club, located 3 miles south of Hillsgrove. The Whistle Pigs now use the quaint, native-chestnut-paneled lodge of the Ogdonia Club for their annual gathering.

John Plowman of Mechanicsburg, a third-generation Whistle Pig and public-relations chairman for the unique organization, explained their common goal. "Our sole purpose is to enjoy the hatches of the Loyalsock and Muncy watersheds in prime time."

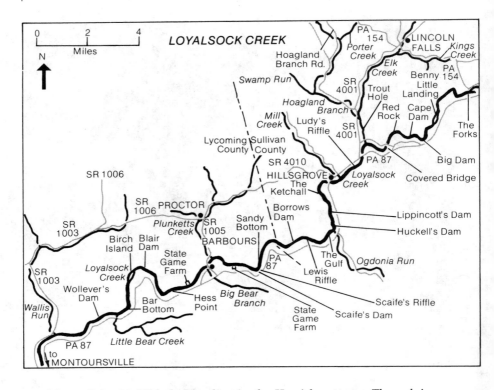

Most of the 25 Whistle Pigs live in the Harrisburg area. They claim among their notables the likes of the late Ned Smith. Many are doctors, preachers, and other professionals.

In a hundred years any organization worth its salt will undoubtedly amass an array of cherished traditions, and the Whistle Pigs have their share. The club screens potential members for two years before they're allowed to join. Each morning in camp someone wakes the members with an early-morning serenade. The club does a great deal for the area and the Loyalsock. They strive to keep local streams open to all anglers, and they work with local sportsmen's organizations and keep in touch with their Sullivan County neighbors of long standing.

If you see up to 25 crazy fly-fishermen elbow to elbow on Ludys Riffle above Hillsgrove in early June, you've met the Whistle Pigs.

The Loyalsock has shared a long and pleasant past with me, too. For years several of us began our meeting-the-hatch season on Loyalsock Creek. On numerous occasions in mid- to late April Dick Mills, Jim Heltzel, and I would travel from the Wilkes-Barre or State College area to be on the stream for the quill gordon and Hendrickson hatches in late April. As an added bonus the blue quill often appeared with one or both

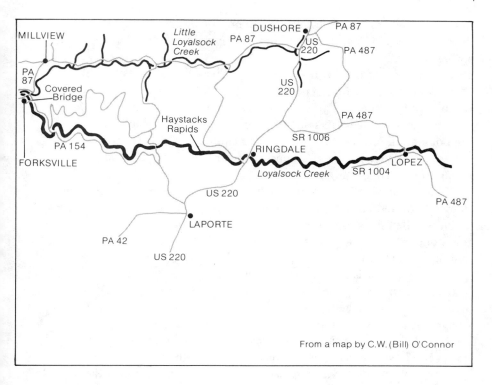

From a map by C.W. (Bill) O'Connor

of the larger mayflies. Some of those trips produced more snow flurries than mayflies, with extremely cold, winterlike air temperatures.

On many of these early trips we witnessed unbelievable hatches, but only occasionally would any trout brave the elements to surface for one of the dazed duns. Temperature readings on this water in mid-April often stay in the low to mid-40s. Often, however, by the time the Hendrickson appears about the third week of April, the water temperature has risen above 50 degrees and dry-fly fishing comes into its own.

Insects like the slate drake emerge in heavy numbers throughout much of June, July, and August on the Loyalsock. However, the water warms quickly. By midsummer much of the lower three-quarters of the stream becomes more smallmouth bass than trout water. Even the fly-fishing-only section at the Lycoming County line is marginal after mid-June. Furthermore, as the Loyalsock's temperature rises, its flow decreases dramatically. I checked the water temperature just below Laporte in the hot summer of 1988. The drought-plagued region had already had 23 days of 90-plus temperatures. The water in the upper end of the Loyalsock in early August registered an incredible 82 degrees. Look for cooler water by fishing below Big Bear, Little Bear, or Hoagland Branches, Mill Creek, or one of a number of other tributaries. Denny Renninger has witnessed hundreds of trout holding in a small area in the main stream where cool springs enter.

The section of the Loyalsock around Hillsgrove has a respectable trico hatch from mid-July into September. Above the bridge at Hillsgrove there can be some productive, albeit short, fly-fishing in July.

The Loyalsock contains abundant mayfly hatches, including a growing population of green drakes. Denny Renninger says that for the past few years the green drake has appeared near Hillsgrove in numbers large enough to produce rising trout.

The stream also harbors excellent stonefly and caddisfly populations. In late April and early May stoneflies emerge in incredible numbers. This hatch is called the great brown stonefly by local fishermen. In addition to this stonefly, there's a good supply of the early brown stoneflies in April, and light stoneflies in early May.

The Loyalsock is a big stream, with its headwaters in Sullivan County near Lopez. Drainage from some of the old subbituminous mines in the area gives a slightly acidic character to the stream in the upper area. Above Lopez the water seems to be of higher quality, and native browns are abundant in some of the feeder streams. From Lopez to Forksville, however, the stream assumes a put-and-take identity.

The fertile Little Loyalsock, beginning near Dushore, enters the main stem at Forksville to produce a much larger stream and creates some 20 miles of prime dry-fly water extending downstream to Barbours. In that section some excellent tributaries like Elk, Mill, and Plunketts Creeks enter. All are freestone but add a supply of fairly cool water all summer long to the main stem. The best of the lot are Elk Creek and its main tributary, Hoagland Branch. The delayed-harvest-only section on the Loyalsock begins at the Sullivan–Lycoming County line and goes downstream for about 2 miles. Below Barbours the water warms quickly in summer.

On rare occasions the Loyalsock can be productive during June and July. Slate drake patterns can be exciting to fish on these summer days in the riffles and pocket water. Wading is dangerous on some stretches, however, and the bottom is littered with various-sized boulders strewn helter-skelter about. Elevated water levels caused by spring runoff can produce treacherous footing as well.

HOAGLAND BRANCH

Access The state stocks 4 miles of Hoagland. The lower 3 miles of the stream flow through state forest lands. A dirt road, Hoagland Branch or

Middle Creek Road, closely parallels the stream and crosses it four times in the lower 4 miles. At the bridges Hoagland forms some deep, productive pools. In addition to these pools the stream forms four or five other deep, ledged pools very similar to those found on Cedar and Slate Runs. Above the fourth bridge you'll find little access but plenty of streambred brook and brown trout. It's worth a hike into the upper end of the stream.

Rating ✷✷

Patterns to Match the Hatches Blue Quill (#18), Quill Gordon (#14), Hendrickson and Red Quill (#14), March Brown (#12), Light Cahill (#14), Slate Drake (#12 and #14), Gray Caddis (#16), Tan Caddis (#16), Little Green Stonefly (#16), Trico (#24)

What great memories Hoagland Branch and Elk Creek harbor for me! More than 20 years ago Lloyd Williams and Tom Taylor of Dallas and I fly-fished at the junction pool where Hoagland joins Elk. On that early-June evening I saw my first great hatch of light cahills. Lloyd, Tom, and I caught and released three limits of trout, and more. The cahill emerges in great numbers on the lower end of Hoagland Branch in late May and early June. By happenstance we selected one of those heavy-hatch evenings to fly-fish the junction pool. That night—that hatch—those rising trout—will forever remain a vivid triumph in our memories of productive fly-fishing trips.

I returned 10 years later to the same pool, hoping to meet that same light cahill hatch. This time, six days into June, slate drakes supplanted light cahills as the hatch to match for the night. That second night proved the value of owning a good cache of White-Gloved Howdy Spinners. An 18-inch brown trout sucked in one of those size-12 maroon spinners that night.

Denny Renninger of Hillsgrove fly-fishes on Hoagland throughout the season. Just this past year in late April Denny caught more than two dozen trout on the stream on a Gold-Ribbed Hare's Ear wet and a Hendrickson dry fly. Hendrickson naturals appeared on the surface that afternoon, and Denny matched the hatch successfully. He's caught trout up to 16 inches long on the branch and has seen trout up to 21 inches caught here.

Denny and I recently traveled Hoagland searching for trout and insects. We traveled up to the third bridge on Middle Creek Road, stopped, and checked a few spiderwebs on the bridge. By checking these webs you can often learn what insects have recently emerged from nearby streams. Denny and I noticed one lone male trico trapped in one web. Certainly no hatch of tricos appeared on this 15- to 20-foot-wide freestone stream. Did the spinner come from the Loyalsock 4 miles below?

I delayed a planned trip to Wilkes-Barre for a day so I could search for tricos on Hoagland and Elk Creek the next day. That morning I arrived at the stream a half mile above its junction with Elk Creek. By 7:30 AM I noticed a few trico duns; then dozens emerged. Within half an hour that section of Hoagland boasted a heavy spinner flight. I headed down to Elk Creek and saw trico flights from Hoagland down to the Loyalsock. If you hit the lower end of Hoagland or Elk in July or August, and the streams contain a decent flow and cool water, you'll be in for some late-season matching-the-hatch fly-fishing with tricos.

Summer brings out the green inchworms on Hoagland. Denny Renninger uses these terrestrial patterns almost any afternoon he fishes here.

Hoagland Branch begins in northwestern Sullivan County where Fall Run joins Hoagland Creek. Three miles downstream Porter Creek joins the main stem and forms Hoagland Branch. A few more miles downstream Swamp Run joins the main stem.

Hoagland Branch remains fairly cool throughout the summer. If you're fortunate enough to appear on the stream when the light cahill emerges on its lower end, you're in for a memorable evening of fly-fishing.

ELK CREEK (SULLIVAN COUNTY)

Access PA 154 crosses Elk at Lincoln Falls, and a blacktop road, Elk Creek Road, parallels the stream to the Loyalsock Creek.

Rating ✱✱

Patterns to Match the Hatches Blue Quill (#18), Quill Gordon (#14), Hendrickson and Red Quill (#14), Gray Fox and Ginger Quill (#12 and #14), March Brown (#12), Light Cahill (#14 and #16), Slate Drake (#12 and #14), Gray Caddis (#16), Tan Caddis (#16), Trico (#24)

Renninger's store in Hillsgrove acts as the local communications center for the area. The building contains a post office, a general store, and a sporting goods store. Because it's the meeting place for fishermen, Denny Renninger, the owner, hears many stories about lunker trout and often sees the evidence of a successful trip. Recently, in late July, a fisherman showed Denny three heavy trout, all over 20 inches long, caught on a local stream within a week. The angler caught all three lunkers on a stream within 3 miles of Hillsgrove—Elk Creek.

Elk contains most of the early-season hatches. Its main claim to fame, however, lies in its late-May and early-June hatches of light cahills and slate drakes in the evening. In addition, however, Elk, like the lower end of Hoagland Branch, holds a respectable trico hatch from mid-July until September. Travel along the lower 2 miles of Elk any midsummer morning and you'll see these tiny mayflies in their typical mating flight 20 feet above the surface. Select a morning when the stream has a reasonable flow and cool water and you're in for some excellent late-season fly-fishing.

Elk begins near Camp Brule in southern Bradford County. The stream flows southeast and picks up the Second Branch just west of Eldredsville. Lloyd Williams lived near the upper end of Elk for years. He recounts stories of large streambred trout caught on the Second Branch. Access above Lincoln Falls is limited but worth the hike into this small stream. This area contains some productive pools. At Lincoln Falls, Kings Creek joins the main stem. The state stocks Elk from this point downstream to its mouth. From Lincoln Falls to Hoagland Branch, Elk flows through a small gorge. Access to this section is difficult. A half mile below Hoagland Branch, Elk forms a large 8-foot-deep pool called the Trout Hole.

Elk ranges from 20 feet wide at Lincoln Falls to 30 to 40 feet wide where it enters the Loyalsock. For its size Elk contains good, productive pools and great hatches.

MUNCY CREEK

Access US 220 just north of Hughesville County Road.

Special Regulations Delayed harvest, artificial lures only—1.1 miles, from the Sullivan property located 600 yards upstream of the T 650 bridge downstream to near the confluence of Big Run at Tivoli.

Rating ✷✷

Patterns to Match the Hatches Little Blue-Winged Olive Dun (#20), Blue Quill (#18), Quill Gordon (#14), Green Caddis (#14), Sulphur Dun and Spinner (#16), Gray Fox and Ginger Quill (#12 and #14), Light Cahill (#14), Slate Drake (#12 and #14), Little Green Stonefly (#16), Hendrickson and Red Quill (#14), Yellow Drake (#12)

Jeff Young of Washingtonville typically begins his fly-fishing year on Muncy Creek, his home stream. Jeff often meets with droves of early-season anglers on this freestone water. Last year he experienced one of those rare opening days when fly-fishermen can entice trout to the surface in mid-April. He caught a dozen trout that day on a size-18 Sid Neff Black Caddis, a size-14 Blue-Winged Olive Emerger, and a size-14 Quill Gordon Cut Wing.

In April the lower 5 or 6 miles of Muncy contain plenty of pocket water and a half-dozen deep pools, with a good flow of water. The creek, however, takes on a completely different look from late May through August. Scant summer rains often reduce it to a boulder-strewn small stream.

I visited this freestone stream recently with Jeff Young, Dave Rothrock, and his son, Dave Jr., of Jersey Shore. We arrived at one of the larger pools on the lower section of the Muncy near the town of Picture Rocks. Barely a trickle of water entered and exited the pool in front of us, but Jeff assured us that this pool, more than 5 feet deep and cool on the bottom, still contained a good number of trout. Even as we glanced at the pool, several trout began to feed on the surface. By 8:45 PM a respectable hatch of yellow drakes appeared on the surface. These mayflies would appear in larger numbers the next week, but a few trout fed on the emerging duns and falling spinners. Dave Jr. tied on a Light Cahill to copy the yellow drake and caught several trout on that—as he had earlier on a green inchworm pattern. On that hot evening, with the water temperature at 74 degrees, I would have wagered that we wouldn't see a trout—but we did.

Jeff says the lower end of the Muncy contains several large pools. These pools contain cool springs and a good supply of trout all season long.

Upstream near Sonestown, in Sullivan County, the stream remains cooler in the summer and contains some streambred brown trout. You can fish the Muncy from Nordmont downstream to the town of Muncy. The stream varies in size from 20 feet in the Nordmont area to 50 to 60 feet wide in the Hughesville–Picture Rocks area. Until mid-May almost any section of the stocked stream can be productive. From mid-May to September, fly-fish around one of the cool, deep pools.

Muncy drops precipitously from Sonestown to Picture Rocks. When traveling US 220 you'll note several fairly flat areas followed by steep inclines. This rapid fall, followed by a gradual fall, provides good holding water and a variety of hatches.

CEDAR RUN

Access A winding dirt road off PA 414 parallels Cedar Run along its entire length.

Special Regulations Trophy-trout project—7.2 miles, from the confluence with Buck Run downstream to the mouth (at the town of Cedar Run).

Rating ✳✳✳✳

Patterns to Match the Hatches Little Black Stonefly (#16), Blue Quill (#18), Quill Gordon (#14), Hendrickson (#14), Gray Caddis (#16), Dark Olive Caddis (#16), Green Caddis (#16), Little Yellow Stonefly (#16), Tan Caddis (#16), Blue-Winged Olive Dun (#14), Green Drake and Coffin Fly (#10), Brown Drake (#12), Slate Drake (#14), Yellow Stonefly (#14), Little Green Stonefly (#16)

When you think of an isolated, untouched, pristine stream teeming with streambred brown trout, some over 20 inches long, Cedar Run comes immediately to mind. This acclaimed cold-water tributary enters Pine Creek at the town of Cedar Run in Lycoming County. Its headwaters, however, originate 12 miles upstream, just northwest of Leetonia, in Tioga County.

Cedar Run is a spectacularly picturesque stream, replete with deep gorges dripping with springwater throughout the year. But beyond that Cedar has some excellent hatches and fine fishing for the first half of the season. During the latter half of the season, from mid-June through August, however, water flow is often low, and trout become extremely wary. After Pine Creek water warms in early June thousands of migrating browns and rainbows inhabit the first couple of pools on Cedar, forced into the colder water from the 70-plus temperature of Pine below. These lower holding pools literally become black with trout that are almost impossible to catch.

Cedar often greets the new fishing season in April with the bevy of fine hatches so common on many of the north-central streams. Select one of the impressive, deep pools on this stream near midday. Fishing over a hatch demonstrates its true merit here, with plenty of blue quills and rising trout. At this time in April synchronous hatches of quill gordons and hendricksons also appear. It's often a fairly predictable event, with blue quills arriving first, quill gordons next, and hendricksons last. You sometimes find yourself fishing to successive hatches for three hours or more.

Cedar Run is an exceptionally cold stream. Often when the first hatches of the year appear, they do so in 45- to 50-degree water. This cold water, plus the likelihood of high water, often works to discourage trout from surface-feeding. On those occasions when few trout surface, use a Quill Gordon wet fly or a Hendrickson or Blue Quill Nymph. If you're fortunate enough to visit Cedar in April, when fly-fishing conditions are right, you're in for some exciting angling.

Like most other north-central streams Cedar takes a break in early May from its previous hatch intensity. But when hatches resume in late May, they do so with incredible vigor. In quick succession insects like the blue-winged olive dun, blue quill *(Paraleptophlebia mollis)*, gray fox, and

March brown emerge much of the day.

Evening is not without its hatches this time of the year, either: In the same period when the daytime hatches appear, the brown drake, slate drake, and green drake move toward the surface in the evening. Fly-fishermen have an added incentive to fish the entire day on Cedar in late May—hatches during the day and evening.

About the middle of June, Cedar evolves into a typical summer free-stone stream with low, crystal-clear water and extremely alert trout. Times like these call for a 12- to 15-foot leader with a 6X or finer tippet.

Cedar Run shelters some huge brown trout, many of them fish that have migrated upstream from Pine Creek. Some, however, are resident fish. My son, Bryan, and I spent a couple of days on Cedar several years ago. It was a Saturday morning in late May, and a sporadic hatch of blue-winged olives rode the surface. I caught several trout from 7 to 12 inches long. All of a sudden I heard Bryan shout from 100 yards upstream, and I saw him hold up a brown trout over 20 inches long. I rushed upstream to get a better look at the lunker Bryan held above his head. It measured 22 inches long and weighed about 5 pounds. Bryan, although he was only 15 at the time, quickly placed the trout back in the water to fight another time for another fisherman.

Cedar's tributaries hold plenty of brook and brown trout. Branches like Fahnstock Run and Mine Hole Run, both entering the main stem from the northeast, possess an abundance of streambred trout.

At its widest point Cedar is about 30 feet wide, but much of the stream is considerably narrower. Wading can be treacherous, because of deep, boulder-filled pools and hidden rocky ledges. More than 7 miles of the lower end of Cedar have been designated a trophy-trout project similar to the one located on Fishing Creek in Clinton County; only two trout over 14 inches long from this section may be kept during the regular season.

Cedar is a picturesque stream with many hatches and some fine trout. Don't miss an opportunity to fish on this scenic water.

LITTLE PINE CREEK

Access Access to the best water is easy: A blacktop road follows Little Pine Creek from Waterville to English Center.

Special Regulations Delayed harvest, artificial lures only—1.0 mile, from 200 yards downstream of Otter Run downstream to the confluence of Schoolhouse Hollow.

Rating ✳✳✳

Patterns to Match the Hatches Little Blue-Winged Olive Dun (#20), Blue Quill (#18), Quill Gordon (#14), Hendrickson (#14), Early Brown Stonefly

(#12), Grannom (#16), Light Stonefly (#12), Sulphur Dun and Spinner (#16), March Brown (#12), Gray Fox (#14), Slate Drake (#14), Blue-Winged Olive Dun (#16), Green Drake (#12), Yellow Stonefly (#14), Little Green Stonefly (#16), Light Cahill (#14 and #16)

It's difficult to single out one trout stream in Pennsylvania as my favorite. For early-spring fly-fishing, however, one stream that would be near or at the top of my list is Little Pine Creek. What earns any stream the reputation that it's the best or the finest? First—for fly-fishermen at least—it must harbor a diversity of aquatic insects, and they must appear in abundant numbers. As we'll see later, Little Pine satisfies these conditions well. Further, an ideal trout stream should flow with water cold enough all summer to hold trout. Little Pine's temperatures above the dam near Waterville are usually below 70 degrees all summer. A final requirement: The model stream should not depend entirely on a stocking program for its fish population, but should hold its own supply of streambred trout. Both native brown and brook trout widely inhabit the water of Little Pine.

With all that going for it, does Little Pine have any disadvantages? It has. Like many freestone streams Little Pine changes into a typical low-water fishery in July and August. Pools that were once too deep can now be waded; riffles that earlier held rising trout now contain only minnows. Huge boulders and submerged hemlock trunks, once hidden from view by the spring runoff, are exposed in the shallow summer water.

When any stream or river has the descriptive *little* in its name, you immediately perceive it as water that is slight. Not Little Pine: In some areas the stream is more than 40 feet wide.

The stream begins several miles above the small town of English Center, where Texas and Blockhouse Creeks join. An excellent private fishing club called the Texas Blockhouse owns most of the water above English Center.

Open fishing begins just a half mile above English Center and extends downstream about 12 miles to Waterville. Several stretches just below English Center are posted, but most of the stream remains open for public fishing. The state has impounded part of the water (the Little Pine Creek Dam) about 5 miles above Waterville. The water below the dam is a typical warm-water fishery created by a dam that has a top-water release. It rapidly becomes marginal for trout after early June.

The most productive area for fly-fishing is the section from just above the dam upstream for about 5 miles. Part of this section, called Carsons Flats, produces fine hatches throughout the year. It's not unusual during the last two weeks of April to witness hatches like the little blue-winged olive dun, the blue quill, the quill gordon, and the Hendrickson emerging simultaneously. Fred Templin and Lambert Swingle once accompanied me on a memorable early-season trip to fly-fish in the Carsons Flats area. In late April on Little Pine you often experience three hours of superb fly-fishing over countless rising trout. Even with water temperatures just barely above 50 degrees, trout rose freely to the struggling duns. Trout no one would have guessed were there an hour before started ravenously gorging themselves on the first plentiful supply of food that season.

But there's more to the character of Little Pine than the first week of the season—much more. For here, when many of the north-central streams have few early-May hatches, you can meet and fish the light stonefly hatching in large-enough numbers to generate an exciting day.

As with most freestone streams, however, Little Pine waits until the latter part of May to unleash some of its most abundant and spectacular hatches. In a period of less than a week you can find the green drake on the water both during the day and at night, thousands of sulphurs emerging in the evening, March browns and gray foxes on the water during the day, and an explosive hatch of blue-winged olives appearing barely a couple of hours after sunrise.

Even into June, Little Pine Creek has its better days, with carryover hatches of slate drakes and cream cahills in the evening and some sporadic hatches of blue-winged olives during the day.

Water temperatures in this freestone stream remain fairly respectable for trout fishing throughout much of June and July, but low-water conditions in midsummer normally produce extremely wary trout. The hour just before dusk is the preferred time to fly-fish after early June. Try a size-14 Slate Drake or a size-16 or -18 Cream Cahill tied onto a long leader with a fine tippet.

Late-season fishing on Little Pine is respectable, with sporadic slate drakes and small blue-winged olives. With the approach of fall and cooler water, trout activity picks up considerably. As with so many north-central streams in Pennsylvania, though, Little Pine is most productive from mid-April until mid-June.

High spring runoff from snowmelt and heavy rains can create hazardous wading on Little Pine. Swollen rapids and pools are often impossible to cross. When waters subside, however, Little Pine presents few wading problems. The water resembles many north-central freestones with its mixture of sandbars and piles of small stones where floodwaters once surged. Little Pine contains an inordinate number of productive pools with productive riffles and pockets above.

Idyllic scenery and excellent water with plenty of pristine pools complete the setting of one of Pennsylvania's finest trout streams.

PINE CREEK

Access Pine Creek passes through some of the most scenic areas in Pennsylvania. Much of the stream is accessible by car on PA 44 near Waterville, and on PA 414 above. US 6 parallels much of the upper part of Pine Creek, from Ansonia to Walton.

Rating ✳✳✳

Patterns to Match the Hatches Hendrickson (#14), Blue Quill (#18), Quill Gordon (#14), Gray Caddis (#16), Dark Olive Caddis (#16), Cream Caddis (#14), Black Quill (#14), Gray Fox (#12), March Brown (#12), Sulphur Dun and Spinner (#16 and #18), Blue-Winged Olive Dun (#14 and #16), Brown Drake Dun and Spinner (#12), Green Drake and Coffin Fly (#10), Slate Drake (#12), Light Cahill *(Stenonema ithaca) (#*14), Chocolate Dun (#16), Gray Drake (#14), Little Blue-Winged Olive Dun (#20), Yellow Drake (#12), Trico (#24)

What Pennsylvania stream contains more than 60 miles of trout water, ranges from 100 to 200 feet wide, and holds huge pools and eddies, some more than a half mile long? What stream possesses mile-long productive riffles? Pine Creek. Nevertheless, fishing Pine Creek can be troublesome. Pine can be one of the best and yet one of the most frustrating waters in the Commonwealth. This Jekyll-and-Hyde stream can literally change from good to bad in minutes. Fish Pine Creek in early May when the cream caddis is in the air, for example, and you can truly become disenchanted with the water. Yet fly-fish the stream from Waterville up to Galeton when the brown drakes or gray foxes emerge and you can experience a once-in-a-lifetime event.

Part of the reason Pine can be capricious is its marginal water temperature, despite tremendous hatches during much of the summer season. Brown drakes, blue-winged olives, and others sometimes appear in water well above 70 degrees. On these occasions heavy hatches and spinner falls prevail, but few trout rise in the warm water.

Pine has another problem as well. Tom Finkbiner of the Slate Run Tackle Shop and Mike O'Brien of Williamsport have lamented the alarming decrease in some of the hatches on the lower half of the stream over the past few years. Tom says that the brown drake and gray fox have appeared only sporadically below Blackwell in that time. What has happened? Look at an earlier indicator of water quality, the Hendrickson. For years the Hendrickson has only appeared in large numbers above Blackwell. The demise of all three hatches below Blackwell leads to only one culprit—Babb Creek, which enters Pine at Blackwell. Years ago the Babb Creek area employed hundreds of workers mining coal. Mine acid

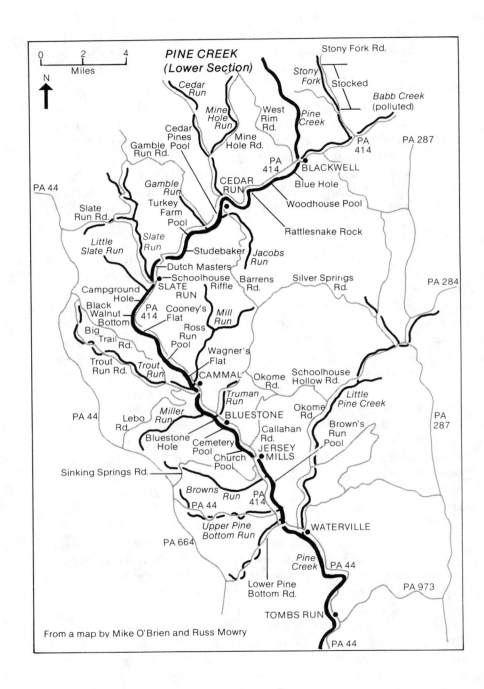

PINE CREEK
(Lower Section)

0 2 4
Miles

N

Cedar Run

Stony Fork Rd.

Stony Fork

Stocked

West Rim Rd.

Pine Creek

Babb Creek (polluted)

PA 414

PA 287

Mine Hole Run

Cedar Pines Pool

Gamble Run Rd.

Mine Hole Rd.

PA 414

BLACKWELL

Blue Hole

Woodhouse Pool

CEDAR RUN

Gamble Run

Turkey Farm Pool

Rattlesnake Rock

PA 44

Slate Run Rd.

Little Slate Run

Slate Run

Studebaker

Jacobs Run

Silver Springs Rd.

PA 284

Dutch Masters

Schoolhouse Riffle

Barrens Rd.

Campground Hole

SLATE RUN

PA 414

Cooney's Flat

Mill Run

Black Walnut Bottom

Ross Run Pool

Big Trail Rd.

Wagner's Flat

Trout Run Rd.

Trout Run

CAMMAL

Okome Rd.

Schoolhouse Hollow Rd.

Little Pine Creek

Truman Run

PA 287

PA 44

Lebo Rd.

Miller Run

BLUESTONE

Okome Rd.

Brown's Run Pool

Bluestone Hole

Cemetery Pool

Callahan Rd.

JERSEY MILLS

Church Pool

Sinking Springs Rd.

Browns Run

PA 414

Upper Pine Bottom Run

PA 664

WATERVILLE

Pine Creek

PA 44

PA 973

Lower Pine Bottom Rd.

TOMBS RUN

From a map by Mike O'Brien and Russ Mowry

PA 44

fills the stream continuously, even though these mines closed years ago. Future generations will suffer the consequences of man's inconsiderate destruction of the land and water.

Recently, concerned anglers and citizens banded together to form three influential organizations to attempt to cope with problems on the Pine Creek watershed—especially with the mine acid in Babb Creek. First, the Pine Creek Headwaters Protection Group (PCHPG) has completed a study on the effects of mayfly numbers in Pine Creek near Babb Creek. Dr. Robert Ross, who conducted the study for the group, found no insects on Pine Creek directly below where Babb Creek enters. Just upstream from Babb Creek he found a diversity of aquatic insects. The PCHPG monitors acidity on all tributaries of Pine Creek in the upper area (Tioga County) of the watershed. A second group, the Pine Creek Preservation Group, monitors all streams in the watershed in the lower section of the stream (in Lycoming County).

A third group, the Pennsylvania Environmental Defense Foundation, deals with the treatment of mine acid in Babb Creek. It has placed a liming device at Bridge Run along PA 287. When the device works it elevates the pH in the stream above 9. Congratulations to the PEDF for challenging and winning a court case against a mining company that polluted the Pine Creek watershed. Please read chapter 11 for more details on these groups and the work they are doing on Pine Creek.

With groups like these active on Pine Creek the future looks much brighter. We must encourage and join groups like this. Hatch intensity has already improved, largely through their efforts.

If you encounter warm water on big Pine try one of its productive tributaries, where temperatures usually remain in the 60s throughout much of the summer. When Pine heats up, thousands of trout migrate to one of the cooler holding pools on Cedar, Slate, or Trout Runs, or to one of a dozen smaller feeders.

The most eventful time on Pine Creek, if the water temperature is cooperative, is the last two weeks in May. Within a couple of weeks you can fish over hatches like the gray fox, the slate drake, the brown drake, the blue-winged olive dun, the light cahill, and the green drake; and over spinner falls like the ginger quill, white-gloved howdy, brown drake, dark olive spinner, coffin fly, and more. Most of the trout in Pine Creek are stocked, but there is an occasional holdover and plenty of lunkers.

The little blue-winged olive dun has not been affected by the mine-acid drainage from Babb Creek. This species *(Dannella simplex)* appears for a few weeks around the middle of June. If the water remains cool, you're prepared with a size-20 pattern, and you're on the stream in the morning you're in for some excellent match-the-hatch fly-fishing.

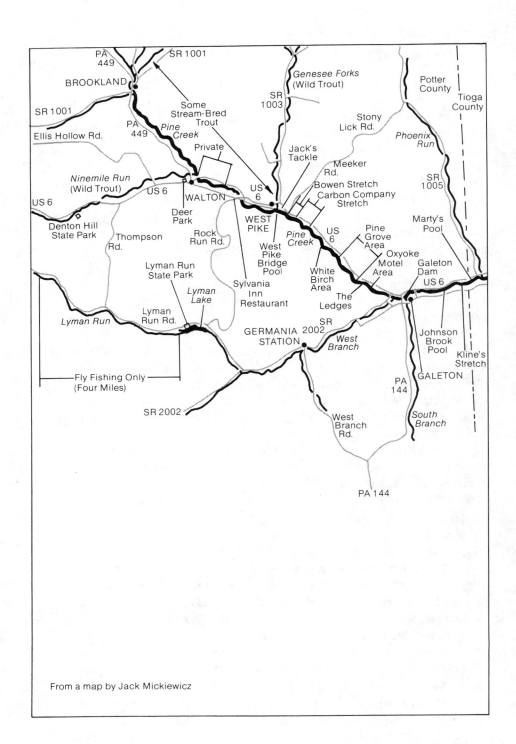

From a map by Jack Mickiewicz

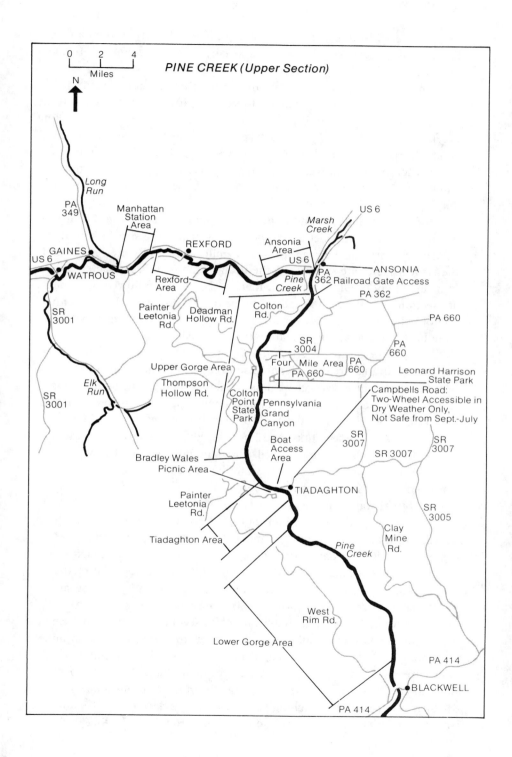

PINE CREEK (Upper Section)

0 2 4
Miles

N

Long Run

PA 349

Manhattan Station Area

GAINES

US 6

WATROUS

REXFORD

Rexford Area

Painter Leetonia Rd.

Deadman Hollow Rd.

SR 3001

Marsh Creek

US 6

Ansonia Area

US 6

Pine Creek

PA 362

ANSONIA

Railroad Gate Access

PA 362

Colton Rd.

PA 660

SR 3004

Four Mile Area

PA 660

PA 660

PA 660

Leonard Harrison State Park

Upper Gorge Area

Thompson Hollow Rd.

SR 3001

Elk Run

Colton Point State Park

Pennsylvania Grand Canyon

Boat Access Area

Campbells Road: Two-Wheel Accessible in Dry Weather Only, Not Safe from Sept.-July

SR 3007

SR 3007

SR 3007

Bradley Wales Picnic Area

TIADAGHTON

SR 3005

Painter Leetonia Rd.

Tiadaghton Area

Clay Mine Rd.

Pine Creek

West Rim Rd.

Lower Gorge Area

PA 414

BLACKWELL

PA 414

Pine Creek is a large freestone stream, more like a river than a creek. From April to early May the water is usually high and cold, with temperatures between 45 and 60 degrees.

Pine warms quickly, however, and without the benefit of cold limestone springs or any heavy canopy to shade it, it becomes marginal trout water early in June. Were it not for the cold water of the tributaries, Pine Creek would be totally a put-and-take stream. Dave and Dana Poust of Tombs Run have reported seeing hundreds of dead and dying trout in Pine Creek when the stream warms in early July. What a great stream this would be if a bottom-release flood-control dam were constructed in the gorge just above Blackwell.

Some heavy hatches and large trout inhabit the area from Cedar Run downstream to the hamlet of Jersey Mills. Much of the stream here flows within 100 yards of the road. In this 20-mile section of water you'll find the typical moderate sections at the head of the pool, a characteristic long slow pool or eddy, a tailout, then pocket water, followed by a moderate section or riffle at the head of the next pool. Many of the pools and sections—like the Dutch Masters near Slate Run, and the Cemetery Pool—have been affectionately named by the local fishermen.

Above Galeton in eastern Potter County, Pine Creek is a cool, moderate stream. In this area the Hendrickson reigns supreme, with some of the heaviest hatches I have ever witnessed. Above Galeton the stream ranges from 40 to 50 feet wide and contains a good supply of streambred brown and brook trout. For its first 10 or 15 miles Pine flows east, adding Ninemile Run, Genesee Forks, and Phoenix, Elk, and Long Runs to its flow.

At Galeton, Pine is impounded. The dam, plus marginal water entering from the West Branch, warms the water below. The West Branch was at one time a fantastic trout stream, but today the dam on Lyman Run creates marginal water on the lower 6 miles of the West Branch.

At Ansonia, just west of Wellsboro, the stream picks up volume from Marsh Creek and heads south, forming the extensive, picturesque Pennsylvania Grand Canyon. Pine exits the gorge 15 miles downstream, just above Blackwell. Early in the season high water brings out plenty of rafters and canoeists on this upper area. It's difficult to fly-fish because of this river traffic on many April and May weekends.

At Blackwell, Pine adds Babb Creek to its volume. Earlier I indicated that Babb carries heavy pollution originating from abandoned coal mines. This mine acid also affects some of the hatches on Pine for many miles downstream. Hendricksons, which are prevalent above Blackwell, become sporadic below. Not until the stream travels another 30 miles does the Hendrickson regain its hatching stature. From Blackwell 10 miles downstream Pine picks up additional volume from Trout Run flowing in from the east and Cedar Run from the northwest. These tributaries, and just about all others, harbor good supplies of streambred brown and brook trout.

Pine travels southwest, adding Slate Run and Gamble Run in the next 6 miles. The section from Cedar Run to Slate Run has spectacular hatches, plenty of heavy riffles with deep pools below, and some heavy trout.

From Slate Run, Pine heads south, picking up Mill Run and another Trout Run at Cammal. This 8-mile section also produces some heavy hatches and large trout. From Cammal, Pine flows 10 miles, picking up Miller, Browns, and Upper Pine Bottom Runs before the Little Pine enters at Waterville. The state plants no trout below Waterville, but many of the stocked rainbows migrate downstream for miles, and fishing in this lower area around Tombs Run can be productive with the onset of the Hendrickson hatch in late April.

Many hatches appear in incredible numbers throughout the year on Pine. Almost from the beginning of the season mayflies, caddisflies, and stoneflies appear. It's not unusual the first week of the season to witness the three early gray hatches somewhere on the stream. The blue quill is often the heaviest hatch of the three, but in some areas the Hendrickson emerges in dense numbers too.

Unlike many state streams, which pause for a respite around the beginning of May, Pine displays one of the greatest caddis hatches in the East, the cream caddis, at that time. Caddis adults can be seen for more than a week, appearing like blizzards from the past winter. Fly-fishing over this hatch, however, produces mixed results.

Spend an afternoon from May 18 to May 25 on Pine and you'll probably encounter the gray fox. This mayfly usually appears sporadically from afternoon until early evening. Numbers are high, and the mayfly is sizable enough to promote some excellent dry-fly fishing.

Just about the time the gray fox diminishes in intensity, the blue-winged olive takes over. At about the same date, but in the evening, appear hatches like the brown drake, green drake, and slate drake. If you have never witnessed a hatch of brown drake mayflies, you're in for a special treat. On the two or three evenings a year when these substantial insects emerge or when their spinners fall, you'll behold one of nature's finest ephemeral displays.

Even though conditions on Pine deteriorate during much of the rest of the season, hatches continue almost without interruption. Throughout late June and July mayflies like the yellow drake, pale evening dun, and even the trico appear on the water. Check the water temperature closely after early June—you might be fishing over a tremendous hatch with only smallmouth bass and fallfish surfacing.

Pine Creek exhibits moments of brilliance, especially from mid-April until early June. Try this massive stream set in a picturesque valley during one of the great hatches it exhibits, and you too will become a Pine Creek convert.

Check with Tom Finkbiner at the Slate Run Tackle Shop for the latest information on hatches on Pine. Tom keeps a daily diary of the hatches on Pine and Slate Run.

WEST BRANCH, PINE CREEK

Access You can access the stream easily off SR 2002. Upstream a few hundred feet above the bridge above Corbett, Sunken Branch enters the West Branch.

Rating ✳✳

Patterns to Match the Hatches Little Blue-Winged Olive Dun (#20), Blue Quill (#18), Quill Gordon (#14), Early Brown Stonefly (#14), Hendrickson (#14), Brown Caddis (#14 and #16), Sulphur (#16 and #18), Green Drake (#10), Brown Drake (#10 and #12), March Brown (#12), Slate Drake (#12), Blue-Winged Olive Dun (#14), Light Cahill (#14), Little Green Stonefly (#16), Little Yellow Stonefly (#14 and #16), Little Olive Stonefly (#16), Yellow Drake (#10)

We traveled up SR 2002 above Lyman Run to fish a stream I had passed dozens of times but never previously fly-fished. "It's an extremely productive Potter County freestone stream," Jack Mickievicz said. "Its fertility is astounding, with plenty of streambred browns and native brook trout." Jack should know. For more than four years he operated Jack's Tackle in West Pike just a few miles from the stream. Jack has often taken anglers to this stream to experience what Pennsylvania native-trout fishing is all about.

It was late season and the two of us headed several miles above where Lyman Run enters the West Branch. Lyman Lake pours heated water from the top of the dam into Lyman Run below. Three miles downstream, Lyman empties into the West Branch. There's about 5 miles of the West Branch from Lyman Run downstream to Galeton where it enters Pine Creek. In this area the stream ranges from 20 to 40 feet wide with good-sized runs and riffles; it holds stocked trout and an occasional holdover. The warm water from Lyman Lake makes this section marginal in mid-summer.

Above Lyman Run the West Branch narrows considerably, flowing through a bottom of fields and hardwoods. Above Lyman you'll begin to find plenty of native fish, including a lot of streambred brown trout. There are about 10 miles of stream from Lyman Run upstream to its headwaters near Cherry Run. The farther up you go, the more brook trout you'll find. You'll find some angling pressure early in the season—but after Memorial Day you'll seldom find another fisherman on the stream.

The West Branch holds many of the great hatches with little of the angling pressure. You'll find most of the early-season hatches on the stream, including the quill gordon, blue quill, and Hendrickson. Hit the stream when the Hendrickson appears and you're in for a great fly-fishing event. Around the end of May you'll see green drakes, sulphurs, and slate drakes. Stoneflies make up an important part of the trout's diet on the West Branch and stonefly nymphs work well.

LYCOMING CREEK

Access Take US 15 north of Williamsport to reach the stream. To reach the upper end, take PA 14 north of the town of Trout Run.

Rating ✳✳

Patterns to Match the Hatches Blue Quill (#18), Quill Gordon (#14), Hendrickson and Red Quill (#14), Early Brown Stonefly (#12), Olive Dun Caddis (#16), Tan Caddis (#16), Gray Fox and Ginger Quill (#12 and #14), March Brown (#12), Slate Drake (#12), Blue-Winged Olive Dun (#14), Light Cahill (#14), Cream Cahill (#14 and #16), Yellow Drake (#12)

Mike O'Brien of Williamsport provides fishing tours and on-stream instruction to hundreds of fly-fishermen annually. Mike, along with Jerry Stercho, publishes the *Mid Atlantic Fly Fishing Guide*. It's published 10 times a year and covers fly fishing in six northeastern states. It's unquestionably the finest publication of its kind in the United States. Mike enjoys fly-fishing on Lycoming Creek. After mid-June Mike and his long-time fishing buddy Wally Larimer of Clearfield fish after dark. Often Mike and Wally begin fly-fishing just as I'm leaving the same stream. The two have had some bizarre experiences in their quest for lunkers at night. They've encountered bats, herons, beavers, and snakes. Once Wally led Mike off a 20-foot-high bank in the pitch black. But they have fun—and they catch an unusual number of heavy brown trout in the summer. Mike recently caught a lunker brown measuring 27 inches and weighing 7.5 pounds on a night-fishing trip in north-central Pennsylvania.

Recently an angler telephoned Mike and asked him where he could go night fishing. Mike suggested an area on the Lycoming Creek above Trout Run. The next morning that same fisherman called Mike back and thanked him. He had caught two heavy brown trout, both about 18 inches long, on the Lycoming after dark. After mid-June the best fly-fishing on the Lycoming is relegated to the hour before dusk—or, as Mike will tell you, after dark.

If you're like me and prefer the more conventional daylight hours for catching trout, then try the Lycoming when one of its major hatches appears, especially early in the season.

Dick Mills of Lehman and I hit the Lycoming one late-April day. We fly-fished on a section at the bridge near Bodines just as a heavy Hendrickson hatch appeared and just after some quill gordons ended their daily appearance. The water was exceptionally high but not off color, and we both looked for rising trout feeding to the second hatch of the day. Periodically one of us would spot trout rising for hendricksons, but not in the numbers we expected given the intensity of the hatch. Each trout that did rise did so almost imperceptibly, and we had difficulty spotting them. Dick continued to look for rising trout, while I switched to a weighted Hendrickson Nymph. This pattern in a size 12 or 14, with its dark brown body, is deadly during a hatch of naturals. I picked up a couple of trout just below a riffle leading to a deep, undercut pool and missed a couple more. Trout fed sporadically on the surface for a couple of hours, but my Hendrickson Nymph continued to be productive well after the hatch had subsided.

My next trip to the Lycoming took place later that same season, near the end of June. In the area where Grays Run enters, the high water I'd found in spring had been replaced by extremely low, crystal-clear water. Huge rocks and boulders, hidden by the snowmelt in April, appeared in full view and dotted the pool. On my way up to Grays Run that evening I stopped at several convenient locations and checked the water temperature. I recorded Lycoming temperatures in the low 70s—marginal water for trout. Some of the Lycoming from Grays Run upstream, however, contains cooler water and some great late-season fly-fishing. Just below where Grays Run enters, the Lycoming registered 67 degrees—perfect for fishing a hatch in the middle of summer.

Nothing much happened until near dusk. Various light cahill spinners danced above the fast stretch at the head of the pool, but none of them even came close to the surface. Just before dusk, however, several large yellow drake duns appeared, then more. Only a couple of trout fed on the dozen or so laggards in the half-light just before dusk. One of the two trout that did rise, though, proved to be a 16-inch brown that had eluded the hooks of many previous bait-fishermen.

The Lycoming is a typical north-central Pennsylvania freestone, with high, clear water in spring and low, crystal-clear water during summer. It has plenty of shallow riffles and deep pools. Locals favor the Camp Susque Pool a few miles above Trout Run. It is a fairly open stream, conducive to fly-fishing, with some great hatches and good water in its upper sections. And it's readily accessible by car for the fly-fisherman who's willing to travel a few miles.

The stream begins near Grover in southwestern Bradford County, picking up volume from Sugar Works Run, Mill Creek, Roaring Branch, Rock Run, and Pleasant Stream before it meets Grays Run at Fields Station. Grays Run contains a 2.2-mile fly-fishing-only section. This tributary also contains many great hatches, including a respectable green drake. The Lycoming continues south through the town of Trout Run, where it picks up a good brook trout stream with the same name as the town. The stream travels southward another 13 miles before it enters the North Branch of the Susquehanna River at Williamsport. There are about 20 miles of good trout fishing before the stream becomes marginal near Trout Run.

Lycoming Creek was hit hard by Hurricane Agnes in 1972. Take a ride along its course and you'll still find many gnarled railroad tracks and damaged bridges, demonstrating the power of the floodwaters.

The Lycoming is a rocky stream with some large boulders. Wading in spring can be hazardous. Try fishing the Lycoming above Trout Run. If you plan a late-season excursion try the stream just below one of its larger tributaries, where you're assured of cool water. Or if you're a night fisherman like Mike O'Brien and Wally Larimer, try the Lycoming after dark.

SLATE RUN

Access You can reach the stream by traveling north on PA 414 to the town of Slate Run. Turn left, cross the bridge over Pine Creek, and proceed onto secondary roads that parallel much of the stream. Most of Slate Run lies in a deep gorge, and there are only a few access points and trails to the stream. Once there, however, you'll find the experience is well worth the effort.

Special Regulations Heritage-trout angling—7 miles, from the confluence of Cushman and Francis Branches downstream to Pine Creek. Francis Branch—2 miles, from Kramer Hollow downstream to the mouth.

Rating ✳✳✳✳

Patterns to Match the Hatches Little Black Stonefly (#16), Blue Quill (#18), Hendrickson (#14), Quill Gordon (#14), Early Brown Stonefly (#12), Gray Caddis (#16), Dark Olive Caddis (#16), Green Caddis (#16), Light Stonefly

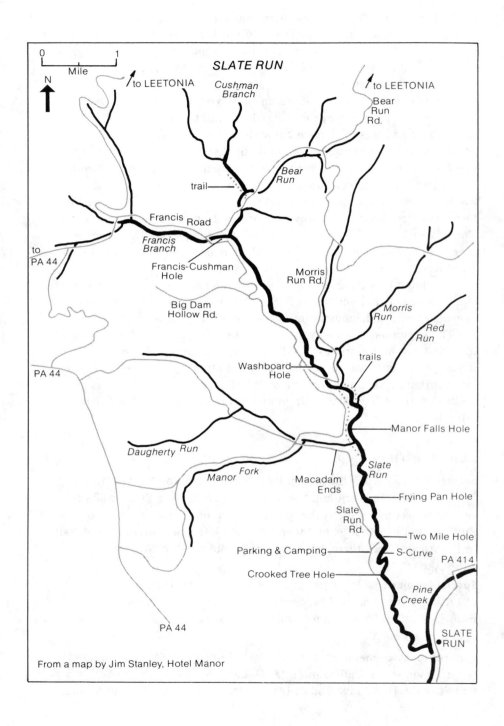

SLATE RUN

0 — Mile — 1

N

to LEETONIA

Cushman Branch

to LEETONIA

Bear Run Rd.

Bear Run

trail

Francis Road

Francis Branch

to PA 44

Francis-Cushman Hole

Morris Run Rd.

Big Dam Hollow Rd.

Morris Run

Red Run

PA 44

Washboard Hole

trails

Daugherty Run

Manor Fork

Washboard Hole

Manor Falls Hole

Macadam Ends

Slate Run

Frying Pan Hole

Slate Run Rd.

Two Mile Hole

Parking & Camping

S-Curve

PA 414

Crooked Tree Hole

Pine Creek

PA 44

SLATE RUN

From a map by Jim Stanley, Hotel Manor

(#12), Tan Caddis (#16), Little Yellow Stonefly (#16), Gray Fox and Ginger Quill (#12 and #14), March Brown (#12), Sulphur Dun and Spinner (#16 and #18), Yellow Stonefly (#16), Blue-Winged Olive Dun (#14 and #16), Green Drake and Coffin Fly (#10), Slate Drake (#12 and #14), Light Cahill (#14), Little Green Stonefly (#16), Olive Caddis (#16), Trico (#24)

Ah, the Good Old Days! In the early 1900s several anglers who fished the Francis Branch, one of the tributaries to Slate Run, reported that they had caught a "bushel" of trout from 12 to 15 inches long. For the next 50 years Slate experienced an onslaught of anglers who kept their catches, particularly in the 1950 season. Regulations on Slate Run had changed the year before, and liberal limits took their toll on the trout population in the stream. Reports told us that the outlook for fishing on Slate Run in 1951 was bleak. Because the future looked so dismal for Slate, a new group formed to protect the stream. The leaders of the Slate Run Sportsmen, Kurt Bonner, L. W. Fetter, Eddie Haines, and Grant Larimer, believed that Slate Run should become a fly-fishing-only stream. What foresight this group had! Were they well ahead of their time?

Mike O'Brien claims Slate as his second home. He first started fly-fishing on the stream at the age of six. He's fly-fished on the stream for more than 40 years. Today, through the Slate Run Tackle Shop, Mike provides on-stream fly-fishing instruction on this water.

From the mid-1960s on Mike has consistently fished this tremendous freestone stream for 45 to 50 days each year, camping out on the stream for weeks at a time in some years. He relates that in those early years he and others would fish the water for a week without seeing another fisherman or hearing another car. Those quiet, deserted days have vanished forever. Slate Run now has a large following, but the stream still holds a sizable native brown trout population. The main stem and most of the tributaries also hold a good supply of brook trout.

Mike recently took me to one of his favorite stretches on Slate Run, where Manor Fork enters. We fished this section on a hot July afternoon. The water temperature on the main stem registered 72 degrees, yet within an hour Mike had caught three native brown trout ranging from 10 to 14 inches long. He caught them on his own ant imitation, which he's dubbed the O'Brien Deer Hair Ant. It's an effective terrestrial with a white poly post that you can actually see on the water.

Several years ago the Fish Commission conducted a survey of the trout population of many of the streams of Pennsylvania. Slate Run was found to possess an unusually high number of trout. On first glance at Slate Run, however, you might appropriately question the high esteem reserved for this piece of water. It's not much different from hundreds of other Pennsylvania streams. Indeed, much of Slate is difficult to reach—some of it is accessible only by hiking into a steep gorge. It's a freestone stream with extremely variable water levels throughout the fishing season. But as the state survey found, Slate contains a hefty supply of native brown and brook trout, some of them well in excess of 20 inches. Part of this concentration of trout is owing to an exceptional supply of mayflies, stoneflies, and caddisflies.

Slate Run flows about 10 miles southwest of Cedar Run and contains just about the same species of insects that the latter does. Even with its poor access, however, Slate gets much more fishing pressure than Cedar, because of its reputation. Fishing pressure is highest on the lower few miles, just before Slate enters Pine Creek. Upstream the number of fishermen diminishes, and the scenic beauty of this spectacular stream blossoms.

Slate begins in southwestern Tioga County, with the juncture of Francis and Cushman Branches. The stream then flows south-southeast, picking up additional volume from four other feeder streams, including Manor Fork, the largest. Slate enters Pine Creek 12 miles downstream at the town of Slate Run.

Hatches on Slate Run often coincide with the first week of the season. With any break in the weather you can witness blue quills and quill gordons that first week, followed closely by female hendricksons and male red quills a couple of days later. Slate also contains the common early-April stonefly hatches. Gray foxes and green drakes appear on this pristine freestone water just after they debut on Pine. Hatches continue throughout the season, with blue-winged olives emerging in late May and June; tricos in July and August; and slate drakes, blue quills, and little blue duns interspersed with other hatches from late May into early October. Slate Run, at times, is a veritable hotbed of hatching activity.

Slate Run is a small stream with extremely clear low-water conditions throughout the summer. If you plan to fish the trico hatch on the lower end of Slate in July, use a long leader and a fine tippet.

The stream is composed of a series of rapids, moderate-flow stretches, and pools, with rocks as numerous as the trout. Many of the pools on this famous water are named. (See map.) The lower 7 miles of the stream from the Manor Hotel upstream are designated fly-fishing-only water.

Slate Run has a reputation for poisonous snakes during July and August. Because I hate snakes, and because of the numerous early hatches on the stream, I most often fish the water in April. The dilemmas often faced then concern which of the hatches the trout are feeding on and what imitation to try. Often by 11:00 AM blue quills in a size 18 already rest on the surface, and trout seem to enjoy these tasty small naturals.

Just prior to the time the blue quill appears, and for a short time thereafter, use a small, dark, brownish black nymph and imitate the movement of the natural up from the bottom. Trout often swirl, then hit the nymph on almost every cast. Wet flies, too, like those copying the quill gordon, perform well the first couple of weeks of the fishing year. Some of the finest fly-fishing of the year occurs the first couple of weeks of the season in Pennsylvania, especially on fertile streams with plenty of hatches, like Slate Run.

Slate can be treacherous to wade, with high water in the spring and with rocks and boulders strewn pell-mell on its bottom. Every once in a while you'll come across a rock ledge in the stream, which also can be difficult to circumnavigate. Slate Run contains plenty of deep pools with productive riffles above. Try the stream either the last week in April or the last week in May for an exciting experience with plenty of hatches, rising trout, and impressive scenery thrown in as a bonus.

Tom Finkbiner at the Slate Run Tackle Shop can give you the latest information on the stream. Tom provides a log of all the hatches on Slate Run, Cedar Run, and Pine Creek from the beginning of the season. You'll also see a chalkboard in his shop showing which hatches are appearing and when and where. Tom updates the hatches weekly. He and his wife, Debbie, even provide a telephone hotline to update fly-fishermen on stream conditions and hatch information.

KETTLE CREEK

Access You can reach the stream by taking PA 144 north out of Renovo.

Special Regulations Delayed harvest, fly-fishing only—1.7 miles, from about 500 feet below the PA 144 bridge upstream.

Rating ✷✷

Patterns to Match the Hatches Blue Quill (#18), Hendrickson (#14), Early Brown Stonefly (#14), Quill Gordon (#14), Little Blue-Winged Olive Dun (#20), Black Caddis (#14, #16, and #18), Sulphur (#16), March Brown (#12), Green Drake (#10), Brown Drake (#12), Slate Drake (#12 and #14), Blue-Winged Olive Dun (#14), Light Stonefly (#14), Little Green Stonefly (#18), Chocolate Dun (#16), Light Cahill (#14), Yellow Drake (#12), Trico (#24)

Jim Dubisz saw a problem and is now trying to do something about it. Jim and others heard that the Pennsylvania Fish and Boat Commission had decided that the area previously designated catch-and-release on Kettle Creek would now be a delayed-harvest stretch. Why? The commission had

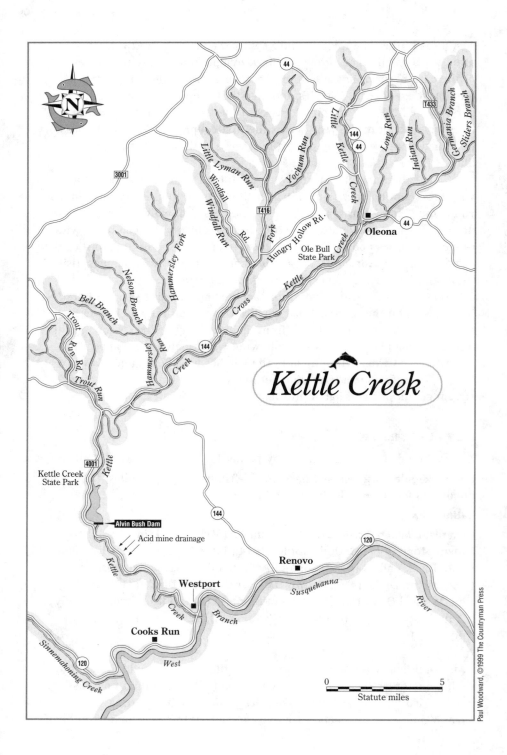

Kettle Creek

determined that the water quality on that stretch did not live up to what's needed for the catch-and-release designation. So Jim, Phil Baldacchino, Charlie Bach, and other interested anglers decided to work on the stream's problems by forming the Kettle Creek Watershed Association. When Jim's not busy with his work as president of the watershed association, he's an accounting supervisor with Adelphi Communications in Coudersport. Phil owns one of the finest fly-shops in the state, the Kettle Creek Tackle Shop. Phil's fly-shop has been open at the same location for 19 years. Charlie Bach has lived in the watershed all his life. He has worked on many stream improvements over the years. The three of them, along with many other anglers in the area, have a vested interest in the future of this great stream. Although the association is only a couple of years old, it has a long list of plans for the stream. Members list as their four goals to restore, preserve, monitor, and protect the Kettle Creek watershed—a truly immense and outstanding plan.

This is an extremely active group and it needs your help. If you can't help physically, it needs donations to complete its comprehensive plan. If you believe in organizations like this then you've got to help—this is the future of our trout fishing.

What are some of Kettle Creek's problems as a viable trout fishery? First and foremost, temperatures on Kettle rise into the high 70s in summer. In July Jim Dubisz, Phil Baldacchino, Charlie Bach, and I checked the entire stream for water temperatures and structure. From Ole Bull downstream we recorded water temperatures in the low to mid-70s on a hot afternoon. Watershed association members plan to do something to lower those temperatures. They've already placed stream improvement devices on the lower end of the regulated water. But they have developed a list of things they plan to do to keep this stream a cold-water fishery year-round. If you visit the stream during summer you'll likely see students like Tara Esposit and Chris Hartley from Lock Haven University recording important data on the stream. They're keeping detailed records of pH, alkalinity, dissolved oxygen, and macroinvertebrates.

Fifteen miles below the regulated water you'll find an impoundment, the Bush Dam, below which the state plants some trout. The dam has a bottom release but the stream below doesn't get its full effects, because the lake is fairly shallow. A few miles downstream from the dam you'll see the telltale signs of mine-acid drainage entering the stream. The watershed association even has plans to lessen the effects of this pollutant.

Recently Jim Dubisz and I spent an afternoon exploring the entire 1.5 miles of regulated water on Kettle Creek. Both the lower and upper thirds hold many more pools and productive riffles than the middle third. As we began fishing at the lower end Jim pointed out the two deflectors that the

Jim Dubicz fly-fishing Kettle Creek.

group had installed just a month before. When Jim recorded a water temperature of 76 degrees at the lower end of the delayed-harvest area I knew we were in trouble. Normally if the water is warmer than 70 degrees I refuse to fly-fish. I made an exception here because I wanted to fly-fish with Jim and find out his plans for the association. In two hours of fishing Jim and I managed to hook a half-dozen trout. We didn't land one of these—but it wasn't bad under those conditions.

Young Womans Creek flows just a few miles east of Kettle, yet it doesn't have the same temperature problem that Kettle does. Much of Kettle's problem is due to its size and its channel. Because the stream runs much wider than Young Womans, the summer sun warms the open water. A lot of Kettle has been channeled throughout the years as a flood-prevention device, too. After the 1972 flood the Corps of Engineers bulldozed a long stretch just above the Leidy Bridge. Even today, if you stand on the bridge and look upstream you'll see the effects of its work. Such channelization has also elevated the temperatures on the stream.

If temperatures rise so high in the summer months, where can you find more active trout on Kettle Creek? Jim, Phil, and Charlie recommend that you try the stream above Oleona. Here it is much smaller and cooler, and holds a lot of streambred brown trout. The salvation of Kettle is its many cool tributaries and springs. It's hard to travel more than a mile and not see springs or tributaries entering the main stem. As Jim, Phil, Charlie, and I took our tour, each would point out pools and sections where a spring or tributary entered.

In *Needham's Trout Streams,* the author indicates that the ideal stream should hold a pool-riffle-pool structure. This type of stream tends to hold a good food supply for the trout. To a great extent Kettle Creek has that type of diversity, and it boasts some of the greatest hatches in the state. Do you want to see some early hatches? Look for the Hendrickson, quill gordon, and blue quill around April 20. Want to see some of the lunker trout in Kettle feed on drakes? Then fish the stream in the latter part of May and early June; you'll probably encounter brown and green drakes appearing in the evening. Of the many hatches the stream holds Phil Baldacchino prefers fishing the March brown on the Kettle. Why? It appears for a couple of weeks through much of the afternoon. Besides, it occurs a week or two before the stream gets crowded with anglers searching for the drakes. By the way, if you stop in at the Kettle Creek Tackle Shop you'll see a display of artificials that copy what's hatching each week.

If you plan to travel to Kettle Creek in the next few years, you owe it to yourself and to the future to help the Kettle Creek Watershed Association, financially or physically, to attain its goals of better fishing on the stream. You can contact the group at RR 1, Box 184D, Coudersport 16915. And while you're at it, stop in at the Kettle Creek Tackle Shop and thank Phil and the association for their efforts.

What does the future hold for this proud stream? On one thing you can rely: With the many folks actively dedicated to improving this cold-water fishery, the future for Kettle Creek looks better than ever.

CROSS FORK CREEK

Access Improved dirt roads parallel much of the 20 miles of water on Cross Fork. A dirt road on the northern side of the stream off PA 144 gives access to the lower end, and another dirt road on the southern side of the stream parallels much of the upper water.

Special Regulations Heritage-trout angling—5.4 miles, from Bear Trap Lodge downstream to the Weed property.

Rating ✷✷✷

Patterns to Match the Hatches Blue Quill (#18), Hendrickson (#14), Early Brown Stonefly (#12), Quill Gordon (#14), Little Blue-Winged Olive Dun (#20), Sulphur Dun and Spinner (#16), Gray Fox (#14), March Brown (#14), Green Drake and Coffin Fly (#10), Blue-Winged Olive Dun (#14), Light Cahill (#14), Slate Drake (#12 and #14), Cream Cahill (#14 and #16), Trico (#24)

Phil Baldacchino spends many days matching the hatches on Cross Fork. He lives only 5 miles from this productive stream. Phil's been on Cross Fork hundreds of times in the past 10 years. He's fished while hendricksons, blue quills, and quill gordons have appeared in enormous numbers. He's witnessed trout rising to the impressive green drake on this stream.

I too have enjoyed the hatches on Cross Fork. My first trip came about purely by chance. About 20 years ago I traveled 150 miles from my home to fish Kettle Creek near the end of May. We experienced a heavy downpour the night before that turned Kettle muddy and bank-high. I had scheduled my trip hopeful that green or brown drakes would appear on Kettle that evening. Now that hope disappeared with the poor fly-fishing conditions on Kettle.

So I drove downstream to the town of Cross Fork, crossed the stream with the same name, and noted that it too was high, but not off color. Fishing this unfamiliar water topped any other strategy I had, so I headed upstream a few miles.

The farther I traveled up the dirt road paralleling part of the stream, the more intrigued I became. Cross Fork is a small stream, replete with plenty of pools harboring native brook and brown trout. In most areas the stream is only 15 to 25 feet wide in spring and less than that in July and August. I got out of the car in midafternoon to explore on foot more of this new water on Cross Fork. Not far from the car, in a well-shaded pool with much of its water flowing under a far bank, I noticed a large mayfly appear—then another. Soon a couple of trout seemed to move out from underneath the bank and start chasing duns on the surface. Several more sizable mayflies struggled on the surface. I started chasing the mayflies in an attempt to identify this afternoon bonus. Finally I caught one, glanced at its cream body and barred wings, and concluded that green drakes had set off this feeding frenzy. Now more drakes rested on the surface in the pool, and trout responded to this impressive source of food by feeding in the middle of the afternoon.

I wasn't too surprised by this afternoon hatch of green drakes. Small streams with heavy canopies often harbor afternoon hatches of this species. On Big Fill and Vanscoyoc Runs in central Pennsylvania, and on Cedar Run in north-central, green drakes emerge all day.

Experiencing a spectacular hatch on a new stream with responsive trout proved too much for me. I ran back to the car, assembled my gear, and headed back to Cross Fork. As I walked along a trail leading to the water, I hurriedly tied on a size-10 Green Drake pattern. At the stream I witnessed more than a dozen native trout taking duns from the surface.

Nearly every trout took my pattern that day—a far cry from one of those frustrating green drake days on Penns Creek, for example, where you're often fortunate to catch one or two trout. In the middle of a late-May afternoon on Cross Fork, trout took that Green Drake pattern for several hours.

Cross Fork begins in southern Potter County near Cherry Springs State Park. It flows almost directly south and picks up additional volume from feeder streams like Boone Run, Bolich Run, Little Lyman Run, Yocum Run, Windfall Run, and Elk Lick Run before it enters Kettle Creek. Some of these tributaries, including Windfall Run, hold excellent populations of brook trout.

There's 5.4 miles of fly-fishing-only water on the stream. Why not declare the entire Cross Fork watershed a catch-and-release area?

HAMMERSLEY RUN (FORK)

Access Hammersley Road, dirt, parallels the lower 2 miles of Hammersley Run. Above that point the only way to reach this stream is on foot. The state recently declared the watershed a wilderness area. There are some large trout on the main stem and on the tributaries, which join about 3 miles upstream from the mouth.

Rating ✳✳✳

Patterns to Match the Hatches Blue Quill (#18), Quill Gordon (#14), Hendrickson and Red Quill (#14), Sulphur Dun and Spinner (#16), March Brown (#12), Blue-Winged Olive Dun (#14), Light Cahill (#14), Slate Drake (#12 and #14), Green Drake and Coffin Fly (#10), Little Green Stonefly (#16)

Back in 1982 the state stocked the lower end of Hammersley Run for the last time. It had found in a survey that this stream held a respectable native brook and brown trout population and felt it no longer needed additional fish. What has happened to the stream since that last stocking? Unwary stocked trout gave way to cautious, discriminating wild trout. Fewer anglers fish the stream since the native trout have become harder to catch. But the trout are there, and some of the hatches are heavy. If you enjoy small, pristine streams loaded with streambred browns and brook trout, you'll enjoy a day on Hammersley Run. Good water quality, some heavy hatches, and a wild population make this a great place to fish.

You'll notice stream improvement devices 2 miles upstream, placed there by the Cross Fork Sportsmen, Kettle Creek–Tamarack Sportsmen,

West Clinton County Sportsmen, and Kettle Creek Chapter of Trout Unlimited. Some of the improvements have withstood more than seven years of high spring waters.

Recently Phil Baldacchino of the Kettle Creek Tackle Shop and I traveled up the lower 4 miles of Hammersley. Phil and I noticed dozens of wild trout and the absence of any kind of worn path along the stream. Almost every stretch contained several undercut banks and rock-ledged pools. Phil declares that if you hit this small water when a hatch appears, the stream comes alive with rising native trout. Hammersley contains a good hatch of early-season mayflies. On occasion in late April you can fish over one of three hatches for several hours.

Bell and Nelson Branches flow from the northwest and Hammersley Fork from the north to form the main stem near the Clinton County line.

If you enjoy small-stream fly-fishing, solitude, scenery, native trout, and some good hatches, you must try Hammersley Run.

YOUNG WOMANS CREEK

Access You can reach Young Womans Creek on a blacktop road off PA 120 at North Bend. A dirt road follows the Left Branch.

Special Regulations Selective-harvest program—5.5 miles, from the state forest property line upstream to Beechwood Trail.

Rating ✳✳✳✳

Patterns to Match the Hatches Little Black Stonefly (#16), Dark Red Stonefly (#12), Little Blue-Winged Olive Dun (#20), Blue Quill (#18), Quill Gordon (#14), Hendrickson (#14), Light Stonefly (#12), Tan Caddis (#16), Gray Fox (#14), March Brown (#14), Sulphur Dun and Spinner (#16 and #18), Dark Green Drake (#8), Green Drake and Coffin Fly (#12), Slate Drake (#12 and #14), Pink Lady and Light Cahill (#14), Little Green Stonefly (#16), Little Yellow Stonefly (#16), *Pteronarcys* Stonefly (#8), Dark Blue Quill (#20)

Back in 1962 Tom Forbes extolled the virtues of catch-and-release fishing in an article on Young Womans Creek included in the popular booklet *100 Trout Streams*. After many interviews with fly-fishermen Tom concluded that this stream was a true paradise, with plenty of good-sized trout. In his story Tom didn't examine the other important ingredient that contributes to making Young Womans a model trout stream: great hatches. Tom talked about the Left Branch of the creek, which enters the main stem 2 miles above North Bend. The Left Branch no longer holds a catch-and-release area. More than 5 miles of the Right Branch are now set aside for fly-fishing only, however.

Although the main stem and the Left Branch are typical small mountain streams with riffles separating pools of various lengths, the water has a good hatch diversity and a good population of brown and brook trout. In the fly-fishing-only section you'll probably catch native brook trout up to a foot long and streambred brown trout up to 15 inches long, with an occasional lunker near 20. The state stocks the Left Branch and sections on the Right Branch above and below the 5.5-mile fly-fishing-only area.

Rich Meyers fly-fishes on Young Womans just about every weekend. Rich caught his first trout more than 40 years ago on Hyner Run, just a few miles from Young Womans Creek. He's fly-fished Cedar Run, Slate Run, and Young Womans Creek since 1961. Rich has observed, identified, and photographed many of the mayflies on the stream. Several of his mayfly photos hang in Tom Finkbiner's store and at the Manor Hotel, both in Slate Run. Rich has studied sulphur nymphs and the way they emerge. As a result of these observations he's developed an emerger pattern with an enlarged yellow thorax that works to perfection during the hatch.

Rich says that the two best hatches for him on Young Womans are the early blue quill and the sulphurs in mid-May. He fishes a Blue Quill for the first two weeks of the season.

In mid-May Rich fishes the sulphurs, green drakes, and more blue quills. He's seen two sulphur species, *Ephemerella rotunda* and *E. invaria,* emerge simultaneously on Young Womans Creek. Green drakes also emerge in large enough numbers on the stream to make this hatch rewarding to fly-fish. Often Rich sees a second blue quill *(Paraleptophlebia mollis)* appear at the same time the green drake does. During any of the prolific hatches on the stream Rich often catches 20 or more rising trout.

You'll also see plenty of stoneflies on this water: little black stoneflies, little yellow stoneflies, little green stoneflies, the large *Pteronarcys,* and the dark red stonefly. The little black stonefly appears as early as late March. Rich matches the dark red stonefly with a size-12 or -14 Red Quill wet fly.

Young Womans Creek has an advantage few of its sister streams in north-central Pennsylvania can claim. In addition to exhibiting many of the hatches found on the Kettle, First Fork, and Pine, Young Womans retains its cool water year-round. A heavy canopy of oak, maple, and pine protects much of its freestone surface from the heating effect of the summer sun. Temperatures rarely exceed 70 degrees except in extreme heat or drought.

There's little trouble wading either branch of the stream except when there's high water in the early season from snowmelt. Small, medium, and large boulders clog the bottom and produce some pools on this small stream that are indescribably picturesque.

Young Womans Creek contains a lot of unproductive water, too. The fly-fishing-only area has few large pools. Stream improvement devices strategically placed throughout the Right Branch would make the water even more productive.

Don't miss fishing this outstanding north-central Pennsylvania stream.

STONY FORK

Access Stony can be reached at Wellsboro. Turn off PA 660 onto the Stony Creek Road. This blacktop road parallels the upper half of the stream. At Draper a good dirt road follows the stream to Painter Run.

Rating ✳✳

Patterns to Match the Hatches Early Brown Stonefly (#12), Blue Quill (#18), Quill Gordon (#14), Hendrickson (#14), Gray Fox (#14), March Brown (#12), Green Drake (#10), Brown Drake (#12), Slate Drake (#14), Blue-Winged Olive Dun (#14)

The chilly morning air quickly warmed under the high late-April sun. For weather, this second day of the season would prove to be a tremendous improvement over opening day, with its flurry-filled skies. Today I planned to arrive at Stony Fork about 10 miles south of Wellsboro by early afternoon to check some of the early-season hatches.

Traveling down the paved secondary road that parallels Stony Fork, then onto a dirt road at Draper, I wasn't impressed with the character of the stream. The upper 5 miles of Stony flow through open pastureland and capture plenty of sunlight to warm the water in summer. Once I hit state game lands and the wooded section, however, the complexion of the stream changed dramatically. In this area rock-ledged pools, some more than 10 feet deep, seemed common. Here the stream resembled another piece of water not more than 6 air miles away, Cedar Run.

I pulled into a parking lot about 2 miles upstream from one of Stony's major tributaries, Painter Run. The state stocks no trout below Painter, because this branch pours mine acid into the main stem. Ten cars were parked in the area, and fishermen lined all the productive spots on the 20-foot-wide stream. I became intrigued with the character of this miniature Cedar Run and hiked downstream a half mile in an attempt to avoid the hordes of bait-fishermen.

I arrived at another deep pool that had evidently been stocked recently. Five or six other fishermen had come before me to this picturesque pool, so I moved downstream another 100 yards, now just exploring the water. When I arrived at this lower pool I noticed a half-dozen trout feeding in front of three bait-fishermen. They saw my fly-rod and encouraged me to try to catch these trout. I scanned the surface of the pool, saw hundreds of blue quills drifting in the eddy, and tied on a size-18 copy of the natural.

The pool had a heavy canopy of hemlocks, and a shadow covered its surface; I had difficulty picking up the drift of my size-18 imitation. On the first cast a heavy brown hit the fly. Soon quill gordons joined the blue quills, and trout began taking the larger morsel. I quickly tied on a size-14 copy, because it would be much easier to see than the size 18. For more than two hours blue quills, then quill gordons and blue quills, paraded across the surface of that small pool, and fish continued to rise throughout the episode. Two hours and 20 trout later I headed back to my car. What a day with the blue quill and quill gordon!

Gary Hall of Wellsboro fly-fishes on Stony often during the season and says that it contains some excellent hatches through much of the early and midseason. There are a few green drakes and even some brown drakes on this picturesque stream. Gary says that the water contains some holdovers, and he hears reports about 20-inch lunkers in some of the deeper pools.

Because of the open farmlands upstream, Stony Fork often warms into the high 70s in July and August. The best area to fish is the 4-mile stretch above Painter Run.

OSWAYO CREEK

Access Take PA 44 north out of Coudersport to Coneville.

Rating ✳✳✳✳

Patterns to Match the Hatch Little Blue-Winged Olive Dun (#20), Blue Quill (#18), Quill Gordon (#14), Hendrickson (#14), Black Quill (#12 and #14), Grannom (#12 and #14), Tan Caddis (#14 and #16), Sulphur Dun and Spinner (#16 and #18), Gray Fox (#14), March Brown (#12), Green Drake and Coffin Fly (#10), Light Cahill (#14), Brown Drake (#12), Gray Drake (#10 and #12), Dark Blue Sedge (#14), Slate Drake (#12), Blue-Winged Olive Dun (#14), Yellow Drake (#10 and #12), Brown Caddis (#14), Trico (#24)

Dr. Peter Ryan practices dentistry in the beautiful Potter County town of Coudersport. On Thursdays, Sundays, and any other time he can find an excuse he becomes Pete Ryan, fly-fisherman. Skip Gibson, who until recently lived in north-central Pennsylvania, on occasion coaxed Pete to vacate his favorite fishing waters near his home to fly-fish on one of the famous south-central Pennsylvania streams like the LeTort or Falling Spring. The trico hatches on these two streams can be spectacular in late July and August.

After a frustrating day of fishing the trico on the LeTort, Pete headed to the Oswayo just 12 miles from his home in Coudersport. He was anxious to fly-fish this cool, productive freestone and its trico hatch—and he was now on his home territory. Forty trout later Pete headed back to Coudersport, satisfied with the hatch, the rising trout, and with the pattern he used to match the hatch.

Only a handful of fly-fishermen frequent the Oswayo regularly. One fly-fisherman who knows the stream and its hatches well is Stewart Dickerson of Shinglehouse. When one of a dozen hatches appears, he fishes the stream four or five times a week. In mid-April Stewart spends any afternoon he can fishing the prolific blue quill and Hendrickson hatches. Often the Hendrickson appears for two weeks on the Oswayo.

By mid-May Stewart spends evenings on the Oswayo near Clara Creek, fishing the prolific sulphur dun and spinner. This hatch lasts for three or four weeks. By late May a fantastic green drake hatch appears on this excellent stream. Stewart recalls many evenings when matching the ephemeral drake produced dozens of heavy trout.

Even in July and August you'll find hatches on the Oswayo. Tom Dewey of Coudersport regularly fishes the yellow drake, which appears on the stream for a month or more. Tom feels the yellow drake, like the green drake, brings up some of the lunker browns on Oswayo. He's had some of his best yellow drake fishing at dusk in early August.

The last hatch of the Oswayo's season, and the smallest, appears for almost two months. Pete Ryan, Stewart Dickerson, and Vic Howard fish the trico hatch, frequently with fantastic results.

Drive 12 miles north of Coudersport on PA 49 and PA 44, and you'll enter the scenic Oswayo Valley. The Oswayo stands out as one of the top trout streams in the state. Deep, pristine pools about every 100 yards, with some productive moderate stretches between, consistently cool water throughout the season, and some of the most abundant hatches in the state make this premier trout water.

The South Branch follows PA 44 and joins the main stem at Coneville. This bushy tributary contains stocked trout and ranges from 15 to 20 feet wide at most places. Whitney Creek joins the South Branch near Coneville. The South Branch warms considerably in summer, with water temperatures sometimes above 70 degrees.

The Oswayo's main stem flows from a state fish hatchery through the village of Oswayo and meets the South Branch at Coneville. Many springs from the upper end cool the main stem above Coneville all summer long. This upper section ranges from 15 to 20 feet wide and contains many pools and a great trico hatch. Much of the stream here flows through open meadows.

A meadow on the upper Oswayo Creek. This section holds a good trico hatch.

From just below the village of Oswayo downstream almost to Clara Creek, the Fish Commission classifies the main stem as wild-trout water. This section needs no additional trout. It contains plenty of streambred browns, some over 20 inches long, and a few brookies.

Below Coneville, Clara and Elevenmile Creeks enter the main stem. Elevenmile gets some stocked trout at its lower end. The state stocks trout on the main stem from Clara Creek to Sharon Center. In this area the Oswayo widens to 40 to 50 feet, with some pools over 10 feet deep, great hatches, and plenty of large trout.

Since the Oswayo contains a good supply of streambred brown trout, it's important to leave the stream the way you came—without any creeled trout. If this stream is to remain a consistently top-quality water, each fisherman must return his entire catch.

Will Pete Ryan ever travel south to fish the trico again? Why should he, with the Oswayo so close to home?

ALLEGHENY RIVER

Access PA 49 follows the Allegheny above Coudersport, and US 6 parallels the river from Coudersport to Port Allegany.

Special Regulations Delayed harvest, artificial lures only—2.7 miles, from Judge Pattersons Pond Road downstream to Ford.

Rating ✳✳

Patterns to Match the Hatches Little Blue-Winged Olive Dun (#20), Early Brown Stonefly (#12), Blue Quill (#18), Quill Gordon (#14), Hendrickson (#14), Black Quill (#14), Grannom (#12 and #14), Light Stonefly (#12), Tan Caddis (#14 and #16), Sulphur Dun and Spinner (#16 and #18), Green Drake and Coffin Fly (#10), Brown Drake (#12), March Brown (#12), Light Cahill (#14), Blue-Winged Olive Dun (#14 and #16), Gray Drake (#14), Yellow Drake (#12), Big Slate Drake (#8)

I had an entire day to spend on the Allegheny River in late April. At noon snow flurries filled the cold, early-season sky. The water temperature at this section, 5 miles below Coudersport, registered 48 degrees. If only the air would warm the water a few degrees, maybe a Hendrickson hatch would appear.

About 3:00 PM I checked the temperature a second time and again recorded 48 degrees. Probably no hatch would appear, I decided. Almost as soon as I returned the thermometer to my fishing vest, I noticed a few hendricksons appear on a moderate stretch just above me. Soon dozens, then hundreds, then thousands of dazed hendricksons and red quills drifted to the eddies and pools below. Almost immediately a half-dozen trout began feeding in unison in the moderate stretch where the duns first appeared. More than a dozen trout joined in on the surface food in the pool below. The trout were extremely selective—maybe a dozen duns floated over each feeding fish before it rose. After countless casts with a size-14 Red Quill pattern over a riser, it might take the dry fly. Soon hendricksons covered the pool, but trout still only surface-fed sporadically. Maybe the cold water slowed the metabolic rate of the trout, and they needed little nourishment.

A size-14 imitation seems a bit large for the hatch on this river. These insects also looked somewhat darker than other Hendrickson hatches.

Three other fishermen arrived in the midst of the hatch. These bait-fishermen/part-time fly-fishermen noticed the number of trout rising and quickly headed back to their car for their fly-rods.

"What are they taking?" they yelled.

"A Red Quill," I said.

"Don't have any of those," they replied.

The tremendous hatch continued uninterrupted for two hours with thousands of duns now covering the surface. With the air temperature below 50 degrees no duns took flight. At 5:00 PM I quit. Trout continued to rise sporadically, but the icy water and cold air numbed my fingers. Even under those adverse weather conditions, and with extremely selective trout, I landed 15 fish during that spectacular hatch.

The Allegheny River contains much more than just a sensational Hendrickson hatch. Vic Howard of Coudersport fly-fishes on the river frequently. He recently retired from teaching to devote his time fully to fly-fishing. After the Hendrickson, Vic often travels to the river for the March brown, sulphur, green drake, or brown drake hatches in late May.

Even into late June he finds some worthwhile hatches on the Allegheny River. About that time the yellow drake appears just at dusk. Early in August, Vic says, the natural imitated by a Big Slate Drake tied on a size-6 hook appears on the Allegheny in numbers. Vic fishes much of the river and vividly recalls many stories of lunker browns caught during the green and brown drake hatches.

Vic and Pete Ryan fish the Allegheny frequently. They both belong to the local Trout Unlimited chapter, appropriately named God's Country. The chapter is one of the few volunteer watchdog organizations dedicated to protecting the water quality of the river. It has developed some stream improvements on Baker Creek, a tributary to the Allegheny.

The Fish Commission stocks about 27 miles of water, including about 11 miles above Coudersport. Above the flood-control project in town, the river ranges from 30 to 40 feet wide. The upper end above Coudersport harbors a good supply of holdover and streambred brown trout. I feel that the river above Coudersport should not be stocked. Given a chance streambred brown trout would thrive in the headwaters. Baker Creek and Peet Brook flow into the Allegheny above Coudersport.

In Coudersport a tremendous wild-trout stream, Mill Creek, enters the Allegheny. US 6 and PA 44 follow Mill Creek to its headwaters. If you have some time and want to fish on a small, productive stream with wild trout, try Mill Creek.

From Coudersport, the Allegheny flows west-northwest and picks up additional flow from Dingman Run, Reed Run, Trout Brook, Laninger Creek, Fishing Creek (stocked), Card Creek, and Sartwell Creek before it enters Port Allegany. Below Coudersport the river widens to 50 to 60 feet, with many deep pools and productive moderate stretches.

Water temperatures above Coudersport remain low all summer long. Below Coudersport, however, the river's temperature rises in the summer, and warm-water fish species compete with the stocked trout. The concrete flood channel through which the river flows in town heats up the water considerably. Water entering the channel is often 10 degrees cooler than water leaving the concrete channel at the lower end of town.

If you like large-water fly-fishing with plenty of trout and some great hatches, try the Allegheny River.

GENESEE FORKS

Access A secondary road off US 6 from West Pike to Loucks Mills parallels Genesee Forks for 8 miles.

Rating ✳✳✳

Patterns to Match the Hatches Blue Quill (#18), Quill Gordon (#14),
Hendrickson (#14), Early Brown Stonefly (#12), Gray Fox (#14), March
Brown (#12), Slate Drake (#12 and #14), Light Cahill (#14), Green Drake
and Coffin Fly (#10), Blue-Winged Olive Dun (#14 and #16), Trico (#24),
Little Blue-Winged Olive Dun (#20), Cinnamon Caddis (#10)

Jack Mickievicz lived and worked in Phoenixville in southeastern
Pennsylvania for years. On weekdays he operated Jack's Tackle, but on
weekends he left southeastern Pennsylvania for God's Country, Potter
County. Jack finally succumbed to the scenic beauty of the West Pike area
of Potter County. He moved his sporting goods store onto one of his
favorite streams, Genesee Forks. Jack could then leave his store, rechris-
tened Jack's Tackle and West Pike Outfitters, walk across US 6, and begin
fly-fishing. Jack has now returned to southeastern Pennsylvania, but he
still fishes Genesee Forks.

In addition to Genesee Forks, Jack fly-fishes several other local wild-
trout streams, including Ninemile Run, Phoenix Run, and the upper end of
Pine Creek. He prefers these smaller streams because he believes few other
fly-fishermen visit them. From past experience he knows that these small
streams boast a good supply of streambred brown and brook trout up to
15 inches long, with an occasional lunker over 20. Jack's favorite streams
flow into Pine Creek between Galeton and Walton near US 6 and hold
excellent stonefly, caddisfly, and mayfly hatches.

Caddisflies like the grannom and little black caddis abound in these
streams. Even into August Jack has found the cinnamon caddis emerging
on Genesee Forks.

Genesee Forks also harbors many mayflies. It has many of the early
hatches but also some of the later ones: tricos, slate drakes, and blue
quills in July and August. Don't expect the same hatch density on
Genesee Forks that you'd witness on Pine below, however.

I followed Jack one day on the Genesee Forks to better understand his
techniques for mastering small-stream fly-fishing. He fly-fished every
inch of the productive pocket water and pools in a 1-mile stretch. On
these small streams Jack uses a 7-foot graphite fly-rod with a 7- or 9-foot
leader. As the fly drifts across pockets of varying velocity he constantly
mends the line to obtain a longer drift.

The water temperature for Jack's and my early-season trip on the

Genesee Forks stayed at 40 degrees throughout the day. Jack attempted to coax trout to the surface with a Royal Coachman, Quill Gordon, Hendrickson, and several other dry flies. Only occasionally would a trout rise for the fly in this cold water, but one that did was a hefty foot-long streambred brown.

Was Jack discouraged with his lack of success on Genesee Forks that day? Not Jack. He fly-fished Genesee Forks throughout the succeeding summer and caught plenty of brook and brown trout up to 14 inches long. If you like solitude, wild trout, and some great hatches, try Genesee Forks. Be prepared with some caddis patterns and even some Green Drakes if you're there around the end of May.

The stream is brush lined at many places and difficult to fly-fish. It's about 20 feet wide with pools positioned about every 100 yards. Throughout its length Genesee Forks contains many overhanging trees and brush, and pools filled with logs, sticks, and twigs. You'll find no fisherman's path along this stream. Few anglers ever fish the Forks much above where it enters Pine at West Pike.

Genesee Forks has one major tributary, California Creek, which enters at Loucks Mills.

NINEMILE RUN

Access Ninemile Run parallels US 6 from Walton to Denton Hill.

Rating ✳✳

Patterns to Match the Hatches Blue Quill (#18), Quill Gordon (#14), Hendrickson (#14), Little Black Caddis (#18), Gray Fox (#14), March Brown (#12), Green Drake and Coffin Fly (#10), Brown Drake (#12), Slate Drake (#12 and #14), Light Cahill (#14), Blue-Winged Olive Dun (#14 and #16), Trico (#24)

Just 100 yards from the rustic Shiloh Lodge flows Ninemile Run, a major tributary to upper Pine Creek. Ninemile's headwaters begin just across US 6 from the Potato City Motor Inn, at an elevation of 2,500 feet. It flows east for 9 miles before it joins Pine Creek at Walton. Flowing in the opposite direction, toward the west, is Mill Creek.

There are about 6 miles of excellent fishing on Ninemile for brook and brown trout. A study by the Fish Commission recently showed a good population of streambred browns from 10 to 12 inches long and brook trout 6 to 10 inches long.

Fly-fishing Ninemile presents many challenges. In the lower mile of water the stream contains a heavy canopy of hemlocks and beeches. In open meadows are brush-lined banks and beaver dams. Here you'll find your fly on a bush or tree as often as it is in the water. At no place is the stream wider than 15 feet. Fallen trees, logs, and twigs form impenetrable logjams. All this makes for challenging casting.

The water temperature in Ninemile rarely exceeds 70 degrees even in July. Wary trout scare easily on this wild-trout stream, and a low profile is a prerequisite.

Near the end of May this diminutive stream presents its pièce de résistance, the green drake. When these large mayflies struggle to become airborne on this small stream, trout seem to lose their timidity and feed voraciously on the insects.

Ninemile contains plenty of hatches other than the green drake. In late April blue quills, quill gordons, and Hendricksons appear.

DRIFTWOOD BRANCH, SINNEMAHONING CREEK

Access PA 120 parallels the Driftwood Branch upstream to Emporium. Take PA 46 out of Emporium to access the upper end.

Special Regulations Delayed harvest, fly-fishing only—1.4 miles, from the Shippen Township Building downstream to near PA 120 west of Emporium.

Rating ✳✳

Patterns to Match the Hatches Early Brown Stonefly (#12), Little Blue-Winged Olive Dun (#20), Blue Quill (#18), Quill Gordon (#14), Hendrickson and Red Quill (#14), Tan Caddis (#14), Green Caddis (#16), Grannom (#16), Sulphur Dun and Spinner (#16), Gray Fox (#14), March Brown (#12), Light Cahill (#14), Green Drake and Coffin Fly (#10), Brown Drake (#12), Blue-Winged Olive Dun (#14 and #16), Dark Green Drake (#8), Little Green Stonefly (#16), Golden Drake (#12), Slate Drake (#12 and #14)

For several years Craig Hudson of Emporium in Cameron County has issued a standing invitation for me to fly-fish with him on the Driftwood Branch. Craig, now an accomplished fly-fisherman, operates the Fisherman's Attic for fly-fishermen out of the basement of his Sixth Street home in Emporium.

Craig, Mark Campbell, Don Perry, and Tom Barton met me at the Driftwood Branch just a few miles above town in the delayed-harvest area. Don and Craig belong to the local Trout Unlimited organization, called the Jim Zwald Chapter. Don currently heads the group, which diligently acts as a watchdog on local trout-stream concerns. The group urged the Fish Commission to change its regulations from "artificials" to "flies only" on the delayed-harvest area of Driftwood, and placed at least six stream improvement devices in the regulated water.

Even as we approached the 40-foot-wide water, we saw green drakes emerge. Craig indicated that they had begun to appear the night before. Within an hour, at 6:00 PM, a major hatch of drakes had developed. Hundreds of struggling duns, ranging from size 8 to 12, appeared on the surface, and many of the trout in this well-stocked area responded with splashing rises.

All five of us began the expected ritual, casting Green Drake dry flies over the rising trout. Several browns, brooks, and rainbows inspected, even nudged my pattern—but I had no true strikes.

Dozens of trout still rose throughout the pool and riffle above. Then on one cast Craig's Drake dry fly sank, and a trout struck. So I began purposely sinking my pattern just beneath the surface—and had five strikes on five casts. As often happens with green drake hatches, trout chase the emerger and ignore the dun on the surface.

By 8:00 PM ginger quill spinners appeared over the riffle at the head of the pool. Craig, Tom, Don, and I switched to appropriate patterns, waiting for the spinner fall. It happened almost at 8:30, and trout occasionally took our imitations. Tom, Craig, and Don yelled, "Tuna," every time they hooked a trout with the Ginger Quill. "Tuna" resounded up and down the valley repeatedly until the spinner fall subsided near 9:00 PM.

What an evening on the Driftwood Branch! Thousands of green drakes on the surface; a few coffin flies appearing at dusk; thousands of black caddis emerging near dusk; and the fitting climax, the ginger quill spinner fall.

The Driftwood Branch contains many aquatic insects with outstanding match-the-hatch fly-fishing. Craig says that hendricksons had appeared in huge numbers the past year. The stream also contains an enormous hatch of brown drakes near the end of May. Within the past few years these drakes have even emerged above Emporium. The hatch and spinner fall lasts for four or five days on the Driftwood Branch. Craig Hudson says that one Trout Unlimited member who has fly-fished many central-Pennsylvania streams believes that the brown drake hatch near Emporium appears in larger numbers than does the green drake on Penns Creek.

The green drake hatch seems to move upstream, like the one on Penns Creek. About five days after it first appears at Driftwood it emerges at Emporium, 20 miles upstream. The little green stonefly appears just at the end of the green drake hatch and becomes an important stonefly to copy almost the entire month of June.

The Driftwood Branch begins in northeastern Elk County. It flows southeast into Cameron County, where it picks up Bobby Run, Cooks Run, Clear Creek, and North Creek. West Creek joins the main stem in Emporium, and Portage Creek at the eastern end of town. Above Emporium water temperatures remain fairly low throughout the summer but sometimes rise into the 70s. When temperatures in the main stem rise, trout migrate to one of the cooler tributaries.

Above Emporium, Driftwood Branch ranges from 20 to 40 feet wide with some productive riffles and pools up to 5 feet deep. Here you'll find some streambred browns and plenty of holdover trout. Below Emporium the Driftwood Branch flows south and adds tributaries like Canoe Run, Hunts Run, Stillhouse Run, and Sterling Run. The latter enters the main stem at the town of the same name and adds a small amount of mine acid to the branch. Driftwood Branch joins the severely polluted Bennett Branch at Driftwood to form Sinnemahoning Creek.

Below Emporium the Driftwood becomes a large stream, widening to 100 feet. Deep pools, heavy riffles, and long, flat sections dominate the lower end of the stream. After June the lower end warms rapidly and becomes a warm-water fishery. In total there are about 40 miles of stocked stream.

The locals have named many of the pools and sections on the Driftwood Branch. Above Emporium are the Township Building, Dodge Hollow, Deflectors, Hertlein, Steel Dam, Fairgrounds, and Water Company Dam. Below Emporium you'll find the Y, Mallorys, Friendly Garden, German Rocks, Memorial Springs, Coke Oven, Canoe Run, Cameron Hotel, and Tunnel Hill.

Above Emporium the delayed-harvest area runs for more than a mile. This regulated stretch needs to be extended upstream a mile or two, to encompass areas where several cool tributaries enter the main stem. In July and August water temperatures in the regulated area often rise above 70 degrees. Trout move out of the delayed-harvest area upstream to one of the cooler tributaries. Here bait-fishermen lie in wait. If the Fish Commission enlarged the delayed-harvest area, these trout could be caught and released all summer long.

6 | Streams of Central Pennsylvania

Central Pennsylvania is blessed with plenty of limestone caverns, limestone springs, and limestone water. This area of the state is a haven for tremendous mayfly hatches and large streambred brown trout. Who hasn't heard of Penns Creek, Spruce Creek, or even Elk Creek? These are just a few of the great streams in central Pennsylvania.

Some of the area's once-polluted waters have reemerged into prominence as top trout waters in the East. The Little Juniata River, for years heavily polluted with tannic acid and upriver sewage, is now free from those contaminants. Spring Creek, once noted as one of the top 10 streams in the East, fell victim to various doses of raw sewage and harmful chemicals over many years. It too has made a gallant attempt to regain some of its earlier brilliance. Both streams now harbor respectable hatches of several mayfly and caddisfly species along with an abundant supply of brown trout.

We'll explore more than 19 central-Pennsylvania trout streams and their tributaries. Try some of these top-notch waters on your next trip.

PINE CREEK

Access SR 2018 parallels the limestone part of Pine Creek, and Pine Creek Road follows the upper section.

Rating ✳✳

Patterns to Match the Hatches Little Blue-Winged Olive Dun (#20), Blue Quill (#18), Sulphur (#16), March Brown (#12), Gray Fox (#12), Light Cahill (#14), Green Drake (#10), Blue-Winged Olive Dun (#14), Tan Caddis (#16), Cream Cahill (#14), Trico (#24)

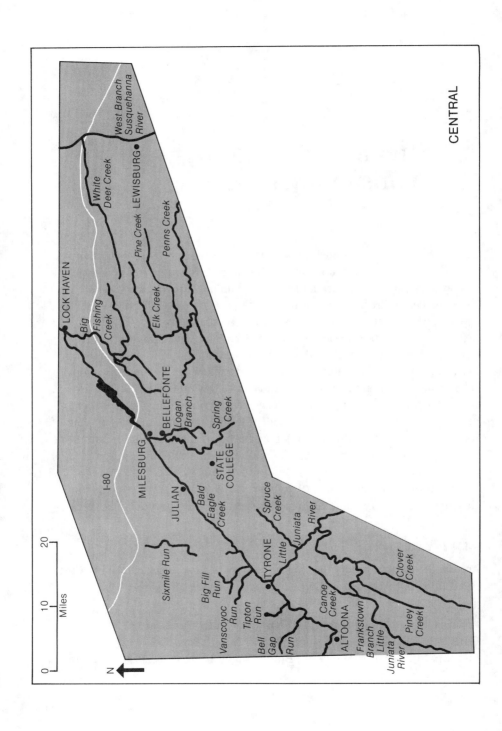

CENTRAL

"It's a classic English-type limestone stream, except here, you enter the water to fly-fish," said Jon Witwer of the Feathered Hook in Coburn as we waded into Pine Creek. "Pine, along with Penns and Elk Creeks, is extremely important to local and out-of-state anglers. Here you have one of the largest and most important limestone aquifers in the United States. Not protecting this valuable resource would be a tragedy for us and future generations," Jon lamented. Jon should know. For the past five years he's guided hundreds of anglers on Penns, Elk, and Fishing Creeks. He lives in Coburn, only a stone's throw from Elk, Penns, and Pine Creeks. Anglers from as far away as England, Canada, and Italy have traveled to Coburn to have Jon guide them.

Pine Creek is a major tributary to the much more familiar Penns Creek. Along with Elk Creek, it provides a needed shot of cool water to Penns Creek throughout the summer. Jon pointed to meaningful statistics he recorded during the summer of 1991 to show the importance of this spring-filled limestone stream to Penns Creek. Penns Creek at Coburn, just upstream from Pine and Elk, registered 78 degrees in mid-July. Just downstream from the mouth of Elk the Penns cooled to 71 degrees. What a difference! During that summer, water from Elk was almost nonexistent. Eighty percent of the cold water entering Penns Creek that summer came from Pine Creek.

Why is Pine Creek so much cooler? If you check the stream from Woodward downstream to Coburn you'll find it fed by two major and about six minor limestone springs. In a meadow just above Dingas Mills in mid-August you'll find temperatures in the high 50s. These springs and in turn the entire aquifer might be impacted if authorities allow a limestone quarry to operate just 3 miles from the stream. The quarry is now operating, but local environmentalists are closely monitoring any effects it might have.

Without a hatch on Pine Creek, fly-fishing this slow, silted limestone stream can be less than productive. Add a sulphur hatch in late May or early June and wait for rising trout and you're likely to have a successful day. During late-fall and winter months you'll often find midges on the surface, and crane flies are important throughout the year. You'd think that Pine would hold a great trico population. It doesn't—but Paul Antolosky of Bellefonte does report seeing a few at the Dingas Mills section.

Just getting around in Pine Creek can be challenging. You'll find weed beds throughout with narrow silted gravel paths between them. When wading the stream always try to walk in areas void of weed growth. Pine Creek has two types of water in its lower 3 miles—slow and slower. Getting a drag-free float under these conditions ranks high if you're going

Jon Witwer fly-fishes Pine Creek.

to have a productive day. Jon Witwer suggests that you use a long, fine tippet, because the streambred browns and native brook trout spook easily. Be careful as you wade—you'll see lunker trout swim out from under the weeds. Several years ago Jon landed an 18-inch brookie, and he's heard of someone taking a 24-inch brown trout.

With assured cold water throughout the summer, few anglers along the stream to contend with throughout the season, and good access to the water you'd think there are no concerns about Pine Creek. Not so—the stream desperately needs some attention. I can't help but wonder what a group of concerned anglers under the guidance of landowners and the Fish Commission could do here. The entire length of Pine from its limestone springs downstream 3 miles has few rocks. As you wade along the stream each and every stone and piece of sunken timber holds dozens of caddisfly larvae. If some rocks and debris were added to the bottom, the numbers of aquatic insects could increase greatly. With gravel added in some areas, trout would be better able to spawn. In addition, the 3 miles of limestone water on lower Pine Creek should have some special regulations placed on it.

Pine Creek begins near the Centre-Union County line. The upper 10 miles are small freestone water with native brook trout and some stocked trout just upstream from Woodward. George Harvey and I frequently fly-fished the freestone headwaters of Pine and have caught plenty of native brook trout. Below Woodward the stream goes underground and reappears just above where it crosses SR 2018.

Jon Witwer often fly-fishes Pine Creek to get away from the crowds on Elk and Penns Creeks. He occasionally sees a few green drakes on the water, but believes the most dependable hatch is the sulphur. "It's an excellent, consistent hatch," Jon says. When trout aren't feeding on one of the hatches they can easily feed on an abundant supply of scuds and cress bugs.

Check with Jon Witwer of Coburn for the latest hatches and conditions on Penns, Elk, and Pine Creeks. Jon and his wife, Jane, also operate a bed & breakfast at their home that caters to fly-fishers.

LITTLE JUNIATA RIVER
By Robert Budd

Access The "Little J" is easily reached by traveling 6 miles south from Tyrone on PA 453. From that point paved secondary roads parallel the stream to Spruce Creek. From Spruce Creek to Barree access is more difficult and is mainly by foot. Access has been somewhat impaired with the construction of a cyclone fence to keep anglers away from the railroad right-of-way. You have to walk a little farther but this section is quite picturesque; once you wade into the river you might just think you are in Montana. From Barree to Petersburg a secondary paved road again parallels the river. Pools are deep and wading can be dangerous. PA 305 crosses the river near Petersburg and 30 yards below, the Little Juniata joins with the Frankstown Branch to form the Juniata River. Here the two rivers form the upper end of the Warriors Ridge Dam, a hydroelectric project.

Special Regulations All-tackle trophy-trout water—13.5 miles, from the railroad bridge at the eastern (downstream) border of Ironville downstream to the mouth.

Rating ✳✳✳

Patterns to Match the Hatches Little Blue-Winged Olive Dun (#20), Early Brown Stonefly (#14), Grannom (#12 and #14), Yellow Caddis (#14), Yellow Crane Fly (#20), Tan Caddis (#14 to #20), Dark Green Caddis (#18), Green Caddis (#14 and #16), Light Cahill Dun and Spinner (#14), Gray Fox and Ginger Quill (#12), Tiny Blue-Winged Olive (*Pseudocloeon* spp.) (#20 to #24), Green Drake and Shad Fly (#10), Dark Blue Quill (#20), Cream Cahill (#14), Blue-Winged Olive Dun (#14 and #16), Blue Quill (#18), Slate Drake (#12 and #14), Yellow Drake Dun and Spinner (#12), Sulphur Dun and Spinner (#16 and #18), Trico (#24), Little White Mayfly (#28), White Mayfly (#16), Little Sulphur (#22), Winged Ant (#20)

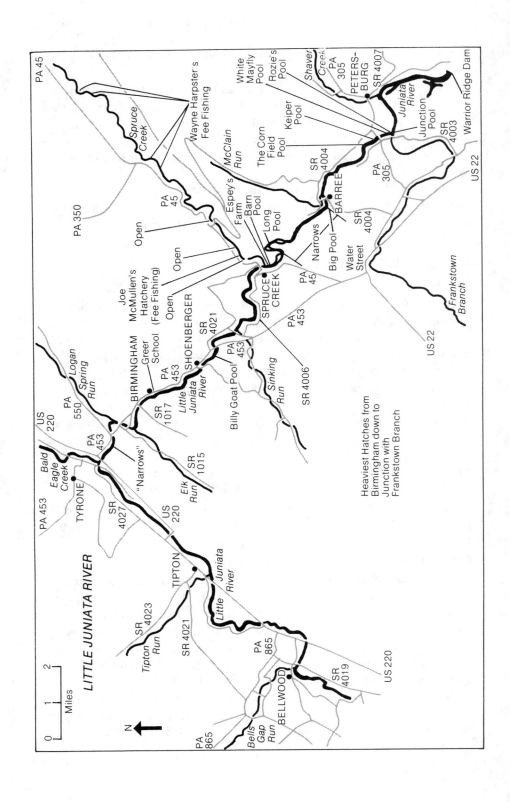

What a checkered history the Little Juniata River has had! Until 1968 the river flowed with a deep brown color from effluent upriver. Between 1968 and 1996 the river experienced several spills that threatened its very existence as a viable trout stream—but it survived.

Yes, the river recovered from pollution before and now has to do so again. Sometime in 1996 an insecticide (presumably) found its way into the water. A biological survey conducted on the Little Juniata documented that an unknown event occurred between the railroad bridge downstream of Ironville and the Honest Hollow Road bridge. This event severely impacted the macroinvertebrae community for at least 10 miles downstream. Fishermen who frequented the stream realized that the mayfly hatches in particular were not what they used to be; hence an aquatic biological investigation was conducted by the Department of Environmental Protection. Future biological surveys are scheduled on a regular basis to monitor recovery. Unfortunately, we will probably never know the who, what, or how of this incident, but fortunately, the river is recovering. In fact, the hatches below Spruce Creek, while not equal to what they were a few years ago, were fair to good in 1998, with the sulphur and cahill emergences leading the way. Above Spruce Creek the hatches are less prolific, but this doesn't seem to have affected the fishing or the health of the fish. A few fishermen told me that they had caught a few lean trout but I believe that may have been a result of random sampling. The fish I caught above Spruce Creek in 1998 were colorful, thick bodied, and as healthy as ever. In fact, the best morning I've ever had on the "Little J" was just this past June when, in a little over three and a half hours, I hooked 15 fish in the riffle water adjacent to the geological station just above the mouth of Spruce Creek. I did encounter some drop-off in the quality of fishing above the "Junkyard Pool" along PA 453 adjacent to the Greer School section.

Aware of what had happened in 1996, and of the disappointing hatches in 1997, I was anxious for the arrival of the 1998 trout season. In mid-April I went down to the Barree stretch to take some insect samples. After a period of prolonged rain, the river was in full spate. I didn't bother to rig a rod. I was accompanied by my son, Christopher, and friend, Lance DeFrancisco. Lance's son, Dave, came along too and insisted on bringing a rod "just in case." We parked at the turnaround at Barree and were preparing to walk upstream when Dave said he saw a rise adjacent to the bank. Ordinarily, this stretch of river is relatively slow, but it was moving fairly quickly now because of the recent runoff. Amazingly, two trout were rising in a back eddy created by a deadfall. This river previously had not had a grannom hatch to speak of, but on this day there were a few around that obviously had the trout interested. I knotted a size-14

Grannom pattern to Dave's tippet. The persistence and enthusiasm of youth overshadowed the pessimism of old age. Dave waded into position behind the two fish and promptly landed both of them. The larger fish was a beautiful 13- or 14-inch brown, nicely colored and in excellent condition.

The rest of the season continued to be a pleasant surprise on the Little Juniata. The usual hatches of caddis (green, yellow, tan, and grannom) and mayflies (sulphurs, March browns, blue-winged olives, green drakes, cahills, and white mayflies) appeared to improve. Even during periods of no apparent hatch activity the brown trout were eager to take dead-drifted Bead Head Pheasant Tail Nymphs in the riffle water that abounds in this river.

With a smaller population of aquatic insects, perhaps the trout at times were looking for terrestrials a bit more eagerly. Fishing terrestrials tight to the shaded banks and under overhanging branches produced plenty of trout. Above the town of Spruce Creek numerous limestone springs enter the river; during warm summer mornings you can actually see a mist on the surface indicating where the cool water enters. Concentrate your efforts here with cricket and beetle patterns and you can have a lot of fun.

Summertime trout fishing on the Little J can actually be quite enjoy-able; I have had some success fishing Little Blue-Winged Olives in the morning. My favorite summertime hatch on the Little Juniata, however, is the white mayfly, which usually appears around the third week of August. By that time of year a lot of the anglers have left for the golf course and you don't need to arrive in the middle of the afternoon to stake out your water, the way you do during the green drake frenzy. My best fish on the Little Juniata was caught during this hatch a few years ago. It was a hefty brown trout measuring 20 inches long (honest—just ask Charlie Meck!). Be prepared to concentrate your efforts on fishing emergers and spent pat-terns right at dark.

I was able to get to the river a few nights in late August and I was quite glad I did. Despite daytime temperatures approaching 90 degrees, the water temperature remained in the mid-60s. From 6:00 to 7:30 PM we found trout taking emerging caddis and white mayflies, as well as a few taking little sulphurs and crane flies; we had to be observant as to the riseform each fish was making. I switched to a Spent White Mayfly pat-tern at dark and did very well. The white mayflies were a bit sparse com-pared to recent years, but the fish were on them. My best Little Juniata trout of the 1998 season came during this hatch—a heavy 16- or 17-inch male that was beginning to sport his autumn colors.

The Little Juniata River flows south from Tyrone to Petersburg in central Pennsylvania. Above Tyrone the main river remains marginal except in sections where the main stem picks up productive tributaries like Bells Gap, Tipton Run, and the large Bald Eagle. Downriver a few hundred yards from the town, the river enters a narrows with high limestone cliffs. At this point the Juniata becomes a limestone river.

By eastern standards this is a large stream, ranging from 30 to 60 feet wide with a moderate drop of about 15 feet per mile. It has many good-sized pools, some of them 100 yards or more long. Riffles and moderate water abound. These sections are especially productive with Bead Head Nymphs. Wading can be dangerous, and felt-bottomed boots are a big help. Some fast-water sections are difficult or impossible to cross even in low to moderate flows.

The last edition of *Trout Streams of Pennsylvania* noted concerns that an upstream sewage-treatment plant was impacting the health of the Little Juniata, but there is hope that this will become less of an issue as more state-of-the-art treatments are employed. Some of the prime water remains private but there is still plenty of fishing available to those who don't wish to pay fees. The other good news is that the creel limits have been changed: you can now keep only two fish over 14 inches per day during the regular trout season. No fish may be kept from Labor Day to the first day of trout season. With new regulations and improving hatches, the Little Juniata River will only get better as a major trout-fishing resource. In 1998 the river was good to excellent. Future years could be awesome.

For up-to-the-minute information on hatches and water conditions call Allan Bright, the proprietor of Spruce Creek Outfitters, at 814-632-3071. His shop is stocked with all the appropriate patterns and tackle necessary to have an enjoyable time on the Little Juniata River. He is one of the best trout fishermen I know, so heed his suggestions well. You'll also find another fly-shop, Six Springs (814-632-7180), in the town of Spruce Creek. Run by Dave McMullen, this shop guides fishermen on the Espy Farm section of the river.

ELK CREEK

Access PA 445, Millheim Narrows Road, parallels much of the open water above Millheim, and SR 2011 parallels the stream from Millheim downstream to Coburn.

Rating ✳✳✳

Patterns to Match the Hatches Little Blue-Winged Olive Dun (#20), Hendrickson (#14), Sulphur Dun and Spinner (#16), March Brown (#12),

Dark Green Drake (#8), Green Drake (#10), Blue-Winged Olive Dun (#14 and #16), Pale Evening Dun *(Ephemerella dorothea) (#18)*, Blue Quill and Dark Brown Spinner (#18), Yellow Drake (#12), Trico (#24)

Talk about memories—this stream holds plenty of them for me. I still remember vividly the day that my son, Bryan, Vince Gigliotti of Punxsutawney, and I arrived at Elk on a late-May morning. It turned out to be one of those miserable early-spring days. It began drizzling before we arrived and continued the entire day. But guess what? From the minute we arrived at the stream at 10 AM until we left at 4 PM we saw sulphurs on the water—along with a continuous show of trout rising to these mayflies. That was six hours of nonstop matching the hatch. I sat back much of the time and took photos while Bryan and Vince caught one streambred brown after another. Not once did the action slow down.

I also remember clearly those summer mornings spent matching one of the several blue-winged olive hatches that this fertile limestone stream holds. I'd sit by the stream for hours and wait for trout to rise to the insects. In the 1970s I spent at least several hours a week on Elk Creek.

But that was then and this is now, and things have changed dramatically on Elk Creek in the past few years. Several owners of land bordering the upper end of the stream attempted a few years ago to place special regulations on the stream. They were upset—and rightly so—at anglers coming onto their property and killing trout. For the past two decades Elk has not received plantings of trout; it depends solely on its streambred population. More recently 2 miles of the upper end of Elk, just above the narrows and Millheim, have become a private club called the Elk Creek Fishing Association. Still, there is some excellent water left open on the stream. You will find some more land posted at Park Road in Millheim.

Elk holds a generous share of hatches throughout the season. In early April you'll see some hendricksons and blue quills, but the best is yet to come. It's the sulphur in May and June and the March brown that bring some heavy Elk Creek browns to the surface to feed. Into June, July, August—and even September—you'll find hatches on this prolific limestone stream. Blue quills appear for more than two months in late summer. I've seen at least three species of blue-winged olive duns (*Drunella* spp.) appear during the day in mid- and late season.

At the upper end of the stream near the town of Smulton you'll find excellent accommodations at the Centre Mills Bed and Breakfast. Proprietor Maria Davison will make you feel at home and help you find your way around area limestone streams.

Pine Creek, another limestone, joins Elk near the town of Coburn. Elk enters Penns Creek just a couple of miles downstream from Pine. The cool water from Elk helps preserve Penns Creek as a top-notch trout fishery.

Elk flows for about 6 miles before it enters Penns. You'll find many productive pockets, riffles, and pools on this 20- to 30-foot-wide stream. Again, much of the upper end of this water has already gone private; please respect landowners on this great limestone stream.

SPRING CREEK

Access Most of Spring Creek is readily accessible by car—much of the creek runs within less than 100 yards of a paved road. The upper end of the stream, from its source to Oak Hall, is posted water. A secondary road from the limestone quarry just below Oak Hall to Lemont parallels the upper end of the creek. PA 26 crosses the stream at Lemont, and PA 550 and 150 bring you close to the stream near Bellefonte and Milesburg.

Special Regulations Heritage-trout angling—1 mile, that section on Fish Commission property known as Fishermans Paradise. Miscellaneous waters special regulations—from the bridge at Oak Hall above Neidig Brother's Limestone Company to the mouth. No-kill zone—unlawful to kill or possess any fish. All fish caught must be returned immediately.

Rating ✳✳✳✳

Patterns to Match the Hatches Blue Quill (#18), Little Blue-Winged Olive Dun (#20), Sulphur Dun and Spinner (#16), Light Cahill (#14), Blue-Winged Olive Dun (#14), Trico (#24), Green Caddis (# 14, #16, and #18), Little Sulphur (#22 and #24), Slate Drake (#12 and #14), Tan Crane Fly (#18 and #20)

I was lucky to have had the opportunity to fly-fish Spring Creek in 1954, when the legendary green drake hatch appeared in late May. How was I to know that I had just witnessed one of the last good hatches of green drakes that this limestone stream would ever display? Thousands of coffin fly spinners fell that last night, as green drake duns greeted me on my first trip to this showcase of the East. Unfortunately, evil days were not far ahead.

Great crimes have been perpetrated on Spring Creek. In the late 1950s Spring received several doses of raw sewage, and many of the trout and most of the hatches vanished forever. Then in the 1960s and 1970s Spring endured additional pollution—this time from chemicals like Depone and Mynex. Shortly after the last contamination the state decided to take the threatened stream off the stocking list and make it a "no-kill" stream. Guess what happened? Some of the hardier, more resilient hatches returned in abundant numbers, and the brown trout population multiplied.

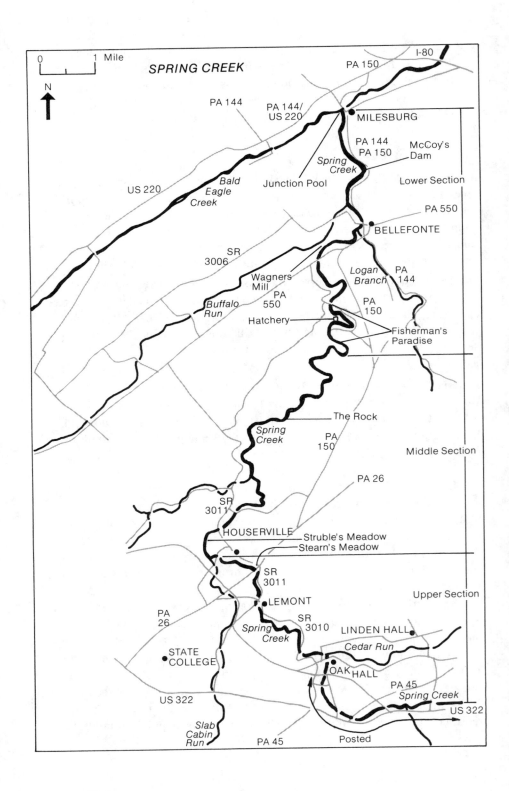

0   1 Mile

N

SPRING CREEK

I-80

PA 150

PA 144

PA 144/
US 220

MILESBURG

PA 144
PA 150

McCoy's
Dam

US 220

*Bald
Eagle
Creek*

*Spring
Creek*

Junction Pool

Lower Section

PA 550

BELLEFONTE

SR
3006

Wagners
Mill

*Logan
Branch*

PA
144

*Buffalo
Run*

PA
550

PA
150

Hatchery

Fisherman's
Paradise

The Rock

*Spring
Creek*

PA
150

Middle Section

PA 26

SR
3011

HOUSERVILLE

Struble's Meadow

Stearn's Meadow

SR
3011

Upper Section

PA
26

LEMONT

SR
3010

LINDEN HALL

*Spring
Creek*

Cedar Run

STATE
COLLEGE

OAK HALL

PA 45
Spring Creek

US 322

US 322

*Slab
Cabin
Run*

PA 45

Posted

Now, 17 years after the last trout was stocked in the water, Spring boasts abundant, hefty streambred browns. Still, it no longer harbors the green drake, brown drake, or yellow drake, or for that matter many of its once-prominent hatches.

It's interesting to visit the Frost Museum at Penn State University, just 5 miles from Spring Creek. Here you can examine vials of mayfly species found in Pennsylvania, including the only remnants of the fabulous hatches Spring Creek once accommodated. Many of these vials house mayflies from Spring Creek before it fell prey to pollution—mayflies that will probably never return.

Luckily, all is not lost, for the stream or for the hatches. Spring Creek has valiantly made a comeback, and three good mayfly and a couple of excellent caddisfly hatches now emerge annually. The sulphur and light cahill seem to be somewhat pollution-resistant species. These were the first two mayflies to appear on the Little Juniata after its bout with pollution, and both have remained on Spring in substantial numbers. The sulphur appears on Spring from mid-May to mid-June. Sometimes when this species first appears in May it does so in the early afternoon. If you're lucky enough to be on the stream at that time, plan to fish over rising trout for several hours. Within a couple of days of its initial appearance, however, the hatch resumes its normal emergence time, after 7:00 PM. The sulphur spinner, with its tan body, can also be important to copy. The spinner is less predictable, since it sometimes appears before the dun, sometimes after, and sometimes is of no consequence at all.

The other pollution-tolerant mayfly, the light cahill, appears about the same time of year as the sulphur but usually earlier in the evening. It's an added bonus to fly-fishing Spring Creek in late May, because you're consistently meeting and fishing over two hatches. The cahill is larger than the sulphur (the cahill is a size 12 or 14, and the sulphur a size 16) and serves as a harbinger of the heavier hatch to come—the sulphur.

The trico hatch and spinner fall are extremely predictable on Spring Creek. The middle section of the stream was almost void of this species until a few years ago, and the upper and lower sections have dependable hatches and falls. The trico falls in large numbers by the second week in July and continues to do so well into September. Spinner falls of this species occur between 7:00 and 9:00 AM on the hottest days and from 9:00 AM to noon in September. On warm, muggy mornings the spinner fall often lasts less than half an hour.

Don't overlook the importance of crane flies and midges on Spring Creek. You'll find the former on the water from March through September in body colors of creamish orange and tan. You can often fish over pods of trout rising to afternoon hatches of midges from November through

February. Carry a Gray Midge pattern in size 24 to match these important winter hatches.

There are three distinct sections of Spring Creek, with different hatches and types of water in each. The upper section, from the source above Linden Hall downstream to Houserville, is a small meadowland limestone stream. This upper section harbors a good number of sulphurs and a healthy trico hatch, but it also has other hatches not present below. Several species of blue-winged olives (*Ephemerella cornuta* and others) appear daily in June and July in this upper section along with several blue quills and several blue duns (*Baetis tricaudatus* and others). Blue duns, or little blue-winged olive duns as they are also called, appear as early as March and April.

The middle section of Spring Creek, from Houserville downstream to the upper end of Fishermans Paradise, was almost totally void of hatches for years, for it was this section that received the brunt of the worst pollution. Within the last few years, however, several mayflies have feebly repopulated this area. The trico now appears but not in the numbers it attains above or below, and the sulphur and light cahill have also reappeared in limited quantities.

The lower section of Spring, from Fishermans Paradise downstream 6 miles to the creek's junction with Bald Eagle Creek, is larger, more productive water. Hatches like the sulphur, trico, and green caddis become important again. Here you'll encounter green caddis hatches copied with a size-16 or -18 downwing almost every morning in July and August. Here too you'll find trout rising in August and September for tan crane flies—very common on the water after midmorning. Fishermans Paradise, once a well-maintained and heavily stocked no-harvest, fly-fishing-only section, has lost much of its previous notoriety.

Spring Creek has a relatively moderate flow with plenty of productive pocket water. The stream ranges from 30 to 40 feet from bank to bank and is fairly easy to wade, although aquatic plants make wading difficult in some areas. Several excellent tributaries enter Spring Creek, and most of them contain streambred brown trout. Cedar Run, a typical pastoral limestone stream, enters Spring at Oak Hall. Downstream, just below Lemont, Slab Cabin Run enters. This too has native trout but was also the cause of much of the pollution; it was a minor tributary to Slab Cabin that carried effluents from the State College sewage plant. Two other important tributaries enter near Bellefonte. Logan Branch holds plenty of large trout and enters Spring in the center of Bellefonte. Buffalo Run, another important native brown trout stream, joins Spring Creek at the lower end of Bellefonte. All of the major tributaries to Spring Creek are productive limestone streams.

Recently a wealthy executive purchased a mile-long section of Spring Creek just above PA 550. He then posted and fenced in this extremely productive section of the stream. The Fish Commission in one of its more prudent moves decided to purchase this land from the owner, and this productive stretch is now open for all to fish.

Since its designation as a no-kill stream, Spring Creek has made a remarkable recovery as a trout fishery, with plenty of healthy streambred browns. The entire stream from Oak Hall to its mouth is classified as a no-kill zone. Try fishing the stream from May 15 to June 10 for some exciting hatches and plenty of trout. Flyfisher's Paradise, in Lemont, can advise you about the conditions and hatches on the stream. Steve Sywensky and Dan Shields know the area streams well.

PENNS CREEK

Access From Spring Mills 6 miles downstream to Coburn there is access to most of Penns Creek. Access to the section from Coburn to Cherry Run is limited. You can reach the upper section by driving to the old railroad tunnel about 3 miles below Coburn, then hiking down the old railroad track. Or you can enter at Ingleby from the north or Poe Paddy State Park from the south, following the railroad upstream or downstream. Access to the Cherry Run section is no problem: A road parallels the creek down to Weikert. The section around Weikert is marginal.

Special Regulations All-tackle trophy-trout water—7.0 miles, from the confluence with Elk Creek downstream to the catch-and-release area. Catch-and-release—3.9 miles, from Swift Run downstream to the R. J. Soper property line. Trout—14-inch minimum size limit, creek limit two per day from opening day to Labor Day. All other species—inland regulations apply.

Rating ✳✳✳✳

Patterns to Match the Hatches Grannom (#10 and #12), Blue Quill (#18), Hendrickson (#14), Quill Gordon (#14), Little Black Caddis (#16), Chocolate Dun and Spinner (#16), Gray Fox (#12), Ginger Quill Spinner (#12), Light Cahill (#14), Sulphur Dun and Spinner (#16), Green Drake and Coffin Fly (#10), Dark Blue Quill (#18), Tan Caddis (#14), Blue-Winged Olive Dun (#16), Yellow Drake Dun and Spinner (#12), Great Stonefly (#10), Trico Spinner (#24), Little White Mayfly (#26), Slate Drake (#12 and #14), Dark Slate Drake and Rusty Spinner (#8), White Mayfly (#14 and #16), Dark Olive Caddis (#14), Dark Brown Caddis (#16)

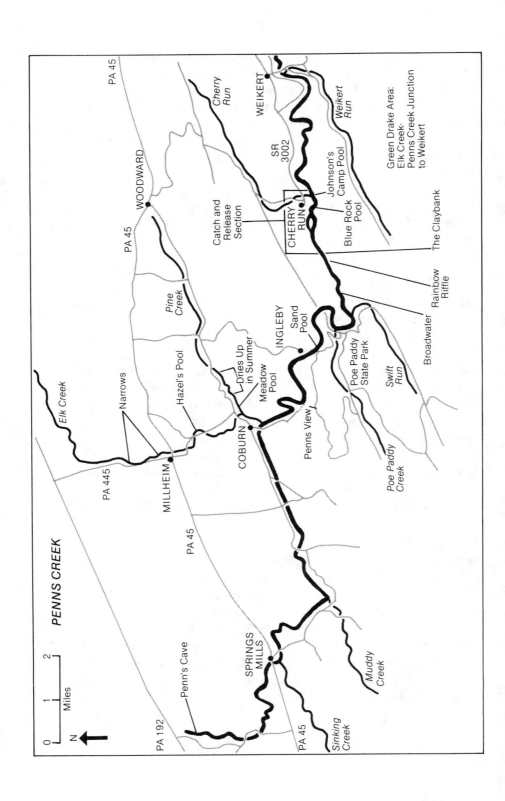

PENNS CREEK

N

0 1 2
Miles

Penn's Cave

PA 192

PA 45

SPRINGS MILLS

Sinking Creek

Muddy Creek

Elk Creek

PA 445

Narrows

MILLHEIM

Hazel's Pool

PA 45

COBURN

Dries Up in Summer

Meadow Pool

Penns View

Poe Paddy Creek

Poe Paddy State Park

Swift Run

Broadwater

Pine Creek

PA 45

WOODWARD

Catch and Release Section

INGLEBY

Sand Pool

Rainbow Riffle

The Claybank

Cherry Run

PA 45

WEIKERT

SR 3002

Weikert Run

CHERRY RUN

Johnson's Camp Pool

Blue Rock Pool

Green Drake Area: Elk Creek-Penns Creek Junction to Weikert

Fourth of July on Penns Creek, the famous but sometimes frustrating limestone stream in central Pennsylvania. By 10:00 AM the temperature had barely reached 58 degrees, and a fine drizzle fell. At the lower end of the catch-and-release section on this holiday, no one was fly-fishing except me. Two other fair-weather anglers had returned their gear to their cars seemingly disgusted with the depressing weather. I was the only nut remaining on the entire stretch of that productive water. I headed up the abandoned railroad bed toward the R. B. Winter estate.

Swallows cruised near the water's surface, crisscrossing upstream, downstream, and across stream. Just in front of me thousands of blue-winged olive duns floated, half dazed, swirling around in an eddy. Normally this species *(Drunella lata)* takes off rapidly from the surface when emerging, but the unusually cold weather today prevented the duns from escaping quickly from the water. Five, 10, 15 trout rose in a small riffle in front of me.

I quickly tied on a size-16 Blue-Winged Olive Dun, nervously finishing the improved clinch knot. The leader slipped out of the second loop, and I had to retie the knot. More and more duns emerged and added to the incredible number already resting on the surface. When it seemed like every trout in that section had taken my Blue-Wing, I moved upstream. Ahead of me lay some moderate water with a boulder-strewn area at its head. Here maybe 15 more trout lined up in a feeding lane and fed in a frenzy on the duns. At least 10 of the trout in that stretch sucked in the dry fly. I continued upstream for about a half mile, fishing every pool, riffle, and pocket that harbored rising trout. Remember, while this unbelievable fly-fishing over a hatch continued, not one other person took part in the excitement—not one other fly-fisherman shared this memorable experience. Three hours, 65 trout, and seven imitations later, I quit.

Not long after I wrote about the preceding incident on Penns Creek I received a letter from Andrew Leitzinger of Collegeville, Pennsylvania. It seems Andrew had experienced that same memorable hatch on Penns that day, 10 years ago. He'd fished the hatch 2 miles upstream from me. He wrote:

> On July 4, 1979, in the late morning after a cold rain, I fished the upper no-kill stretch of Penns Creek from the Broadwaters to the Upper Island. I found the surface covered with tiny blue-winged olive mayflies. I fished this stretch with a size-20 Midge Adams and hooked and released 30 trout between 10 and 17 inches long. I missed many, many more. The water surface was quite broken as far as you could see with feeding fish.
>
> I fished that day in complete solitude (I thought). I was cold, happy, and alone. I can remember how my shoulders ached from so

many hours, and my thumb had become tattered by the teeth of the many trout that I had released. I stopped fishing at about 5:00 PM because I had reached a state just short of exhaustion. I exalted the cold gray heavens above me and gave thanks for a wonderful and unique gift.

So when I read your book and came across the passage on your experience at Penns Creek, I wondered what the odds were that such conditions had occurred more than once on a Fourth of July in the past 10 years: a cold rain, a great hatch of blue-winged olives, and a nearly deserted stream. If our two days were separate in time, then a statistical phenomenon has occurred to be noted! But if, as I hope, those two days were one and the same, then I am glad to know that one other person was able to share the exhilaration I felt that day. Those days, when all things come together, are few and far between and should never be taken for granted.

Andrew and I experienced the same hatch on the same day just 2 miles away from one another. If you're fortunate enough to hit a blue-winged olive dun hatch under the same circumstances, do it.

What makes Penns Creek such an excellent trout stream? Hatches? Number and size of trout? Good water conditions all year long? Beautiful scenery? Plenty of open space to fly-fish? All of the above. What fly-fisherman hasn't heard of the great green drake on this hallowed stream? What fly-fisherman hasn't had reports of the lunkers caught during this hatch or the following spinner fall?

Penns Creek has received much notoriety in the last few decades, and much of it is warranted. To many fishermen, including fly-fishers, Penns Creek is productive only until the green drake has finished its annual ritual, about the first week in June. Nothing could be farther from the truth. You saw earlier that Penns contains some prolific, productive late-season hatches like the blue-winged olive duns in June and July. Few fly-fishermen take advantage of another late-June hatch, the golden drake. This mayfly (*Potamanthus* spp.) appears nightly for a week on Penns near the end of June. Tricos succeed in July and August, and slate drakes are found well into October.

Superb fly-fishing develops early on Penns Creek. The lower section around Weikert has a decent Hendrickson hatch around April 21, and most of the stream contains a concentrated hach of caddisflies called grannoms at about the same time. Joe Dougherty of Lewisburg has fished the Hendrickson hatch near Weikert for years. He says the hatch never gets extremely heavy, but still it brings plenty of trout to the surface. The grannom on Penns can be as frustrating and unrewarding as the cream caddis is on Pine Creek. Thousands of caddisflies in the air this early in the season thrill many fly-fishermen but often don't persuade many trout into rising. Many times the air is filled with the large dark grannoms on this fertile limestone stream, but no trout appear.

Penns Creek emerges from a limestone cavern at Penns Cave just a couple of miles north of Spring Mills in Centre County. It is a cold, productive alkaline stream for its first 5 miles, but much of the water north of PA 45 is posted. The section with the heaviest hatches and the largest trout, however, is the 15-mile segment that extends from Coburn to Cherry Run.

Just upstream from Coburn, Penns is slowed by several small ponds and lacks any protective canopy. As a result this section warms quickly. But just a few hundred feet below Coburn a cold limestone tributary, Elk Creek, enters. Elk injects a generous amount of cold water into the main stem, creating a great trout stream for the next 20 miles.

The Fish Commission has set aside a 4-mile section near Cherry Run as a catch-and-release area. Fly-fishing on this part of Penns produces lunker trout during the green drake hatch.

Penns is most often renowned for its green drake hatch in late May. Fish the stream when the "shad fly" is on and you'll meet hundreds of fly-fishermen on the water, each with his own favorite pattern to match the upcoming hatch. It often happens that, when the green drake appears, five or six other significant aquatic insects arrive on the water at the same time. Anglers may become frustrated with this diversity of insects, but many continue to use a Green Drake even though trout are feeding on another phase of the same insect (like the emerging nymph), or are surfacing for a light cahill, sulphur, sulphur spinner, gray fox, ginger quill, or one of many other species. More times than I care to remember I've quit the stream in disgust in these confusing circumstances. Like so many others who plan to fish the hatch, I use a Green Drake pattern no matter what else takes place that evening—a serious blunder when you're fishing the hatch on Penns Creek.

It's mid-June, however, and the hordes that have visited Penns are gone for another year. What happens now? You already know that Penns hosts a fantastic blue-winged olive hatch. But it contains more hatches even later in the season. Slate drakes (*Isonychia matilda*) emerge on many September afternoons in enough numbers to bring trout to the surface one more time. By that time of year the water is still in the mid- to high 50s in the afternoon, and the air is cooler. These cool days prevent the slate drake duns' typical speedy escape from the surface. Fishing when this hatch appears can be your one last triumph of the season.

Penns drains six main tributaries. Sinking Creek enters at Spring Mills, adding tannic acid and warm water to the main stem. Sinking

Creek's headwaters are in the boglike area of Bear Meadows. Downstream 10 miles the largest and most influential tributary to Penns, Elk Creek, joins. In the Poe Paddy State Park area, Poe Paddy Creek and Swift Creek flow into Penns. At the lower end of the catch-and-release area Cherry Run, another excellent tributary, adds volume. A few more miles downstream Weikert Run enters.

Wading on Penns can be treacherous. In some areas deep pools lined with huge hidden boulders present obvious problems to the angler. Other sections, especially from Coburn downstream for about 5 miles, are easier to traverse.

BALD EAGLE CREEK (JULIAN)

Access US 220 parallels the stream from Port Matilda to Milesburg.

Rating ✳✳

Patterns to Match the Hatches Little Black Stonefly (#18), Little Black Caddis (#16), Quill Gordon (#12 and #14), Blue Quill (#16 and #18), Hendrickson (#14), Black Quill *(Ameletus ludens)* and Early Brown Spinner (#14), Pale Evening Dun (#16 and #18), Gray Fox and Ginger Quill (#14), Slate Drake (#14), Blue-Winged Olive Dun (#14), Light Cahill (#14), Yellow Drake Dun and Spinner (#12), White Mayfly (#16), Dark Slate Drake and Dark Rusty Spinner (#6 and #8)

For more than 15 years I have begun the trout-fishing season on the Bald Eagle near Julian in central Pennsylvania. Normally my son, Bryan, Mel Neidig, Fred Templin, and a few other anglers join me in that first-day ritual. All those years we have started the season with hundreds of other fishermen just below Julian. When 8:00 AM arrives all of us cast our weighted Woolly Buggers and Muddlers into riffles and pools teeming with recently stocked trout. Meanwhile, the anglers near us cast assorted spinners, minnows, worms, salmon eggs, cheese, or anything else that seems to catch trout.

Opening day the past few years has seen warmer-than-usual water on the stream. This past year the water temperature at the start of the season was 52 degrees. Woolly Buggers proved to be effective early in the morning, but by 10:00 AM most of the trout in the section we fished had either been caught or frightened by the anglers' commotion. Soon the crowded stream emptied, and we sat back and decided what our next move should be.

While we sat on the bank a few hendricksons began to emerge. Soon the few turned into an all-out hatch, with hundreds of duns on the pool in front of us. First one trout rose—the first of the year—then several joined in the search for food on the surface. Mel couldn't wait and quickly tied on a dry fly to imitate the emerging dun. One cast and he had a trout. Soon he aroused our interest with a second trout on the imitation. Within minutes all four of us tied on dry flies and began casting to rising trout— trout that were rising two hours before noon in the middle of April.

The hatch lasted for five hours that day, and trout continued to rise in concert with the hatch. All of us continued to catch trout throughout the afternoon. What an opening day on the Bald Eagle!

The Bald Eagle flows just 5 miles northwest of Spring Creek, but the two streams are very different. Water temperature on the Bald Eagle rises rapidly in the heat of summer, the stream loses much of its volume, and it holds few if any holdover trout. Spring Creek, on the other hand, remains relatively cool throughout the summer, retains a fairly constant water flow, and holds only streambred brown trout. Why the great discrepancy between these two neighboring streams? Spring Creek has been blessed with plenty of limestone springs, whereas the Bald Eagle is a typical flat freestone stream.

From Port Matilda to Milesburg, almost 20 miles, the Bald Eagle is a freestone stream that becomes a marginal trout stream in early June. What a pity, since this upper water has some fantastic late-summer hatch-es like the yellow drake, the white mayfly, a light cahill *(Heptagenia mar-ginalis)*, and many, many pale evening duns *(Heptagenia* spp.). On many occasions when the yellow drake appears in late June and early July, the water temperature approaches 80 degrees.

You saw earlier how Hendrickson duns catch many anglers by sur-prise on the opening day of the trout season, and how those who are ade-quately prepared for a hatch experience unbelievable dry-fly fishing. A 50-degree or higher water temperature on the creek provides a sure sign that the hatch will appear. Shortly after the Hendrickson appears, the black quill emerges on the slower sections of the stream. The Bald Eagle holds the only concentrated hatch of black quills in the area. Shortly after the middle of May the gray fox begins its sporadic appearance on the Bald Eagle. The large mayflies usually emerge in the afternoon, but on warm spring days they sometimes appear with a burst just at dusk. The spinner of the gray fox is the ginger quill. Predictable and heavy spinner falls occur nightly at 8:30.

The upper 20 miles of the stream flow within 200 yards of US 220. In this area the Bald Eagle is easy to wade and contains a bottom of com-pressed shale with few boulders. The stream ranges from 20 to 30 feet wide, with many deep pools but few fishable riffles. There are a few areas on this marginal upper section that provide cool water throughout the year. Cool mountain springs seeping from Bald Eagle Mountain to the

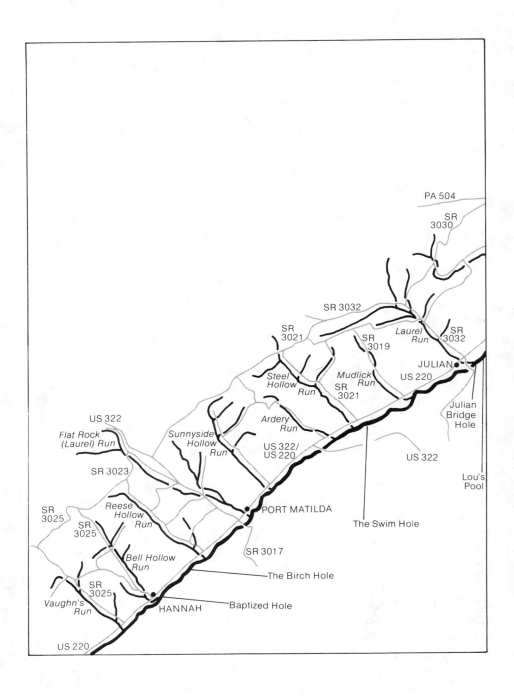

PA 504

SR 3030

SR 3032

SR 3021

SR 3019

Laurel Run

SR 3032

Steel Hollow Run

Mudlick Run

SR 3021

JULIAN

US 220

US 322

Flat Rock (Laurel) Run

Sunnyside Hollow Run

Ardery Run

US 322/ US 220

Julian Bridge Hole

US 322

Lou's Pool

SR 3023

SR 3025

Reese Hollow Run

SR 3025

Bell Hollow Run

PORT MATILDA

The Swim Hole

SR 3017

The Birch Hole

SR 3025

Vaughn's Run

HANNAH

Baptized Hole

US 220

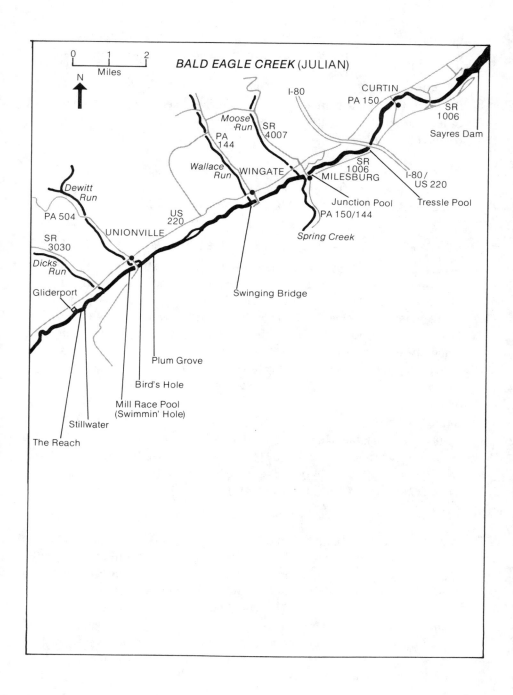

BALD EAGLE CREEK (JULIAN)

0   1   2
Miles

N

CURTIN
PA 150

I-80

SR
1006

Sayres Dam

Moose
Run   SR
PA   4007
144

SR
1006
MILESBURG

I-80 /
US 220

Wallace
Run   WINGATE

Junction Pool   Tressle Pool

Dewitt
Run

PA 150/144

PA 504

US
220

Spring Creek

UNIONVILLE

SR
3030

Dicks
Run

Swinging Bridge

Gliderport

Plum Grove

Bird's Hole

Mill Race Pool
(Swimmin' Hole)

Stillwater

The Reach

southeast provide some relief to the stream. And some fine tributaries with good supplies of brown and brook trout maintain low temperatures throughout the season. Travel up one of these branches in late July and you'll likely see many trout that have migrated upstream from the Bald Eagle.

All the streams entering the Bald Eagle do so from the escarpment to the northwest, the Allegheny Plateau. Branches like Flat Rock Run (also called Laurel) at Port Matilda, Laurel Run at Julian, Dicks Run near Unionville, and Wallace Run at Wingate feed some cold water into the Bald Eagle.

When fishing the extensive Bald Eagle, your choices are simple. If you plan to fish the stream before mid-May, try the water from Port Matilda to Wingate. After the middle of May, fish the lower end near Curtin.

LOWER BALD EAGLE CREEK (BELOW MILESBURG)

Access You'll find access to the lower Bald Eagle in Milesburg (on the northwestern side of the stream); a half mile below Milesburg (off SR 1006); where I-80 crosses Water Street (SR 1006); above and at Curtin Bridge; and at Dowdys Hole. The entire 6 miles of water hold plenty of large trout. Plan to walk quite a bit. Once in the water you can usually wade up- or downstream. Even if you get away from the access areas you should find plenty of trout in this productive limestone stream. It has been getting more attention recently so expect to see other anglers—even in late summer.

Rating ✳✳✳✳

Patterns to Match the Hatches Little Black Stonefly (#18), Little Blue-Winged Olive Dun (#20), Sulphur (#16), March Brown (#14), Slate Drake (#12 and #14), Dark Blue Quill (#20), Yellow Drake (#12), Blue Quill (#18), Trico (#24), Green Caddis (#14 and #16), White Mayfly (#14), Pale Evening Dun (#16)

When the Pennsylvania Fish and Boat Commission does something really significant to positively affect the future of a trout stream it's important to give the group credit. The quality of fishing on lower Bald Eagle Creek might be forever altered by its decision to stock fingerling trout in the summer of 1998. This could be a giant step forward in the management of this fishery for trout.

In that year the commission began stocking approximately 34,000 3-to 4-inch brown trout in this 6-mile stretch. Tom Greene, Coldwater Unit Leader of the Fisheries Management Division, will evaluate this fingerling stocking program over a five-year period and come up with permanent recommendations.

Will stocking these fingerlings on the lower Bald Eagle work? Only time will tell, but Tom Greene said that the Fish Commission is taking advantage of the continuous cold water from Spring Creek. In the 25 years I've fly-fished this stream I have never seen water temperatures rise above 72 degrees. Only on the hottest days of summer have I seen temperatures higher than the 60s.

What about the food supply for these fingerlings? The stream does hold some good hatches, but it remains to be seen whether this supply is

John Randolph with a holdover brown trout taken during a trico fall on the Bald Eagle below Milesburg.

heavy enough for all of these trout. The lower Bald Eagle holds a fairly good sulphur hatch that begins in mid-May and continues through mid-June. At the same time of the year you'll see an increasing number of March browns emerging. Late in the season the stream hosts a fair trico hatch and spinner fall every morning from mid-July through September. I've already hunted ducks in mid-October just above the Sayers Dam, and while hidden under cover near a fog rising from the stream, I've seen trout rising to a few tricos and blue quills.

A fairly new hatch, the dark blue quill, has just begun appearing on the Bald Eagle in the past couple of years. This size-20 dun emerges in the evening and the almost black spinner falls early in the morning in early and mid-June.

What about downwings? The lower Bald Eagle has its share. I'll never forget the time I fly-fished just below Dowdys Hole in early May. That afternoon thousands and thousands of size-16 green caddis emerged, and I saw a pod of about 10 fish on the far side rising to them. I hiked upstream, waded across, and headed back downstream to where these fish rose. I cast above one rising almost imperceptibly and, on the first drift, it took my downwing pattern. The heavy fish headed downstream and only after a 10-minute struggle did I land it. In my net I saw a 5-pound carp. Yes, a carp. Those fish rising to caddisflies were all carp.

The lower Bald Eagle has a good number of holdover trout. Annually I land a couple of trout on this stream in the 20-inch category. I still remember vividly my New Year's Eve fishing trip to the lower Bald Eagle with Bob Budd. On that late-afternoon fishing trip Bob landed—well, almost—two heavy rainbows.

This stream holds some of the deepest pools and most productive riffles of almost any trout stream I know. Some pools are over 10 feet deep and hold deep riffles and glides in their upper reaches. On occasion I've seen anglers float down this 40- to 60-foot-wide stream in canoes.

During summer about three-quarters of the flow in the lower Bald Eagle comes from Spring Creek and some of its limestone tributaries. In Bellefonte, Logan Branch and Buffalo Run, both great limestone streams, enter Spring Creek. Spring Creek then enters the upper Bald Eagle just above the bridge in Milesburg. The upper Bald Eagle warms quickly in summer and trout seek out cool springs and tributaries. Spring Creek, in contrast, boasts 60-degree temperatures all summer long. It's interesting to stand on the bridge in Milesburg in January and look upstream. To your right you'll see the freestone Bald Eagle entering. To your front left Spring Creek joins. Usually you'll see the upper Bald Eagle ice covered while Spring Creek flows clear.

Will stocking fingerlings on lower Bald Eagle Creek truly affect the quality of fishing on this stream? I predict that it will become one of the top streams in the state—thanks in large part to the foresight of the Pennsylvania Fish and Boat Commission.

BALD EAGLE CREEK (TYRONE)

Access US 220 parallels the Bald Eagle–Tyrone near Tyrone.

Rating ✳✳

Patterns to Match the Hatches Little Blue-Winged Olive Dun (#20), Blue Quill (#18), Quill Gordon (#14), Hendrickson (#14), Sulphur Dun and Spinner (#16), Green Drake (#12), Slate Drake (#14), Pale Evening Dun and Spinner (#18), Yellow Drake (#12)

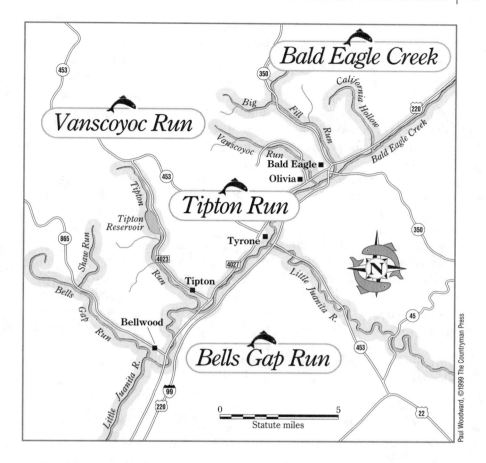

There's a section of the Bald Eagle–Tyrone near Vail that I fish often. It contains a pool about 100 yards long with a productive riffle above. I regularly visit this area in mid-April just before noon when I can depend on seeing the blue quill emerge. Thousands of these dependable mayflies appear in the riffle and drift to the pool below. A size-18 imitation consistently performs well during this extensive hatch.

The Bald Eagle–Tyrone (I'll refer to it as the BET) is a productive tributary to the Little Juniata River. Although it and the Bald Eagle near Julian begin in the same valley, the BET is better, having a healthy supply of native brook and brown trout. These two Bald Eagle Creeks have their headwaters in a swampy area a few hundred feet from each other. The BET, however, seldom has temperatures above 70 degrees all summer, because it drains two highly productive and sizable cold-water tributaries, Big Fill and Vanscoyoc Runs. Both streams have a good supply of native brown and brook trout, and their summer temperatures rarely go above 65 degrees. Both tributaries flow into the BET within a mile and create a cold, productive stream about 30 feet wide, though barely 5 miles long. But the BET harbors many great hatches.

After an initial spurt of blue quills, quill gordons, and a few hendricksons, few mayflies appear again until late May. Then within the span of a couple of weeks mayflies like the green drake, slate drake, and, by mid-June, yellow drake produce rising trout.

Sulphurs too are important on the BET. The smallest of the three (*Ephemerella dorothea*) appears most abundantly. This size-18 sulphur usually appears throughout most of the month of June, just at dusk. The yellow drake emerges on the BET in numbers equal to the hatch on the other Bald Eagle, but here trout feed on the drakes freely, since the water temperature in late June is usually in the mid-60s. As with many Pennsylvania streams, the BET is fished continuously from the beginning of the season until early June. For the remainder of the season the once heavily worn paths along the stream are restored to their natural appearance. Much of the best fly-fishing occurs after early June, however. Some of the water above the town of Bald Eagle is posted. The BET is easy to wade and has only a few large boulders. It contains the characteristic riffle-pool-riffle-pool sequence. Try this stream in late June when the showpiece appears, the yellow drake.

BIG FILL RUN

Access PA 350 parallels most of the Big Fill. You reach this road at the town of Bald Eagle. There's about 4 miles of fishable stream before it flows into the Little Bald Eagle.

Rating ✳✳

Patterns to Match the Hatches Early Brown Stonefly (#14), Hendrickson (#14), Quill Gordon (#14), Blue Quill (#18), March Brown (#12), Sulphur (#16 and #18), Slate Drake (#12 and #14), Light Cahill (#14), Green Drake (#10), Chocolate Dun (#16)

Just how hot did it get that July day when Matt Evey and I fly-fished Big Fill Run in central Pennsylvania? Would you believe it was so hot that we had to eat our lunch in an air-conditioned car? Matt's outdoor thermometer on the car registered 91 degrees and we estimated the humidity at 80 percent. As soon as we got out of the stream we both made a mad dash for the cool environs of the car. And yet we fly-fished Big Fill Run all morning and afternoon.

Matt is a real estate broker by day for the John Hill Company in Altoona. But give him some time off from work and he becomes an avid and skillful fly-fisher. He lives in nearby Hollidaysburg and one of his favorite streams for the past 10 years has been Big Fill Run. He's had many eventful days on that stream with hatches like the green drake and March brown. But some of his best fishing occurs early in the season when early brown stoneflies appear by the thousands on this small stream. Matt copies the stonefly with a Hare's Ear Elk Hair Caddis and usually does well. He's caught trout in the 15-inch category on this wild-trout stream.

Until 15 years ago Big Fill received state plantings of trout. Then the Fish Commission declared it a wild-trout stream and quit stocking it. I mentioned in a previous edition of *Trout Streams of Pennsylvania* that many of these streams, shortly after receiving their new wild-trout designation, went private. Yet Matt Evey has discovered the secret to fishing much of this stream and many other nearby posted waters—he asks for permission. Once Matt finds a stretch he'd like to fly-fish he tries to find the owner of the land bordering the stream. He then tells the owner he fly-fishes and that he won't keep any trout. Matt tells me that the majority of landowners gladly allow him to fish their stretch of water. Matt's simple courtesy to owners might be a lesson for all of us: Treat a landowner with understanding, respect, and courtesy and he just might let you fish.

When we first entered this 15-foot-wide freestone stream around 9:00 AM I checked the water temperature. Would you believe this stream was at a respectable 59 degrees? The water was extremely low and in each pool and riffle we spooked skittish trout.

We headed upstream to a pool where a week earlier Matt had caught several large trout. The water flow had lowered considerably in those seven days. As Matt approached the pool from downstream he crept the last 30 feet so he would present a low profile. The dry fly landed on the surface and we both saw waves on the surface caused by nervous trout. Finally Matt cast his ant pattern upstream where a small deep riffle entered. Here a heavy trout hit and Matt missed it. Matt picked up a brook trout in some pocket water just upstream from the deep pool. The two of us landed a few more trout before the heat got to us and we headed for the air-conditioned car.

If you plan to fish this productive freestone stream with plenty of native brook trout and streambred browns, try it in spring. This 15-foot-wide water holds hatches that appear almost continuously from late March until mid-June. Try fishing when the water volume is fairly high and the trout less spooky. And—above all—do what Matt Evey of Hollidaysburg does on the Big Fill and every other Commonwealth stream:

He asks for permission to fish this small, productive trout stream, and he releases all his trout. You should be willing to do the same.

VANSCOYOC RUN

Access SR 4027 crosses Vanscoyoc near the town of Bald Eagle.

Rating ✸✸

Patterns to Match the Hatches Blue Quill (#18), Quill Gordon (#14), Hendrickson (#14), Green Drake (#10), Dark Green Drake (#10), Sulphur (#16), March Brown (#12), Slate Drake (#14)

If you thought the Big Fill was a small stream then try to fish Vanscoyoc Run, just 2 miles southwest of the town of Bald Eagle. Much of the water above old US 220 is too narrow and too brush covered to fly-fish, but below the old route the stream holds several large pools, some excellent hatches, and a good trout population.

Green drakes, slate drakes, quill gordons, hendricksons, blue quills, and dark green drakes make up only a small portion of the potpourri of hatches found on this water, and on the main stem into which it flows, the Bald Eagle. Since the stream at its widest is less than 15 feet across, select one of the pools or upstream riffles to fly-fish. Between the railroad and its merger with the Bald Eagle lie some productive pools with plenty of cool water throughout the summer.

WHITE DEER CREEK

Access To find White Deer, exit I-80 at Mile Run. Turn left on SR 1010 to reach the lower end and right to reach the upper end.

Special Regulations Delayed harvest, fly-fishing only—3.1 miles, from Cooper Mill Road upstream to the Union-Centre County line.

Rating ✸✸

Patterns to Match the Hatches Blue Quill and Dark Brown Spinner (#18), Quill Gordon (#14), Hendrickson and Red Quill Spinner (#14), March Brown (#12), Gray Fox (#14), Green Drake (#12), Sulphur Dun and Spinner (#16), Blue-Winged Olive Dun (#14), Slate Drake (#12 and #14)

During my 25 years of service with Pennsylvania State University I traveled extensively throughout the Commonwealth, frequently visiting all 20 university campuses. At least once a week I traveled I-80 east. I must have crossed White Deer Creek dozens of times before I finally gave in to temptation and exited the thruway at Mile Run to fish.

White Deer Creek is a small freestone stream located in central Pennsylvania's Centre and Union Counties. The upper end, reached by an improved dirt road, contains a 2-mile delayed-harvest fly-fishing-only section, heavily stocked and rewarding for the persistent angler. The stream in the upper area is tiny, and fishing it requires constant caution, a low profile, and a long, fine leader.

Although I-80 parallels White Deer Creek, much of the stream is relatively untouched by anglers after Memorial Day. Below the fly-fishing-only section are 10 more miles of productive water with a diversity of hatches throughout the year and plenty of native brown and brook trout to complement the early stocking program. Fishing is decent to the town of White Deer, where the stream enters the Susquehanna River. Much of the stream is narrow, lined with rhododendrons, and almost impossible to fly-fish. White Deer contains some good pocket water, however, and adequate holding pools, especially for the heavy hatches that appear in spring.

One of the heaviest hatches on White Deer is also one of the earliest. The first blue quills of the year to appear do so in unbelievable numbers for such a small stream. Late morning and early afternoon in the third week in April, you can almost assuredly witness a hatch of these mayflies. Hendrickson duns and spinners often intermingle with the blue quills and dark brown spinners to produce some of the finest small-water fly-fishing in Pennsylvania. Red quill spinners, the mating adults of the Hendrickson, perform their mating ritual in the late-afternoon and early-evening hours. And there's more—the quill gordon also appears on this fertile freestone stream. On these early-season days carry patterns of the three duns and the dark brown and red quill spinners: use the Dark Brown Spinners in size 18 to imitate the adult of the blue quill; select the Red Quill Spinner to copy the images of the Hendrickson and quill gordon.

Occasional stoneflies and caddisflies continue to emerge on White Deer into mid-May. When mayfly activity returns after the earliest hatches, it does so with an exciting array of aquatic insects. First to appear after the respite following the blue quill, Hendrickson, and quill gordon is the large, sporadic March brown. Since this species ordinarily appears throughout much of the day, it can be a boon to the persistent angler. Be prepared to wait for the March brown to emerge, search for rising trout, and you'll be rewarded. The large naturals often start dashing toward the surface around 10:00 AM the third week in May. If you're fortunate enough to meet the hatch, you'll experience productive fly-fishing until late afternoon.

The green drake, a size or two larger than the March brown, usually appears on White Deer around May 25 or 26. As the drake does on so many smaller freestone streams, it emerges throughout much of the day, again making daylight fishing over large trout possible. (A heavy canopy of oaks, maples, and evergreens hides most of White Deer's surface from continuous exposure to sunlight.) Green drakes appear sporadically throughout the day and into the evening, when another important species, the sulphur, appears. *Sulphur* is a catchall term used to describe dozens of yellow-bodied species ranging in hook size from 16 to 20. On White Deer the sulphur *Ephemerella rotunda* requires a size-16 or -18 imitation to copy the size of the natural.

If you prefer wet flies and nymphs, you might try a Hendrickson Nymph early in the season or a Green Drake or Sulphur Nymph with its dark brown body in late May. All are effective fish catchers at that time.

White Deer is a small stream. Its width ranges from 15 to 25 feet. Wading, however, can be treacherous, because the stream hides plenty of huge boulders. Pools on the stream are small, but many of the riffles and pocket water harbor rising trout.

By late June White Deer evolves into a clear, freestone stream with extraordinarily wary trout. At this time you need a fine tippet on a long leader and a low profile. With these precautions trout can be caught all summer long on this relatively underfished and highly productive water.

FISHING CREEK

Access PA 64 crosses Fishing Creek at Lamar, and numerous secondary roads take you within walking distance above and below.

Special Regulations Trophy-trout project—5 miles, from the bridge at the Tylersville Fish Hatchery downstream to Flemings Bridge at the Lamar Fish Hatchery.

Rating ✻✻✻✻

Patterns to Match the Hatches Blue Quill (#18), Quill Gordon (#14), Hendrickson (#14), Black Caddis (#14 and #16), Little Blue-Winged Dun (#20), Little Blue Dun (#20), Sulphur Dun and Spinner (#16), March Brown (#14), Dark Green Drake (#8), Green Drake and Coffin Fly (#10), Slate Drake (#12 and #14), Light Cahill (#14), Pink Lady (#14), Green Caddis (#14), Blue-Winged Olive Dun (#14), Pale Evening Dun (#16), Trico (#24), Blue Dun (#20)

Pennsylvania probably contains dozens of streams with the same names. There are many Pine Creeks, Cedar Creeks and Cedar Runs, Bear Creeks, and, yes, quite a few Fishing Creeks. But none of the so-called Fishing Creeks is more productive, contains more hatches, and has consistently colder water all season long than does Fishing Creek in Clinton County. This Fishing Creek originates near Loganton in southern Clinton County, then flows west and north for 15 miles until it enters the Susquehanna River near Lock Haven. A few miles below Tylersville and a couple of miles above Lamar, Fishing Creek enters a section affectionately called the Narrows by many fly-fishing enthusiasts. The Narrows is about 4 miles long and carries trophy-trout regulations. This section is the most productive, but also the most heavily fished.

Special regulations end at the lower hatchery at Lamar. From this point almost to Mill Hall, Fishing Creek is classified as a wild-trout stream and receives no state stocking. It depends totally on natural reproduction for its trout population. This section, about 7 miles long, has plenty of browns and brook trout and great hatches. From Cedar Run downstream through Mill Hall, Fishing Creek is stocked with large numbers of trout annually. This section too has excellent hatches and is seldom fished after June.

Fishing Creek is one of those few streams in the state that doesn't need as many friends as it has. Heavy angling pressure has placed a premium on fishing spots here, and has elevated tensions between anglers and landowners. The Narrows is now closed on Sunday; more pressure might produce even more drastic steps.

What can you do to alleviate this situation? First, if you see anyone fishing an area you planned to try, move on to another area. Second, avoid the stream during some of the better-known hatches like the green drake. And finally, be considerate of the landowners and their property. Only with your cooperation will this top-notch stream stay open for everyone to enjoy.

Throughout its entire length Fishing Creek retains cool water all season long. Mid-July temperatures in the Narrows remain in the low 60s. Cool limestone springs create these ideal temperatures. Fishing Creek picks up additional cooling water below the Narrows from its limestone tributaries. In succession, going downstream, Fishing Creek picks up cooling water from Cherry Run (a freestone stream) in the Narrows, Little Fishing Creek at the town of Lamar, and Cedar and Spruce Runs just above Mill Hall.

Fishing Creek reminds me somewhat of the Henrys Fork in Idaho because of the diversity and intensity of its hatches. The season begins almost immediately with the opening of the trout season. First-day fishermen are often greeted with the blue quill, quill gordon, and Hendrickson. But this limestone stream doesn't pause after the early hatches, as so many other Pennsylvania streams do. The third week of April produces a fantastic black caddis hatch that can be gratifying for the patient fly-fisherman. The most effective pattern for the caddis is an emerging-pupa

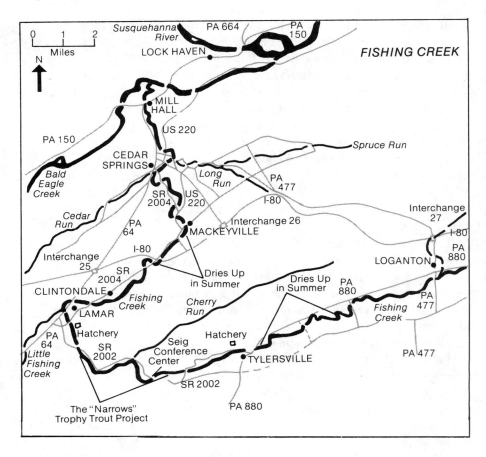

imitation. During the hatch fish the pattern just under the surface. Trout sometimes swirl at the wet fly and miss it. There are plenty of other caddis species on the stream. Check the stream bottom, and you'll see all types of caddis larvae. Fishing Creek contains some massive green caddis larvae (*Rhyacophila* spp.) that measure 20 millimeters long. Many are bright green, and a green-bodied larval imitation on a size-10 hook works well.

The sulphur hatch begins early on Fishing Creek, almost the same day it first appears on the Little Juniata River. By May 13 or 14 the hatch is heavy enough to bring trout to the surface. This sulphur has a distinct olive cast to its orange-yellow body. In my book *Meeting and Fishing the Hatches* I indicated many times that the size of insects of the same species varies from stream to stream. The coloration of insects, especially mayflies, also varies from stream to stream. The sulphur emerges from the Narrows downstream until mid- to late June.

Fishing Creek is probably best noted for its green drake hatch, which appears about a week later than the one on Penns Creek. When the drake appears in late afternoon and evening, any section of the Narrows is productive, and the trout seem to take the imitation more willingly than on Penns Creek. Fishing over the drake during its peak emergence can be a three-hour event, and catching a dozen or more trout on the imitation is commonplace. As with Penns, however, when the word gets out that the hatch is on, dozens of fly-fishermen show up for the spectacle and crowd much of the suitable fishing space. The March brown and the sulphur emerge simultaneously with the green drake, so if you miss the drake hatch you will probably see one of the other two.

By mid-June Fishing Creek is still alive with insects. Yet to appear are several species of blue quills (*Paraleptophlebia* spp.), slate drakes, some blue-winged olive duns, light cahills, and a great hatch of tricos beginning in mid-July. Tricos and blue-winged olive duns continue well into September. Dave Rothrock of Jersey Shore looks forward to the slate drake hatch on Fishing Creek. Dave's developed an excellent pattern for the nymph and finds it especially effective on this stream.

Even during July and August, Fishing Creek near Lamar holds good hatches and heavy trout.

Fishing Creek is almost like three separate streams in its water conditions and hatches. Tricos, for example, don't appear on the upper section in the Narrows. They do, however, emerge from Mackeyville downstream, and for the patient late-season angler they can be a boon. Green drakes and blue quills are most prominent in the Narrows. Therefore, even though this stream contains a great hatch of a given species, it's important to know just where that hatch occurs. Often the least-productive section is that area just above Mackeyville where much of the stream moves underground in July and August.

Fishing Creek has a dependable Hendrickson hatch in the Narrows. For years this hatch has annoyed me because it often appears before the first week of the season, well ahead of its normal appearance on other local streams, and also because the body color of the local Hendrickson is much darker than that of other hendricksons. The species has since been identified as a subspecies of the true Hendrickson.

The tributaries of Fishing Creek produce adequate hatches and harbor some large streambred trout. Cedar Run near Mill Hall has some sulphurs and tricos and a healthy population of streambred browns. Much of the stream is posted, however. Ask permission before fishing on this small limestone stream. Little Fishing Creek, which enters the main stream at Lamar, is heavily stocked by the state and holds a decent trout population all season. Little Fishing is a typical meadow limestone stream. If you were a gambler, you'd bet that it contains a heavy trico hatch. It should, but it doesn't. There have been reports that this stream does hold some green drakes. Cherry Run, which enters in the Narrows section, is lined much of the way with rhododendrons, making it difficult to fly-fish, but it does contain some large trout.

Wading in much of the Narrows can be dangerous. The stream is filled with large rocks and boulders, and the bottom is uneven. The Narrows also has many deep pools and productive riffles.

You can spend weeks on Fishing Creek and still not know the true character of this stream. Try it almost any time of the year and you will be impressed with the quality of the stream, the quantity of the hatches, and, most of all, the trout population.

PINEY CREEK

Access A secondary blacktop road parallels much of the Piney's lower water and PA 866, the upper end. The Fish Commission maintains two access areas on the stream.

Rating ✳✳✳

Patterns to Match the Hatches Little Black Stonefly (#18), Little Blue-Winged Olive Dun (#20), Blue Quill (#18), Sulphur Dun and Spinner (#16), Gray Fox and Ginger Quill (#14), Trico (#24)

If you want to fish a real sleeper, try Piney Creek in Blair County. This small but exceptionally productive limestone stream is seldom fished after Memorial Day, and infrequently before that by fly-fishermen. Piney has many streambred brown trout over 15 inches long. Because of its size and brush-cluttered banks, however, Piney can be difficult to fly-fish.

Piney is noted for three abundant hatches that occur over a good part of the season. Other than some blue quills and blue-winged olive duns, the first two notable hatches occur simultaneously in mid-May: Within a day or two of each other the gray fox and the sulphur emerge. If you plan your trip accordingly, you can fish over hatches during the afternoon and early evening in the latter part of May and early June. Gray foxes usually appear shortly after noon and sporadically the rest of the day. After 7:00 PM sulphur duns and spinners appear. Theoretically various duns and spinners may be on the water anytime from early afternoon until dusk. There's a two-week period from late May to early June where you're almost assured of fishing over at least two hatches.

To be a consistent stream, Piney should be productive late in the season, and it is, with a passable trico hatch. Granted, many Pennsylvania streams exhibit much heavier trico hatches, but the one on Piney is adequate. Besides, many other streams with trico hatches suffer from marginal if not downright warm summer water. Not so with Piney, whose headwaters emanate from consistently cool limestone springs.

Piney is a small stream beginning just a few miles northeast of Martinsburg in Blair County and flowing northeast 15 miles before it enters the Frankstown Branch of the Juniata River just west of Williamsburg. The lower half of the stream, beginning about 6 miles upstream from Williamsburg, offers good brown trout fishing.

Some anglers have reported excellent fly-fishing on the Frankstown Branch just below where Piney enters. This section is cooled somewhat by the flow from Piney, and it contains some sulphurs. Piney picks up only one small tributary on its 15-mile journey to the Frankstown Branch of the Juniata River. What it lacks in tributaries it picks up in limestone springs. Wading is no problem on this 15-foot-wide stream. Piney has some deep pools and plenty of small pocket water and riffles where sulphurs emerge.

If you like fishing cool water all summer long with a good supply of streambred brown trout and limited but adequate hatches, and if you don't mind fly-fishing on a small, tree-lined limestone stream, then try Piney.

CLOVER CREEK

Access Take SR 2011 south of Williamsburg to reach the stream.

Rating ✷✷

Patterns to Match the Hatches Little Blue-Winged Olive Dun (#20), Quill Gordon (#14), Blue Quill (#18), Gray Fox and Ginger Quill (#14), Sulphur Dun and Spinner (#16), Yellow Drake (#12), Trico (#24)

Ed Gunnett of Williamsburg in Blair County invited me to fly-fish a stretch of his club's private water on Clover Creek a few years ago. It happened to be the Memorial Day weekend, and Ed asked me to talk to his club's members on some of the hatches of Pennsylvania. We made certain that the talk and fishing demonstration ended by 7:00 PM so we'd have plenty of time to fish the sulphur hatch so prevalent on this stream that time of the year.

Ed and I headed upstream a few hundred yards to the upper end of the club's posted water. Here we waited for the hatch to begin. Warm weather the past few days delayed the hatch until just before dark. When the sulphurs appeared, they did so by the thousands on this 20-foot-wide stream. Trout eagerly took our dry flies that evening, but the action only lasted for half an hour. Then the hatch diminished, and total darkness set in. Before we quit, however, we had witnessed a tremendous hatch and seen maybe two dozen rising trout.

Clover has many of the same hatches as Piney. We saw that it contains a respectable sulphur hatch, but it also holds a consistent trico hatch on its upper end near Henrietta. The trico combines with cool summer water in its upper end to produce dependable fly-fishing over rising trout every day. The sulphur is the heaviest and longest hatch of the year on Clover, lasting for almost a month. Some yellow drakes appear in the latter part of June. In mid-October I've seen Ed Gunnett and Danny Deters fish over trout rising to little blue-winged olive duns, on a day when 50-degree air temperatures delayed duns in escaping from the surface in their normal rapid fashion. Trout rose on Clover throughout the afternoon to dazed *Baetis* spp. duns.

Piney and Clover are two fine limestone streams tucked in between Tussey and Lock Mountains in southeastern Blair County. Piney Creek is the smaller of the two and lies 5 miles to the northwest of Clover Creek. These two little limestone streams make a good weekend trip for any fly-fisherman who likes to fish new water with few other anglers.

SPRUCE CREEK

Access PA 45 parallels the stream from Graysville to the town of Spruce Creek.

Special Regulations Catch-and-release—0.5 mile, Pennsylvania State University Experimental Fisheries Area (George Harvey Area, about 0.6 mile above the village of Spruce Creek).

Rating ✳✳✳✳

Patterns to Match the Hatches Grannom (#16), Blue Quill (#18),

Walt Young ties a fly at Six Springs Fly Shop.

Hendrickson (#14), Little Blue-Winged Olive Dun (#20), Blue Dun (#20), Little Blue Dun (#20), Sulphur Dun and Spinner (#16), Gray Fox (#14), Green Drake (#10), Slate Drake (#12 and #14), Light Cahill (#14), Blue-Winged Olive Dun (#14 and #16), Cream Cahill (#14), Olive Sulphur (#14), Yellow Drake (#12), Trico (#24), Little White Mayfly (#28)

Andre Lijoi of York, Pennsylvania; Jim Herde of Tuscon, Arizona; and Doug Pierce of Nashville, Tennessee, make an annual pilgrimage to this almost holy limestone stream. They plan their trip for the first week in June so they can hit some of the stream's major hatches and lunker trout. They take plenty of photos of large fish, and they share their memories of a successful fishing episode until next year's journey. These are three extremely busy men, so in some years this might be the only fishing trip they make the entire season. But they always come back to this stream. They have been making the trip for more than 10 years. What stream holds such indelible memories for these three busy doctors and for many other anglers across the United States? It can be only one stream—Spruce Creek in central Pennsylvania.

What a fantastic limestone stream! Situated in a scenic rural valley in central Pennsylvania, Spruce Creek continuously ranks as one of the top in the nation. But most of this 13-mile limestone stream is private—and has been for decades. So why write about it? First, because the stream is one of the top in the state—no, make that in the East. Second, it is a special stream, even though the special-project water owned by Penn State University is the only section open to the public. Third, there are at least three stretches on Spruce that you can fish—for a fee.

One of those private stretches is run out of Six Springs Fly Shop, located in the town of Spruce Creek. Dave McMullen runs the shop and also a guiding operation, with Jim Gilson, called Angling Fantasies. I recently had an opportunity to fly-fish one of the five beats that the two operate and just sat back and watched Dave cast. He's one of the most skilled fly-casters with whom I've had the opportunity to fish. Dave covered the near shore, then the far shore. I watched him make perfect casts—the first time—into an opening of only a few inches between two bushes. Dave contends, and I heartily agree, that the first cast is often the most important. Not only can he cast well, but Dave's also an excellent instructor. He has been guiding on Spruce Creek for more than 18 years. It shows—he knows where just about every trout lies in the entire section of his stream. By being guided by Dave on Spruce Creek you can get more than just the opportunity to fly-fish a top stream—you get the bonus of some excellent instruction on the finer points of casting, reading water, and pattern selection.

Dave and I also recently fly-fished the section of the stream directly behind his fly-shop. We agreed to meet at 7:30 AM in late July to fish over trico spinners. As we entered the water we saw only a few trout feeding on spent spinners. Dave tied on a beetle and began casting toward the bushes lining the far shore. He made each cast almost perfectly, getting

within an inch or two of the submerged brush. He landed several heavy trout and handed me the rod. Now the pressure was on! He pointed to a spot on the far side where a trout fed and cautioned me against spooking it; the trico hatch had ended and the surface-feeding activity had slowed considerably. Dave tied on an ant pattern and I cast within an inch of the far shore. An 18-inch brown took the fly in almost immediately. What a

Dave McMullen lands a brown trout on Spruce Creek.

morning of fly-fishing! You can contact Dave at 814-632-7180 to make arrangements to fish his stretch of water.

One of Dave's workers at Six Springs Fly Shop, Walt Young, has won several fly-tying championships in Pennsylvania and New Jersey. Walt has created three patterns—Walt's Worm, the Golden Pheasant Nymph, and the Halloween streamer—that work well on local streams. He's been tying for the past 35 years.

Spruce Creek Outfitters, also located in Spruce Creek and owned by Allan Bright, guides on a private stretch of the stream called the Colerain Club. You'll also find heavy trout in this section. You can contact Allan at 814-632-3071.

The third private section that you can fish—again for a fee—is the Wayne Harpster farm. Wayne has a cabin and a cottage on the stream that he rents to anglers. The upper cabin is located in a meadow setting and the stream is 20 to 30 feet wide. The two popular hatches here are the sulphur and the trico. The lower cottage usually houses Jimmy Carter when he travels to the area to fish. At the lower cottage, 5 miles downstream from the upper cabin, the water is a bit wider. Each section has a mile or more of water filled with plenty of heavy browns and rainbows. You can contact Wayne at 814-632-5925.

Fees vary at the three private stretches, so check with them for their current prices.

Hatches abound on Spruce Creek. Beginning in late March you'll see plenty of little blue-winged olives. You'll continue to see this hatch throughout the year. But four hatches predominate on Spruce Creek. First, there's a great sulphur hatch in the latter half of May and early June. While sulphurs are still around, the green drake appears on this productive limestone stream. In August you'll be greeted every morning with a trico hatch on much of the stream. And just a year ago I met a hatch I had never seen before—I call the female dun the olive sulphur. Scientists call it *Ephemerella needhami*. The hatch begins appearing just as the regular sulphur wanes. It's heavy for a couple of weeks, and an olive pattern is important to match it.

Spruce Creek begins as a huge limestone spring near Pennsylvania Furnace. The stream then flows about 13 miles paralleling PA 45, until it empties into the Little Juniata River at the town of Spruce Creek. If you want to experience what a productive limestone stream can hold—try Spruce Creek.

SIXMILE RUN

Access You can access Sixmile Run by taking Sixmile Road off US 322; or you can find it off PA 504 east from Philipsburg, or PA 504 west from Unionville.

Rating ✳✳✳

Patterns to Match the Hatches Quill Gordon (#14), Little Blue-Winged Olive Dun (#20), Hendrickson (#14), Early Brown Stonefly (#14), Blue Quill (#18), Giant Stonefly (#6), Little Yellow Stonefly (#16 and 18), Light Quill Gordon (#14), Slate Drake (#12 and #14), Pale Evening Dun (#16), Green Drake (#10), Yellow Drake (#12), Gray Drake (#12)

Upstream less than 100 yards I had just landed six heavy trout. Three of these had never seen the bottom of a hatchery truck. Now I looked at the mouth of this proud, productive stream and saw it quickly disappear into a heavy dose of deep yellowish tan mine-acid drainage into Moshannon Creek. I wondered what this polluted stream would hold were it not for man's cruel and thoughtless devastation of his once-vast natural resources. I also wondered how many more hatches Sixmile Run would now hold if it had a clean connection with a downstream source.

Nevertheless Sixmile Run is a gem of a trout stream in central Pennsylvania. It holds a diversity of hatches with which even some of the more fertile limestone streams to the south can't compare. It holds some green and yellow drakes; most of the early-season hatches; some unusual hatches not mentioned in fly-fishing literature before; and plenty of stoneflies. Check the water temperature almost any summer day and you'll find it in the low to mid-60s. I occasionally recorded mid-June temperatures in the high 50s.

Hatches begin early on Sixmile Run. Almost from the opening day of the season you can see quill gordons and a few hendricksons. I've seen major fishable hatches of quill gordons on this stream as late as June 10. How's that for an extra-long early-season hatch? In June the quill gordon emerges around 4:00 PM, and the spinner becomes active near dusk. Midseason brings some green drakes, sulphurs, giant stoneflies, blue quills, and gray drakes—yes, I said gray drakes. I've seen this species *(Siphlonurus mirus)* on this stream in large-enough numbers to bring trout to the surface. Look for the spinners to fall on the stream around 8:00 PM.

Fish any of the lower 5 miles and you'll find a good number of native brook trout up to 10 inches long mixed in with streambred browns of up to a foot. With the good number of trout, great hatches, and cool temperatures, you'd think all was right with Sixmile Run. Not so!

Sixmile doesn't hold many natural deep pools. In the stretch upstream from PA 504 you will find three small impoundments. On the lower one, just a couple of hundred feet above PA 504, you'll see plenty of rising trout in the evening throughout the season. From PA 504 downstream to Sixmile's juncture with Moshannon Creek, you'll find some productive pockets and small man-made pools. This section could be enhanced tremendously by adding some stream improvements throughout.

Sixmile Road closely parallels the stream for its entire 6-mile fishable section—most of the time within a few feet of the stream. Because of this close proximity you'll find plenty of angling pressure on this stream from opening day through much of June.

Not only does Sixmile have angling pressure and few deep pools, but even the most accomplished angler will find some stretches difficult to fly-fish. Especially in the upper half, you'll find plenty of alders hugging the banks and ready to grab any fly that you cast nearby.

Still, this small, productive stream is worth a try. It lies on the Allegheny Plateau at an altitude of 1,800 feet.

LOGAN BRANCH

Access Logan Branch flows north along PA 144 and enters Spring Creek 6 miles downstream at Bellefonte.

Rating ✳✳✳

Patterns to Match the Hatches Little Blue-Winged Olive Dun (#20), Sulphur Dun and Spinner (#16), Blue-Winged Olive Dun (#14), Blue Quill (#18), Trico (#24)

I first fly-fished on Logan Branch 18 years ago. When I arrived at the stream that day, I just about turned around and went home. Why? Logan is a narrow limestone stream running through almost its entire length within a couple of feet of a busy highway. Litter and debris tossed out of cars clutter the banks.

That first encounter with Logan occurred on June 13 at 6:00 PM. A few sulphurs had already appeared, and trout fed on the surface through the milky limestone water. More of these size-18 duns emerged, and more trout fed, especially in the short moderate stretches just above the abbreviated pools. No other fishermen appeared that evening. Sulphurs continued to emerge nightly on Logan Branch until early July.

Each year anglers catch several trout over 20 inches long on this miniature but extremely productive stream. Logan Branch contains only a few hatches, but the sulphur is prolific enough for more than a month, and it produces some fine opportunities for matching the hatch. The stream harbors a decent blue-winged olive dun near the end of May, some blue quills, and some little blue-winged olives (*Baetis* spp.).

Without a hatch to match, however, Logan Branch can be difficult to fly-fish. Check the rocks along the stream, and you find a plentiful supply of sow bugs and scuds. If you plan to fish the stream when no hatch appears, you will want to use an imitation of those isopods and fish it on the bottom.

Logan slows its flow just enough on its way to Spring Creek to create many small, productive pools. At places along the stream you can almost jump across Logan—at many points it's barely 15 feet wide. Logan develops from several springs near Pleasant Gap in Centre County. Water temperatures remain fairly constant year-round because of Logan's limestone springs. If you're in the central part of the state in late May or June, and you don't mind fishing small water, don't miss this fertile stream.

TIPTON RUN

Access Take SR 4023 north of Tipton to reach the stream.

Rating ✳✳

Patterns to Match the Hatches Early Brown Stonefly (#12), Little Blue-Winged Olive Dun (#20), Blue Quill (#18), Quill Gordon (#14), Hendrickson and Red Quill (#14), Black Stonefly (#14), Sulphur Dun and Spinner (#16), Light Cahill (#14), Little Yellow Stonefly (#16), Little Brown Stonefly (#16)

Do you want to fly-fish for native browns and brooks on a picturesque mountain stream? Do you enjoy fishing over rising trout? If so, Tipton Run might be the perfect stream for you. Even before the trout season begins on this wild-trout water, trout begin surface-feeding on early brown stoneflies. I've seen terrific hatches and rising trout on Tipton as early as April 3—a good two weeks before the stream opens for fishing.

Tipton Run flows southeast from its headwaters in Cambria County 8 miles to the town of Tipton, where it enters the Little Juniata River. Most of its 8-mile trip parallels an improved blacktop road. Four miles upstream from Tipton's mouth lies the Tipton Reservoir. This large impoundment tends to warm the water below. Above the dam lie 4 miles of wild native brook trout fishing. Below the dam, pools, pockets, and riffles teem with both native brown and brook trout. The stream hasn't been stocked for years, because the state has designated it a wild-trout stream.

BELL GAP RUN

Access Take PA 865 north out of Bellwood to reach the stream.

Rating ✳✳

Patterns to Match the Hatches Little Blue-Winged Olive Dun (#20), Blue Quill (#18), March Brown (#12), Light Cahill (#14), Slate Drake (#12), Little Yellow Stonefly (#16), Little Brown Stonefly (#16)

Do you remember your first time casting a fly? Paul Weamer of Ashville remembers that first time vividly. He even remembers what caused him to use a fly. Guess what? One day while fishing on Bell Gap Run he ran out of the garden hackle and had to resort to a marabou streamer. On one of his initial casts a respectable native brook trout hit the streamer and he landed his first trout on a fly. That occurred four years ago and Paul has since become an avid fly-fisher.

Recently Paul and I returned to Bell Gap Run. We selected one of the worst days of the fishing season to test the merits of this stream. No rain had fallen for more than a week and the stream flowed with less than half of its mid-April volume. As we approached the crystal-clear water in early September Paul remarked on how low it was. Pools and riffles that had held trout eager to take a fly earlier in the season now held just a few easily spooked trout. As we hiked along the stream above the reservoir we saw hundreds of little brown stoneflies appear. Despite choosing this poorest of times to fish Bell Gap Run we did catch a sizable number of native brook trout.

Below the reservoir Bell Gap looks like a different stream. Jack dams and other stream improvement devices dot its course in the Bell Gap Valley floor. These slow Bell Gap Run only momentarily in its rush to meet the Little Juniata River 3 miles downstream. The Bellwood Sportsmen's Association, under the leadership of Dick Amrhein, Herb Jones, Chub Dillen, John Gunsallus, Don Johnson, Rick Sprankle, and Bob Slee, developed these stream improvements. Sections void of trout several years ago now hold recently stocked browns and rainbows and a fair supply of holdovers. But that's not all—the club recently established a cooperative nursery with the Pennsylvania Fish Commission. This nursery is one of 187 operated throughout the state by 154 different sportsmen's groups and husbanded by diligent volunteers. These cooperative nurseries released over a million and a half trout and salmon during 1996–1997.

Bell Gap Run lies in a fragile watershed. Abandoned strip mines located around its headwaters still discharge silt into the stream all too frequently. Recent silt deposits cover much of the streambed, even in the lower sections of the stream below the reservoir. Tributaries like Bear Loop Run, Shaw Run, and Tubb Run are still affected by past mining practices in the area. But wait! Just recently several environmental groups got together and formed the Shaw Run Water Improvement Project, funded by the Heinz Endowment, the Western Pennsylvania Watershed Protection Program, and the US Environmental Protection Agency. The future looks bright for Bell Gap Run.

The state stocks 4 miles of Bell Gap Run below the reservoir. Add to this several stockings by the Bellwood club and clearly the stream contains a good supply of trout. Above the reservoir are 5 good miles of native brook trout water that remain cooler in midsummer than the section below the reservoir. Temperatures on the lower end often rise into the 70s during July and August from water the reservoir warms.

In some years the stream releases a respectable green drake hatch; in others this same mayfly appears in diminished numbers.

The Bellwood club has also provided a small pond on its premises for kids under 15. It stocks the pond with plenty of hefty trout for the youngsters.

CANOE CREEK

Access A paved secondary road off US 22 at the town of Canoe Creek follows the upper section of stream up to the state game lands. You can reach the lower stretches by taking a paved road on the western side of the stream. The upper end is reached by a blacktop road on the eastern side. A dirt road gives access to 2 miles of the upper end off the blacktop road. You have to hike into the headwaters.

Rating ✳✳

Patterns to Match the Hatches Blue Quill (#18), Hendrickson and Red Quill (#14), Sulphur Dun and Spinner (#16), Gray Fox and Ginger Quill (#12 and #14), March Brown (#12), Green Drake and Coffin Fly (#10), Slate Gray Caddis (#12 and #14), Light Cahill (#14), Cream Cahill (#14 and #16), Trico (#24)

Ed Gunnett of Williamsburg called a couple of years ago to encourage my son, Bryan, and me to experience the green drake hatch on a new stream in central Pennsylvania. I had vowed never to travel to Penns Creek again, because the drake hatch there draws such a crowd and because I was frustrated with the hatch—six or seven other mayfly species emerge with the green drake. Ed assured me that few fly-anglers fish the drake hatch on Canoe Creek, less than 10 miles from Altoona, and also that few other species appear at the same time. I decided to give it a try.

We met Ed at the stream about 2 miles upstream from Canoe Lake. I had fished Canoe Creek several times before but not this late in the season. Low, clear water had already replaced the high spring waters.

As Bryan and I crossed a footbridge to meet Ed, Ed yelled, "They're on already!"

We glanced upstream and saw a half-dozen duns struggling to take flight. Several duns didn't make it—trout aborted their attempts to become airborne. Ed headed upstream and Bryan downstream to fish the hatch. I stood on the bridge, taping the hatch with my video camera. The hatch increased in intensity as 8:00 PM approached. Upstream from Ed, in a small riffle entering the pool, five trout fed on the duns. In short order he caught or missed all of the rising trout. Downstream Bryan experienced the same success with a Green Drake pattern. In a deep riffle below the pool at the bridge two trout rose for naturals. Bryan hooked both.

By 8:30 dusk had arrived, but green drake duns continued to appear. Both Bryan and Ed headed to a long, deep pool 100 yards above the bridge. About every five minutes I heard Ed or Bryan yell that he had one on. What a great night! What a great green drake hatch! The Canoe Creek hatch indeed had proved more rewarding than the one on Penns Creek,

The New Creek area of Canoe Creek below the Canoe Creek Dam. The Blair County Chapter of Trout Unlimited has constructed many stream improvement devices here.

because fewer mayflies appeared.

Ed Gunnett and Danny Deters often fish this overlooked stream in summer. Although it's small, Canoe holds a good holdover-trout population, even though anglers neglect it a few days after the hatchery truck has unloaded its last fish in the stream. The Green Drake hatch appears on Canoe Creek about a week ahead of Penns.

Canoe boasts hatches other than the green drake. Blue quills early in the season produce some productive early dry-fly fishing. Sulphurs appear on Canoe from mid-May nightly into early June. Bob Beck of Ruskin Drive in Altoona has fly-fished Canoe for 10 years. Bob often sees the slate gray caddis emerging on Canoe at the same time the green drake appears. Bob says this downwing appears on both the creek and Canoe Lake.

Canoe Creek's headwaters begin in northeastern Blair County in Brush Valley. The upper end, flowing through state game lands, contains some streambred brown and brook trout. There are about 7 miles of fishable water in the game lands. Several beaver dams in this area warm the water and provide homes for pickerel rather than trout.

The state recently impounded an area of Canoe Creek a mile north of US 22. The state also stocks the lower section below the dam. This area, however, warms quickly in summer, suffering from the dam's top release and from the lack of any canopy. Just a few hundred yards below the dam New Creek enters the main stem. New Creek's temperature always stays 5 to 10 degrees below that of the main stem. Many of the stocked trout move up the branch when the main stem warms. The lower end of New Creek contains some late-season blue quills and a few tricos. Mary Anns Creek enters Canoe at the dam. This tributary holds a good number of native brown trout.

The Blair County Chapter of Trout Unlimited has installed several stream improvement devices a few miles above the lake. Just below the dam, where New Creek enters, you'll see other devices installed by the local TU chapter.

7 | Streams of South-Central Pennsylvania

Cool limestone waters abound in south-central Pennsylvania. Many south-central streams keep a constant cool flow all summer long. I've fly-fished successfully on these streams when summer air temperatures were at 90-plus degrees. Different streams in the region also host the same aquatic insects. Just about all of them display sulphur, trico, and little blue-winged olive hatches. Only a few of the northern streams in the area house many green drakes, however.

Not all streams in this region boast limestone aquifers. York County has Muddy and Codorus Creeks, which, though freestone in character, produce some fine trout fishing. Juniata County also contains some good trout streams with excellent hatches. East Licking and Lost Creeks have green drakes near the end of May.

LAUREL RUN

Access Laurel Run Road closely parallels the entire stream above the dam. Below the dam you'll find a couple of access points. You can enter just below the dam and fish downstream. Or you can reach the stream near the Whipple Dam Store on PA 26. The lower section warms in summer, but does hold some deeper pools and riffles.

Rating ✸✸

Patterns to Match the Hatches Hendrickson (#14), Blue Quill (#18), Black Quill (#14), Early Brown Stonefly (#14), Dark Green Drake (#10), Little Green Stonefly (#18), Yellow Stonefly (#16), Little Blue-Winged Olive Dun (#20)

Sometimes I wonder how a stream got its name. There must be at least ten Fishing Creeks in Pennsylvania, several Cherry Runs, and, yes, at

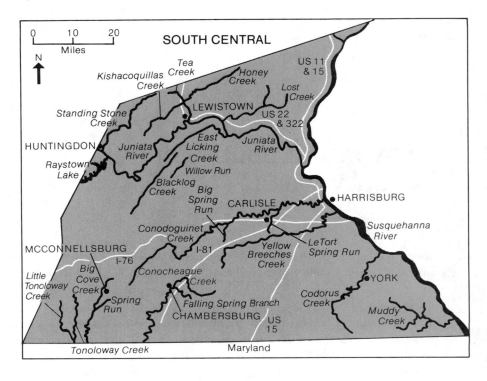

least four Laurel Creeks or Runs. With the Laurel Run in northern Huntingdon County, however, there's no question how it got its name. An even more appropriate name would be Rhododendron Run. Walk along many areas of this stream and you're confronted with casting in a narrow area between dozens of these huge bushes.

Recently I wanted to fly-fish on a central Pennsylvania trout stream—any stream—after four days of rain. The Little Juniata River and Spruce Creek were muddy. Bald Eagle and Penns Creeks ran full and off color. Finally I decided to hit a mountain stream, Laurel Run. When I arrived I had guessed correctly—the stream ran a bit high but was almost crystal clear. I headed above the impoundment.

There are really two parts to Laurel Run—above and below the Whipple Dam. When the state constructed the impoundment they probably thought they did a great thing. Not so! This top-release dam warms the stream below and makes it a marginal trout water in summer. Were it not for the springs below the dam, lower Laurel Run would be void of trout.

The upper area, above the dam, holds a good number of native brook trout up to a foot long. Here you'll find a stream about 20 feet wide with fairly slow water and a few 2- to 3-foot-deep pools. Watch yourself in this area—you'll find plenty of tree falls. You'll have to climb over a number of them to reach the stream. This section of Laurel Run also holds some planted trout that move upstream from the dam in summer and fall.

Laurel Run holds trout for several miles above the Whipple Dam. The Pennsylvania Fish and Boat Commission plants trout about 2 miles above the dam and approximately 3 miles below it. The upper area holds a good number of productive riffles and pools, but the stream here is extremely small. Talk about tight casting!

Don't overlook this stream for some great late-season fly-fishing. The Pennsylvania Fish and Boat Commission often plants some large brookies in early October. Several years ago I combined a cast and blast near Laurel Run: I hunted grouse in the morning and fly-fished for trout in the afternoon. I landed several heavy brook trout that afternoon on a Green Weenie pattern.

GREEN SPRING CREEK

Access Green Spring Creek can be difficult to find. To reach it take PA 641 to the town of Green Spring. If you're traveling east go across a small bridge in town and turn left onto Bullshead Road (T 398). Bullshead Road closely parallels Green Spring Creek until it empties into Conodoquinet Creek near Steelstown Road. In the mile of regulated water Bullshead Road crosses the stream twice.

Special Regulations Delayed harvest, fly-fishing only—1.0 mile, from the mouth upstream to near the confluence with Bulls Head Branch.

Rating ✳✳✳

Patterns to Match the Hatches Little Blue-Winged Olive Dun (#20), Dark Gray Midge (#26), Hendrickson (#14), Sulphur (#16), Cream Midge (#26), Trico (#24)

On most summer days you'll find Jerry Armstrong of Chambersburg guiding fly-fishers at the Upper Canyon Outfitters near Alder, Montana. He retired from the Big Spring School District a few years ago to pursue his dream of fly-fishing and guiding on the Ruby River. When Jerry returns to Pennsylvania in fall to fish, though, one of his favorite streams is Green Spring. He started fishing this fertile limestone stream in 1970. He looks forward to the great trico hatch and the early-season Hendrickson. When no hatch appears Jerry prefers using a Woolly Bugger. He feels this is one of the most challenging limestone streams because of the weeds—in the water and in the fields—and the subtle currents. Jerry says that anyone who wants to fish a classic eastern limestone should find Green Spring a good choice.

Practice, practice, practice! Before you fish Green Spring Creek, make certain you've become a fairly good fly-caster. Why? Green Spring is a small stream that often features only a narrow channel flowing through dense aquatic weeds. Tall grass lines both sides of the shore. Make certain you cast high—if you don't, you'll find yourself pulling your dry or wet fly from this bothersome grass. But if you make a good long cast and don't get tangled in the weeds, you're often rewarded with a strike.

I recently had an opportunity to fly-fish this productive limestone trout stream in late June. I thought that I'd encounter few trout, because authorities had declared the section I fly-fished delayed-harvest, fly-fishing-only. On Pennsylvania's delayed-harvest sections anglers can keep three trout from June 15 to Labor Day. But evidently anglers who fly-fish this regulated area do exactly what I constantly preach—catch and release. If you read this book and if you decide to fish this stream, then you've got to promise to return every trout back where it belongs—to the stream.

I arrived at the upper end of Green Spring Creek shortly before noon. I had difficulty reaching water even though it flowed only 100 feet from the road—I had to struggle through chest-high grass. I finally got there and sat back and watched. In front of me three trout fed on small terrestrials. I tied on a Patriot; 18 inches behind it I tied on a size-16 Dark Olive Bead Head. I made a long, high cast to a deep run 40 feet upstream. On that first cast it looked like two trout fought over the Bead Head; one struck, and I set the hook. I landed a healthy 12-inch stocked brown trout. Four or five casts later a trout took the dry fly, the Patriot. I set the hook and this time landed a 12-inch brookie that looked like it had been in the stream for quite a while. I next caught and released a 13-inch rainbow. Wow! On maybe a dozen casts I had caught a brook, brown, and rainbow trout. That's probably a first for me. No matter where I fly-fished on that stream I caught trout. Sometimes I landed two or three trout in the same general section before I spooked the others.

I quit after a little more than an hour of fishing and catching more than a dozen trout. What was the secret to my success? I think it was using the tandem. Fishing a wet fly in this water is almost impossible; on every cast the fly seems to get tangled in the aquatic weeds. But attach the wet fly 1½ feet behind the dry and you can easily fish much of the stream. Three brook trout took my dry fly, but nine browns and rainbows took the wet.

As I suggested earlier, Green Spring doesn't seem to have much angling pressure. I believe that's because of the challenge of casting here. I traveled up and down Bullshead Road, which parallels the stream, and never saw another angler. You'll find the upper third of the regulated water flowing through a meadow with occasional willow trees. Watch out

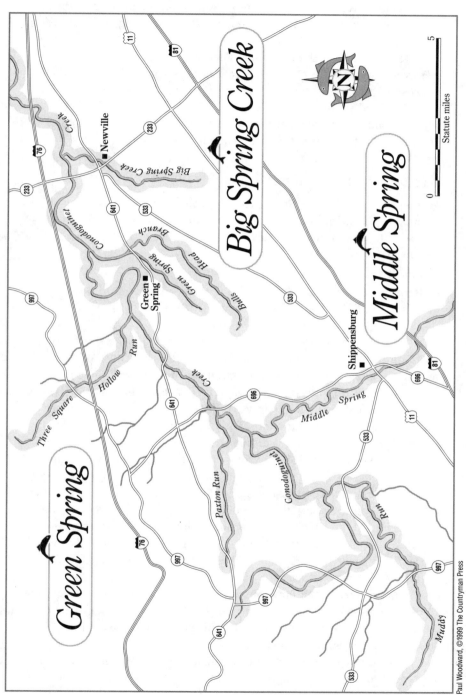

Green Spring

Big Spring Creek

Middle Spring

Three Square Hollow Run

Green Spring Run

Green Spring

Conodoguinet Creek

Newville

Big Spring Creek

Green Spring Head Branch

Bulls Head

Paxton Run

Middle Spring

Conodoguinet

Shippensburg

Muddy Run

Run

Statute miles

0   5

Paul Woodward, ©1999 The Countryman Press

for the poison ivy growing in among the weeds. The lower two-thirds of the stream flow through a more wooded setting. Casting in this lower area still presents many problems.

Green Spring Creek holds some good hatches. Just about every summer evening you'll see plenty of cream midges appear. The stream also holds some mayfly hatches like the trico, Hendrickson, little blue-winged olive dun, and sulphur.

Don't miss this excellent limestone trout stream. And remember—you promised to return every trout you caught to this stream.

MIDDLE SPRING CREEK

Access Access to Middle Spring can be difficult. No road parallels the stream, so you have to depend on those intersecting it. T 626 and SR 4018 intersect the stream near the town of Middle Spring. T 306 crosses the stream just north of Shippensburg.

Rating ✳✳

Patterns to Match the Hatches Little Blue-Winged Olive Dun (#20), Green Caddis (#16), Sulphur (#16), Tan Caddis (#16), Trico (#24)

The anticipation of the first cast on a new stream always does something to me. Will I catch a trout in this stream quickly? Will I catch one on the first cast? Are there any trout in this stream? These and other questions went through my mind as I entered this cool limestone stream for the very first time late in July. My first cast landed perfectly, just behind a bush near the far shore. The tiny Trico pattern drifted slowly for a couple of seconds before it disappeared. I set the hook and missed the fish. Guess what happened? My four-piece fly-rod suddenly became a two-piece one. As I looked at a tree above me I saw the other two pieces dangling from a piece of heavy monofilament line. Some angler earlier in the season had messed with that same oak tree—and lost. What to do now? If I broke off my leader I'd probably lose the two pieces of the fly-rod in the tree. Finally, after 15 minutes of pulling and jerking the two pieces came loose from the line and fell in the water. So much for the enthusiasm of the first cast!

I looked over to the far shore and saw a fish feeding on spent tricos. My second cast worked out better than the first. The spinner drifted a foot before the strike. I landed a 12-inch brown trout that looked like it had been planted a couple of months before.

I waded downstream and saw a half-dozen trout rising in a 3-foot-deep pool to tricos. I managed to land two of those before I spooked the rest. I had fished Middle Spring for a little over an hour and found it full of trout—in late July. The 58-degree temperature encouraged trout to feed on the meager hatch of tricos that morning.

Middle Spring is another one of those cool limestone streams that enter the Conodoquinet Creek from the south. Green Spring and Big Spring enter farther downstream (to the east). The state stocks the stream for about 6 miles, from Shippensburg downstream. Look out for some private land along this stream. Middle Spring has plenty of 3-foot pools and riffles; it averages 15 to 20 feet wide. Don't expect it to be the same kind of stream as Green Spring, Big Spring, Falling Springs, or the LeTort. All of the latter are somewhat weed choked, while Middle Spring has sections that look more like a freestone stream.

This small stream does have some decent hatches, including a fair trico hatch from July through September. You'll also find sulphurs and little blue-winged olives.

Try this one after the hordes of spring anglers have left. When the trico appears on this stream most anglers have long since abandoned it waiting for next year's stocking trucks to appear. I hope you look forward to your first cast with the same kind of enthusiasm that I do—especially on a new stream like this.

LOST CREEK

Access You can access this Juniata County stream from Cuba Mills Road (SR 1002). Three miles upstream (still on SR 1002) from US 322, Ridge Road accesses the stream. You'll also find access near Pine Grove off SR 1002 and at the Oakland Mills Golf Course.

Rating ✳✳

Patterns to Match the Hatches Blue Quill (#18), Grannom (#14 and #16), Black Quill (#12 and #14), Gray Fox (#12), Sulphur (#16), Gray Drake (#14), Green Drake (#10), Slate Drake (#12), Tan Caddis (#14), Green Caddis (#14 and #16)

Recently I stopped at Lost Creek to check for rising trout and emerging mayflies. It was midafternoon on a section near Oakland Mills. As I scanned the surface downstream from the bridge I noted a half-dozen gray foxes emerge and trout feeding on them in the riffle. I quickly grabbed my gear and cast to the nearest riser. Within half an hour I had landed and released five heavy planted brown trout on this section of Lost Creek. In the three hours I spent on the recently stocked stream that day I did not see one other angler fishing.

You'll find few fly-fishers on Lost Creek. Bill Hubler of Port Royal is one of the few who fly-fishes this stream throughout the summer. Bill has been fishing this 30- to 40-foot-wide, meandering stream for more than 25 years. He knows which sections get warm, and where he can find holdover and streambred trout all summer long. Bill finds trout especially responsive to terrestrials in June, July, and August. Although you'll find trout downstream to US 322, Bill prefers to fish above Oakland Mills. He finds the stream around the Juniata Saddle Club near Oakland Mills especially productive.

Bill used to look forward to the sulphur hatch that appeared on Lost Creek. Recently this hatch has diminished, though, probably because of the siltation from the farms along the watershed.

Lost Creek has some decent hatches including gray foxes and gray drakes. You'll find both on the surface in mid- to late May. You'll find tan caddis on the water at the same time.

LITTLE TONOLOWAY CREEK

Access I-70 parallels much of the upper Little Tonoloway and US 522, PA 655, and SR 2004 the lower end.

Rating **

Patterns to Match the Hatches Little Blue-Winged Olive Dun (#20), Quill Gordon (#14), Little Black Caddis (#16), Hendrickson (#14), Early Brown Stonefly (#14), Blue Quill (#18), March Brown (#12), Sulphur (#16 and #24), Light Cahill (#14), Slate Drake (#12), Blue-Winged Olive Dun (#14), Cream Cahill (#14)

If they're not hunting for deer or turkey, they're fly-fishing. Most of the time you'll find Bob Lynn and his son, Bobby, stalking trout on a relatively small but productive freestone stream in western Fulton County, Little Tonoloway Creek. Bob feels that this small stream, tucked away on the western side of Fulton County and paralleling I-70, sees few outside fly-fishers.

Both Steve Frey and Bob Lynn look forward to spring days fishing this stream. However, when July and August appear they seldom come here to fly-fish. In midsummer you'll often see temperatures in the mid-70s and only a trickle of water. The stream flows into the Potomac River near Hancock, Maryland. In many sections the flow ranges from 15 to 30 feet wide.

I met Bob and Bobby and Steve on the Little Tonoloway in late July to see if the stream held any trout at that time of the season. Even though

Bobby Lynn fly-fishes the Little Tonoloway Creek in late July.

we had experienced a good rainfall in July all three complained about the extremely low flow. We hiked downstream past a few unproductive riffles to a 3-foot-deep pool with a slate ledge on its far side. Bob pointed to one trout in the pool that had survived. We headed downstream another 100 yards to the next pool on the stream. This too held a ledge on its far side. We scanned this 3-foot-deep pool and spotted three trout on the bottom. Even under the low-water conditions trout had survived much of the summer. In late summer you'll see few if any anglers here. Streamside paths that in April had been trampled by hordes of anglers were now choked with weeds.

Even as the season begins in Pennsylvania you'll find some hatching activity on the Little Tonoloway. In April it holds quill gordon and black caddis hatches. From late May throughout the summer you'll find slate drakes appearing nightly on the stream. The Little Tonoloway holds at least two species of blue quills. Because they are common on this stream Steve finds a Blue Quill Nymph and Blue Quill dry fly to be effective patterns.

The Little Tonoloway begins about 8 miles southeast of Breezewood and flows south 15 miles, then joins Tonoloway Creek at Johnsons Mill. Tonoloway Creek flows south through Needmore. This stream gets extremely warm in midsummer. Bob and Steve feel the best section of the Little Tonoloway is the lower 6 miles. Near the town of Wardfordsburg the

Little Tonoloway flows through limestone quarries and loses some of its freestone identity. Fishing the hatches in Wardfordsburg can be rewarding.

WILLOW RUN

Access The best way to reach Willow Run is to turn off PA 35 onto Turkeyhill Road (T 314), then head upstream on T 387 to the state game lands. The farther you hike upstream the better you'll find the fishing.

Rating ✳✳✳

Patterns to Match the Hatches Little Blue-Winged Olive Dun (#20), Blue Quill (#18), Quill Gordon (#14), Early Brown Stonefly (#14), Sulphur (#16), March Brown (#12), Gray Fox (#12), Green Drake (#10), Slate Drake (#12), Light Cahill (#14), Brown Caddis (#14), Slate Stonefly (#18)

Bob Hockenberry of Port Royal decided almost 30 years ago that he wanted to learn to fly-fish. He knew some local streams that held great numbers of trout, but he didn't know how to catch them on flies. Bob searched for someone who could teach him fly-fishing techniques quickly. Within a couple of miles of home he found fly-fishing enthusiast Jim Gilson. Jim agreed that if Bob would share some of his trout hot spots he would show him some of the basics of fly-fishing.

One of the streams Bob shared with Jim was Willow Run at Reeds Gap. For more than 20 years Bob, Jim, and Bill Hubler fly-fished almost every weekend—many of them spent on Willow Run. If you ever stop by Jim's office you'll see proof that he's been a longtime advocate of Willow Run. "That's the last wild trout I ever kept on a Pennsylvania trout stream," he told me as he proudly pointed to a mounted 21-inch stream-bred Willow Run brown trout. Jim and Dave McMullen run Angling Fantasies, a guide service for central-Pennsylvania limestone streams.

Jim and I headed for a test run on the stream on which he cut his teeth. He eagerly pointed to a limestone spring partially choked with watercress crossing PA 35 in Peru Mills. "That's the headwaters of Willow—do you see now why it's so cool throughout the summer?"

We headed downstream to State Game Lands 215, hiked upstream a mile, and began fly-fishing on this 20-foot stream. Each pool along the way held memories for Jim. "See that pool—20 years ago I'd catch two or three trout in it 12 to 14 inches long." Jim cautioned me not to expect that kind of success now. The Fish Commission decided to stock trout in the headwaters of Willow Run in the late 1960s and 1970s. These trout plantings brought in hordes of bait-fishermen, who decided they had to kill everything they caught. Anglers not only dispatched stocked trout but also killed many of the streambred browns and native brookies. Since the Willow was classified a wild-trout stream in the early 1980s the state has stopped stocking trout. It will take years for the stream to recover, however—if it ever does.

As Jim and I fly-fished our way upstream I pointed out several tracks made by recent anglers. "That's why the fishing's bad today—several anglers were through here today," Jim said. We did manage to catch a couple of streambred Willow Run brown trout. When we arrived back at the car we saw four bait-fishermen fishing the stream at a bridge—on a weekday in early August. One of these anglers complained that since the state had stopped stocking trout in Willow Run it was difficult to catch a limit.

Lift up any of the rocks in Willow Run and you'll see why the stream holds plenty of streambred trout. Fish the stream in late May and you'll find great hatches of green drakes and impressive hatches of March browns. Throughout the summer slate drakes emerge in the early evening.

In July and August you'll find plenty of terrestrials on Willow Run. Jim fishes polycelon beetle patterns extensively and does well with them in the middle of summer.

Willow Run flows northeast for 8 miles before it enters Tuscarora Creek. The section from McCullochs Mills downstream is marginal. You'll find plenty of 3- and 4-foot-deep pools throughout with fallen hemlocks and undercut banks providing plenty of cover for trout. Although Willow contains some limestone springs in its headwaters, it looks like any typical central-Pennsylvania freestone stream.

Will Willow Run ever return to what it was when Bob Hockenberry, Bill Hubler, and Jim Gilson fly-fished it weekly? Only if authorities decide to make it catch-and-release. This small but productive stream can't afford to lose its trout. It takes too long to replace them.

LETORT SPRING RUN

Access PA 34 and 74 cross the stream just east and south of Carlisle.

Special Regulations Heritage-trout angling—1.5 miles, from 300 yards above the bridge on T 481 downstream to the Reading Railroad Bridge at the southern edge of LeTort Spring Park.

Rating ✱✱✱

Patterns to Match the Hatches Little Blue-Winged Olive Dun (#20), Sulphur Dun and Spinner (#16), Trico (#24)

What fly-fishing history this magnificent limestone stream embraces! Visit the meadow by Charlie Fox's home on the outskirts of Carlisle, and you'll see initials of great fly-fishermen carved in a picnic table next to the stream. There Charlie Fox, Vince Marinaro, Irv Swope, Don DuBois, and many others casually met. These great anglers spent hours near the table observing how trout fed and what they fed on. These observations on the LeTort led to tremendous fly-fishing innovations. Vince Marinaro has departed, but he's not forgotten: Just a half mile upstream from Charlie's place, in a meadow, his friends recently dedicated a plaque in memory of Vince.

In 1978 the fine group of anglers who frequented the LeTort formed an organization called the LeTort Regulars. From the name you might think this group was dedicated to the history of the Civil or Revolutionary War. Not so. These anglers meet in an informal way not only to discuss all aspects of fly-fishing but also to dedicate their organization to the preservation of this fine limestone stream.

The regulars meet monthly with unusual camaraderie. The membership list reads like a *Who's Who* in American fly-fishing: Lin Black, Don DuBois, Jack Eshenmann, Ben Felix, Larry Foster, Tom Henry, Jack Hunter, Lefty Kreh, Gene Macri, Andy McNeillie, Monroe Mizel, Gary Mortensen, Bill Porter, Gene Shetter, Norm and Rich Shires, Al Smeltz, Irv Swope, Tommy Thomas, Ross Trimmer, Gene Utech, Dave Wolfe, Sam Wilks, and Dave Williams (II and III).

The LeTort begins near Bonnie Brook, just a few miles south of Carlisle. It flows 7-plus miles through Carlisle before entering the Conodoquinet just northeast of town. A 1.5-mile segment of the stream has been designated as limestone-springs wild-trout water. Throughout, the LeTort maintains a steady flow of cool limestone water and ranges from 30 to 40 feet wide.

The LeTort has not been without its calamities. Intensive upstream farming, with the resultant runoff, has added unwanted chemicals to the stream. In addition, urban development in the Carlisle area has outpaced that in many other areas of the state. Several years ago the stream received a shot of pesticides from upstream watercress farms. All have had a deleterious effect on the watershed. As a result both the mayfly hatches and the trout population have suffered.

Once on the LeTort, however, you're in for some challenging fly-fishing. Tricky variable currents with slower eddies on the right or left enter into long, smooth glides. Endless weed beds of spirogyra, watercress, and pondweed often prevent casting anywhere but in a small open channel near the center of the stream. The LeTort presents classic terrestrial water through most of the summer months. Add to this imitations of cress bugs and scuds and you'll likely match what a trout finds in the stream. Tricos, sulphurs, and little blue-winged olives still appear, but not in their previous numbers.

Other interested citizens besides the LeTort Regulars look upon this stream as a national landmark. Recently the National Land Trust of Media, Pennsylvania, has become interested in the preservation of this national shrine. This group is currently working with watershed landowners to provide an open area along the stream. Both the LeTort Regulars and the National Land Trust need our support to preserve this prominent, historic limestone stream.

BIG SPRING RUN (CREEK)

Access Take PA 641, 233, or 533 to Newville. Head south on SR 3007 to the stream.

Special Regulations Heritage-trout angling—1.1 miles, from 100 feet below the source downstream to the Strohm Dam.

Rating ✳✳✳

Patterns to Match the Hatches Little Blue-Winged Olive Dun (#20), Tan Caddis (#14 and #16), Sulphur Dun and Spinner (#16), Trico (#24)

I prefer fishing a dry fly over a wet, nymph, or streamer any day. But Gene Macri of Waynesboro taught me an important lesson to remember when fly-fishing on many of the south-central-Pennsylvania limestone springs like Big Spring Run. I tried several dry flies while Gene went on the bottom with cress bug and Light Sulphur Nymph patterns. We fly-fished the section just below the hatchery that many locals refer to as the Ditch. In an hour Gene picked up several heavy browns, brooks, and rainbows. I stubbornly clung to my floating pattern throughout our trip to Big Spring, even after fishing for an hour without a strike. The moral: If you plan to fish any of these streams, take plenty of cress bugs and scuds with you, and be prepared to fish on the bottom. (See Falling Spring Branch, page 252, for more details.)

If you're properly prepared for a trip to Big Spring Run, you can experience an exciting day catching some hefty trout. In the short time Gene and I fished the Ditch, we saw several fly-fishermen catch trout of over 3 pounds. One rainbow, caught by Allen Hepfer of Newville, measured 23 inches long and weighed over 4 pounds.

Big Spring Run begins halfway between Carlisle and Shippensburg just north of US 11. Back in the 1970s the state completed a hatchery where the spring emerges. Fishing's prohibited in the first 100 feet of the stream; the Fish Commission has designated this as a spawning area for brook trout. Below lies the Ditch. Here you can see hundreds of brooks, browns, and rainbows—some over 20 inches long. The Ditch, plus a mile of water below, constitute a section designated limestone-springs wild-trout water. Regulations on this section differ from other limestone streams with the same designation, however. In Big Spring you may take two trout over 15 inches long daily (in the designated section only). Please don't. Release these fish immediately so someone else can enjoy catching them later.

Allen Hepfer, of nearby Newville, holds a 4-pound-plus rainbow caught on a cress bug on Big Spring Run.

A couple of miles below the hatchery the Fish Commission has constructed a weir to prevent browns and rainbows from moving upstream into an area designated wild brook trout water. Above the weir and a small dam are flat, silt-filled shallows with little cover and few trout. A solution to the problems of this area just above the dam would be to narrow the streambed and add rocks and a canopy along the bank.

Mayflies and caddisflies appear on Big Spring Run. Gene Macri says that the middle part of the stream, a few miles above Newville, exhibits a decent trico hatch from early July into September. There's also a tan caddis, according to Gene, which can be important to match early in the season.

YELLOW BREECHES CREEK

Access The Yellow Breeches is easy to reach by car. PA 174 parallels much of the upper end of the Breeches, and Creek Road much of the lower end.

Special Regulations Catch-and-release—1.0 mile, from Boiling Springs downstream to the vicinity of Allenberry.

Rating ✳✳✳

Patterns to Match the Hatches Little Black Stonefly (#16), Tan Caddis (#14), Little Blue-Winged Olive Dun (#20), Blue Quill (#18), Hendrickson and Red Quill (#14), Sulphur Dun and Spinner (#16), Gray Fox and Ginger Quill (#12 and #14), Blue-Winged Olive Dun (#14), Slate Drake (#12 and #14), Cream Cahill (#14 and #16), Yellow Drake (#12), Trico (#24), Big Slate and Rusty Spinner (#8), White Mayfly (#14 and #16), Little Black Caddis (#18), Little Sulphur (#24)

Bryan Meck and I hiked down the steep hill behind the Allenberry Inn around 7:00 PM. No need to arrive on the Yellow Breeches too early on this late-August evening—the white mayfly, or white fly, most often appears just at dark this time of year. Bryan and I headed toward a run where he, Ed Koch, and Craig Josephson had fished just two nights before. On that previous trip the three did fairly well with this often frustrating hatch on the Breeches. For the next hour we saw only an occasional trout rise to various minutiae, including some size-24 winged ants. I asked Bryan whether there really were as many trout in this glide as he said the three had seen just a few nights before. Then the hatch came—first a few low-flying, pellicle-trailing size-14 male white flies, then hundreds. Trout acrobatically rose a foot out of the water trying to catch those nearest the surface. I wanted to see if these trout, during this emergence of burrowing mayflies, fed on the emerging nymph. I tied on a floating, size-14 White Fly, attached a 2-foot piece of tippet material to the bend of the dry's hook, and secured it with an improved clinch knot. To the end of the tippet I tied a size-14 weighted grayish tan nymph. The floating White Fly acted as both a strike indicator and a copy of the dun.

On one of my first few casts the White Fly sank. I set the hook and landed a 12-inch brown on the nymph. Five other trout took the nymph readily before I hooked any trout on the floating pattern. Meanwhile Bryan, just a few feet downstream from me, experienced the same success with the bi-cycle or double rig. He too landed a half-dozen trout before darkness and the diminishing hatch prompted us to head back to the car.

The white mayfly is an extremely dependable hatch on the Breeches. Once the hatch begins you can expect to see it continue every evening for at least two weeks. Because it is so reliable and because anglers see plenty

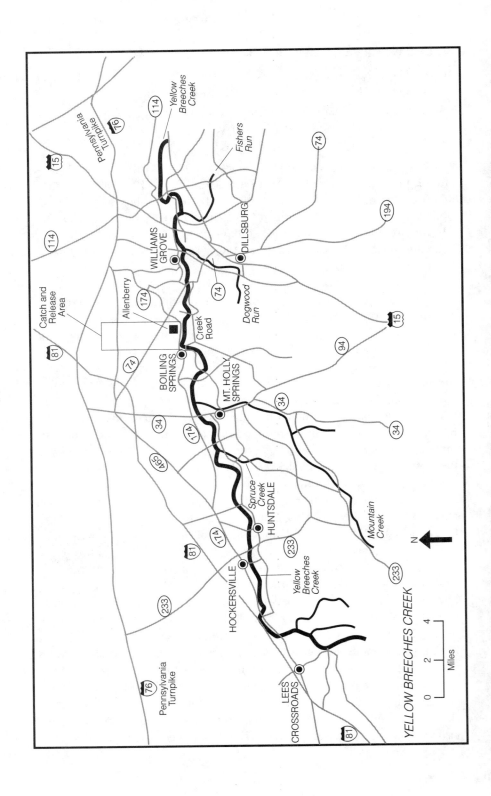

YELLOW BREECHES CREEK

of feeding trout, you can expect to see angling pressure reminiscent of opening-day crowds. This final observance of the fly-fishing year has almost a carnival atmosphere—similar to the green drake hatch on Penns Creek. Fishing access near Allenberry at the time of the hatch is at a premium. As dusk progresses on these late-summer evenings, the white flies emerge. They seem to do so later on the Yellow Breeches than on the Little Juniata River. As with the hatch of green drakes on Penns Creek, the catch on the Yellow Breeches is not up to the standards you'd expect for the event, and the festivity often becomes more important than the catch.

Granted, this spectacular hatch stimulates many trout to rise, but the Yellow Breeches is more than a one-hatch stream. Many of the concentrated hatches occur in April, May, June, and July. The stream boasts a good tan caddis in April that few anglers see, a good little blue-winged olive dun hatch in September, and much more. If you want to see the Breeches at its finest then fish when one of these lesser-known, lesser-fished hatches appears.

Rick Shreve, formerly with Chet Patterson's Sporting Goods in York, looks forward to the early-season tan caddis hatch on the Breeches. "I often fish over the tan caddis for two or more weeks in late March and early April," Rick claims.

The Yellow Breeches begins near Lees Crossroads in southern Cumberland County. It flows east-northeast for about 30 miles before entering the Susquehanna River at New Cumberland. On its path to the Susquehanna, the Yellow Breeches picks up additional volume from tributaries like Mountain Creek, Spruce Run, Fishers Run, and Dogwood Run. Most of these enter the main stream from the south. Mountain Creek has recently experienced problems with acid rain. Near the Huntsdale Nursery the stream ranges from 20 to 25 feet wide; by the time it flows to Allenberry it runs 50 to 60 feet from bank to bank.

The most heavily fished section of the Breeches is the 1-mile catch-and-release area near Boiling Springs. The lower section, below Williams Grove, becomes marginal in summer. Sections above Boiling Springs Run also become marginal in July and August. Boiling Springs Run cools the Breeches for a mile below, making it productive through much of summer.

What can be done to make the Breeches an even better stream? Herb Weigl, who owns Cold Stream Anglers in Carlisle, believes it's one of the finest streams in the state. Herb says, "More than 20 miles of quality trout water are available to anglers, but most anglers concentrate on the no-kill section at Boiling Springs. This 1-mile beat holds plenty of trout all year long because it is stocked well, the water quality is good, and, most important, because trout must be returned to be caught again. Increasing the miles of no-kill or limited-kill on the Yellow Breeches would do more

to improve the stream's long-term fishing quality than anything else."
Excellent words from a man who makes his livelihood from fly-fishing.

Gene Utech of Huntsdale is an expert wet-fly fisherman. He's fly-
fished on the Breeches for years. Gene uses soft-hackle wets almost exclusively on this limestone stream. He agrees that fly-fishing on the Yellow
Breeches can produce trout throughout the year.

FALLING SPRING BRANCH

Access You can reach the Falling Spring by a secondary road near I-81 in
Chambersburg. Four access points take you to the stream: Quarry Road,
Edwards Avenue, Skelly Farm, and just below Fry's Dairy.

Special Regulations Heritage-trout angling—2.4 miles, from the Briar Lane
bridge downstream to a wire fence crossing the Thomas L. Geisel property.
Delayed harvest, artificial lures only—1.1 miles, from Walker Road to the
Fifth Avenue bridge in Chambersburg.

Rating ✳✳✳

Patterns to Match the Hatches Little Blue-Winged Olive Dun (#16 to #20),
Little Black Caddis (#16 and #18), Tan Caddis (#14 and #16), Golden
Caddis (#14 and #16), Sulphur Dun and Spinner (#16 to #20), Light
Cahill (#14), Yellow Drake (#10), Trico (#24)

Twenty years ago I fly-fished a small, productive limestone stream near
Chambersburg. I first fished with the late Vince Marinaro, along with
Barry Beck and Dick Mills, on Falling Spring in the middle of a heavy
trico spinner fall. It was early September, and the mayfly spinners
appeared on the water almost as heavily as they had in late July. Vince
uttered some language almost in a whisper, discouraged that so many
trout rose to the trico spinners but rejected his lifelike imitation. Barry,
Dick, and I gathered around Vince to hear some wisdom on tricking these
selective trout. Instead we heard nothing but grumbling. All three of us
selected fishing spots nearby, tied on trico imitations, and began casting
to dozens of surface-feeding trout—and all of us experienced the same
lack of success Vince was having. What was the problem? We all had
size-24 dark-bodied Trico patterns; we were all using fairly lengthy leaders, about 12 feet long; and we had all tied on fine tippets, about .005 or
6X. Why were all of us experiencing frustration? It's a lot like the goose
season on the Chesapeake in Maryland. For the first few weeks of the
goose season the birds fly within shotgun range; after those first few weeks
the geese seem to fly higher, sensing trouble. Similarly, fly-fish over the
trico hatch in early July and you'll likely experience many rises to your
imitation, and many catches. Evidently trout become more discriminating

as the season progresses, though. And tricos appear on this fertile stream until November. In fact, at that time Falling Spring once had the heaviest hatches of tricos in the United States.

But that was 20 years ago. Ten years ago Gene Macri of Waynesboro asked me to meet him on the stream in early July. I was anxious to discuss the stream with Gene and to fish the famous trico hatch after a hiatus of 10 years. A few years ago Gene completed his master's thesis at Shippensburg University: *A Study of Falling Spring, A Limestone Trout Stream: The Invertebrate Fauna with Aspects of Geology, Land Use, Substrate Diversity, and Fishery.* While completing his studies Gene spent 340 days on Falling Spring and found that the water had deteriorated significantly within the preceding 10 years. Tricos, once so prevalent on the stream from late June through October, had dramatically decreased in numbers. The sulphur hatches that had appeared from late April until early September were only about a quarter as abundant as they once were.

What had happened to this highly acclaimed stream? Siltation appears to have had a major role in the decline of Falling Spring. Many of the pools and riffles I remembered fishing with Vince, Barry, and Dick had

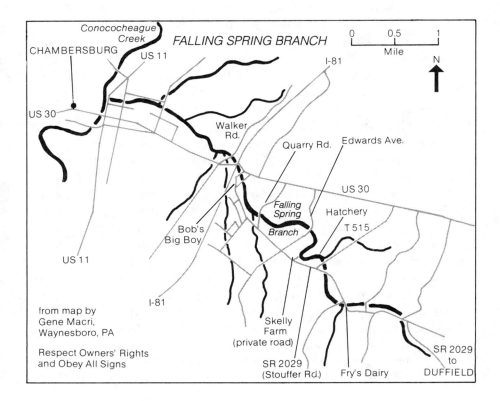

filled in with silt. The Glory Hole, 6 feet deep 20 years ago, barely held 3 feet of water and contained a silt bottom. Intensive upstream farming, headwaters housing developments, and excavation for a sewage line in the early 1980s appear to have caused the siltation.

Jim Gracie and Dennis LaBare, stream restoration experts, however, felt that the problem was not that so much excess sediment reached the stream, but that long-term channel restrictions had not allowed the stream to transport its sediment properly. This in turn buried important stream-bottom habitat for insects.

But wait—something happened to this great stream in 1989. Area anglers also noted the decline of Falling Spring and joined together to produce a more viable Falling Spring fishery. The Falling Spring Chapter of Trout Unlimited and an environmental group called the Falling Spring Greenway have actively become involved in the future of this great lime-stone stream.

The greenway group actively participates in stream restoration proj-ects, promoting stream access, and informing groups on the objectives of the greenway. Falling Spring Greenway has fulfilled one of its major mis-sions, keeping livestock out of the stream, by fencing off the Quarry Meadow. The greenway has produced a brochure entitled *10 Ways You Can Help Save the Falling Spring*. Together, the local chapter of Trout Unlimited and the greenway group have brought Falling Spring back on a path to total recovery. The greenway includes Pat Pastor, Bill White, Susan Armstrong, Jerry Armstrong, Bill Horn, Dick Tietbohl, and Dennis LaBare. To continue to improve Falling Spring, the greenway needs your help—both physical and financial. You can contact this group at Falling Spring Greenway, Inc., P.O. Box 961, Chambersburg 17201.

Have the conservation efforts of the greenway group and the Falling Spring Chapter of Trout Unlimited helped? Has the problem of sedimenta-tion lessened? This past year Ken Rictor and Bugs Stevens, both of Chambersburg, witnessed good yellow drake hatches on the lower end of the stream. This is the first burrowing mayfly to reinhabit the stream and bodes well for the group's efforts in reducing the sedimentation problem.

Recently it looked as if the entire lower project water smack in the middle of Chambersburg might be posted to fishing. Landowners had to constantly pick up garbage thrown along the streambank by anglers. One of those landowners, Jack Good, approached a group of fly-fishers. He felt there were two options to remedy the clutter near the stream: Either the lower section would be designated a special project or it would be closed. Bill White, a landowner and fly-fisher along the same section, worked with the Fish Commission to designate the area as delayed harvest.

Since then landowners couldn't be happier—they now find little if any

An early morning fog hovers over Falling Spring in Chambersburg.

debris along their streambanks. This is an experiment that has been totally successful for both anglers and landowners. This lower section will remain open for all to enjoy.

Ken and Kathy Rictor recently invited me to revisit Falling Spring and fly-fish on this newly designated delayed-harvest area in Chambersburg. Joining us that morning were John Newcomer, Bill and Gerry Gram of Orrstown, and Bill and Grace White. Ken Rictor practices family medicine out of nearby Scotland; Bill Gram is a colonel at Letterkenny; and Bill and Grace White carve and paint birds for a living—what a combination of talented people! All are members of the Falling Spring Chapter of Trout Unlimited and the Falling Spring Greenway. John Newcomer and Bill White have fished Falling Spring for a combined total of more than 100 years. Both know where every trout feeds during the trico hatch and have caught and released the majority of them. Just a few nights before John had lost a heavy trout that tangled onto some brush in the project water.

Ken, John, and I headed downstream to fish the trico hatch. As John pointed out some stream improvement devices put in place by the local Trout Unlimited chapter, I noted a swarm of tricos in the air. Soon several trout began actively feeding on the spent spinners. What a refreshing morning with a great group of people devoted to a better future for Falling Spring! Because of the efforts of these people and others in the area, the future of this stream looks bright.

Falling Spring begins near Duffield, with part of it coming from a limestone cavern. It is an extremely small limestone stream. Wading is no problem; the stream is no wider than 25 feet at its widest point. Falling Spring flows northwest, entering Conococheague Creek at Chambersburg.

Falling Spring has only 6 miles of fishable water, and some are posted. About midway up the stream is a 2.4-mile stretch of limestone-springs wild-trout water. You'll occasionally catch streambred rainbows over 20 inches long in this section. Water temperature remains fairly constant, ranging from 60 degrees in summer to 46 in winter.

The sulphur hatch lasts for several months on Falling Spring. It begins in early May and continues well into September. Gene Macri found in his study that all of the sulphurs were *Ephemerella rotunda*. Their predictable appearance just before dusk and their extensive hatching period make this sulphur an attractive hatch to fish and match.

Will Falling Spring ever regain its prominence as one of the top limestone streams in Pennsylvania? Will the sulphur and trico ever appear in their former numbers? It looks like this stream is well on the way to recovery thanks to the help of the Falling Spring Chapter of Trout Unlimited and the Falling Spring Greenway.

MUDDY CREEK

Access PA 425 crosses Muddy Creek at the village of Woodbine. Take Bridgeton Road off PA 425 to reach the delayed-harvest area.

Special Regulations Delayed harvest, fly-fishing only—2.0 miles, from the SR 2032 bridge in Bridgeton up to Bruce.

Rating ✷✷

Patterns to Match the Hatches Little Black Stonefly (#16), Early Brown Stonefly (#14), Green Caddis (#16), Sulphur Dun and Spinner (#16), March Brown (#12), Gray Fox (#14), Blue-Winged Olive Dun (#14), Green Drake (#10), Trico (#24), Big Slate Drake (#8), White Mayfly (#14)

When John Taylor was the outdoors editor of the *York Dispatch,* he wrote an excellent article extolling the trout-fishing virtues of a southeastern York County stream. He's fished this water for more than 20 years, experienced some hatches on it, caught some heavy holdover brown trout, and likes the solitude of a stream so near a metropolitan area. Yes, Muddy Creek means much to John and many York County anglers.

In his story about the water, John wrote a detailed history of the efforts of some local anglers to maintain Muddy Creek as a respectable fishery. Years ago, he relates, a group of interested anglers became the

Muddy Creek Trout Stocking Committee (MCTSC). The MCTSC ensures that all 8 miles of the main stem receive trout. Although Muddy Creek has little access by road, and some of the roads that approach it are poor, the MCTSC struck an agreement with a company back in the 1950s to use a railroad that parallels the stream for stocking.

Muddy Creek presents some dilemmas that will test its ability to remain a viable trout stream. Siltation appears to be its main curse. Muddy suffers from severe doses of silt caused by upstream state and township road work, farming practices, and housing developments. Travel along the South Branch of Muddy Creek and you'll see the siltation. Even minor storms quickly discolor the South Branch. During June, July, and August temperatures on Muddy and its branches often rise into the high 70s, causing cold-water fish to die or seek areas where cool springs appear.

The good news for Muddy Creek is that after years of frustration, Jan Pickel, Jim Hersehey, Steve Knopp, and other conservation-minded York County residents recently formed a Muddy Creek Chapter of Trout Unlimited—something that John Taylor encouraged through his editorials for years. Now Muddy Creek will receive the careful supervision it deserves.

The North and South Branches join at the small village of Muddy Creek Forks to form the main stem. The branches range from 20 to 40 feet wide and contain plenty of moderately fast water with some deep pools below. The main stem runs from 40 to 60 feet wide and contains plenty of long, deep pools. The state has designated a 2-mile area near Bridgeton fly-fishing-only water. One of the landowners on this stretch would like to revert the section to an open area, however, so the future of the fly stretch seems to be in jeopardy.

March browns, gray foxes, sulphurs, and tricos make up a large part of the mayflies on Muddy. Combine these with some caddisflies and stoneflies and you can experience good fly-fishing days on the stream. Many of the best fly-fishermen on the stream, like Fred Bridge, use nymphs almost exclusively. Check the rocks on any of the riffles and you'll note a wide variety of nymphal life, including a good quantity of March brown nymphs. That pattern should prove an effective selection for Muddy.

On its flow to the Susquehanna River, Muddy picks up tributaries like Toms Run (stocked), Bald Eagle Creek (stocked), Neill Run, Fishing Creek, Orson Run, and South Creek.

CODORUS CREEK

Access Take PA 116 to the village of Iron Ridge. Take Iron Ridge Road (SR 3047) to the stream.

Special Regulations Selective-harvest program—3.3 miles, from SR 3047 downstream to PA 116.

Rating ✳✳✳

Patterns to Match the Hatches Little Blue-Winged Olive Dun (#20), Tan Caddis (#14 and #16), Hendrickson (#14), Gray Caddis (#14 and #16), Cream Caddis (#14 and #16), Sulphur Dun and Spinner (#16 and #18), Gray Fox (#14), March Brown (#12), Light Cahill (#14), Yellow Drake (#10), Blue Quill (#18), Tiny Blue-Winged Olive (*Pseudocloeon* spp.) (#20 to #24), Cinnamon Caddis (#12 and #14)

Walk along this southern York County tailwater and you'll note many weed-clogged pools and a hint of off-color, almost chalky water typical of many of the state's prime limestone waters. Check the water temperature on Codorus in June, July, or August and you're really in for a surprise. In the hottest part of the summer the water temperature in this part of the stream rarely rises higher than the low 60s—ideal for some late-summer fly-fishing.

But Codorus Creek has no limestone aquifer. It's totally a freestone stream. Lake Marburg, a few miles above Porters Sideling, empties into the Codorus. This lake contains a bottom release that maintains a productive trout fishery all year.

Recently Andre Lijoi, Bryan Meck, and I fly-fished for a couple of hours one late-August morning. I wanted to determine once and for all if this small tailwater held a trico hatch. Andre and Bryan frequently fish the Codorus. As we entered the 30-foot-wide stream Andre checked the temperature and told us it registered 49 degrees. I searched for more than an hour and didn't find a trico above the stream. I did, however, find dozens of jenny spinners (*Paraleptophlebia* spp.) above the water. Anglers often confuse this species with the trico.

The stream holds a 3.3-mile stretch designated a delayed-harvest area. One landowner on this regulated stretch planned to close his property to fishing until the special regulations were posted. A major force in setting this stretch aside was Brian Berger, a waterways patrolman in the area until recently. Codorus only lately has been designated a special project, but the quality of the fishery already is apparent. Already many Maryland anglers frequent this stream only a few miles from their border.

The more times I fish the stream and the more people I talk to, the more I'm convinced that the Codorus needs a change in the regulations the Fish Commission has placed on it. Delayed harvest is a good designation for a stream that becomes marginal in summer. But water temperatures on the Codorus rarely rise much above 60 degrees even on the

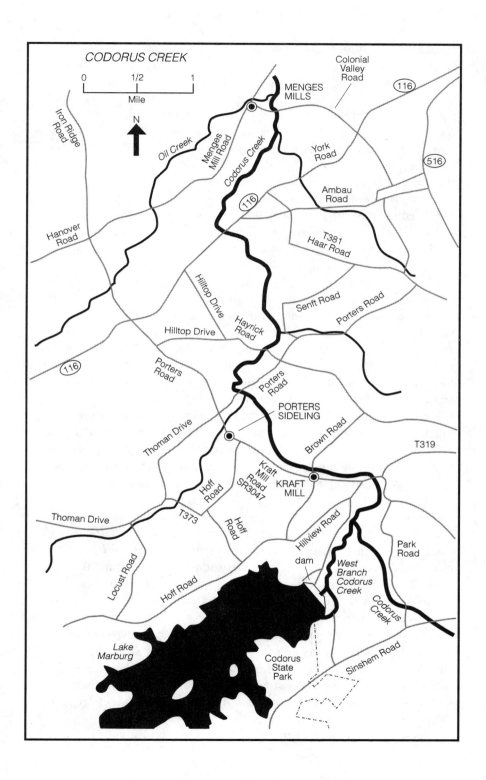

CODORUS CREEK

0   1/2   1
Mile

N

hottest July afternoon. Too many anglers presently poach the stream, catching fish out of season, and others take trout after the middle of June. The Codorus has a lot of fishing pressure throughout the season. Into July and August you'll see several cars parked along the specially regulated water. A trophy-trout designation would preserve the trout for all to enjoy for the entire season. Many of the members of the Codorus Chapter of Trout Unlimited agree that the stream should be redesignated a trophy-trout stretch.

The Codorus contains some good hatches. Rick Shreve, who until a few years ago worked at Chet Patterson's store in York, says that the tan caddis constitutes the first major hatch of the season. Rick also looks forward to the hendricksons that often emerge the first week in April. "Once the Hendrickson begins you can expect almost two excellent weeks of matching-the-hatch fishing," Rick says.

Fly-fish on any evening from May 12 into June and you'll probably encounter many sulphur duns and spinners. If you're fortunate enough to hit the stream on a cloudy day in mid- to late May, you're apt to witness sulphurs emerging sporadically all afternoon, although the Codorus exhibits its heaviest hatch of this mayfly shortly after 8:00 PM. Fish this productive water for that hour just at dusk and you'll have some excellent trout fishing. March browns, gray foxes, and several other mayfly species add to the fly-fishing on the Codorus.

Eric Laskowich of Brodbecks has fly-fished the Codorus more than 50 times a year for the past seven years. He gets excited every time he talks about this stream and its hatches. He especially enjoys fishing when the Hendrickson, sulphur, gray fox, and yellow drake appear. Eric says the sulphur hatch lasts more than a month. He believes that the stream holds two or three species all commonly called "sulphurs." He matches the early sulphurs with a size-16 pattern and later hatches with a size-18 fly. He cautions all who fish the stream to be prepared for downwing hatches like the tan, cream, gray, and cinnamon caddis that cover the surface. Eric also cautions all who fish the stream to carry some copies of crane flies in sizes 18 and 20 to copy those with yellow, tan, and green bodies.

Furnace Creek, Long Run, and West Branch flow into Lake Marburg near Blooming Grove. These form the Codorus, which flows north, picking up Oil Creek and the South and East Branches just southwest of York.

Codorus Creek doesn't compare in size with other streams below dams with bottom releases, like the Allegheny River, Tulpehocken Creek, or Pohopoco Creek. The present stream ranges from 25 to 30 feet wide in most places. It does, however, contain many pools 5 to 6 feet deep with short, productive riffles between.

Fly-fishing on much of the stream will severely test your skills. You'll

Bryan Meck fishes Codorus Creek.

find a low, heavy canopy over much of the stream. The Codorus Chapter of Trout Unlimited formed just a few years ago but already has carved its mark on the stream. You'll see a stream map, signs, and, more significantly, many man-hours of streambank restoration work done by the local chapter. The chapter has also worked with state authorities to clean up a dump on one of the tributaries. All Codorus anglers should join this club.

The Codorus has a good supply of holdover trout and streambred brown trout. John Morrison of York said that in the past couple of years he's been seeing more and more streambred brown trout. Eric Laskowich feels the stream now holds streambred rainbows.

The East Branch already has two dams—Lake Williams and Lake Redman. A third dam on this branch is planned upstream from the other two. This will further damage the trout fishery on this tributary.

Check in with Sportabout in York or the Olde Village Fly Shop in Shrewsbury for information on the condition of the stream and hatches appearing on the Codorus.

KISHACOQUILLAS CREEK

Access The Kishacoquillas flows south from Reedsville, through Yeagertown, entering the Juniata at Lewistown. PA 655 follows the West Branch from Belleville to Reedsville, and US 322 parallels the main stem from Reedsville to Lewistown. Use waders and watch your step on the lower end of the stream.

Rating ✳✳

Patterns to Match the Hatches Grannom (#16), Green Caddis (#16), Olive Caddis (#16), Tan Caddis (#16), Sulphur Dun and Spinner (#16), Slate Drake (#12 and #14), Green Drake and Coffin Fly (#10), Little Blue-Winged Olive Dun (#20), Slate Drake (#12 and #14), Trico (#24), Blue Quill (#18)

Lewistown-area residents Denny Sieber, Bill Force, and dozens of other anglers who habitually travel to Penns Creek sometimes overlook excellent fly-fishing right in their own backyard on Kishacoquillas Creek. The Kish, as some of the locals call it, contains great hatches, heavy limestone water, and some large trout. But, like Rodney Dangerfield, it gets no respect. The local Trout Unlimited chapter meets within a couple of feet of where the Kish flows, and yet the chapter's named the Penns Creek Chapter.

Walk along Kishacoquillas in early spring and you'll meet plenty of bait- and spin-fishermen. But after the last in-season stocking you'll have much of this large stream to yourself. The heaviest hatches and most productive water begin at Reedsville and continue downstream past Yeagertown. At Reedsville two other productive limestone streams, Honey and Tea Creeks, enter the West Branch of the Kish to form the main stem. When these three combine the stream widens to 40 to 50 feet, with plenty of deep pocket water. A mile below Reedsville the Kishacoquillas enters a mile-long section called the Narrows by the locals. Similar to the Narrows sections on Fishing Creek and Elk Creek in central Pennsylvania, the section on Kish contains plenty of huge boulders scattered throughout the stream bottom.

The West Branch begins just west of Belleville in Mifflin County. On its 12-mile trip to Reedsville it picks up several limestone tributaries, including the Coffee. (Yes, Coffee, Tea, and Honey really are tributaries of the Kish.) Most of Coffee is posted, while much of Alexander Springs, another tributary, remains open to public fishing. Both branches range from 10 to 15 feet wide and contain plenty of streambred brown trout. Most of the West Branch around Belleville remains open to anglers—but some owners prohibit Sunday fishing. The West Branch flows east through Amish farmland to Reedsville. Some of the lower sections on this branch are posted and warm considerably in the summer. This branch ranges from 20 to 40 feet wide with plenty of pools and productive riffles. Several years ago the West Branch received an ammonia spill that devastated the vertebrate and

Kishacoquillas Creek near US 322 holds a good number of planted and streambred trout.

invertebrate biota. Even with the warming in summer and the chemical spill, though, the West Branch contains some hatches and heavy fish.

Travel through Reedsville or Yeagertown in mid- or late May and you will often see thousands of displaced sulphur spinners hovering above the roads. Fish the main stem in the Narrows in the evening at that time and you'll probably experience a great sulphur hatch. Just prior to and during the sulphur hatch you'll also see many caddis on the Kish. Use a size-16 dark brown, green, olive, or tan body color to copy many of these insects.

I've found a good number of streambred browns on Kish directly under the US 322 bridge. On occasion I've fished this stretch into late August and caught some streambred trout.

HONEY CREEK

Access The main stem of Honey flows about 5 miles before it enters Kishacoquillas at Reedsville. A blacktop road parallels Honey from Reedsville upstream.

Rating ✳✳✳

Patterns to Match the Hatches Blue Quill (#18), Quill Gordon (#14), Hendrickson and Red Quill (#14), Grannom (#14), Tan Caddis (#16), Blue Dun (*Pseudocloeon* spp.) (#20), Sulphur Dun and Spinner (#16), Blue-Winged Olive Dun (#16), Gray Fox (#14), March Brown (#12), Green Drake and Coffin Fly (#10), Brown Drake (#12), Slate Drake (#12 and #14), Little Blue-Winged Olive Dun (#20), Perla Stonefly (#12)

Clouds of coffin flies filled the late-May air. The green drake hatch the previous night had been nothing short of spectacular. Fishermen from all around the Lewistown area met on Honey Creek to fly-fish during this sensational annual occurrence. But that happened 30 years ago—and that's how great fly-fishermen like Reed Gray of Lewistown remember the last great hatches of this species on Honey.

The abundant emergences of the green drake, and others such as the Hendrickson, abandoned this once-fertile stream in the mid-1950s. Around that time some of the local limestone quarries washed concentrated limestone into the stream. Reed Gray and others feel that the concentrated limestone destroyed the mayfly population on Honey Creek.

Recent reports indicate that the green drake may be making a comeback and within a few years might again be abundant on the stream. Even now enough drakes have returned on the lower end to create some fantastic fly-fishing for a few days in late May. Denny Sieber of Lewistown built a cabin near one of the tributaries of Honey, and fishes the stream frequently. Two years ago he witnessed a hatch of green drakes reappear on Honey. Enough emerged one evening to bring trout to the surface.

As with many central-Pennsylvania trout streams, much of Honey Creek's fame now rests with its sulphur hatch. From mid-May into early June matching the sulphur dun and spinner can still produce some exciting, quality matching-the-hatch time.

Honey Creek begins near Reeds Gap State Park in northeastern Mifflin County and runs southwest to Reedsville, where it enters the Kishacoquillas. Two major tributaries, Treaster and Havice, are freestone in nature in their headwaters, but near Siglerville take on a limestone character. Near Siglerville the Penns Creek Chapter of Trout Unlimited has installed numerous stream improvement devices. It plans several more.

Upstream the state stocks these tributaries. Each branch ranges from 10 to 20 feet wide. In the freestone headwaters, Reed Gray reports, several hatches emerge that are absent in the limestone water below. Typical fast-water freestone mayflies like slate drakes and quill gordons are common on Treaster and Havice, less so on Honey below. Branches like Treaster, Havice, and Laurel, as well as the main stem of Honey, flow underground in areas.

The state classifies Honey as a class A wild-trout water, and the stream receives no stocked trout. Honey contains an adequate supply of stream-bred browns up to 20 inches long. Its lower end ranges from 30 to 40 feet wide and contains plenty of deep pools and many productive riffles.

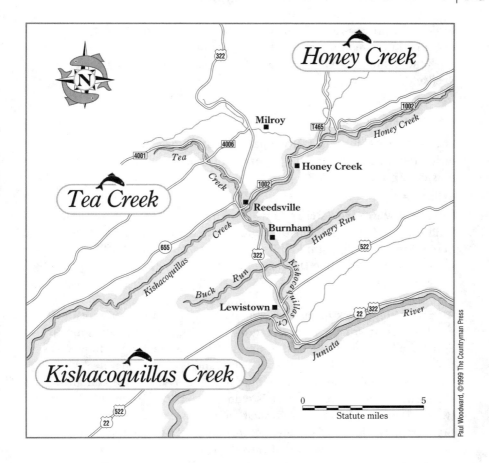

TEA CREEK

Access You can reach Tea Creek at Reedsville from SR 1005.

Rating ✶✶✶

Patterns to Match the Hatches Blue Quill (#18), Little Blue-Winged Olive Dun (#20), Sulphur Dun and Spinner (#16 and #18)

Reed Gray of Lewistown fly-fished area streams for more than 50 years. One of the streams near his home that he fished frequently was Tea Creek. The state no longer stocks Tea Creek but it contains a good population of streambred brown trout. The native trout almost resemble salmon with their silver-sided bodies. What a pity this 10- to 20-foot-wide limestone stream doesn't contain a no-kill area. How can this small stream replace valuable trout killed in it? The Tea flows cold all summer long with temperatures in the upper end rarely getting out of the 50s. Tea Creek would be an excellent stream in which to place some stream improvement devices. At present most of the open water contains small pockets that could be improved by placing stone deflectors, log deflectors, tip deflectors, and gabions. There's only a mile of open water—all below US 322 in Reedsville.

EAST LICKING CREEK

Access East Licking Creek Drive parallels much of the water. It's paved upstream to the dam and dirt beyond. You can reach this access road just outside Mifflin from PA 35.

Rating ✸✸

Patterns to Match the Hatches Early Brown Stonefly (#12), Blue Quill (#18), Quill Gordon (#14), Sulphur Dun and Spinner (#16), Gray Fox (#14), March Brown (#12), Light Cahill (#14), Green Drake and Coffin Fly (#10), Little Blue-Winged Olive Dun (#20), Perla Stonefly (#12), Trico (#24), Big Slate Drake (#8)

East Licking Creek means a lot to Jim Gilson. He lives only a stone's throw away from the lower end of this Juniata County stream near Port Royal. He's been fly-fishing on the stream since long before it was fashionable to fly-fish in Juniata County and is well acquainted with the water, its hatches, and the streambred and holdover trout it contains. Jim's one of those rare individuals whose avocation became his vocation. He and Dave McMullen have formed a business called Angling Fantasies that arranges trips for fly-fishermen to England, Scotland, Alberta, Alaska, the western United States, and Pennsylvania.

But Jim keeps coming back to his roots—East Licking Creek. This mountain stream flows for more than 20 miles in an isolated, uninhabited, scenic valley. About halfway up the valley you'll see the Clearview Reservoir—the locals call it the Big Dam. Below the impoundment there are about 10 miles of stocked water before the stream enters Tuscorora Creek, which in turn enters the Juniata River at Port Royal. This lower end flows through some farmland and contains many long, flat sections, some more than 6 feet deep. It warms in summer, but contains some holdover trout. Several spring-fed streams like Johnstown Run enter this water, adding a limestone base to the last 5 miles.

Drive above the dam on East Licking Creek Drive and you'll note an entirely different stream. Above the reservoir there's 12 miles of heavily forested water that rarely rises above 70 degrees in summer. Even though it's heavily canopied, this upper section presents few problems for the fly-fisherman. There's little brush near the banks to catch an errant fly. In this upper section you'll see plenty of rapids, riffles, and small pools, a diversity of hatches, and many stocked and streambred trout. Jim Gilson feels that there are larger trout below the dam, but some natural reproduction above. The state developed the Karl Guss Picnic Area on this upper end.

Hatches on the two sections vary almost as much as the stream. On the lower end there's a decent hatch of tricos, but the warm water in July and August often reduces the number of rising trout. On this same section Jim says there's a tremendous hatch of big slate drakes in mid-August. The water above the dam harbors few of these huge *Hexagenia* spp. mayflies. Few green drakes appear in the lower section, yet there is a fishable hatch upstream.

Even though East Licking Creek contains a diversity of hatches, Jim believes that the density of some of the hatches has declined noticeably in the past 10 years. He says acid rain is the culprit. Below the dam the hatch density hasn't been affected because of the limestone springs entering the main stem.

Annually Jim catches 16- to 20-inch trout on East Licking Creek on a variety of patterns. Some of the most effective copy *Stenonema* spp. nymphs found in the stream. In July and August when hatches are scarce, Jim often resorts to terrestrials like the ant, cricket, beetle, or inchworm when he fishes above the dam.

BIG COVE CREEK

Access US 522 gives access to the upper end of Big Cove Creek, and PA 928 follows the stream below Big Cove Tannery.

Rating ✳✳

Patterns to Match the Hatches Little Blue-Winged Olive Dun (#20), Quill Gordon (#14), Gray Caddis (#16), Sulphur Dun and Spinner (#16), March Brown (#12), Blue-Winged Olive Dun (#14), Cream Cahill (#14 and #16), Light Cahill (#14 and #16), Slate Drake (#12 and #14), Yellow Drake (#12), Trico (#24), Little Brown Stonefly (#16)

Big Cove Creek, a respectable trout stream that few anglers fly-fish, begins near McConnellsburg and flows south just west of US 522. In its upper 4 miles Big Cove flows through open meadowland and averages 20 to 30 feet wide. Because of its lack of any canopy, this area warms quickly in the summer sun. The upper end of Big Cove would be much more productive with a system of stream improvement devices, and an agreement with the farmers to keep their cattle out of the water.

Near Big Cove Tannery the main stem adds Back Run, Roaring Run, and Spring Run to its flow. Spring Run is a sleeper. This cold limestone stream contains some heavy hatches and a good supply of trout through-

Big Cove Creek near McConnellsburg holds a good slate drake hatch in late July.

out the season. Spring Run above Webster Mills boasts a good trico hatch from mid-July through September. During this period Spring's temperature often holds in the low 60s, but you'll see few fishermen on the stream in late summer. Spring Run, plus the next downstream tributary, Spring Creek, provide cool water to the main stem of Big Cove for a mile. The Fulton County Sportsmen's Association operates a cooperative nursery on the upper end of Spring Creek that supplies additional trout to Cove and other local streams.

From Big Cove Tannery the main stem contains a good canopy, with a generous greenbelt along the stream. Two miles downstream Cove enters Buchanan State Forest. Below this half-mile section Cove is almost inaccessible. Some cold springs from Dickeys Mountain enter the lower 4 miles, but the area still becomes marginal after June. Cove has a total of about 14 miles of stocked water.

Ed Lehman of McConnellsburg often fly-fishes the stream in October and November, catching dozens of trout. He's seen many holdovers on the main stem and heard of trout up to 24 inches long being caught on Cove.

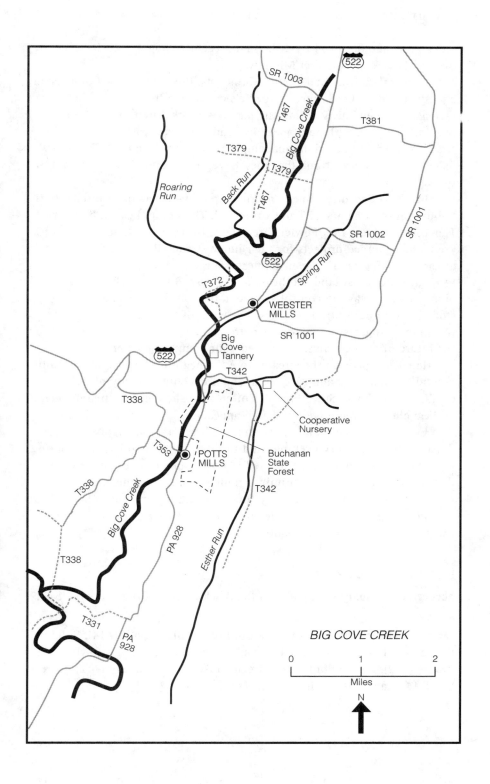

BIG COVE CREEK

Steve Frey, another local fly-fisherman, recently caught a 26-inch brown trout in Cove on a Muddler Minnow.

Cove suffers from some severe problems. Bob Lynn of McConnellsburg has fly-fished on Cove since 1970. He's concerned that siltation has increased tremendously within the past few years. Intensive upstream farming on Cove, with open meadows and few trees, could threaten the stream's future. In addition, poaching on Cove is widespread. Too many fishermen in the area think that they have to go home with their limit of trout.

But wait! Recently some concerned area fly-fishers have formed the Fulton County Chapter of Trout Unlimited. The group, headed by Gerry Timko, Steve Frey, Don Fowler, Grey Hays, Garey Sprowl, and Allen Cover, has planned projects for their home stream, Big Cove Creek. They're already working on a delayed-harvest project for the stream where it runs through state forest land southeast of Big Cove Tannery. The club also plans to study ways to control sedimentation on the stream and float-stock Fulton County trout streams. The work of this group, along with a farsighted, progressive waterways patrolman, Jan Caveney, bodes well for the future of area streams. They need your complete cooperation.

Hatches appear on the stream from the beginning of the season until late fall. In late May and early June you'll encounter plenty of light cahills on Big Cove. Steve Frey has often fly-fished on the stream when a prolific blue-winged olive dun hatch appears in late May or early June. Fish Cove even in July or August and you'll see a good supply of slate drakes appearing every evening. Add to this a good trico hatch on Spring Run and on Big Cove 1 mile below Big Cove Tannery and you can see that hatches continue almost uninterrupted throughout the season.

Cove above Big Cove Tannery flows through open meadowland. Below it ranges from 30 to 50 feet wide with plenty of undercut banks, productive riffles, and ledge-lined pools.

BLACKLOG CREEK

Access A secondary road parallels the Blacklog from Orbisonia off US 522.

Rating ✳✳

Patterns to Match the Hatches Blue Quill (#18), Black Quill (#14), Sulphur Dun and Spinner (#16), Gray Fox and Ginger Quill (#12 and #14), March Brown (#12), Light Cahill (#14), Green Drake and Coffin Fly (#12), Cream Cahill (#14 and #16), Yellow Drake (#12), Trico (#24)

John Gordon of Huntingdon caught 98 trout on one June afternoon three years ago. Many of these trout ranged from 6 to 12 inches long, and all but a few were native browns and brooks. John, like a growing number of fishermen, returns most of his trout. He used a small spinner and promptly released all of these fish to fight for another angler at another time. He caught them on a stream few anglers ever fly-fish: Blacklog Creek, in a secluded valley in Juniata and Huntingdon Counties.

Recently John and I met on Blacklog. We fished the upper end of the stocked area about 12 miles above Orbisonia. Here you find not only stocked trout but also many holdovers and an abundant native-trout population.

The late-June day we selected to fish Blacklog could not have turned out to be a poorer choice. The stream level had fallen rapidly the week before, and by now Blacklog ran a foot below normal. Native trout scattered when we approached the bank. John used a small spinner, and I tied on a Cream Cahill, size 14. We alternated fishing pools on the 10-foot-wide stream. We caught trout in almost every pool, even a few streambred browns. We headed upstream to fish the remains of a beaver dam abandoned several years before. Blacklog contains many active and abandoned beaver dams in its 20-mile flow. In one small pool I caught four heavy brook trout and missed two more. John agreed that there's an advantage to fly-fishing on small streams. After he caught one trout in a pool or riffle, other trout in that section refused his hardware. Not so with a dry fly.

Phil Stewart of Allenport fly-fishes Blacklog weekly throughout the season—one of the very few fly-fishermen on the stream. Phil often uses Bivisible or Adams patterns. He's caught some large holdover trout in October. Phil often fishes Blacklog with special success in late May, when a sporadic green drake hatch appears in the narrows just above Orbisonia.

Blacklog flows southwest from Juniata to Huntingdon County. It picks up few tributaries on its 20-mile trip to Shade Creek, then into Aughwick Creek near Orbisonia. Some of the upper 10 miles of water are posted. Shade Creek enters near Blacklog, close to Orbisonia. This tributary seems to contain more hatches than Blacklog. I've seen a decent black quill hatch near the Catholic church in late April on Shade Creek. Blue quills appear every morning during summer just below Shade Gap.

Although Blacklog flows in an isolated valley, it has a siltation problem that affects the hatches it contains. Silt flows into the main stem from poor road drainage and timbering in the headwaters.

STANDING STONE CREEK

Access Standing Stone Creek begins above Alan Seeger Park and flows into the Juniata River at Huntingdon. There are about 23 miles of water between those two points. PA 26 parallels the lower 16 miles of the stream. A dirt-and-blacktop road to Alan Seeger Park gives access to the upper end of Standing Stone. An excellent tributary, Laurel Run, enters the main stem near McAleveys Fort. Laurel Run holds a small impoundment, the Whipple Dam. Above this lake you'll find plenty of streambred trout.

Rating ✳✳

Patterns to Match the Hatches Little Blue-Winged Olive Dun (#20), Blue Quill (#18), Quill Gordon (#14), Hendrickson and Red Quill (#14), Black Quill (#14), Sulphur Dun and Spinner (#16), Gray Fox and Ginger Quill (#12 and #14), March Brown (#12), Light Cahill (#14), Slate Drake (#12 and #14), Yellow Drake (#12), Cream Cahill (#14 and #16)

Standing Stone has faced some major problems in the past few years. Like Spruce Creek just a few miles away, it suffered from a liquid-manure spill into the main stem just above McAleveys Fort. Within the past few years much of the East Branch, a productive tributary with a good population of streambred trout, has been closed. Standing Stone also suffers from major siltation from farming and, in the lower half, from warm marginal water. The last 7 miles of stream become smallmouth bass water in late summer.

Despite all of these difficulties Standing Stone contains a good supply of stocked, holdover, and streambred trout. From Jacksons Corner upstream to Alan Seeger Park, you'll find native brook and brown trout. The farther you travel upstream, the higher the ratio of brook to brown trout you'll find.

Hatches on the stream often produce rising trout. By mid-April you'll probably encounter some hendricksons. Even into late June you'll see trout feeding on yellow drakes and cream cahills. After early June try the upper end of the stream, where water temperatures stay fairly low.

8 | Streams of Northwestern Pennsylvania

The streams of northwestern Pennsylvania present great contrasts. Small, productive streams like Thompson Creek and Little Sandy Creek provide fly-fishermen with plenty of opportunities to fish the hatches. Large trout waters also flow through the northwestern sector of Pennsylvania. Oil Creek and Slippery Rock Creek present large water with some decent hatches—the light cahill in early June, for example. The largest potential trout water in the area, the Allegheny River below the Kinzua Dam, is in jeopardy. This big water with its lunker trout might revert to a warm-water stream. It is imperative for all of us to see that this doesn't happen.

WEST BRANCH, TUNUNGWANT CREEK

Access To reach the delayed-harvest stretch of the West Branch, from Bradford take PA 346 (Washington Street) west to Dorothy Lane. Turn left on Dorothy Lane; a right or left on Campus Drive will then take you to the regulated water.

Special Regulations Delayed harvest, artificial lures only—1.2 miles, from the T 499 bridge downstream to the pipeline crossing near the confluence of Gates Hollow.

Rating ✶✶

Patterns to Match the Hatches Little Blue-Winged Olive Dun (#20), Blue Quill (#18), Hendrickson (#14), Black Quill (#14), Black Caddis (#16), Tan Caddis (#14), Slate Drake (#12 and #14), Light Cahill (#14), Pale Evening Dun (#16)

Move over, Penn State—make room for the University of Pittsburgh at Bradford. Why? Pitt-Bradford boasts a unique setting in the Allegheny Mountains. Through the beautiful 125-acre campus of this

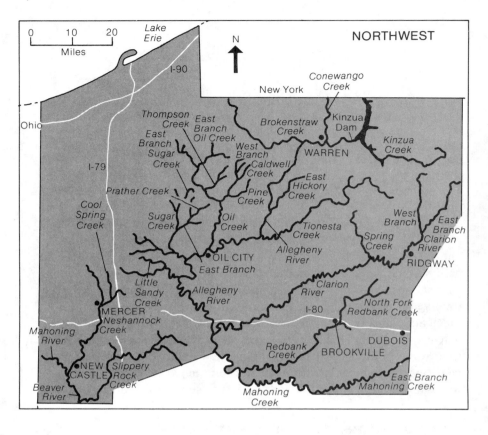

four-year liberal arts college flows a viable trout stream, the West Branch of Tunungwant Creek. Add to that setting the fact that the president of the college, Richard McDowell, and the vice president and dean of academic affairs, Carol Baker, are both avid fly-fishers and you can see that the future looks bright for this trout stream—and this college!

Carol Baker recalls a time a few years back when she saw a student fly-fishing on the college grounds during finals week. She vividly recalls how she worried about this student and his grades. She happily responds that the student not only passed the tests that semester, but he also became president of the freshman honor society. Carol often fly-fishes on the campus waters for an hour or two before she goes home.

How committed is the college to fly-fishing? Pitt-Bradford offers a Kinzua Fly Fishing Camp in summer, and it conducts a one-credit course entitled "Fly-Fishing and Fly-Tying," usually in fall. Both programs are under the skillful hands of Carl Zandi and Steve Svarka. Many of the students attending Pitt-Bradford actively fly-fish on the 1.2-mile section of delayed-harvest water.

I recently had an opportunity to fly-fish the delayed-harvest section on the West Branch a few days after the stream became catch-and-kill. (Anglers can kill fish in these regulated waters after June 15.) When I first entered the stream I checked the temperature. Seventy-six degrees—wow! That's too warm. But wait—the air temperature hit a record in Bradford that day, 91 degrees. Even with these high temperatures, though, I saw a few trout feed that evening.

I waited until the next morning to fly-fish the section again. By early morning the stream had cooled to 70 degrees and trout rose in the fast, oxygenated water in the rapids above. I still had a Patriot dry fly tied on my line, so I cast that pattern toward the rising fish. In half an hour I had caught and released three heavy brown trout on the dry fly. How does this stream hold up during July and August? Carol Baker says it does get marginal in the hot days of summer.

But wait again—I told you the administrators of this college were avid fly-fishers. Three miles upstream from the project water there's Reservoir #5, used by the Bradford Water Authority. Richard McDowell and Carol Baker approached the authority about a bottom release for this dam.

Guess what? They agreed. The college has recruited two Trout Unlimited chapters, the Pennsylvania Fish and Boat Commission, employees of Pitt-Bradford, and the Boondocs Program working with the McKean County Juvenile Justice Program to work on the project. In addition, the group plans to install stream improvement devices on the regulated water. If all goes well, water should be released from the bottom of this 60-foot-deep dam sometime in late 1999.

A sign designating the West Branch of Tunungwant Creek on the Pitt-Bradford Campus.

The West Branch is 20 to 30 feet wide with plenty of slow, deep pools and some fairly deep productive riffles. Temperatures on hot summer days can vary as much as 13 degrees from the East Branch to the West Branch. You will see some hatches on the West Branch. Look for cahills, blue quills, and yellow drakes during the summer. In the early and late season you'll find some blue-winged olive duns and slate drakes.

In the native American language *Tunungwant* means "pretty stream." Most locals call the stream by a shortened, easier-to-say name: Tuna.

What does the future have in store for this marginal trout stream? Who knows? But given the zeal and hard work of Pitt-Bradford administrators it could be bright.

EAST BRANCH, TUNUNGWANT CREEK

Access You can access the East Branch in the town of Lewis Run. The specially regulated water begins at Main and Egbert. Travel up Egbert a half mile to access the lower end of the stream. Upstream a couple of miles is a second access area, Droney Road. Take LR 4001, Lafayette Street, in Lewis Run to access the stream.

Special Regulations Trophy-trout project—3.0 miles, from the confluence with Pigeon Run downstream to the Main Street bridge in the town of Lewis Run.

Rating ✶✶

Patterns to Match the Hatches Blue Quill (#18), Hendrickson (#14), Little Blue-Winged Olive Dun (#20), Light Cahill (#14), Pale Evening Dun (#16), Yellow Stonefly (#16), Little Green Stonefly (#18), Slate Drake (#14)

Guess when I chose to fly-fish the East Branch for the first time? Just my luck, on the hottest day of the summer—and to beat it all I arrived on the stream near midday. By the time I gathered my gear I'm certain the temperature had risen to near 90 degrees.

I selected one of only a couple of access areas to the stream, just below the Droney Road bridge (T 329). I hiked downstream a half mile and then fished my way back upstream to the bridge. In that hour of fishing I didn't have a strike—I didn't even see a trout.

I almost quit, but instead I decided to head upstream, above the bridge, for an hour or two. The East Branch takes on a completely different appearance a couple of hundred yards above the bridge. Below, the stream is somewhat open—but above the bridge it's a different story. In this upper area much of the stream sees little sun; it's shaded by a dense growth of hemlocks. I didn't have to wait long to see if the East Branch held trout. On my second cast, in a deeply shaded pool, a 5-inch brookie hit my Patriot. A second small trout took the pattern on my very next cast. The next three riffles and pools upstream also yielded native trout.

Water temperatures stayed respectably cool on that hot afternoon. I recorded a 63-degree reading—in the middle of 90-degree day! The East Branch seems to hold temperatures about 10 degrees cooler than the West Branch. There are more differences between these two streams as well. The East Branch is, at 20 to 25 feet wide, smaller than the West Branch. And the East Branch has fewer slow pools than its sister to the west.

Even in June you'll find some hatches—rather sparse—on the East Branch. The stream boasts a good number of stoneflies. In early summer you'll see plenty of yellow and little green stoneflies appearing each evening. On summer mornings blue quills appear. You'll see the spinners of these mayflies undulating above fast-water sections of the stream throughout the day.

The East Branch has a trophy-trout designation. The stream is small and the water flow during the summer is minimal to maintain trophy-trout water. A better classification might be delayed harvest—fly-fishing only.

THOMPSON CREEK

Access The upper end of Thompson intersects PA 89, and the lower end crosses PA 8. A paved secondary road parallels much of the water.

Rating ✳✳

Patterns to Match the Hatches Little Blue-Winged Olive Dun (#20), Blue Quill (#18), Hendrickson and Red Quill (#14), Brown Drake (#12), Gray Fox (#14), March Brown (#14), Green Drake and Coffin Fly (#10), Slate Drake (#12 and #14), Light Cahill (#14), Cream Cahill (#14 and #16), Trico (#24)

This beautiful stream contains great hatches. You can start early in the season with blue quills and Hendricksons; fish midseason with March browns, green drakes, and brown drakes; and finish the season in early September with the trico. Thompson Creek has them all. What a shame that this productive stream, with its many holdover and streambred trout, has a large section not open to the public. About 3 miles upstream from PA 8 there's a prime section of the stream, almost 1.5 miles long, posted by the Titusville Rod and Gun Club. It's a pity this water can't be open to the public as a catch-and-release area.

Several years ago Jerry Honard of Fairview invited me to meet him on Thompson Creek. As regional director for continuing education at Penn State University, I traveled to Behrend College in Erie at least once a month. On each of those trips I crossed Thompson Creek at PA 8. Each time I did I wondered about its fishing. Therefore it didn't take much coaxing to induce me to meet Jerry on Thompson Creek one late-July morning.

Jerry showed me jars of mayfly duns and spinners he'd collected over the years from Thompson Creek: March browns, gray foxes, hendricksons, and brown drakes. Other jars contained many other aquatic insects that I couldn't identify because their color had faded in the alcohol solution. I was impressed with the variety of insects Jerry had gathered on this water. What amazed me most was the collection of brown drakes. I had experienced this species on Kettle, First Fork, Pine, and the Allegheny River, but I had not heard of it on Thompson Creek.

It was 8:00 AM by the time we gathered our gear for a morning of fishing. Jerry told me to expect a respectable trico spinner fall, so I tied on a size-24 female Trico Spinner. By 8:30 AM the trico spinners swarmed about 10 feet above the fast water at the head of the pool where we entered the stream. While we waited for the spinners to fall, I checked the water temperature on this warm morning. The thermometer showed 69 degrees—higher than what I had expected this early in the day. We flyfished on the lower end of the stream anyway, and Jerry assured me that upstream several miles the water would be cooler. Soon some female tricos returned to the surface spent, and an occasional trout rose to the sparse food supply. For more than half an hour only a few trout rose, and then the hatch ended as quickly as it had begun. Jerry and I had only three trout to show for our hour of watching and fishing, but we agreed that the unusually low water and elevated temperature evidently deterred trout from feeding.

As with so many other Pennsylvania streams, hatches on Thompson Creek have diminished in intensity the past few years. Is it because of upstream farming and siltation, or has this reduction resulted from natural causes?

Like many freestone streams, Thompson Creek warms in summer. Despite this it harbors some holdover trout in its main stem and especially in its two major tributaries, McLaughlin Creek and Shirley Run. Thompson Creek is a relatively short stream, only about 6 miles long. It begins with the merger of Shirley Run and Hummer Creek near the small town of Shelmadine Springs. Downstream Thompson picks up McLaughlin Creek— an extremely productive tributary. Thompson flows southwest and empties into Oil Creek at Hydetown.

Thompson's stream bottom contains mainly small rocks and shale and is not difficult to wade. Some of the pools are fairly extensive, and some of the riffles above are productive.

Do you want to experience some early-season success with the Hendrickson and the March brown, and see the brown drake? Try Thompson Creek.

CALDWELL CREEK

Access Caldwell is a small stream, especially in midsummer, with a relatively moderate fall of 15 feet per mile. The main stem begins near Torpedo and flows southwest along PA 27 to Titusville. The upper end can be reached via PA 27, the lower half by Dotyville and Flat Roads. An old railroad bed follows the stream near the regulated area. The main stem flows about 15 miles before it enters Pine Creek, another trout stream, 2 miles east of Titusville. Pine Creek flows into Oil Creek near the Drake Museum in Titusville.

Special Regulations Delayed harvest, fly-fishing only—1.4 miles, from the Selkirk highway bridge downstream to near the Dotyville bridge. West Branch of Caldwell Creek—catch-and-release—3.6 miles, from the West Branch bridge upstream to Three Bridge Run.

Rating ✳✳

Patterns to Match the Hatches Early Brown Stonefly (#12), Blue Quill (#18), Hendrickson and Red Quill (#14), Sulphur Dun and Spinner (#16), March Brown (#12), Gray Fox (#14), Slate Drake (#12 and #14), Green Drake and Coffin Fly (#10), Yellow Drake (#12), Light Cahill (#14), Trico (#24)

Jack Busch of Erie and I sat patiently by the stream, waiting for something to happen. In late April Caldwell Creek should have been alive with insect activity by early afternoon, and by 2:00 PM hundreds of early brown stoneflies returned to the water's surface to complete their life cycle by laying eggs. As the stoneflies laid their eggs, dozens of blue quills escaped rapidly from the surface in the warm afternoon sun. Still no fish appeared. In a 100-yard section in front of me no trout rose to this increase in insect activity. Jack assured me that this water still contained plenty of trout, even though we saw cluttered remains of fish guts strewn about the stream bottom. By 2:30 PM Jack suggested we leave Caldwell Creek and head to Sugar Creek and the grannom hatch on that stream. I suggested that we wait until 3:15.

About 3:00 PM the riffle ahead of me came alive with hendricksons and red quills escaping rapidly in the warm spring air. With this assortment of hatches in the air and on the water, however, only two trout rose. I caught both surface-feeders on a size-14 Red Quill, and the pool and riffle above became quiet again. Probably the 48-degree water slowed feeding.

Jack suggested that we head upstream 2 miles to the delayed-harvest area. We parked at the lower end of the regulated stretch and walked upstream. In the first couple of pools we saw about two dozen trout rising to blue quills and hendricksons. Within a few minutes the Hendrickson hatch ended as abruptly as it had begun half an hour before, but the blue quill continued for two more hours. In almost every pool Jack and I caught trout rising to our size-18 Blue Quills. Why so many trout rising in the regulated stretch and so few below? In the open water below most fishermen keep their catch. What a fantastic stream Caldwell Creek would be if the entire stream were catch-and-release water—or at least delayed harvest.

Northwestern Pennsylvania fly-fishermen consider Caldwell a prime trout stream, one that maintains fairly cool temperatures all season. Caldwell contains plenty of holdover and a good supply of streambred browns and some brook trout in its headwaters.

Caldwell Creek in July is like most other state freestone streams: low and at some places marginal. There are, however, many springs feeding into the main stem, and fishing at those or just below them in late summer can be rewarding. Besides, on its West Branch this stream contains over 3.5 miles of catch-and-release water, and the main stem includes more than a mile of delayed-harvest water.

Caldwell exhibits many of the state's common hatches, including plentiful blue quills and hendricksons in April. Often when these two hatches appear on this stream, snow flurries arrive as a last blast of winter. Blue quills too dazed to take flight ride the surface from pool to pool. Water temperatures on these late-April days often hover near or below the 50-degree mark. If you're so fortunate as to be on Caldwell or the West Branch when the water temperature rises above 50 and trout rise to stunned mayflies, you'll probably experience tremendous fly-fishing.

March browns and gray foxes appear on Caldwell during the latter part of May. Both species are large enough to bring trout to the surface of this small stream. Trout up to 20 inches long often surface-feed to the green drake hatch common on Caldwell around the end of May. Even in late June, if you find cool water, yellow drakes appear in the evening for some good late-season fly-fishing. On those late-season mornings blue quills and light cahills appear daily on the West Branch, on the main stem, and on Pine Creek. Tricos appear every morning throughout the late summer.

Caldwell contains some unbelievably large pools for its size, and each seems to harbor a good supply of trout, especially those with undercut banks and logjams. Much of the stream has a good overhead canopy of hardwoods and hemlocks. In many areas the bank is lined with thick groves of alders, making fly-fishing frustrating. Although Caldwell is lined with rocks, wading is fairly easy.

Area anglers have noticed a dramatic reduction in the intensity of hatches on Caldwell Creek the past few years. Talk with a Caldwell Chapter member of Trout Unlimited, like Barry Johnson of Spartansburg, and he'll tell you he feels the cause of this decline is surface oil draining from nearby oil wells.

Nevertheless, if you enjoy small and moderate streams with many large trout and some good hatches, try Caldwell or its main tributary, the West Branch. Both have special-project water to ensure an adequate supply of trout through much of the season.

SUGAR CREEK

Access Just west of Chapmanville, PA 427 parallels Sugar Creek to its mouth.

Rating ✳✳

Patterns to Match the Hatches Early Brown Stonefly (#12), Blue Quill (#18), Hendrickson (#14), Grannom (#16), March Brown (#12), Green Drake (#10), Slate Drake (#12 and #14), Trico (#24)

Jack Busch met me at Titusville on a cool late-April morning. We had come for a day of fly-fishing during the grannom hatch. I hoped I'd planned the trip correctly so as finally to witness the heavy emergence and egg laying of the caddisfly I had heard about for years.

Jack fishes Sugar Creek almost continually from mid-April until late November and knows the hatches on the stream well. In late April the grannom constitutes one of the major hatches, and this is an excellent time to find rising trout—that is, if conditions like water temperature and flow are satisfactory.

When we met at the Pizza Hut in Titusville, Jack carried several vials full of insects with him. "They're on," he said.

"The grannoms?" I asked.

"Yes, they started four days ago."

I examined the vials of preserved grannoms, with their brownish black bodies, tan-and-black legs, and dark, mottled wings, and urged Jack to head to the stream.

We arrived at Bradleytown, gathered our fishing gear from the car, and headed for a pool behind the church. Hundreds of adult grannoms greeted us as we followed the worn path to the creek. At the stream we saw thousands of caddisflies in the air and on nearby bushes, and dozens laying eggs on the water surface. But with all this food available, no trout rose in the deep pool and rapids in front of us. We continued to walk upstream, exploring more pools and pocket water for rising trout. In the next pool under a low-lying hemlock branch a solitary trout rose sporadically to the enormous supply of insects on the surface. Trout seemed lethargic because of the 46-degree water temperature and four days of intense feeding on the insects.

About 1:00 PM several trout began to rise to the grannoms. Jack cast over the nearest downstream fish. He caught two of the five risers and saw two more look at his imitation and refuse it. We were both confused and dejected at the lack of rising trout during this heavy hatch, but caddis hatches are often disappointing. Only a steady flow of grannom naturals on the water kept us on the stream.

We waited until 4:00 PM and headed upstream a couple of miles above Bradleytown. Jack told me to hike downstream a half mile and work my way back up to the car. The first pool I entered contained a half-dozen freely rising trout taking grannoms. Each one took my size-16 Grannom on the first accurate cast. I lost the last trout when an overhanging alder on the far bank snagged my leader. I hurriedly tied on another downwing imitation and headed up to the next productive-looking pocket. Here a holdover trout of about 14 inches sucked in my imitation. Each pool upstream held two or three rising trout, and most took the imitation.

Jack fished upstream from the car and experienced the same success. He too landed a holdover about 15 inches long. The surface action lasted for about an hour and then subsided. Pools and riffles that had earlier come alive with rising trout now were silent. Grannoms appeared in the air and on the water until dark, but few trout rose to this magnificent hatch after 5:00 PM.

Sugar Creek begins in southeastern Crawford County and flows south into Venango County to the town of Sugarcreek, where it enters French Creek. There's a total of about 12 miles of stocked water on Sugar. On its way to French Creek, Sugar picks up volume from Little Sugar, a few miles above Bradleytown. At Cooperstown, Lake Creek enters the main stem, and a mile upstream the East Branch joins Sugar. In the Bradleytown area Sugar ranges from 25 to 40 feet wide, with some productive runs, moderate pools, and a good supply of holdover browns. Some of these holdovers range from 15 to 20 inches long. At Cooperstown, Sugar doubles in size and ranges from 60 to 70 feet wide, with long, deep pools and runs, some a couple of hundred feet long.

Sporadic mayfly and stonefly hatches appear on Sugar throughout the year. Blue quills and early brown stoneflies often appear on the opening day of the fishing season. But in late April when the grannom appears, it's time to fly-fish on Sugar.

PINE CREEK

Access PA 27 crosses Pine Creek at Enterprise. Take SR 3002 to reach the stream.

Rating ✳✳

Patterns to Match the Hatches Early Brown Stonefly (#12), Hendrickson and Red Quill (#14), Grannom (#16), Blue Quill (#18), March Brown (#12), Green Drake and Coffin Fly (#10), Sulphur Dun and Spinner (#16), Light Cahill (#14), Brown Caddis (#14)

Pine Creek lies just to the southeast of Caldwell Creek. It too contains plenty of sizable pools for holdover trout. Much of the section above Enterprise contains streambred browns, but below they are limited. The upper end, before Caldwell enters, ranges from 30 to 40 feet wide, with the section above Enterprise about 20 feet wide.

The best time to fly-fish Pine is near the end of May. By that time most other anglers have vacated the stream, and the hatches bring up some large trout. With the sulphur and green drake hatches, late May is an ideal time to fish this water. In June, Pine harbors light cahills in the evening; in September and October you can experience some late-season fly-fishing with a size-14 Brown Caddis.

Caldwell joins Pine near East Titusville. Below, Pine widens considerably, to 60 feet in some areas. It enters Oil Creek near the Drake Well Memorial Park in Titusville.

OIL CREEK

Access PA 8 runs parallel to and within a mile of Oil Creek above Titusville and within a few miles of the area below. Only four points allow access to the stretch of Oil Creek from Titusville to Petroleum Center. You can reach the upper end at the Drake Well Memorial Park and the middle section by way of a poor dirt road, Miller Farm Road; near the lower end on Pioneer Road; and at the lower end, Oil Creek State Park at Petroleum Center. A 14-mile paved bike trail runs along the creek from Titusville to Petroleum Center and also provides access. Picnic spots, resting areas, and historical markers dot the trail.

Special Regulations Delayed harvest, artificial lures only—1.6 miles, from the Petroleum Center bridge downstream to the railroad bridge at Columbia Farm.

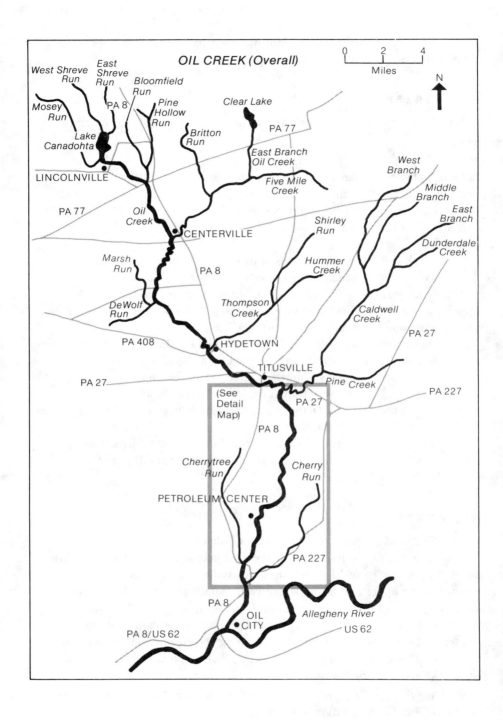

OIL CREEK (Overall)

0 2 4
Miles

N

West Shreve Run
East Shreve Run
Bloomfield Run
Mosey Run
PA 8
Pine Hollow Run
Clear Lake
Lake Canadohta
Britton Run
PA 77
LINCOLNVILLE
East Branch Oil Creek
West Branch
Five Mile Creek
Middle Branch
East Branch
PA 77
Oil Creek
CENTERVILLE
Shirley Run
Dunderdale Creek
Marsh Run
PA 8
Hummer Creek
DeWolf Run
Thompson Creek
Caldwell Creek
PA 27
PA 408
HYDETOWN
TITUSVILLE
Pine Creek
PA 27
PA 227
(See Detail Map)
PA 27
PA 8
Cherrytree Run
Cherry Run
PETROLEUM CENTER
PA 227
PA 8
OIL CITY
Allegheny River
US 62
PA 8/US 62

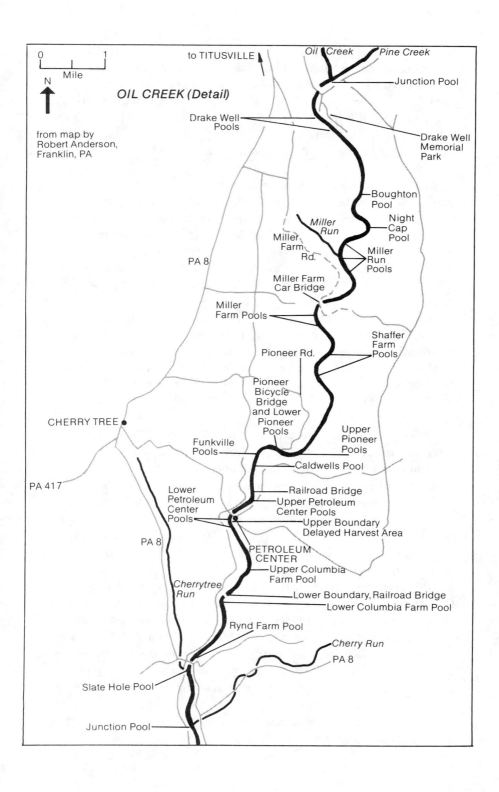

Rating ✳✳✳

Patterns to Match the Hatches Little Black Stonefly (#16 and #18), Little Blue-Winged Olive Dun (#20), Quill Gordon (#14), Blue Quill (#18), Green Caddis (#14), Grannom (#14), Black Quill (#14), Tan Caddis (#14), Gray Fox (#12), March Brown (#12), Sulphur Dun and Spinner (#16), Light Cahill (#14), Yellow Drake (#10), Trico (#24), Slate Drake (#12), Big Slate Drake (#8), Big Slate and Rusty Spinner (#8), White Mayfly (#14 and #16)

It's one of the biggest trout streams in Pennsylvania. The state stocks more than 33 miles of water with 16,000 to 30,000 trout annually. It's more than 100 feet wide at many points and has plenty of deep, half-mile-long pools with productive, moderate riffles scattered between. Access is limited, except by bike or a hike down a bike path. This bike trail follows the stream for 14 miles of isolated beauty. Marshall Young calls the water Pennsylvania's Beaverkill. Most people, however, call it by its proper name—Oil Creek.

Don Foltz of Lincolnville and Marshall Young of Union City recently formed the Caldwell Creek Chapter of Trout Unlimited. Their goal for the organization is to preserve and even improve the quality of trout water in northwestern Pennsylvania. They have created stream improvement projects on French Creek and plan to construct some on Caldwell. At the urging of the Oil Creek Chapter, the state designated a delayed-harvest area on Oil Creek in 1989.

Weekly, throughout the season, Don and Marshall fly-fish on this extensive, underrated stream. These two outstanding fly-fishermen, using a combination of emerging-pupa and dry-fly patterns, catch hundreds of trout annually. Almost from the beginning of the season you can find them on the stream matching a caddisfly or mayfly hatch. Into July and August they fish Oil Creek, even though the water temperature sometimes rises into the high 70s. At this time of year Don and Marshall search the stream for cool springs or streams entering the main stem. Don has caught trout up to 2 feet long during summer.

Oil Creek lacks many of the common mayfly hatches found on other Commonwealth streams. It has no green drake or brown drake. Consider, however, that it's not many decades since Oil was extremely polluted. From the 1880s until 1915 some companies discharged various pollutants into this potentially productive trout stream. Some companies poured acid into the stream, others floated logs down the water, and still others ejected shots of petroleum and refined gasoline into the stream. Oil Creek has recovered from these careless acts of man, but hatches remain sparse.

Caddis hatches often monopolize the surface activity on Oil Creek. These insects appear almost every day of the season. In May tan- and cream-bodied caddis predominate. Throughout the season emerging-caddis-pupa imitations work well on the stream. By late May some heavier hatches of mayflies appear. At that time sulphurs provide some great dry-fly fishing.

Near the end of May you'll find a good brown drake hatch. Mike Laskowski of Oil Creek Outfitters in Petroleum City says that the lower ends of the delayed-harvest and Miller Farm areas hold good brown drake populations. In June, light cahills appear in the evening and persuade some heavy trout to surface-feed. Marshall Young says the big slate drake and the rusty spinner frequent the surface in mid-August. This huge mayfly dun usually emerges after dark, but the spinner can be found over riffles as early as 7:30 PM. In early August you'll also encounter what the locals call Canadian soldiers, or the white mayfly hatch. Many seasons Oil Creek's temperature at the time this prodigious hatch appears is just too warm to see rising trout. Temperatures in the high 70s and low 80s in summer are not uncommon.

Oil Creek begins near Don Foltz's home in Lincolnville, in northeastern Crawford County. Its tributaries are Mosey Run, West and East Shreve Runs, Bloomfield Run, and Pine Hollow Run. The East Branch, also stocked, joins the main stem at Centerville. On its trip south Oil Creek picks up additional volume from Thompson Creek at Hydetown and Pine Creek near Titusville.

Above Titusville, Oil Creek ranges from 40 to 80 feet wide. After picking up Pine it widens to more than 100 feet in places. On its path to the Allegheny River at Oil City, the main stem adds Cherrytree and Cherry Runs.

Wading on Oil can be extremely hazardous because of the slippery, coated rocks. Use a wading staff and chest waders to effectively cover the entire stream.

Check with Mike Laskowski of Oil Creek Outfitters (814-677-4684) in Petroleum Center for stream conditions and hatches. His shop borders the delayed-harvest area on the stream.

SLIPPERY ROCK CREEK

Access You can get to the upper end of Slippery Rock via PA 108, PA 8, and PA 308. You can reach the lower end in Lawrence County off US 19 and US 422, and from secondary roads like Heinz Camp and Mountville Roads.

Special Regulations Delayed harvest, fly-fishing only—0.5 mile, from Heinz Camp property downstream to 0.25 mile below the SR 2022 bridge.

Rating ✷✷

Patterns to Match the Hatches Little Blue-Winged Olive Dun (#20), Blue
Quill (#18), Green Caddis (#16), Grannom (#16), Tan Caddis (#16), Dark
Olive Caddis (#16), Sulphur Dun and Spinner (#16), March Brown (#12),
Light Cahill (#14), Brown Drake (#12), Slate Drake (#12 and #14), Green
Drake and Coffin Fly (#10), *Pteronarcys* Stonefly (#6), Yellow Drake (#12),
White Mayfly (#14 and #16)

How did this substantial stream get its name? Try wading it sometime
and you'll quickly see. This oversized stream contains a variety of
rocks and boulders, all covered with mud and organic matter and all bent
on creating hazardous wading for the angler.

Tony Palumbo of Hermitage and Ted Fauceglia of Sharpsville travel to
Slippery Rock Creek from their Mercer County homes at least a dozen
times a year. They usually fish the lower end of the stream, which houses
a delayed-harvest area. It's only a 45-minute trip for them to this stretch.
Frequently they meet many anglers on the section from the Pittsburgh
area, only 50 minutes from Slippery Rock Creek.

Tony prefers the heavy pocket water in the regulated area and usually
fishes caddis or crane fly patterns. His wet crane fly works exceptionally
well on the stream. While Tony's fishing the heavy water, Ted moves
downstream to one of the slow pools and uses midges. Both do well on
Slippery Rock, each using his own style of fly-fishing. Midges, crane flies,
and caddisflies are all important items on the trout's menu in Slippery
Rock Creek.

Almost 30 years ago Slippery Rock Creek received a super-slug of
mine acid after a heavy rainfall. Before the cloudburst only slight
amounts of acid bled into the stream from abandoned mines. The heavy
discharge killed most of the trout in the stream and decimated the aquatic
life. The Department of Environmental Resources has since added a liming
device near Harrisville to help alleviate the mine-acid problem on the
stream. Tony says the hatches seem to get heavier each year. If you're on
the stream around the end of May, you might even see the few green
drakes that now emerge. Add to this several caddisflies, some light cahills,
sulphurs, little blue-winged olives, brown drakes in the upper end, and
white mayflies in late August and you see that matching the hatch can be
fun on Slippery Rock Creek. Tony says that the little blue-winged olives
become important to match in April and September on this water.

Slippery Rock resembles the Little Juniata River in many spots. It even
has cloudy water like the Little Juniata's, created by an upstream limestone
plant that empties some of its effluent into the stream. Water temperatures
rise above 70 degrees during June, July, and August. At those times trout
look for one of the cool tributaries like the one just below Heinz Bridge,

or Hells Run a half mile upstream. Here trout rest in the main stem just next to the bank and take advantage of the cool influx from the springs.

Slippery Rock begins in northern Butler County near Higgins Corners. It picks up Seaton Run, Blacks Creek, North Branch (stocked), McMurray Run (stocked), South Branch, Long Run, Glade Run, Big Run, and Wolf Creek in Butler County. Continuing its flow southwest into Lawrence County, Slippery Rock adds Jamison Run, Taylor Run (stocked), and Muddy Creek. The stream enters Connoquenessing Creek near Ellwood City. The state stocks the stream from the Armstrong Bridge at the lower end of the delayed-harvest area upstream to a point just below PA 173 in Butler County—about 15 miles.

On the lower end of the stocked water there's a delayed-harvest area accessible by Heinz Camp Road. Here the stream averages 80 to 100 feet wide, with long, flat sections and some deep pocket water. Seven miles upstream from this point Slippery Rock flows through a gorge filled with huge boulders. This section is dangerous, and wading is extremely challenging. Upstream, where Slippery Rock crosses US 19, the stream narrows to 60 to 70 feet.

The delayed-harvest segment at the lower end of Slippery Rock is only a half mile long. Additional length must be added to this regulated water. Since the stream is only a 50-minute drive from Pittsburgh the regulated section gets extreme fishing pressure, while the remainder of the stream seems void of fishermen. What a stretch this would be if the delayed-harvest area were extended upstream a couple of miles!

The stream has a siltation problem—it discolors quickly after a storm and stays off color for several days.

NESHANNOCK CREEK

Access US 19 parallels the upper end of Neshannock Creek, and Creek Road the middle section to Volant. PA 956 crosses the stream near Neshannock Falls. The Neshannock varies from a small stream above Volant, ranging from 30 to 40 feet wide, to one over 40 feet wide below.

Special Regulations Delayed harvest, artificial lures only—2.7 miles, from the base of the Mill Dam in Volant downstream to the covered bridge on T 476.

Rating ✳✳

Patterns to Match the Hatches Tan Caddis (#16), Olive Caddis (#16), Dark Brown Caddis (#16), Green Caddis (#16), Sulphur Dun and Spinner (#16), March Brown (#12), Light Cahill (#14), Brown Drake (#12), Red Quill (#16), Blue-Winged Olive Dun (#14), Green Drake and Coffin Fly (#10),

Slate Drake (#12 and #14), Big Slate Drake (#8), White Mayfly (#14 and #16)

Who would believe that Neshannock Creek in Mercer and Lawrence Counties contains an abundant brown drake hatch? The same brown drake that you find on the Allegheny River, First and Driftwood Forks of the Sinnemahoning, and Kettle and Pine Creeks. The same mayfly that brings large trout to the surface to feed.

Near the end of May Tony Palumbo, Ted Fauceglia, and I visited Neshannock Creek Outfitters (now called the Outdoor Shop) in Volant. Chris Horn, then the store manager, told us the brown drakes had appeared for the last three days on the stream. Ted and I rushed over to the bridge in Volant to see if we could spot any drakes. Ted wanted to photograph a dun and spinner. I hoped that I would see the brown drake on Neshannock and authenticate it. As Ted and I walked to the bridge we examined several spiderwebs. Each contained dozens of still-struggling brown drake duns and spinners. The Neshannock did contain a brown drake hatch, then, and given the number at the bridge, a sizable one. As with all other eastern streams, the hatch of drakes on the Neshannock lasts for three or four days.

The state stocks 25 miles of the Neshannock. There's an intense belief on the part of local fishermen that you should catch and keep your limit—consequently, areas near stocking points like bridges see an undue amount of pressure, especially shortly after opening day and after in-season stockings. Fly-fishermen would do well to avoid these stocked areas and fish sections in between. Chris Horn and Wayne Edwards, until recently managers of the Neshannock Creek Outfitters, urged the Fish Commission to designate a 2-mile delayed-harvest area from Leesburg Station downstream to the Volant Dam. The state finally agreed and the area is now in place below Volant. Fly-fishermen would enjoy fishing over the brown drake hatch when the water still teemed with trout.

The Neshannock begins where Cool Spring and Otter Creeks combine at the eastern end of Mercer County. The stream then flows southwest through Mercer and Lawrence Counties, picking up tributaries like Beaver, Pine, Indian, and Potter Runs, and the Little Neshannock near Neshannock Falls. The Neshannock enters the Shenango River in New Castle. The water temperature on the Neshannock often rises into the high 70s and low 80s in late June, July, and August. When it does the stream quickly becomes a warm-water fishery.

"If you know where the springs are in late summer, you can find trout," Chris Horn says.

If you plan to fly-fish on this stream check with Bob Veltre, Wayne Edwards, Bill Duncan, Debbie Michaels, or Ron Olsescyski at the Outdoor Shop on Main Street in Volant for the latest information on stream conditions and hatches.

COOL SPRING CREEK

Access Cool Spring flows just east of Mercer and is reached off US 62: Take Airport Road to McCullough Road and then to Cool Spring Road.

Special Regulations Delayed harvest, artificial lures only—1.25 miles, from the SR 2014 bridge upstream to the abandoned railroad grade.

Rating ✳✳

Patterns to Match the Hatches Green Caddis (#16), Brown Caddis (#16), Sulphur Dun and Spinner (#16), Gray Fox (#14), Brown Drake (#12), Little Blue-Winged Olive Dun (#20), Slate Drake (#12 and #14)

If you get an opportunity to fly-fish on Cool Spring Creek in the delayed-harvest area, you'll notice plenty of work completed by the local Trout Unlimited group. The Neshannock Chapter provided access to the stream. Before the group completed its project, access to some stretches was difficult, but now it's merely a short walk along a path and some footbridges built by the organization's members.

Once you reach the stream you see plenty of trout, especially in the hole the locals call the Glory Hole. Here you'll probably see a dozen trout rising—especially if you arrive before June 15. The stream contains some pools and short but productive riffles. In the regulated area the stream ranges from 20 to 30 feet wide and contains a good canopy of alders and hardwoods. Cool Spring does, however, warm into the 70s in summer.

Who would believe that this small stream contains a decent brown drake hatch? If you're lucky enough to meet that hatch or the little blue-winged olive dun in early June, you're in for some good small-stream fly-fishing. The state stocks 5 miles of water. The delayed-harvest area allows fishing with artificial lures.

LITTLE SANDY CREEK

Access US 62 crosses the stream at the town of Polk.

Special Regulations Delayed harvest, fly-fishing only—1.3 miles, from SR 3024 at Polk upstream to the old bridge at the Polk Center pump house.

Rating ✳✳

Patterns to Match the Hatches Little Blue-Winged Olive Dun (#20), Blue

Quill (#18), Quill Gordon (#14), Hendrickson and Red Quill (#14), Grannom (#16), Beetle (#20), Sulphur Dun and Spinner (#16), Gray Fox (#14), March Brown (#12), Blue-Winged Olive Dun (#14), Green Drake and Coffin Fly (#10), Slate Drake (#12 and #14), Dark Green Drake (#8), Light Cahill (#14), Chocolate Dun (#12 and #14), Yellow Drake (#12)

In 1958 the Fish Commission poisoned Little Sandy Creek to kill all the brown trout in the stream. Some anglers and residents remember vividly that sorry day. They saw huge brown trout lying belly-up on the surface throughout much of the stream. For the next 20 years the state stocked only brook trout in this fertile freestone stream. What a crime was committed against this miniature insect factory!

In 1978, under pressure from the Neshannock Chapter of Trout Unlimited, the Fish Commission finally allowed the group to plant fingerling browns back in the stream. Tony Palumbo and Ted Fauceglia recall that initial stocking well. Tony proudly displays three large mounted brown trout—all taken from Little Sandy. Ted's an accomplished photographer. One of his most cherished photos shows a 19-inch brown that he caught on this stream.

For its size Little Sandy contains some massive and unusual hatches. This diminutive stream holds heavy, productive quill gordon, blue quill, slate drake, and green drake hatches, but it also hosts a decent supply of dark green drakes that often appear concurrently with the green drakes. Members of the genus *Baetisca* also appear in numbers on the stream. Examine some of the exposed rocks in Little Sandy and you'll see evidence of shucks from these humpbacked nymphs. If the need arises to match the *Baetisca*, use a Chocolate Dun in a size 12 or 14.

Little Sandy has a good number of holdover trout and streambred browns and brookies. Temperatures seldom rise above 70 degrees on this heavily canopied stream. Heavy cover throughout and a narrow stream make casting a dry fly difficult.

Little Sandy begins just east of Lake Wilhelm in eastern Mercer County. The stream flows southeast to Polk, where it enters Sandy Creek. There are about 5 miles of stocked water. Above Polk the stream is narrow, about 20 to 30 feet wide; it widens at Polk to 30 to 40 feet. Throughout its length it contains a heavy covering of hemlocks, alders, and hardwoods. The stream has plenty of small pools and productive riffles. The section near the old railroad bridge on the hospital grounds at Polk contains several deep, productive pools that harbor some large brown trout.

The last 1.3 miles of Little Sandy have been designated fly-fishing-only water. The Oil Creek Chapter of Trout Unlimited has placed many worthwhile stream improvement devices in this regulated section.

The brown trout population has rebounded from the disaster that occurred in 1958. Little Sandy is home to many streambred and holdover browns.

ALLEGHENY RIVER (BELOW KINZUA DAM)

Access The Allegheny River is easy to get to. PA 59 follows the river from US 6 to Warren.

Special Regulations Miscellaneous waters special regulations—8.75 miles below the Kinzua Dam, from the outflow of the Allegheny Reservoir to the confluence with Conewago Creek.

Rating ✷✷✷

Patterns to Match the Hatches Dark Tan Caddis (#14 and #16), Light Cahill (#14), Little Blue-Winged Olive Dun (#20 and #26), Olive Caddis (#18), Trico (#24), Tan Caddis (#16)

The Allegheny River below the Kinzua Dam is a river that's searching for an identity. Will the 8 miles from the breast downriver to the Warren bridge be managed for trout, or will the stretch revert to a warm-water fishery?

The fate of this section rests with the Pennsylvania Fish Commission and the Army Corps of Engineers. Current indications from the commission are that the river will be managed to return to "historic flows and temperatures." The corps attempts to maintain a summer temperature in the upper tailwater of 71 degrees.

What a pity the tailwater isn't a few degrees cooler! Look at the summers of 1988 and 1998. Record heat and drought conditions devastated many of the state's streams and rivers. Only a handful of large-water trout survived those unusual summers. Fishermen had few choices if they wanted to fish for trout.

One of the very few large waters that held trout in those summers was the Allegheny River. Now this important water may be lost to trout fishermen. The dam above contains miles of warm-water fishing, and more than 100 miles of the river below Warren hold warm-water species. And yet the Fish Commission insists that the 8 miles below the dam can't be retained as a cold-water fishery. A productive cold-water fishery on the Allegheny would bring untold anglers and dollars into the Warren-area economy.

Hank Foradora of Brockway, one of the anglers who frequents the Allegheny, is concerned about the future direction of the fishery. Hank hunts and fishes year-round. In fall and early spring you'll find him in the woods calling in a big gobbler. The rest of the year Hank fishes—much of

The Allegheny River below the Kinzua Dam holds some lunker trout.

that time on the Allegheny. He started fishing the river below the dam one year after the corps completed it in 1965. He used live bait in February and caught browns over 2 feet long. Then Hank switched to fly-fishing in spring and summer. He's often caught rainbow trout up to 18 inches long on a Picket Pin or other favorite pattern. Hank refers to any trout over 18 inches long on the Allegheny as a "sawlog."

I had an opportunity to fish with Hank recently. After the usual cheerful send-off by his wife, Fedora, Hank, his son John, Bryan Meck, and I headed for the Allegheny, 60 miles from the Foradoras' Brockway home. We planned to be on the river before 8:00 AM. John told me several weeks before that he had seen small mayfly spinners in the air early in the morning, and I wanted to identify them.

We arrived on the river and waded across near Putnam Eddy. Sure enough, small spinners began appearing at the head of the eddy shortly after we arrived. Soon tricos filled the air. Then another species appeared, even smaller than the size-24 trico. During all of this mayfly activity not one trout rose. Hank indicated that these trout were fickle, just like those on the Delaware River. The water temperature might have been the culprit. At 8:00 AM it registered 73 degrees—not good for an area several hundred feet below a bottom-release dam.

All four of us stood waiting for rising fish. Nothing happened. Finally Hank motioned for me to come downriver. He had spotted what he thought was a large muskie swimming just 20 feet out from him. I waded closer to the big fish, saw brown spots, and yelled to all three that it was a large brown trout. Hank and I agreed that this sawlog would measure 28 to 30 inches long and would weigh close to 10 pounds. Bryan and John immediately cast dry flies, then wet flies, and finally streamers in front of the lunker.

Finally Bryan yelled, "I got him," and the fight was on.

The trout headed upstream, then toward the far shore, making Bryan's reel sing as the fish fought to free itself of the fly. Bryan waded toward the center of the pool until water poured into his waders. Now the trout surfaced near the far shore. Bryan was into his backing, which became tangled. With a final leap the monster said good-bye. Bryan sat stunned on the shore for 15 minutes, thinking about what he would have done with this heavy brown trout. Would he have released it? This was certainly one of Hank's Allegheny River sawlogs.

The Allegheny contains plenty of caddis throughout much of the season. Hank says that the dark tan caddis appears from mid-May until almost the Fourth of July. Abundant mayflies on the stretch include the light cahill, trico, and little blue-winged olive dun. Tricos and little blue-winged olives emerge many mornings from July through September.

NORTH FORK, RED BANK CREEK

Access US 322 reaches the lower end of this stream in Brookville. To reach the upper end, take PA 36 north to SR 4006 (Moore Bridge Road).

Special Regulations Delayed harvest, fly-fishing only—1.9 miles, from US 322 in Brookville upstream 1.9 miles, except a 50-yard section from the Brookville Water Authority Dam downstream to the wire across the creek.

Rating ✳✳

Patterns to Match the Hatches Hendrickson and Red Quill (#14), Sulphur Dun and Spinner (#16), Gray Fox and Ginger Quill (#12 and #14), March Brown (#12), Brown Drake (#14), Dark Tan Caddis (#14 and #16), Green Drake and Coffin Fly (#12), Light Cahill (#14), Slate Drake (#12 and #14), Little Green Stonefly (#16), Yellow Drake (#12), Cream Cahill (#16 and #18)

What a great stream this must have been years ago! Old-timers rave about the fly-fishing on the North Fork back in the 1930s and 1940s. Recently the stream has suffered some setbacks. Acid rain, hot summers, and severe drought have taken their toll. Fifteen years ago the North Fork experienced a severe fish kill. Some anglers feel acid rain prompted the calamity. Visit the stream almost any day in July or August and you'll probably see that the volume of water in the North Fork is but a trickle compared to its strong flow in April and May. To make matters worse, this often marginal stream appears to receive entirely too many brook trout and too few brown trout in its stocking program.

No road parallels the North Fork, so access is limited to bisecting roads. Local fishermen have named many of these access areas after towns or bridges. The state stocks upstream 12 miles from Brookville to the Blowtown Bridge. In this upper area the North Fork flows slowly, often forming sandy, tree-laden pools. Here you'll find tricky wading in swamps and beaver dams in a stream about 30 feet wide.

Downstream about 1.5 miles you'll find the next access area, Ryan Road, or Jones Bridge. Here you'll see a half-dozen dilapidated log dams, a good canopy over the stream, and tough fly-fishing. The next access, Egypt Bridge, crosses the stream another 1.5 miles below Jones Bridge. This too contains a good canopy, high-velocity water, and a couple of log dams. Jones Bridge and Egypt Bridge lie on state game lands. The next access below Egypt the locals have dubbed the Humpback Bridge. This area contains deep, slow water.

The North Fork empties more than a dozen tributaries in its travels to join Red Bank Creek in Brookville. Some, like Clear, Craft, Shippen, and Pekin Runs, contain streambred brook trout. Others, like Manners Dam Run, drain tannic acid into the main stem. You'll see farms on the upper ends of many of the tributaries. A number of headwater streams have little canopy, and consequently these branches warm rapidly in summer.

Brent Rearick of Brockway believes that the best fly-fishing runs from the Richardsville Bridge downstream to the delayed-harvest area. Below Richardsville you'll find the Big Old Dam Access and the Moore Bridge Access, both maintained by the Fish Commission. A dirt road in Brookville gives access to the upper end of the delayed-harvest area. The regulated water begins at Brookville and runs upstream for 2 miles. You have to walk to reach the upper end of the project water. The lower end of the project water is located at the Water Works at Dick Park, in Brookville.

Despite its drawbacks the North Fork contains some good hatches. It's one of a handful of state streams that hold all three drake (*Ephemera* spp.) hatches. Brent Rearick has fished the green drake hatch on the stream for years, and he follows the hatch upstream for a week. Brent has caught as many as 20 trout on some of his better nights on the stream. He's caught trout as large as 16 inches during the green drake hatch. Later in the season ants and other terrestrials provide plenty of food for trout on the North Fork.

Brent's fly-fished the North Fork for nearly 20 years and feels the section below Richardsville would hold many more trout with some well-placed stream improvement devices.

No surface mining occurs in the North Fork drainage area, although for years operators have tried to mine some of the valley's rich coal fields. If sportsmen and conservationists keep up their vigilance the stream should continue to provide good hatches and fly-fishing for years. With some stream improvements and more brown trout North Fork could become even better.

CLARION RIVER

Access US 219 reaches the trophy-trout section from Ridgway to Johnsonburg. PA 949 offers access to the river below Ridgway.

Special Regulations Trophy trout—from the bridge at Johnsonburg downriver to the upper end of Ridgway. *Note:* This portion of the river was designated trophy trout in 1998. Check your *Summary of Fishing Regulations and Laws* for exact details.

Rating ✳✳✳✳

Patterns to Match the Hatches Little Black Caddis (#16), Little Blue-Winged Olive Dun (#20), Hendrickson and Red Quill (#14), Gray Caddis (#16 and #18), Sulphur (#16), Tan Caddis (#16), Yellow Drake (#12), Green Caddis (#16), Gray Fox and Ginger Quill (#12 and #14), Brown Caddis (#16 and #18), Light Cahill (#14), Cream Caddis (#14), Trico (#24), Blue Quill (#18), Slate Drake (#12 and #14), White Mayfly (#14)

Craig Josephson grew up in Ridgway. He enjoys floating the Clarion River near his home. We had explored the upper stretch of this river, from Johnsonburg to Ridgway, in the morning. Now we wanted to experience the 9 miles of water from Ridgway to Portland Mills from the water.

Craig and I left Love's Canoe Rental in Ridgway and headed downriver. Just a mile from the canoe rental things went bad—really bad. We had just passed through a series of rapids when my fly got hung up on a rock. We tried to get the fly loose. Splash! I went under. I lost my fly-rod, my fly-box, and, most important of all, my $400 camera. There in front of

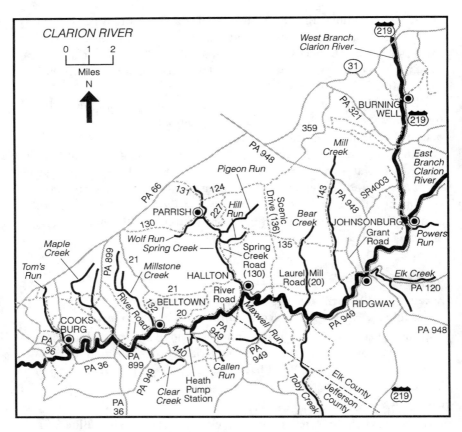

me I saw my fly-rod sinking to the bottom, my camera floating away in
its canvas bag, and my fly-box filling with water. Do you realize how
much damage a split-second dumping into the water can do? Do you have
any idea how quickly water gets into everything you have on the canoe?
We walked to the shore, shook ourselves off, gathered our gear and the
canoe, and sat on the bank for half an hour trying to dry out. Thank
goodness the water temperature at the time was 70 degrees. I quickly
opened my camera—and it was ruined. I'd lost my camera, but most of all
my enthusiasm for seeing the Clarion by canoe. We arrived at the exit
point four hour later and quite a bit drier.

At least that morning had been better on the river—and we weren't in
a canoe. Kurt Thomas of Ridgway had guided us on our morning fishing
trip on the upper end of the Clarion River. Kurt has been fishing the river
for more than 25 years. He's caught seven trout of over 30 inches there.
He keeps an extensive photo album of some of his largest fish from the
river. He's one of the most skilled fly-tiers and fly-fishermen I've had the

opportunity to fish with in the past decade. He ties a Mohair Leech that's deadly on the Clarion. Kurt fishes this river almost the entire year. Even in winter you'll find this expert using Woolly Buggers and catching lunker trout. The Clarion River is Kurt's home water and few anglers know the stream better than him.

Kurt prefers to fly-fish the Clarion from Johnsonburg to Ridgway. He feels that the water below warms considerably during summer; trout fishing becomes spotty downriver to Belltown. This upper end harbors plenty of brown trout over 20 inches long.

Kurt, Craig Josephson, and I had entered the river in the morning near the paper mill to fish for a couple of hours. Kudos to this paper mill for doing some great environmental work to improve the river. It recently demolished a dam on the East Branch of the Clarion, and it has made some substantial efforts to clean up the river. However, more needs to be done. Thermal pollution is the single most important factor impeding the Clarion from being one of the top trout waters in the state—or even in the East. This mill pours thousands of gallons of 93- to 98-degree brownish red water into the river just a half mile downstream from the plant. Below the effluent the river warms considerably in summer. We fished above the effluent, where water temperatures stay much cooler in the summer.

Kurt, Craig, and I spread out on the river. Above the effluent the water was extremely clear with a temperature of 60 degrees. It didn't take long for Craig to catch a heavy 15-inch brook trout that had probably come downstream from the East Branch. Kurt picked up three nice trout in his first half hour of fishing. As we were about to leave I made several final casts into a heavy glide just upriver from me. I saw a huge boil on the surface, I set the hook, and a heavy trout splashed for a second then broke my Patriot dry fly from my delicate tippet. I estimated the brown trout to be over 20 inches long.

The three of us headed downriver and fished at Love's Canoe Rental in Ridgway. Just a year before I had landed a 20-inch brown trout on a Patriot dry fly in that same riffle. Each of us caught a half-dozen fingerling trout near Love's. The state stocks more than 100,000 fingerlings each year on this river, from Powers Run downriver to Belltown. No catchable trout are stocked in this area.

The Clarion holds some good hatches—many of them upriver from Ridgway. As early as April you'll find trout rising to hendricksons. In May trout readily take sulphur emergers, duns, and spinners. And don't give up on the river in June: It's this time of the season when you'll find lunker trout feeding in the last hour before dark on a heavy yellow drake hatch. It even boasts some tricos in July, August, and September.

The Clarion River at Johnsonburg holds plenty of big trout.

As this book went to press the state had just designated a trophy-trout section from the bridge at Johnsonburg to the upper end of Ridgway. If its water quality improves this stretch could become one of the top trout waters in the East.

You'll find great fly-fishing for the Clarion's first 6 miles, from Johnsonburg to Ridgway, then spotty trout fishing downriver to Cooksburg. If you fish here during July or August, bring a thermometer. Keep checking for cool tributaries and springs entering the river. If you find them, you'll find trout. Several years ago Craig Josephson and I caught a number of trout in the Portland Mills section. We're certain these trout had found a spring entering the river.

The river ranges from 60 to 80 feet wide. In the trophy-trout section you'll find plenty of deep pockets and pools and some very productive riffles. Below Ridgway the river holds many long, slow pools and an occasional riffle. If you fish below Ridgway in summer, concentrate on the oxygenated riffle water.

The main stem of the Clarion River begins near Johnsonburg, at the junction of the East and West Branches. Both branches contain stocked trout from the northern Elk County line to Johnsonburg. Just below the junction of the East and West Branches, Powers Run enters the Clarion. Local fishermen consider this a good trout stream. Elk Creek, once polluted, enters in Ridgway. Below Ridgway the river adds several stocked streams to its flow: It picks up Toby Creek, Big Mill, Bear Creek, Maxwell Run,

Spring Creek, Callen Run, Millstone Creek, Clear Creek, Maple Creek, and Toms Run before it flows to Cooksburg and under PA 36. Big Mill Creek has a 1-mile fly-fishing-only section. All these streams are stocked.

Bear Creek contains a good hatch of green drakes, and Spring Creek a decent one. Callen Run, entering the river at the Heath Pump Station, holds decent hatches of green and brown drakes. Big Mill Creek has a great green drake hatch around the end of May.

What does the future hold for this potentially tremendous river? Only time will tell, but if the work of local anglers, the Pennsylvania Fish and Boat Commission, and the local paper mill's recent efforts are any example, then the future looks extremely bright. Fish this great stream soon and you too will applaud the efforts of all who have worked together to make this fishery a reality.

SPRING CREEK

Access Spring Creek begins in northeastern Forest County with the combination of the East and Watson Branches. The stream flows south, picking up Wolf Run at Parrish and Pigeon Run below. You can get to the stream on an improved dirt road, Spring Creek Road, at Hallton. A dirt road parallels the creek for 8 miles from Hill Run downstream to the Clarion River.

Rating ✳✳

Patterns to Match the Hatches Blue Quill (#18), Hendrickson and Red Quill (#14), Yellow Caddis (#16), Green Caddis (#16), Sulphur Dun and Spinner (#16), Gray Fox and Ginger Quill (#12 and #14), Green Drake and Coffin Fly (#10), Light Cahill (#14), Brown Caddis (#16)

Tom Crawford of Falls Creek has fly-fished on Spring Creek for years. The stream has heavy fishing pressure from opening day to Memorial Day, then it becomes practically void of fishermen for the rest of the year. Bill Rowley of Ridgway fishes the Parrish area, 10 miles upstream from the Clarion River. Here he finds deep pools, heavy riffles, and a good supply of native brown trout.

Spring Creek has some decent hatches. One of the earliest and heaviest is the Hendrickson, which appears on the stream the last week in April. By late May you'll witness a sporadic hatch of green drakes throughout the day.

Spring ranges from 15 to 20 feet wide in the Parrish area to 30 to 40 feet wide just before it enters the Clarion. If you plan to fish the stream in April, May, or October, try the lower end near the river. If you plan to fly-fish in June, July, or August, move upstream 5 to 10 miles so you're certain of cooler water.

EAST BRANCH, CLARION RIVER

Access Glen Hazel Road parallels much of the East Branch from Johnsonburg to Glen Hazel. At Glen Hazel a dirt road leading to state game lands follows part of the upper 2 miles.

Special Regulations Delayed harvest, artificial lures only—1.3 miles, just below the East Branch Dam.

Rating ✸✸

Patterns to Match the Hatches Sulphur Dun and Spinner (#16), Light Cahill (#14), Little Yellow Stonefly (#16), Green Caddis (#14 and #16), Blue Quill (#18), Dark Brown Stonefly (#16)

What a fly-fisherman's paradise! Trout fishing and spectacular mayfly hatches flourished in the 1930s on the East Branch. Many area fly-fishermen called the fly-fishing area on this branch the Glen Hazel Paradise. Blackie Veltri of Brockway remembers those productive days well. Almost anyone could catch his limit of six trout over 9 inches long on the stretch. By the late 1940s and early 1950s, however, strip mining slowly contaminated the waters of the East Branch. The state no longer stocked trout in the river. In the mid-1950s the Army Corps of Engineers completed a dam on this Clarion tributary about 8 miles upriver from Johnsonburg. This 100-foot-deep dam contained a bottom release. Nevertheless, mine acid continued to pour into the watershed.

Showing great foresight, the Department of Environmental Resources in 1980 added a limer to one of the more visibly polluted tributaries, Swamp Creek. The river has slowly regained some of its former prominence. The state now stocks the 8 miles below the dam with legal-sized trout and fingerlings.

Where else in Pennsylvania can you fish over trout with water temperatures no higher than the mid-50s in July and August? The East Branch has returned through a cooperative effort of the Fish Commission and the work of the Corps of Engineers. Too many of us criticize the corps and the commission too readily. In this instance they deserve our praise for an excellent reclamation job.

Drive along the river above Glen Hazel and you'll immediately notice strategically located stream improvement devices scattered for miles. These devices should function as a model for groups interested in stream improvement. The Civilian Conservation Corps originally built these contraptions in the 1930s. The Fish Commission and Elk County have upgraded and maintained them since that time. Controlled releases from the dam protect these devices from the devastation of floods.

The East Branch flows out of the dam just above Glen Hazel. The dam's bottom release keeps the water below cool for its 8-mile trip to the junction with the West Branch at Johnsonburg.

The East Branch holds a few hatches. Recently Mike Veltri of Reynoldsville and I fly-fished on the stream. In one morning in late July Mike and I saw a decent hatch of blue quills and little yellow stoneflies and sporadic hatches of green caddis and light cahills. In two hours of fishing Mike and I picked up three browns over 10 inches and dozens of fingerling brook and brown trout up to 6 inches long. If fishermen give these small trout a chance to grow, the East Branch will develop into a tremendous fishery.

Above the dam major siltation has damaged Sevenmile and Fivemile Runs, Crooked Creek, and Middle Fork. Below the dam, because of the controlled bottom release, siltation is not a problem. Swamp Creek (entering at the dam) and Johnson Run empty varying amounts of mine acid into the branch. (See chapter 11 for a more detailed discussion of the treatment plant on Swamp Creek.) Some of the East Branch tributaries contain good supplies of native brook trout.

Congratulations to the Pennsylvania Fish Commission, the Army Corps of Engineers, and the Pennsylvania Department of Environmental Resources for a job well done. The East Branch has returned. Over time it will have a chance to develop into one of the top fisheries in the state.

WEST BRANCH, CLARION RIVER

Access US 219 follows the West Branch from Johnsonburg to the Elk County line.

Special Regulations Delayed harvest, fly-fishing only—0.5 mile, from intersection of US 219 and SR 4003, upstream to Texas Gulf Sulphur property. Fishing is permitted from the eastern shore only. No wading permitted.

Rating ✷✷

Patterns to Match the Hatches Hendrickson and Red Quill (#14), Sulphur Dun and Spinner (#16), Gray Fox and Ginger Quill (#12 and #14), March Brown (#12), Light Cahill (#14), Little Green Stonefly (#16), Green Drake (#12), Yellow Drake (#12), Slate Drake (#14), Trico (#24), Dark Tan Stonefly (#16)

Mike Veltri of Reynoldsville and I approached the West Branch of the Clarion River on a cool, overcast late-July morning. We arrived at the stream by 8:00 AM in anticipation of a trico hatch. Mike said he had seen a few tricos on the West Branch and I wanted to experience this diminutive hatch on another freestone stream.

We approached the delayed-harvest area of the West Branch with much trepidation. We had just experienced two months of hot, dry summer weather. Would there be any water or trout left in the stream? What would the water temperature be on this fairly open stream?

When we arrived at the eastern bank I immediately lowered my thermometer into the stream to check the temperature. Here, next to an underground spring, the thermometer registered 62 degrees. We moved downstream to obtain a more representative reading and found the water at 65. The temperature and the water flow were a pleasant surprise.

Mike and I sat and waited for a trico hatch. Only a very few appeared that morning, but slate drakes and dark tan stoneflies emerged in good numbers. Several trout rose to midges, and Mike and I noted more than a dozen trout feeding. That's not bad for a delayed-harvest area a month after you're allowed to keep fish.

The West Branch contains a half-mile-long delayed-harvest section. In this area you can fly-fish only from the eastern bank; you're allowed neither to wade the stream nor to fish from the western bank. This makes fly-fishing extremely difficult and roll-casting a necessity. Above the delayed-harvest stretch some wading is allowed. Check the signs and regulations before you start fishing.

Hatches on the West Branch seem more numerous than on the Clarion's main stem, with a good supply of yellow drakes, light cahills, March browns, and slate drakes.

Sam Guaglianone says that in the upper reaches of this branch you can still find some streambred brown trout 5 to 6 inches long. The main stem is stocked from Johnsonburg upstream to the Elk County line, about 11 miles. The state stocks a main tributary, Wilson Run, for about 8 miles. The West Branch below Wilcox averages 40 to 50 feet wide, with some deep runs, fishable riffles, and a few pools more than 5 feet deep.

BROKENSTRAW CREEK

Access PA 426 follows the stream from Corry to Garland, and PA 27 and US 6 parallel the Brokenstraw to Youngsville.

Rating ✳✳

Patterns to Match the Hatches Hendrickson and Red Quill (#14), Dark Olive Caddis (#16), Sulphur Dun and Spinner (#16), Blue-Winged Olive Dun (#14), Light Cahill (#14), *Pteronarcys* Stonefly (#6), Slate Drake (#12 and #14), Yellow Drake (#12)

How many Pennsylvania streams do you know whose headwaters are considered a warm-water fishery while the lower half is stocked with trout? The upper half of Brokenstraw harbors plenty of pike and muskie, but from Spring Creek downstream to Youngsville the state stocks thousands of trout annually. Two reasons for this atypical condition stand out. First, Brokenstraw changes from a slow, sluggish stream in its upper half to one with plenty of riffles and rapids in the lower reaches. Second, some cool tributaries, including Spring Creek, Blue Eye Run, and Little Brokenstraw, enter the main stem in the stocked section.

Spring Creek harbors a great green drake hatch and a good supply of light cahills around the end of May. It enters Brokenstraw at PA 426 and Cemetery Road. Blue Eye displays a good Hendrickson hatch in late April and a decent light cahill near the end of May. Blue Eye comes into the main stem near Garland. Little Brokenstraw enters the larger stream at Pittsfield. It warms in summer, but the state stocks 11 miles of this branch.

Brokenstraw contains many long, flat, deep pools with some deep riffles in the lower half. At Garland the main stem ranges from 40 to 50 feet from bank to bank and widens to 60 to 80 feet at Youngsville. Until a few years ago the area near Garland contained a fly-fishing-only section.

The stream contains a few respectable hatches. In April it does on occasion display enough hendricksons to allow fishermen to match the hatch. In May and June you will see some sulphurs and light cahills. In mid-June the yellow drake appears. If the water temperature hasn't risen too high, you're in for some excellent fly-fishing on Brokenstraw when this drake appears.

Brokenstraw Creek begins in New York State and flows south into northeastern Erie County. It then flows southeast and picks up volume from tributaries like Hare Creek, Spring Creek, Blue Eye Run, Coffee Creek, Andrews Run, Mead Run, and Matthews Run.

Don Foltz of Lincolnville feels the best pattern on Brokenstraw is a Dark Olive Henryville. He's even caught holdover trout in the stream on this pattern.

Wading the Brokenstraw can be challenging. It compares with the rigors of wading the Little Juniata River, Yellow Creek, Slippery Rock Creek, and others.

KINZUA CREEK

Access Kinzua can be reached at the lower end by PA 321, then FR 122 (dirt, northern side) or FR 321 (dirt, southern side). FR 122 has deteriorated from use by logging trucks. Upstream, US 219 crosses the stream at Tally Ho.

Special Regulations Delayed harvest, artificial lures only—2.3 miles, from US 219 to Camp Run.

Rating ✳✳

Patterns to Match the Hatches Blue Quill (#18), Hendrickson and Red Quill (#14), Tan Caddis (#16), Gray Fox (#14), March Brown (#12), Slate Drake (#12 and #14), Chocolate Dun (#12 and #14)

When you look at this large freestone stream set in an isolated area of McKean County, you'd bet that it is one of the top streams in the state. If you fish the water, however, you may change your opinion. Kinzua has some water-quality problems that stem from a mud-and-tar bottom in its upper end caused by an old chemical plant. Near PA 59 the bottom of the stream is coated with a tarlike substance.

Kinzua contains some decent hatches, one of them quite unusual. It harbors some March browns, gray foxes, and slate drakes, but it also contains plenty of mayflies in the genus *Baetisca*. The nymphs of these species act much like those of the genus *Isonychia,* both climbing out of the water and emerging on exposed rocks. I have never seen a pattern specifically imitating this species, but a size-12 or -14 Chocolate Dun would match the duns.

Kinzua has an undue amount of fishing pressure. It's located within the Allegheny National Forest and gets added pressure during the summer from campers. The stream averages 40 to 50 feet wide at many places in its lower end and has a good canopy of pines and mixed hardwoods that hold down the water temperature. Don Foltz and Marshall Young catch streambred browns and holdovers in the Kinzua.

Kinzua begins near Mount Alton in McKean County. On its path south, then east, the main stem picks up dozens of small, cool tributaries, mostly entering from the northern side of the stream. Runs like Threemile, Windfall, Wintergreen, Camp, Turnup, and Thundershower flow into the main stem. Just as Kinzua joins the Allegheny Reservoir, South Branch enters. South Branch is a good trout stream in its own right.

EAST BRANCH, MAHONING CREEK

Access Access to the East Branch is limited on the lower 3 miles. You can reach the lower mile on a paved road off US 119 at the northern end of Big Run. The next access is 3 miles upstream at a bridge on a township road.

Rating ✳✳

Patterns to Match the Hatches Little Blue-Winged Olive Dun (#20),

Hendrickson and Red Quill (#14), Tan Caddis (#14), Brown Caddis (#14), Sulphur Dun and Spinner (#16), March Brown (#12), Green Drake and Coffin Fly (#10), Brown Drake (#10 and #12), Yellow Drake (#12), Trico (#24)

The East Branch of Mahoning Creek saw one of its first fly-fishermen in 1928. A hefty brook trout struck a Silver Doctor wet fly on Laurel Run one day that year (Laurel is one of the East Branch's main tributaries). Bob Davis of Big Run caught that trout, more than 60 years ago. Bob died in 1997 and he will be sorely missed by the many anglers he befriended. Until the time he died Bob fished the East Branch and its tributaries. He lived a stone's throw from this productive stream.

What hatches did Bob most often meet on the East Branch? Bobo, as his friends called him, usually waited until mid- to late May and fished the two famous drake hatches on the stream. East Branch holds heavy hatches of both green and brown drakes. He found the greatest number of brown drakes on the lower 3 miles of water and the green drake on the lower 8 miles. Bob said the brown drake appears in unbelievable numbers near the water plant just a mile upstream from the town of Big Run.

The stream holds the third drake hatch also, the yellow drake. In many places where the yellow drake appears, it does so in marginal water with temperatures above 70 degrees. On the East Branch water temperatures normally cooperate with the fishermen, even when the yellow drake appears in mid-June.

The East Branch holds a good number of aquatic insects, a good number of holdover trout, and some natural brown trout reproduction. Two tributaries, Laurel and Clover Runs, contain native brook trout. Bob Davis said that Clover flows about 10 degrees cooler than the main stem in the summer, and many stocked trout move up this tributary.

The quality of water on the East Branch and its tributaries at first glance might seem like an enigma. Ten years ago the streams in this watershed seemed destined for destruction from mine-acid seepage. Enter a local concerned-citizens group, the Allegheny Mountain Chapter of Trout Unlimited. This group, first formed by Al Gretz and Bob Davis, has policed area mining operations on the watershed. The Allegheny Mountain Chapter awarded Bob Davis its first Golden Reel Award for meritorious service to the club and the community. Since Bob passed away the chapter has formed a Bob Davis Scholarship Fund, which sponsors teenagers in worthy conservation programs.

Ten years ago you'd find the East Branch's water with an acidic pH of near 6—now the pH is near 7.2, or neutral to slightly alkaline. Why?

Bob Davis spent sixty years fishing one of his favorite streams, the East Branch of the Mahoning Creek.

Liming by upstream strip miners has upped the pH, temporarily, on the stream.

The East Branch begins near Luthersburg in Clearfield County. The stream flows southwest into Jefferson County and enters Mahoning Creek at the town of Big Run. The state stocks the lower 8 miles of water. Near the Clearfield County line the stream averages 30 feet wide, with hawthorn and alder growing next to the water. At the lower end near the water plant East Branch broadens to 40 feet.

If you fish the East Branch in late May or June, enjoy the scenery, the quality of water, and the hatches on this stream. And above all remember the work Bob Davis or any member of the Allegheny Mountain Chapter of Trout Unlimited has done to help preserve this stream. Thank them for their perseverance in keeping the East Branch of Mahoning Creek clean and productive.

TIONESTA CREEK

Access There's easy access to Tionesta. PA 666 parallels the stream from Kellettville to Barnes; at no point is the stream more than a couple of hundred yards from the road. Below Kellettville the water warms early, the stream isn't stocked, and the Corps of Engineers has built Tionesta Lake. Below the lake the stream enters the Allegheny River at Tionesta. You'll cross the lower end on PA 36.

Rating ✳✳

Patterns to Match the Hatches Blue Quill (#18), Hendrickson and Red Quill (#14), Tan Caddis (#14), Light Stonefly (#14), March Brown (#12), Chocolate Dun (#12 and #14), Light Cahill (#14), Slate Drake (#12 and #14), Brown Drake (#10 and #12)

The first two decades of the 20th century were unkind to Tionesta Creek. "Black Creek" would have been a better name for the stream during those years of decadence. The water appeared black from the tannic acid and chemicals poured directly into it by chemical plants in Mayburg and tanneries in Sheffield.

Over the past few decades nature has revitalized this once-polluted creek. Insects in limited numbers now inhabit the stream. Trout stocked by the state can be found in most of the water.

The Tionesta drains a huge land area: the southeastern half of Forest County, much of southeastern Warren County, and a portion of southwestern McKean County and northwestern Elk County. Tionesta Creek warms quickly in the summer, but its watershed contains 12 branches and tributaries also stocked with trout. Many of these smaller streams hold trout all year long. Jack Busch of Erie fly-fishes on Two Mile Run in McKean all season long and catches trout.

The Tionesta near Kellettville is more a river than a stream. Here the stream averages 60 to 80 feet wide with plenty of deep runs and long holding pools. In the Kellettville–Mayburg–Porkey–Lynch area you'll see long riffles flowing into some deep pools and flats over 100 yards long. This section contains deep pools at Kellettville, Balltown, Minister Run, and Porkey. From Lynch upstream to Barnes the stream narrows. Near Barnes the South and West Branches join to form the main stem. Both branches and many of the tributaries, including Six-, Four-, and Two Mile Runs, contain trout.

A beautiful rock-ledged stream, Bluejay Creek, enters the main stem near Lynch. This stream holds hatches like the Hendrickson, quill gordon, and blue quill early in the season. Bluejay contains a heavy canopy of evergreens and hardwoods throughout its drainage area.

Dick Koval of Brockway has fly-fished the Tionesta for more than 40 years. He cautions that you should not expect to see the variety and density of hatches on the Tionesta that you'll find on First Fork or Kettle. Early in the season you're likely to see a decent Hendrickson hatch appear and produce some rising trout. But caddisflies are the main source of food on the stream. Dick, however, has fly-fished when light stoneflies appeared in early May and when slate drakes emerged in early June. In both instances he's done well matching the hatch. Dick's caught trout up to 18 inches long on the stream and has seen other anglers catch trout up to 2 feet long.

For the past two years Dick Koval, along with George Falkenstern of Pennsylvania Furnace, has met a great brown drake hatch on Tionesta Creek. Dick said the hatch and spinner fall, which appear on the stream in early June, lasted almost a week. He found the hatch especially heavy around the Mayburg area.

If you enjoy large streams and scenic wilderness, and you don't mind fishing for stocked trout, you'll enjoy Tionesta Creek. Tom Greenlee at the Forest County Sports Center in Tionesta knows the stream and its hatches well. Check in with him before you fish the Tionesta.

EAST HICKORY CREEK

Access East Hickory flows into the Allegheny River just 10 miles north of Tionesta. PA 666 parallels the lower 3 miles of the stream. Above that a dirt road follows the stream up to Queen Creek. There's a 1.7-mile delayed-harvest area from the Otter Creek bridge to the Queen Creek bridge. Above the junction with Queen Creek access to the main stem is limited to trails and Allegheny National Forest Highway 119.

Special Regulations Delayed harvest, artificial lures only—1.7 miles, from the Queen Creek bridge downstream to the Otter Creek bridge.

Rating ✷✷

Patterns to Match the Hatches Blue Quill (#18), Quill Gordon (#14), Hendrickson and Red Quill (#14), March Brown (#12), Green Drake and Coffin Fly (#10), Light Cahill (#14), Slate Drake (#12 and #14), Yellow Drake (#12)

East Hickory contains plenty of history, spectacular scenery, lots of native trout in its main stem and tributaries, and some great hatches.

During World War I the Wheeler and Dusenberry Lumber Company operated a "fishermen's paradise" at the junction of Coalbed Run and Queen Creek. This tributary to East Hickory Creek teemed with trout. That same lumber company operated a railroad up East Hickory to supply its two sawmills upstream.

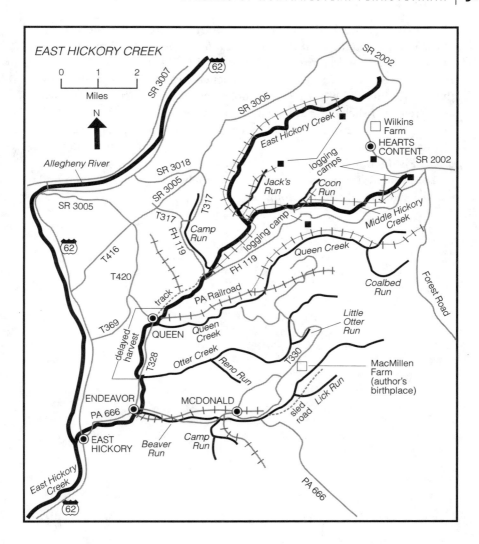

Ted Kiffer and his father before him have spent many days on East Hickory and all of its branches. Ted's dad remembers 1912, when state game authorities used the railroad to stock 20 deer brought in from Michigan. The railroad has long since ended operation, but the old grade, still visible along much of East Hickory, remains as a reminder of the activity the watershed once held.

Hike up Queen Creek and you'll see huge blue spruce planted years ago. Near the headwaters on the main stem you'll find 400 acres of virgin white pine.

Ted Kiffer has fly-fished just about every mile of East Hickory and its many tributaries: Beaver Run, Queen Creek, Coalbed Run, Otter Creek, and

Middle Hickory Creek. His family has lived in the area since the War of 1812. Ted has caught 18-inch brook trout at the Saw Mill Dam on Beaver Run. He remembers the first time he resorted to fly-fishing at that dam. He used a telescoping steel rod and a snelled wet fly. The first time he cast the wet fly into the water he saw a dozen brook trout race to take it. Now Ted often fly-fishes the main stem just above where Queen Creek enters. From this area upstream the main stem usually holds trout all season.

East Hickory boasts a good Hendrickson hatch and a superb green drake. Fly-fish this water in late May and you'll see how spectacular the drake can be. With the heavy canopy on much of the stream, green drakes emerge sporadically all day long.

9 | Streams of Southwestern Pennsylvania

If you live in Pittsburgh or Greensburg and want to experience some great hatches and fish productive trout water, how far do you have to travel? Central Pennsylvania? North-central Pennsylvania? Neither one. You can stay in your own area and enjoy some of the finest fishing Pennsylvania has to offer.

The southwest presents diverse streams and rivers. Two of the best limestone streams in the state lie on the eastern border of the region: Cove and Yellow Creeks contain abundant green drake and sulphur hatches. Less than two hours southeast of Pittsburgh lies the extensive, prolific, always-cool Youghiogheny River. You can fly-fish on this water any time of the year and find it an excellent trout river. Travel a few miles below Confluence or upriver a couple of miles above Ohiopyle and you'll probably not see another fisherman.

You also have other streams in your area from which to choose: Little Mahoning, Loyalhanna, and Laurel Hill Creeks. All three become marginal by mid-June, but all three contain some unusual hatches and trout throughout much of the early season.

In the southwest you can experience green drake, brown drake, trico, and many other hatches. On the Youghiogheny River you'll likely see caddisflies emerging all summer.

Would you like to fly-fish over streambred trout in the southwest? The two major limestone streams, Cove and Yellow, contain remarkable populations of native brown trout. Two of Loyalhanna's tributaries, Furnace and Laughlintown Runs, even hold some streambred rainbow trout.

Southwestern Pennsylvania trout streams have their problems. Acid rain in the Laurel Highlands affects streams like the Loyalhanna and Laurel Hill. Mine-acid drainage affects the Casselman River and many others.

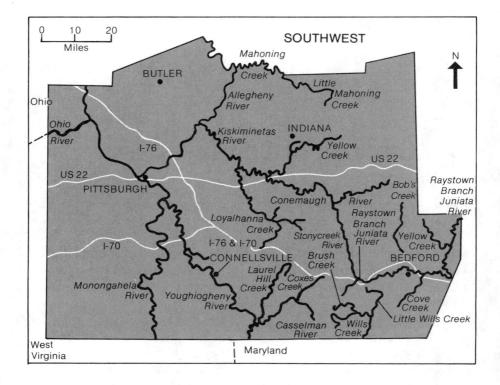

BUFFALO CREEK

Access Buffalo Creek is located just 40 miles north of Pittsburgh and is easy to reach. You can access it off US 422 just west of Kittanning on SR 4035. It flows in Armstrong and Butler Counties. With the exception of its upper 300 yards, the delayed-harvest section is located in Armstrong County. You can reach the upper end on Fennelton Road. Morrow Road crosses the delayed-harvest area near the Butler County line. You can easily reach the middle section from Nichola Road (SR 3013). You'll find slower water in the middle and upper sections of the delayed-harvest area. The lower section, just above Craigsville, has the least accessibility. Here you'll find a deep valley with some faster stretches and few roads to reach the stream. The delayed-harvest section has a heavy canopy throughout.

Special Regulations Delayed harvest, artificial lures only—3.7 miles, from Little Buffalo Run downstream to 0.6 mile above SR 4035 in Craigsville.

Rating ✷✷

Patterns to Match the Hatches Little Black Stonefly (#18), Tan Caddis (#16), Blue Quill (#18), Sulphur (#16), Brown Drake (#12), March Brown (#12), Light Cahill (#14), Slate Drake (#12 and #14)

Question: Which Trout Unlimited chapter is perhaps the most active in the state? From my point of view it's got to be the Arrowhead Chapter in Armstrong County. Why? Look at the contributions this group has made in just the past couple of years. Each year it conducts fly-tying courses for local anglers, raises trout in a local hatchery, and float-stocks one of the better streams in the area; it has also constructed 58 stream improvement devices. Where do these folks expend much of their energy? On Buffalo Creek, just a few miles west of Kittanning.

Recently Mark Transue, owner of Transue's Tackle in Kittanning Highlands, and I spent a couple of hours exploring the delayed-harvest section of Buffalo Creek. Mark has fished Buffalo for more than 25 years. He's caught some lunker trout on the stream. He's caught and released numerous trout in the 20-inch range.

As we traveled along the Buffalo in mid-September we saw a stream starved for precipitation. Yet despite the low-water conditions we saw trout. Why this late in the season? Because of the work the local Trout Unlimited chapter has done in the past few years.

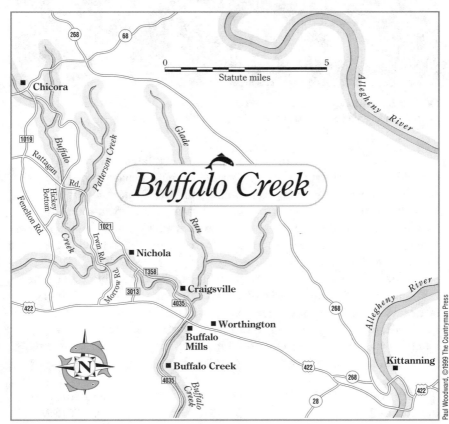

On Buffalo Creek you'll find plenty of stream improvement devices placed there by the Arrowhead Chapter of Trout Unlimited.

As we traveled along the entire specially regulated stretch Mark gave me his thoughts about the changes in the stream the past few years: "It's come a long way. It sure is great to have this stream near my house. I used to fish the project water on the Little Mahoning Creek—but now I have Buffalo Creek just a few miles away. For many years I wouldn't fish this stream—it had few hiding places for trout. But since the club has done so much work on the stream I like it."

Buffalo Creek boasts some respectable hatches. Probably one of the best and most unusual is the brown drake that appears on the stream in late May. These large mayflies appear for just a few days, but often bring some of the heavier trout to the surface to feed. Probably the heaviest hatch on the stream appears in late May and early June—the light cahill. But the stream boasts more—and Mark Transue believes the hatches are becoming heavier.

The stream has plenty of productive pools thanks to the Arrowhead Chapter of Trout Unlimited. Stop in at Transue's Tackle and talk to Mark

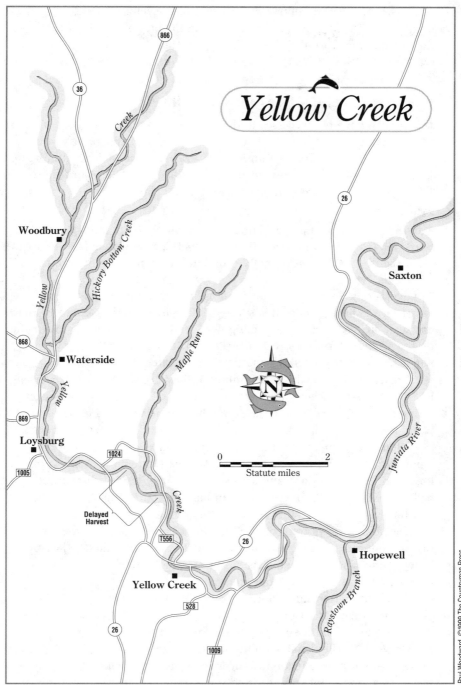

Yellow Creek

866

36

Creek

Woodbury ■

Hickory Bottom Creek

Yellow

26

Saxton ■

Maple Run

868

■ Waterside

N

Yellow

869

Loysburg ■

1024

Juniata River

0   2
Statute miles

1005

Creek

Delayed
Harvest

T556

26

Hopewell ■

■
Yellow Creek

528

Raystown Branch

26

1009

Paul Woodward, ©1999 The Countryman Press

about the stream conditions and hatches. Mark even sells Patriot dry flies in his shop. Thank him and the Arrowhead Chapter of Trout Unlimited for the outstanding work they have done on Buffalo Creek. You can also reach Mark at his Web site (http://www.kittanning.com/transue.htm).

YELLOW CREEK (INDIANA COUNTY)

Access You have two accesses to the open water on Yellow Creek. You can park on either side of the PA 954 bridge and hike upstream, or you can access the stream at Ferrier Run Road (T 627). To reach Ferrier Run Road take PA 954 toward the town of Indiana for about 2 miles. Turn right onto T 604, then right again onto Ferrier Run Road.

Rating ✴✴

Patterns to Match the Hatches Little Black Stonefly (#16 and #18), Little Blue-Winged Olive Dun (#20), Blue Quill (#18), Slate Drake (#12 and #14), Light Cahill (#14), Giant Stonefly (#6), Little Brown Stonefly (#16 or #18)

Travel along Yellow Creek on opening day of the trout season and you'll see how popular this spot is among local anglers. Steve Renosky has seen dozens of cars line the highway, and anglers shoulder to shoulder on the stretch of Yellow Creek near PA 954. Almost any time of year you'll find cars parked along that stretch of water.

I recently fly-fished that section of Yellow Creek just upstream from PA 954. The stream here flows 50 to 60 feet wide, has plenty of pocket water and pools, and even in late June holds a few trout. I checked the water temperature on that warm summer day: 72 degrees at around 3:00 PM. I didn't think much of the stream—even less after I checked the thermometer. I decided to give it an hour. By luck I entered just 300 yards upstream from the bridge and almost immediately landed three trout. Not bad—three trout in 72-degree water in half an hour! I moved upstream and for the next hour didn't have another strike.

The stream flows from the Yellow Creek Lake, which has a mixture of top and bottom releases. The water at the Black Hawk Dam (Yellow Creek Lake) is only about 60 feet deep, so the stream below doesn't get the complete benefits of a deep bottom release.

About a quarter mile below the dam the stream enters private land. The Yellow Creek Trout Club stocks trout in this 3-mile section. Mike Renosky and his son Steve operate this artificial-lures-only, catch-and-release section. They charge an annual fee. Here you'll see plenty of trout in the 20-inch-plus category. If you live in the area, fishing the club waters is an excellent way to catch some trophy trout in a beautiful setting just a few miles from home.

After the private water you will find several miles of open fishing before Yellow Creek enters the Homer Creek Reservoir. This area is Craig Josephson's and Pat Mayer's old fishing grounds. For years Craig and Pat fished this stretch, where there's about 6 miles of open water, early in the season. What a fantastic delayed-harvest area Yellow Creek could hold! Yellow Creek would be an excellent stream for the Pennsylvania Fish and Boat Commission to designate a 2-mile section delayed harvest, artificial lures only.

Below the reservoir you'll find a couple more miles of fishing before the stream flows under PA 954.

Don't overlook the stream above the dam. Woody Banks runs the Indiana Angler, a local fly-shop, and tells me that although the stream is small above the lake, you'll find planted trout and even some streambred trout upstream.

Mike Renosky, owner of the Yellow Creek Trout Club, has worked with the Yellow Creek State Park to lower temperatures on the creek below by adding more bottom-release water to the mixture. Authorities at the dam must release 500,000 gallons per day.

You won't find spectacular hatches on Yellow Creek like you'd see on Pine or Penns Creeks. But the stream does hold some aquatic insects, including a good number of stoneflies. In late May and early June you'll even see good numbers of the giant stonefly. Steve Renosky says that they'll fly in your face when they emerge. Yellow also holds light cahills and slate drakes.

Early in the year you should find plenty of trout in Yellow Creek. It becomes a marginal stream after Memorial Day, but even after that time you can find an occasional trout.

SOUTH BRANCH, TWO LICK CREEK

Access You can access South Branch, Two Lick Creek off PA 580 or PA 240. The former runs south of the stream and the latter, a few miles north.

Rating ✳✳✳

Patterns to Match the Hatches Blue Quill (#18), Little Blue-Winged Olive Dun (#20), Tan Caddis (#16), Yellow Stonefly (#16), Little Green Stonefly (#18), Slate Drake (#14), Light Cahill (#14)

❝**W**hy don't you include more trout streams in the Clearfield, Jefferson, and Indiana County area in your book?" That's the first question that Jim Fleming, a teacher who lives in Lumber City and one of a growing number of area fly-fishers, asked me when we met. I answered that question by telling Jim that many of the potentially good trout streams in that area have been degraded to some degree by mine-acid drainage.

As a result of Jim's prodding, though, I took an expedition through the three counties, trying to find a stream or two that would fit into the criteria for inclusion in this book. For every stream I've included in the past, I've rejected another that I thought would not be suitable for fly-fishing. For previous editions of *Trout Streams of Pennsylvania* I've fished Little Clearfield Creek, Cush Creek, Mill Creek, and many more. I thought none of these were of any quality to be included in this book. But this latest trip—and what I found—amazed me. After fly-fishing many of the Commonwealth's greatest streams I found some quality fishing in the Indiana area. Let me explain.

My wife, Shirley, did the driving while I did the navigating. We headed down one dirt road after another trying to find South Branch, Two Lick Creek. We took two wrong turns and ended up at what I had originally thought was Two Lick Creek. It wasn't—it was a nearly dried-up tributary. Thank goodness. Finally, we took a sharp right turn off PA 580 onto Alder Road (T 916), traveled a half mile on dirt, and crossed a small bridge on the real South Branch of Two Lick Creek. On my first glance from the bridge the stream didn't look like much: It looked slow moving and difficult to fly-fish.

But what the heck—why not try it for a few minutes? I assembled my gear and headed upstream. As I entered the water on this 85-degree, late-June afternoon, I put my hand into the flow. It felt cool enough to hold trout. I plunged my thermometer into a small riffle and waited a couple of minutes. Wow! I recorded a temperature of 62 degrees at 3:00 PM, in late June. Maybe the stream did hold trout.

Still, I didn't like the color of the water. It's the typical tannish color that you see on many of the area streams that have been affected to some extent by mine-acid drainage. In fact, part of this stream had been taken off the stocking list a few years before because of the influx of acid. Anyway, I decided to try Two Lick for an hour or so before I condemned it to oblivion.

In the second riffle upstream I saw a fish rise. I cast over it, but it refused my pattern. Up in the next pool three more fish rose just where the riffle flattens out into the deeper water. Were these trout? Or, as I surmised, were they just your run-of-the-mill chubs? Finally, one of these risers took my Patriot dry fly and I landed it. I yelled for my wife to get the camera and take a photo of a 10-inch native brookie. What a beautiful trout! Would there be more? You bet there were. The first five trout I caught were brookies that had never seen the inside of a stocking truck. The next seven I caught all seemed to be streambred brown trout—some of

Yellow Creek in Indiana County.

them were 12 inches long. Does Two Lick hold trout? It not only holds trout, but it's probably one of the best trout streams I've ever fly-fished in the southwestern part of the state.

Why does this small, nondescript stream hold so many fish? First, much of it flows through a dense forest of hemlocks that block out even the strongest rays in summer. You can barely see the sun under this heavy canopy. Second, the stream holds food for these fish. Check some of the spiderwebs along the stream and you'll see thousands of cream midges. Mayflies like the blue quill, light cahill, and slate drake also inhabit the stream. And downwings—like the tan caddis—provide additional food for the trout.

If you plan to fish this stream it's imperative that you use a barbless hook and return these precious trout back where they belong—to the South Branch of Two Lick Creek.

CHEST CREEK

Access Chest Creek closely parallels PA 36. To access the delayed-harvest area take PA 36 north out of Patton. Turn right onto SR 4024 to the bridge at Thomas Mills. This bridge is the lower boundary of the delayed-harvest water. You'll find plenty of trout in the regulated area throughout the year.

Special Regulations Delayed harvest, artificial lures only—1.8 miles, from the northern Patton borough line downstream to SR 4022 at Thomas Mills.

Rating ✳✳

Patterns to Match the Hatches Little Blue-Winged Olive Dun (#20), Tan Caddis (#14), Light Cahill (#12 and #14), Sulphur (#16), Green Caddis (#16), Chocolate Dun (#16), Slate Drake (#12 and #14)

I'm proud of my first impressions. I'm always correct on them—well, almost always. Let me explain.

It certainly doesn't look like a trout stream. One quick glance will tell you why: Chest Creek looks suspiciously like some mine-acid drainage seeps into it somewhere upstream. It's off color and cloudy most of the time. It almost gives the appearance of dirty dishwater. Once you're on the stream you'll be convinced that this ugly creek holds no trout. Each rock under the surface is covered with a greasy slime certain to upend you if you're not careful.

I recently fished the delayed-harvest section of Chest Creek in early June. I entered at the bridge at Thomas Mills and waded upstream. The first 200 yards looked unimpressive and yielded no trout. No strikes, disgusting-looking water, and the lack of any deep runs, riffles, or pools

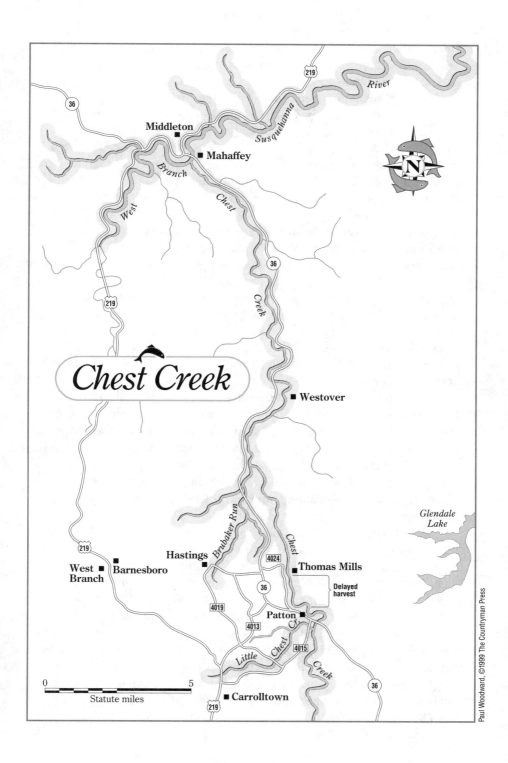

Middleton

Mahaffey

Susquehanna River

219

36

West *Branch*

Chest

36

Creek

Chest Creek

■ Westover

Glendale Lake

219

Brubaker Run

Hastings

Chest

4024

■ Thomas Mills

West ■ Branch Barnesboro

219

36

Delayed harvest

4019

Patton ■

Chest Cr.

4013

4015

Little *Chest*

Creek

36

0   5
Statute miles

219 ■ Carrolltown

almost persuaded me to head back to my car. But you know how anglers are—just one more pool, just a couple of hundred more feet to see what's around the bend.

Then I came upon a deep pool with a short riffle at its head. On my first cast into that pool I had a strike, and I landed a 12-inch palomino. I hate palominos—I think they look like goldfish, and I don't want to fly-fish for goldfish. My impression of Chest Creek didn't change after that first trout—I still had no respect for this stream. On my fifth cast, though, I caught a second trout, this one a 14-inch rainbow. Maybe, just maybe, I was wrong about this stream. In the next hour I landed a half-dozen more trout from that section.

Such success urged me to fish farther upstream. Two hundred yards up I came upon another fly-fisher, Nicholos Somogi of Mentcle. He bemoaned the fact that even though dozens of trout were swimming in front of him, he was having difficulty catching any of them. I looked into the pool myself—it looked like a hatchery. I tied on a Green Weenie and handed one to Nicholos. We both tied it on a tandem rig, using Patriots as our dry flies. Within minutes the action began. We hauled more than 30 trout out of that section. Isn't it strange how quickly time passes when you're having fun? We spent two hours fishing over those trout and still kept catching fish.

At one point more than a dozen trout rose to terrestrials blown off trees. I tied on an ant pattern and quickly picked up four trout in the flat water above the pool. Here trout fed in water no deeper than 6 inches. Finally the cool air and chilly wind reminded me that it was time to quit.

Ask Nicholos what he thinks of the Green Weenie pattern. He'll tell you about the frustrating day he had before he tried that pattern on Chest Creek. This was only Nicholos's fourth trip fly-fishing, and it's one that he'll remember forever.

Surprisingly, Chest Creek holds some mayfly and caddisfly hatches. But ask Brian Lamont of Carrolltown about the hatches he saw here when he was young. Brian says the stream held a fairly good green drake hatch then. Sedimentation and acid-drainage problems have eliminated that hatch. But the stream still holds some aquatic insects. While I fished I saw a few mayflies emerge. During the afternoon a few chocolate duns appeared, and late in the afternoon some light cahills. Some of the old-timers who've fished this stream for years talk about the great light cahill hatch. Look for this hatch in the evening in late May and early June.

There's good fishing below the delayed-harvest section; look for deep pools and riffles. The water does warm in summer.

Chest Creek is stocked for more than 20 miles, from well above Patton downstream to Mahaffey. In the lower end the stream widens to 30 to 40 feet, while in the Patton area it ranges from 25 to 30 feet. You'll find plenty of slow, fairly deep pools throughout.

Does Chest Creek hold trout? You bet it does! Will I return? I certainly will! Will I ever badmouth it again? Well—just maybe.

BOBS CREEK

Access PA 869 parallels the lower end of Bobs Creek. To reach the upper end, take a road officially called T 652 out of the town of Pavia.

Rating ✳✳✳

Patterns to Match the Hatches Little Blue-Winged Olive Dun (#20), Blue Quill (#18), Quill Gordon (#14), Hendrickson (#14), Spotted Sedge (#16), March Brown (#12), Green Drake (#10), Giant Stonefly (#8), Slate Drake (#12), Little Green Stonefly (#16), Little Yellow Stonefly (#16), Light Cahill (#14), Sulphur (#16), Rusty Caddis (#10), Trico (#24), Autumn Sedge (#14)

Tom Wolfe lives less than 4 miles from the stream. He learned to fly-fish on this productive water. He's one of the few who really know each pool, riffle, and trout the stream holds. "I caught a 17-inch brownie behind that log," Tom explained as we hiked downstream. "There I landed a 15-inch brookie last year on a wet fly," he proclaimed as we set a fast pace hiking to a section he wanted us to fish. Tom knows his home stream well and claims he's one of the few to consistently fly-fish on this water, Bobs Creek.

What a setting for a trout stream! The upper 6 to 8 miles of this heavily canopied stream flow through state game lands and you have to hike in from the top from Berkheimer Road (SR 3001) or travel up the gravel road from Pavia (on T 652), park, and walk upstream. Either way you're in for some great fly-fishing over stocked and native browns and brookies—some over 15 inches long. In this upper section of Bobs Creek you'll find a game land access road within a few feet of the stream. This road is both a blessing and a curse. When it rains in the watershed, mud from the road discolors the stream more quickly than would happen without it. The access, however, provides a hiking trail for you to follow.

But modern times have been harsh to this mountain stream situated in northern Bedford County. On the same day that Wills Creek experienced a heavy downpour in 1984, so did Bobs Creek. Tom Wolfe toured his favorite stream the same day the flood occurred and vividly remembers a 10-foot-high surge of water flowing down the valley. Tom and his wife, Mary, monitor the acidity of the stream and fear for its future. Tom monitors the stream for a group from Dickinson College called ALARM. He's seen the pH of this productive stream fall from 7.5 (slightly alkaline) to recent readings of 5.5

(acidic) in the headwaters. What bothers Tom even more is the rapid reduction in the alkalinity of Bobs Creek. Ten years ago Tom found 40 parts of alkalinity per million (ppm). In 1992 Tom recorded 0 ppm on six different occasions. He's concerned that acid-rain events on the watershed have had an effect on the quality and quantity of aquatic insects found in the stream.

What can be done to help this great resource? First, the stream needs more fly-fishermen. If more interested anglers consistently fish this great stream they too will get involved with its well-being. Second, the state should replace with limestone the huge sandstone boulders placed along some of the washed-out banks for stream containment. Even the upper end suffers from man's indiscretion. Two miles from its beginning Bobs Creek flows through pastureland. This open land elevates summer water temperatures; you'll seldom see many brook trout.

With some acid-rain problems in its upper reaches you'd assume that Bobs Creek would hold only marginal hatches. It does contain an excellent early- and late-season blue quill hatch and some quill gordons. But you can expect more. Many years Tom waits until late May or early June to match the green drake that inhabits the stream. This huge mayfly entices even Bobs Creek lunkers to feed on the surface. At about the same time the drake appears you can expect to see March browns and giant stoneflies. Into July and August you'll find slate drakes and blue quills.

Tom says one of the best caddisflies on the stream is the rusty caddis, which appears in July. It also holds little yellow and green stoneflies, appearing in June.

Since much of the upper area of Bobs Creek is canopied, most sections of the stream support trout all year long. You'll find native, stocked, and holdover brook and brown trout on the upper 11 miles of the stream—above Pavia. Just below Pavia, Bobs Creek receives a needed shot of limestone from an outcropping, elevating the pH. You can access the stream below Pavia on PA 869. In this lower area the stream flows through farm country and expands from a 15- to 20-foot mountain stream to one that ranges from 30 to 60 feet wide. Twenty miles downstream from its headwaters Bobs Creek enters Dunning Creek near Reynoldsdale.

Recently I checked the pH of Bobs Creek in late July. Below Pavia I found readings of 6.6 to 7.3—higher as I traveled farther downstream. Above Pavia I checked several locations and recorded readings from 6.5 to 7.0. Water temperatures at noon in late July ranged from 64 degrees above Pavia to 68 degrees several miles downstream.

Try this excellent small stream just southwest of Altoona. Once you see the number of streambred trout, you, like Tom Wolfe, will fish it again and again. Fish upstream from Pavia and you'll see why I've rated Bobs Creek a 3-star stream.

COXES CREEK

Access SR 3015 parallels Coxes Creek from Somerset to Rockwood.

Special Regulations Although there are no Fish Commission regulations on Coxes Creek, the Rockwood Sportsmen, the Casselman Watershed Association, and the landowners along the stream have agreed on the following restrictions. From Bando upstream to source—artificial lures only—only trophy trout allowed over 20 inches. From Rockwood upstream to Bando—live bait allowed—one trophy trout over 20 inches. From Rockwood downstream to Casselman River—no restrictions.

Rating ✳✳

Patterns to Match the Hatches Little Black Stonefly (#16), Little Black Caddis (#16), Blue Quill (#18), Sulphur (#16 and #18), Light Cahill (#14), Tan Caddis (#14 and #16), Giant Stonefly (#8), Little Sulphur (#18 and #20)

❝As a kid I always dreamed about catching trout on Coxes Creek. But for many years it remained only a dream—partially treated sewage from Somerset and acid drainage from abandoned soft-coal mines continued to pour into the stream for decades. No one cared about the stream—it was a dead waterway. I still remember bringing home perch and sunfish that I caught in a dam or pond and placing them in Coxes Creek just behind my shop. Guess what—about 10 years ago these transplanted fish began to live in this highly neglected stream," said Dick Stoner, owner of the S&S Sport Shop.

When Dick saw the panfish survive in 1984 he spent some of his own money and got the Rockwood Sportsmen to plant some trout. The trout not only lived, but many of them held over the next year. Dick brags about a 27½-inch brown trout, the biggest trout caught on the 8-mile stream.

Coxes Creek hasn't fully recovered—it will face problems for years to come—but it has returned from a stream void of trout and hatches to one with plenty of rising trout and some respectable hatches.

Recently Chuck Furimsky of Rockwood and I spent a day on this recovering stream. Chuck, who runs a fine-leather shop, has developed a series of fly patterns from a thinned leather that he calls Bugskin. At several of the access points Chuck and I watched more than a dozen trout sipping chironomids from the surface. These trout, placed in the stream in May, looked extremely healthy in early October. Chuck proceeded to land three healthy trout from the stream on a combination of terrestrials and nymphs.

Hatches will remain borderline for years to come. If you plan to fish Coxes Creek make certain you carry some midge patterns and plenty of downwings. Dick says that a Peacock Caddis is a real killer on the stream.

Donald Dunn Jr. of nearby Berlin fly-fishes Coxes Creek close to 100 times a year. He's seen some good hatches on the stream and enjoys Coxes because of the catch-and-release regulation. Don also recommends a Green Beetle pattern during the summer to copy some of the terrestrials found on bushes along the stream.

Coxes Creek still has its share of problems. Many local anglers feel that poaching and mine-acid drainage remain as the two major problems to yet surmount. The effluent from the Somerset Sewage Plant on the East Branch of Coxes Creek seems to have elevated the pH in the stream, which in turn has lessened the mine-drainage problem. More angling pressure will diminish the poaching problem. Those who fish the stream will help police it.

You won't find Coxes Creek on the Fish Commission's list of approved trout waters. But it does hold a good number of trout and is open to public fishing if anglers abide by the local regulations.

Stop in at S&S Sport Shop and ask Dick or Rich Stoner about the stream and its hatches and where to fish. While you're there thank Dick for caring enough to help the stream recover.

CASSELMAN RIVER

Access You can reach the river at Rockwood, Casselman, Markleton, Harnedsville, Fort Hill, or Confluence. The only way to access the remainder of the river is by the old railroad bed or by floating—and the latter is almost impossible because of the many shallow rapids. PA 281 parallels the northwestern side of the river from about 5 miles away and SR 3011 the southeastern side from the same distance.

Rating ✷✷

Patterns to Match the Hatches Little Black Stonefly (#16), Sulphur (#16), Light Cahill (#14), Tan Caddis (#14 and #16), Green Caddis (#14), Giant Stonefly (#8)

Chuck Furimsky of nearby Rockwood and I waded a deep, treacherous, boulder-lined pool of the Casselman River near the Pinkerton Tunnel. Gingerly wading past huge boulders and over limy rocks, we cast flies searching for trout that might have wandered into the main stem of this recently recovered river. This section of the river had only been stocked with fingerlings for the past couple of years. Until a couple of years before much of the lower 30 miles of the Casselman had contained no fish or hatches for the past half century.

In May 1993 mine-acid drainage again entered the Casselman River.

For several years the future of this great resource looked rather dim. But through the efforts of locals who joined together to form the Casselman Valley Watershed Association, along with the state mining department, the river has been revitalized. The Pennsylvania Fish and Boat Commission planted 25,000 fingerlings in the river in 1997 and 35,000 in 1998.

Recently I spoke with Fish Commission employees Rick Lorson, Area Fisheries Manager, and two of his assistants, Chuck Eisel and Tom Shervinskie. Rick indicated that at present they consider the river from Boynton down to Rockwood polluted water because of the concentration of mine-acid drainage; from Rockwood they term the water transitional and suggest trout will stay there on occasion; from Markleton to Confluence they consider the quality of the river good enough to hold trout. The lower 5 miles, from Fort Hill to Confluence, they consider a better smallmouth bass fishery than one for trout.

The Fish Commission has planted trout in the 6-mile stretch from the Maryland-Pennsylvania state line downriver to Boynton for several years. Anglers like John Shields of Connellsville and Rege Rubis of Uniontown have fly-fished the Salisbury area for more than five years. John feels one of the most effective patterns on this upper section of the Casselman is the Green Weenie.

The biggest impediment to total recovery for the Casselman remains the continuous flow of mine drainage from several abandoned mines and tipples around the Boynton area and the Shaw Mines at Meyersdale. Until authorities control these hot spots, the river will remain marginal.

Chuck Furimsky believes that the Casselman River is one of the most spectacular rivers in the East. He should know—he's been fly-fishing the rivers of the United States for many years. Several years ago Chuck began offering symposia to fly-fishers and fly-tiers at several locations in the East. His New Jersey show proved so successful that authorities made him close the doors after a record-setting 7,000 anglers showed up.

Walk along the river near Markleton and you'll see several personalities to the river. You'll see long, smooth 3- to 4-foot-deep pools; falls formed from water flowing over ledges; miles of deep pocket water; huge boulder-lined riffles; and much much more. You can still see the scars left from years of abuse to the river, too. You'll note a green color to the bottom of deep pools and small amounts of mine drainage oozing in at various points along the river.

Just recently a group purchased a huge section of the old Western Maryland Railroad right-of-way. Called the Allegheny Highlands Trail Project, local groups assisted by the National Park Service purchased and improved a section of the railroad from Rockwood downriver to the Pinkerton Tunnel, 2 miles below Markleton. This path will provide the

The Casselman River reminds many anglers who fish it of a Western river.

only access to miles of the river that would otherwise remain inaccessible. Eventually the trail will run from Confluence to Cumberland, Maryland. The Somerset Rails to Trails Association can take a lot of credit for bringing the access trail to fruition.

Some first-class tributaries help cool the Casselman on its flow to the Youghiogheny in Confluence. These tributaries also help lessen the effects of upriver mine drainage. The state stocks many of these tributaries; on some of them you'll find streambred browns, plenty of wild brook trout, and some great hatches. The best of the lot seems to be Isers Run, which enters the Casselman just below Markleton. This tributary holds good blue quill, green drake, and little blue-winged olive hatches. Hatches on the main stem of the Casselman are often inadequate. Lift up rocks and you're bound to see plenty of caddis larvae, and look into the air above the river almost anytime and you'll see plenty of chironomids—but relatively few mayflies until the stream improves.

If you plan to wade the river always carry a wading staff, and definitely use felt waders. The rocks on this river carry a slime coating destined to sweep you off your feet. Check in at S&S Sport Shop in Rockwood for the latest information on the river.

Fly-fish the rivers of southwestern Pennsylvania? If you were to try that several decades ago you would have been thought a lunatic. But just look at the number of streams and rivers that have recovered or are in the process of doing so: the Youghiogheny in the mid-1970s, the Stonycreek

River in the late 1970s, and the Casselman River and Indian Creek in the 1990s. That's a total of nearly 65 miles of cold-water fisheries added to this section of the state. Congratulations to all those involved in the cleanup campaign, including the Department of Environmental Resources and the Fish Commission. It's now up to us to make certain these rivers are never ravaged again, and that they continue to improve by any means possible.

STONYCREEK RIVER

Access The best trout fishing on Stonycreek River is above US 30 and in the remote section locals call the Upper Gorge. Since access is severely limited in much of this section you have to hike in at spots along a railroad or a trail. Be prepared to walk, and walk some more. But also be prepared to see few other anglers and plenty of trout. Above the gorge you can access the river at Shanksville (SR 1001) and above from SR 1007, which follows the river. You can access the top end of the Upper Gorge from Glessners Covered Bridge (T 565). The next access is in Kimmelton (SR 1008). Be careful not to walk on posted property—the eastern side of the river in this section is posted.

Rating ✳✳

Patterns to Match the Hatches Tan Caddis (#14 to #18), Sulphur (#16), Gray Caddis (#14 to #18), Light Cahill (#14), *Pteronarcys* Stonefly (#8), Cream Cahill (#14), Slate Drake (#12), Autumn Sedge (#14 and #16)

❝It's no 'Madison of the East,' but it's great," Len Lichvar of nearby Stoystown boasted as he gently released a hefty 15-inch holdover brown trout back to the deep pocket water from where it had come. At the same instant, 200 feet upriver, Len's longtime fishing friend Randy Buchanan of Johnstown released a holdover rainbow trout.

Len, Randy, and I spent a late-July evening on this once-decimated, now partially restored classic freestone river in Somerset County in southwestern Pennsylvania. Len is proud of the triumphant return of the Stonycreek River. He should be—he's stream improvement chairman for the Mountain Laurel Chapter of Trout Unlimited, a board member of the Stonycreek–Conemaugh River Improvement Project (SCRIP), a freelance outdoor writer, and projects and operation director for the Greater Johnstown Watershed Association. Len also monitors Stonycreek for the Alliance for Acid Rain Monitoring.

Randy Buchanan is also committed to the total recovery of the Stonycreek River. Besides being one of the most focused nymph-fishers I have ever seen, Randy serves as vice president of the Mountain Laurel Chapter of Trout Unlimited and has created a special fly for Stonycreek called the Apricot Stone Nymph. Together Len and Randy know just about the entire 7 miles of productive trout water on the river.

Darkness crept in quickly that night as we fly-fished just below the Kimmelton bridge. Before it did, and after only two hours of fly-fishing, the three of us caught and released more than 20 trout—a few over 10 inches, but the majority fingerlings.

Hatches on the Stonycreek remain sporadic. You'll find several species of mayflies present, but the best time to match an upright hatch is near the end of May with the light cahill. Until water quality improves fly-fishers will have to be content copying one of the few mayflies or one of the heavier downwing hatches. In early June you'll see hundreds of the large stoneflies that resemble the western salmon fly on the fast-water sections that predominate on this river. This eastern version *(Pteronarcys dorsata)* appears sporadically throughout the summer. In May, gray and tan caddis-

Len Lichvar holds a holdover brown trout caught on the Stonycreek River.

flies provide some matching-the-hatch opportunities.

When there's no hatch to match Len Lichvar suggests you try stonefly nymphs, caddisfly larvae, streamers, Woolly Buggers, or crayfish imitations.

How has this once-neglected river reversed its decline to now hold plenty of trout? Some mine reclamation in the headwaters near Berlin has helped. But it has been individuals and organizations such as the Quemahoning Rod and Gun Club, Fish Commission employees past and present like Blake Weirich, Rick Lorson, Bud Flyte, and Tom Qualters, and hard-working groups like the Somerset County Fly Fishers and the Mountain Laurel Chapter of Trout Unlimited that have provided the impetus.

But the job is only half completed—there's much more work to be done with this river. Sections below Kantner still suffer from highly acidic

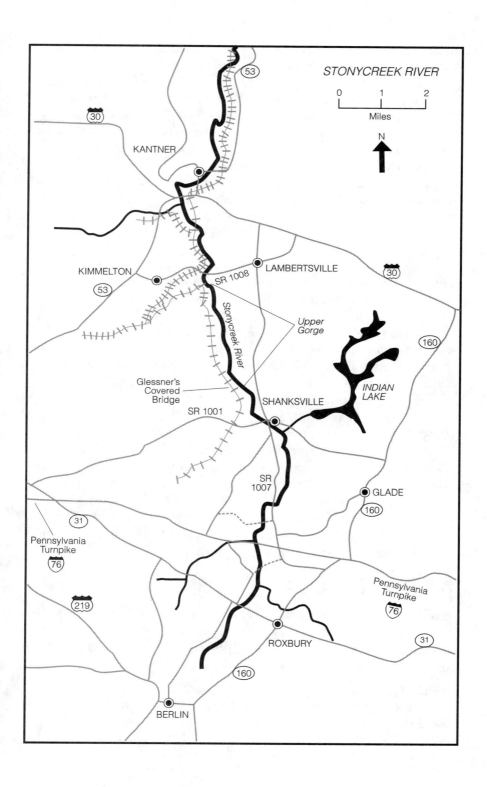

STONYCREEK RIVER

0   1   2

Miles

N

53

30

KANTNER

KIMMELTON

53

SR 1008   LAMBERTSVILLE

30

160

Upper
Gorge

Stonycreek River

Glessner's
Covered
Bridge

SR 1001

SHANKSVILLE

INDIAN
LAKE

SR
1007

GLADE

160

31

Pennsylvania
Turnpike

76

Pennsylvania
Turnpike

76

31

219

ROXBURY

160

BERLIN

tributaries like Oven and Pokeytown Runs. Who will complete this her-culean task of cleaning the entire Stonycreek and Conemaugh Rivers? Enter another important group of concerned citizens—the aforementioned Stonycreek–Conemaugh River Improvement Project (SCRIP). Formed by Congressman John Murtha, the 14-member board consists of representa-tives of industry; sportsmen; environmental groups; county conservation districts; the Southern Alleghenies Resource, Conservation, and Development Program; and elected representatives. The group devotes all its energy to ridding both the Stonycreek and Conemaugh Rivers of their mine-drainage problems. It hopes to achieve its goal in 20 years through the active use of wetlands. All who would like to see this vast effort come to fruition need to support this conservation-minded umbrella group.

Don't go near Stonycreek unless you're well prepared with a wading staff and felt soles. Jagged, slippery rocks and huge half-submerged boul-ders make any wading experience in the river one to remember.

Len Lichvar feels the prime trout water on Stonycreek is found from Glessners Covered Bridge downriver to Kimmelton. Do you like to dry-fly fish on good-sized pools? Or maybe you like to nymph in heavy pocket water or deep riffles. Stonycreek has all of them. It reminds me of one of Virginia's better-known trout streams, the Rapidan River. Len says that much of the summer, water in the Upper Gorge runs gin clear.

Future plans of the Fish Commission call for stocking only fingerlings in much of the Upper Gorge. Recent surveys in this area suggest four-year classes of fingerlings have survived.

If you want a real experience fly-fishing what many of us feel is a classic freestone trout water, then you've got to try the Stonycreek River. When you do you'll realize that you owe a debt of gratitude to countless people and organizations who have banded together to produce a tremen-dous fishery. For starters, people like Len Lichvar and Randy Buchanan deserve your commendations, but there are many many more who have worked diligently so you can enjoy this scenic fishery.

LOYALHANNA CREEK

Access All of the Loyalhanna's 10 miles of open public water flow within feet of US 30, although parking for many areas of the stream is limited.

Special Regulations Delayed harvest, artificial lures only—1.5 miles, from SR 711 downstream to SR 2045.

Rating ✷✷

Patterns to Match the Hatches Gray Fox (#12), March Brown (#12), Sulphur Dun and Spinner (#16), Green Drake and Coffin Fly (#10), Brown Drake and Spinner (#12), Light Cahill (#14), Blue-Winged Olive Dun (#16), Golden Drake (#12), Trico (#24)

Russ Mowry, who lived near the Loyalhanna in Latrobe, just recently passed away. He had a very positive effect on me. He was a true gentleman and a friend of every angler he met. This third edition, in fact, has been dedicated to the memory of this great man.

Russ tied some of the finest trout flies in Pennsylvania. His copies of the brown drake have gained prominence throughout the Commonwealth as top producers during the drake hatch near the end of May. Russ, who ran Mowry's Fly Box, a fly-fishing supply shop in Latrobe, normally concentrated his fly-fishing on Pine Creek in north-central Pennsylvania. He did, however, on occasion fish the Loyalhanna.

Ken Igo and Tim Shaffer of Latrobe accompanied Russ and me to the creek several years ago. The late-March day turned out to be one of the first warm days of spring. Early-morning water temperatures in the low 40s slowly rose to near 50 degrees by noon. Even at this early date occasional little black stoneflies danced above the surface, and gray midges by the dozens rested in the back eddies on some of the slower pools. Both Tim and Ken started the day with an unusual chartreuse-colored fly that the locals call the Green Weenie. It was the first time I'd seen this fly. It reminded me of the San Juan Red Worm that Mike Manfredo and I had used on Montana's Big Horn River. The fly is nothing more than a piece of chenille looped at the tail, then wound around the shank of the hook to the eye. Others call it an inchworm pattern.

What trout would take this odd pattern, I wondered, especially before leaves appeared on the trees? Ken, Tim, and Russ proceeded to catch two dozen trout with the Green Weenie on the Loyalhanna that March morning. Ken knows the hatches on the Loyalhanna well. He says the brown drake, green drake, and golden drake are the most abundant on the stream, but those aren't the only hatches this water contains; the stream also harbors a decent trico hatch from mid-July until September, and a respectable sulphur hatch appears for a month or more during May and June.

The Loyalhanna has more than just mayflies. At least five separate caddis species appear in enough numbers to create some matching-the-hatch possibilities with downwings. Caddis with body colors of tan, yellow, green, cream, and brown emerge in May and June. Tie caddis patterns for this stream in sizes ranging from 12 to 16.

With its diversity of hatches, the Loyalhanna would seem to be a great stream all season long. In fact it is not, because water temperatures often reach 80 degrees in July and August. The stream contains some springs and several decent tributaries that temper the water of the main stem. Branches like Linn Run, Rolling Rock Creek (also called McGinnis Run), and Furnace Run flow into the Loyalhanna above Ligonier. Between Ligonier and Latrobe, Mill, Coalpit, and Fourmile Runs add volume to the main stem.

The Rolling Rock Club owns and posts most of the Loyalhanna upstream from Ligonier. The Fish Commission stocks the stream from Ligonier downstream to the Kingston Dam. The Lloydsville Sportsmen's Association and the Forbes Trail Trout Unlimited Chapter add more trout to the stream with their stocking programs. This Trout Unlimited chapter recently built deflectors and other stream improvements on the Loyalhanna under the Fish Commission's Adopt-a-Stream program.

The Loyalhanna flows out of the Laurel Mountains in Westmoreland County. It is a fairly large freestone, 30 to 40 feet wide at most places. It contains some moderate pools, many rocks, and some productive riffles. Fishing pressure is high from early March until late June in the specially regulated section. This delayed-harvest area runs for 1.5 miles from the PA 711 bridge in Ligonier downstream to the Two Mile bridge. Fishing in this area is open year-round.

LAUREL HILL CREEK

Access SR 4001 parallels Laurel Hill Creek upstream from PA 31. PA 653 crosses the stream at Barronvale.

Special Regulations Delayed harvest, artificial lures only—2.2 miles, from Laurel Hill State Park at the BSA camp downstream to T 364.

Rating ✷✷

Patterns to Match the Hatches Little Black Stonefly (#16), Hendrickson and Red Quill (#14), Cream Caddis (#14 and #16), Black Quill (#12 and #14), Little Black Caddis (#16), Sulphur Dun and Spinner (#16), Olive Caddis (#14), March Brown (#12), Gray Fox and Ginger Quill Spinner (#12), Blue-Winged Olive Dun (#16), Light Cahill (#14), Slate Drake (#12), Golden Drake (#12), Gray Stonefly (#12)

Tim Shaffer of Latrobe has had only one trout mounted in his lifetime. That trout, a brown, came from a highly productive stream in southwestern Pennsylvania, Laurel Hill Creek. Tim recalls the day he saw the lunker feeding on terrestrials under a low-lying branch. Large trout always seem to find a difficult lie, and Tim tried several times before he got a perfect cast to that one. The ant drifted directly over the brown without any rise until it was a foot or so below the fish. The heavy trout then turned around, lunged at the terrestrial, and Tim felt the hit. About 10 minutes later he netted and kept a 19-inch brown.

Nate Rascona and Ken Sarver of Somerset, and John Sanner of Rockwood, also fly-fish on Laurel Hill Creek frequently. Total the years these three have fished the stream and you'll get well over 100. All three have also caught heavy trout on the stream. John landed a 21-inch brown; Ken a 20-incher; and Nate a 19-inch, 3-pound fighter.

But Laurel Hill Creek has fallen on hard times the past few years. Rainfall in its headwaters has diminished drastically. At points along its flow Laurel Hill represents only a shadow of its former character. Laurel Hill experienced a severe fish kill in 1987—the second summer of inadequate rainfall. Again in 1998 the stream suffered from an extremely dry fall. Walk along Laurel Hill in the delayed-harvest area in the summer months and you'll immediately notice that the water level has dropped 2 feet below its height at spring runoff. At many points along the upper end the stream appears stagnant.

The Somerset County Fly Fishers have not given up on Laurel Hill, however. Along with Nate Rascona, Ken Sarver, John Sanner, and Dick Knupp, the club's 50 other members have accomplished much with the stream. In particular they have worked for four years trying to get a delayed-harvest area designated. Nate says that Clair Walker of Somerset instigated the letter to the Fish Commission to start the special-project water on the creek. The stream now contains a specially regulated area in Laurel Hill State Park. Travel along this section of the stream, even in late June, and you'll see plenty of fishermen. And look at the trail that follows the stream along the delayed-harvest area. Unlike areas of the stream where few trout remain and paths have grown over, the delayed-harvest area even in late June remains well traveled and fairly heavily fished. If you walk along the stream even in low-water conditions, you'll see that this section still contains a good trout population. It should. In addition to a heavy state stocking program, the Somerset Fly Fishers add some 14- to 17-inch trout. The Fly Fishers also monitor conditions on the stream and protect the delayed-harvest section from would-be poachers.

Much of the stream below Laurel Hill Lake becomes marginal trout water in early June, because a top release from the dam warms the water below. By the time it enters the Casselman River near Confluence, Laurel Hill has become smallmouth bass water. Although the state stocks most of the stream, Laurel Hill in its lower end flows through open land and warms quickly. Many of the tributaries add a shot of cold water to the stream, however, and most are stocked by the state. Clear Run, Shafer Run, Jones Mill Run, Allen Creek, Blue Hole Creek, Fall Creek, and Sandy Run receive stocked trout. Although Jones Mill is small, it provides plenty of cool water to the main stem.

Recently, when a group of fly-fishers attended an entomology workshop they checked Laurel Hill Creek and Jones Mill Run for insect life. Headed by Gregory Hoover, these anglers found to their amazement a population of green drakes on Jones Mill Run.

Because of its location just off the Pennsylvania Turnpike, Laurel Hill Creek receives heavy fishing pressure from Greensburg and Pittsburgh residents, especially in the delayed-harvest area. This area contains 2.2 miles of deep, flat sections alternating with small riffles. Casting a fly in this heavily canopied area enveloped with dead trees scattered about the banks is difficult. The delayed-harvest water begins at the upper end of Laurel Hill Lake (Old Forge Bridge).

Hatches have suffered from the most recent drought. Still there are some slate drakes, golden drakes and light cahills in mid- and late June. In mid-March you can fish over the little black stonefly.

YOUGHIOGHENY RIVER

Access PA 281 takes you from Somerset to Confluence. Follow SR 2012 from Confluence to Ohiopyle to reach the lower end. It's only a 40-minute drive from Somerset and less than a two-hour drive from Pittsburgh to the Youghiogheny. Confluence and Ohiopyle lack overnight facilities, but Somerset has plenty of motels. If you have the time and enjoy solitude, you might want to hike or bike down the bicycle trail on the Fayette County side. Halfway between Confluence and Ohiopyle, about 5 miles downriver, there's another productive mile-long stretch of flat water at Bidwell Station that contains plenty of heavy trout. There are two bicycle-rental shops in Confluence.

Special Regulations Miscellaneous waters special regulations—from the confluence with the Casselman River to the mouth.

No closed season on trout. Daily limit opening day of trout season to Labor Day—eight trout; day after Labor Day to succeeding opening day of trout season—three trout.

Rating ✷✷

Patterns to Match the Hatches Black Caddis (#16), Olive Caddis (#14 and #16), Blue Dun (#20 and #22), Sulphur Dun and Spinner (#18), Light Cahill (#14), Blue-Winged Olive Dun (#14), Chocolate Dun (#16), Gray Caddis (#16), Slate Drake (#12), Yellow Drake (#12), Cinnamon Caddis (#14), Perla Stonefly (#12), Blue Quill (#18), Dark Gray Caddis (#18)

In early April I scheduled a trip with Art Gusbar for late June on the Youghiogheny River. Art lives in Friedens, near Somerset, Pennsylvania. He agreed to share some of his hot fishing spots with me.

Between April and late June a heat wave unfolded in southwestern Pennsylvania, along with a severe drought. By late June the area had experienced seven days with 90-plus-degree temperatures. I called Art the day before the trip to make certain the river would still be fishable.

"Better bring your neoprene waders," Art commented. "The water temperature rarely rises above the low 60s."

Why does this 200-foot-wide river remain so cool from Confluence to Ohiopyle? Back in the 1940s the Corps of Engineers placed a dam on the river at Confluence. Someone had the foresight to build a bottom release on this 125-foot-deep lake. As a result, water released from the dam stays in the 50s to low 60s downriver for miles. Select any hot summer day and you can fish in predictably cool water filled with rainbow and brown trout. Unlike the Delaware, which depends on cold-water releases from upriver reservoirs, the Yough remains cool from a fairly constant flow throughout the summer. On hot summer days the water temperature averages 50 to 55 degrees at the release site.

Just below the lake two trout streams, Laurel Hill Creek and the Casselman River, enter. By the time both join the Yough they become marginal trout streams.

The state stocks 2 miles of the Yough just below the dam with plenty of legal-sized trout. It stocks this section weekly into August. From this point to Connellsville the river depends on fingerlings planted annually. As an experiment the state placed the first fingerlings in the river in late August 1973. The program has continued, and now the state plants more than 100,000 fingerlings at Confluence and Ohiopyle annually. This mixture of browns and rainbows has adapted well to the river. Fingerlings from a June stocking average 6 to 8 inches long by late summer.

If you plan to fish the Yough between Confluence and Ohiopyle, you have three choices: You can hike or bike down an abandoned railroad track or float the river. Thanks to the efforts of the Western Pennsylvania Conservancy, access via the bike trail will remain in public hands forever. Since there are 9 miles of isolated river accessible by this trail, you won't see any crowd once you've traveled a couple of miles below Confluence or a few miles up from Ohiopyle.

Once on the water you'll experience serious wading problems. The bottom contains square rocks, round rocks, huge boulders, and pebbles of all sizes. Each rock is well coated with a slippery surface prepared to take you off your feet at any moment. There are few places in the river where you have secure footing. Never wade the Yough without felts and a wading staff.

Under drought conditions the river was at least a foot lower than usual. Under normal conditions, many of the rising trout can be impossible

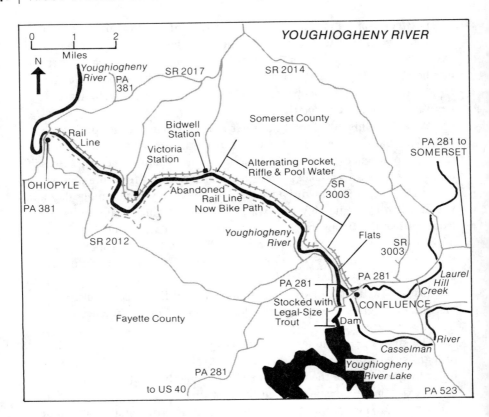

to reach. Still, there's excellent trout fishing downriver to Connellsville, although access to the water from Ohiopyle to Connellsville presents major problems. You can raft down the white water and fish some of the lower eddies—but this is treacherous and I don't recommend taking expensive equipment with you. As I've mentioned there's plenty of water, good access, and very few fishermen from Confluence to Ohiopyle, but this 9-mile stretch contains some sizable pools over 15 feet deep that are impossible to fly-fish. On the plus side, some stretches in this area contain miles of pocket water that are productive most of the day.

Art Gusbar and I began fly-fishing on an area he selected just a mile below Confluence, which represents a typical section of the Youghiogheny River. The water in front of us reminded me of many rivers I had fly-fished before—all of them western. In front of us lay 2-foot-deep pocket water with the typical drag problems associated with varying currents. Just downriver a fast, deep riffle led into a short, 10-foot-deep pool. Above us a 200-foot rapids flowed out of a half-mile-long, deep flat-water section. The river contains several other long flat sections between Confluence and Ohiopyle. The water averages a moderate drop of 11 feet per mile between those two towns.

I struggled to keep my footing in the pocket water, but it didn't seem to bother Art. Shortly after we began fishing an intermittent olive caddis hatch emerged. The caddis takes on extreme importance in this river as a prime source of food for the trout. Many of last year's fingerlings made splashing rises at the emerging pupae. Art tied on an olive soft-hackle wet fly while I tied on a size-14 Olive Caddis dry. For the next two hours we saw several dozen trout rise to the caddis, and we caught 20—all fingerlings. Art assured me that the Yough contained plenty of larger trout and that when we fished the flats upriver in the evening, we'd see these fish rise.

I spent much of the afternoon collecting aquatic insects. During that time I witnessed a sporadic hatch of size-20 or -22 blue duns and saw a few light cahills emerge in the pocket water in front of me. Caddisflies appeared in the largest numbers that afternoon, however. Art assured me that downwings take on tremendous importance on the river.

Art recommended that we move up to the flat section around 6:00 PM, and we headed upriver a half mile. Art felt this area might produce some mayfly activity that evening. Mayflies don't appear in large numbers on the Yough, although Art feels that these insects have increased in the past four years. Once on the flat water we waited two hours for something to happen. Only a few sulphurs and light cahills appeared on the surface—not enough to create any surface-feeding. In those two hours of waiting and observing on this 4-foot-deep flat water, we saw no more than two or three trout rise.

By 8:30 PM a few more mayflies had appeared. Some sulphurs, chocolate duns, blue-winged olive duns, light cahills, and even a couple of slate drakes paraded past us. Now several trout started feeding 100 yards above us. They fed in pods, the way trout feed on some western rivers. Art yelled, "They're feeding," and we both waded upriver after the rising trout. Soon two more pods of risers appeared. Within 15 minutes Art and I had 30 to 40 trout rising within our casting reach.

With just one trip to the river, I caught Yough Fever. I returned two weeks later to learn more about this fantastic trout water. Art again accompanied me, along with Dave Bruner and Pat Docherty, both of Grafton, West Virginia. Pat is the Monongahela Resource Manager for the Army Corps of Engineers—a good fly-fisherman who provided me with information on the excellent job the corps is doing on the Youghiogheny. On this second visit to the river we made an excruciating hike down the bike trail 2 miles below Confluence. By 2:00 PM the air temperature rose over the century mark. Certainly there'd be no trout fishing in the middle of this unbearably hot midsummer afternoon. When we arrived at the 2-mile marker on the bike trail we headed for the river. Pat suggested that

I check the water temperature. About 4 miles below the dam, on this extremely hot afternoon, the Youghiogheny along the shore registered 63 degrees! All afternoon the four of us caught trout—most in the 6- to 10-inch category. All afternoon, also, we saw sparse hatches of slate drakes, blue duns, light cahills, and several caddis species. During that hot afternoon, when nobody should have attempted to fish, we caught trout.

The Youghiogheny River lacks one ingredient, however, without which it cannot be rated as a truly spectacular river—heavy mayfly hatches. Although we saw a smorgasbord of mayflies—seven different species— none appeared in numbers reminiscent of hatches on many other streams. Probably more slate drakes (*Isonychia* spp.) emerge on the Yough than any other group of mayflies.

Mayflies have increased on the river in the past few years, however. In a survey conducted by the Fish Commission in 1970 only two species were found below the dam. Now there are at least seven mayfly species indigenous to the river.

The best strategy for fly-fishing the Yough is to fish the fast pocket water and riffles during the day when the caddis emerge. In the evening move to one of the flats and wait for insect activity and rising trout. Don't quit too early; feeding may not start until dusk.

Because of the cold water, hatches appear about three or four weeks later on the Yough than on other area streams. Slate drakes appear in largest numbers in July. Yellow drakes begin emerging in early July. The cold water also seems to affect the time of day when some of the hatches appear. We observed many blue-winged olives emerging near dusk and slate drakes emerging in the afternoon.

Art Gusbar fly-fishes the river through much of winter. The water in January and February averages 45 degrees just below Confluence. Art says that on many winter days he's seen tremendous midge hatches. Midges can be seen almost every day throughout the year on the Yough.

Are you tired of looking for productive cool water on big streams in the East in July or August? Are you longing to get away from the crowds? Or maybe you'd like to extend your season into winter. Either way, once you fly-fish this river you too will catch Yough Fever.

LITTLE MAHONING CREEK

Access Take US 119 to Hamill, then SR 1035 to the stream.

Special Regulations Delayed harvest, fly-fishing only—4.1 miles, from SR 1034 at Rochester Mills upstream to Cesna Run.

Rating ✳✳

Patterns to Match the Hatches Hendrickson and Red Quill (#14), Grannom (#16), Sulphur (#16), March Brown (#12), Green Drake and Coffin Fly (#10), Light Cahill (#14), Brown Drake (#12), Yellow Drake (#12)

"It's nothing but a ditch!" That's what a friend of Terry Powers calls the Little Mahoning. But to thousands of anglers in western Pennsylvania and Ohio, this stream resembles an oasis in the middle of a desert.

The Little Mahoning flows north, then west through much of northern Indiana County. Many of the streams in this area and in the surrounding counties of Clearfield, Jefferson, and Armstrong have been ravaged by man's careless quest to mine coal. In the aftermath of these mining operations many streams in the area have suffered years of contamination from mine acid. The Little Mahoning, however, remains relatively free of the pollution from strip mining, although it does suffer from severe siltation, which in turn affects the aquatic life on the stream. Small upstream farms and strip mining contribute to this silting problem. Rocks and boulders through much of the stream contain a heavy coating of mud. Wading these mud-covered rocks can be challenging. Even small storms cause the water to discolor quickly.

The Little Mahoning begins near Deckers Point and flows north for 10 miles, where it picks up a major tributary, the North Branch. In its headwaters the creek resembles a small, meandering farmland stream ranging from 10 to 20 feet wide. Before it adds the North Branch, the stream enters a forested area. For the next 7 miles a heavy canopy of mixed hardwoods and pines shades the water. The stream picks up additional flow from more tributaries, including Brewer Run, Broadhead Run, and Leasure Run, before the main stem flows through Rochester Mills. Special-project water begins near Rochester Mills and continues upstream for 4 miles. The state stocks the stream above Smicksburg for 15 miles. From Rochester Mills you can gain access to the stream by a dirt road that goes to Smithport. The locals have named many of the pools, especially in the fly-fishing-only stretch. There's a Millstone Pool, a Gas Well Pool, and a Swimming Hole Pool—among others.

The late Bob Davis of Big Run fly-fished on the Little Mahoning for over 30 years and knew the hatches on the stream well. He felt that along with a few caddis species, the March brown and the green drake produce the heaviest hatches of the year. In contrast to many limestone streams like Penns Creek, the green drake on the freestone Little Mahoning produces plenty of risers and cooperative trout. Bob said that if you hit the green drake on the stream, you'd probably experience a great evening of fly-fishing.

Terry Powers of Colver and Dennis Horn of Penn Run met me on the Little Mahoning recently. Dennis spends his spare time fly-fishing on nearby streams and working with the local Ken Sink Chapter of Trout Unlimited. Beginning in 1982 this chapter, with the cooperation of the Fish Commission, installed 26 stream improvement devices on the fly-fishing section of the Little Mahoning. These improvements still prevent bank erosion. Terry heads up the Western Pennsylvania Fly Fisherman's Association in Barnesboro. This volunteer organization does much work on local streams to improve their quality. His organization recently installed stream improvement devices on another Cambria County stream, Blacklick Creek.

"Henryville Specials, Honey Bugs, and floating nymphs work well on this stream," Dennis said as we set out to fish. Terry tied on a Green Weenie, and Dennis a Honey Bug. I tied on more conventional patterns like the March Brown and Light Cahill.

Throughout the day March browns emerged sporadically. After 3:00 PM a dozen green drakes appeared. The drake here almost reaches the size of its counterpart on Penns and Yellow Creeks. The dark yellow abdomen of the drake here, however, differs from the lighter belly of this species on most other streams.

We traveled upstream to be in place on the Swimming Hole for the last hour of fishing before dusk. Thousands of great red spinners returned to the surface to lay their eggs, but only a handful of coffin flies reappeared. The green drake hatch we had expected to materialize didn't—probably in another night or two the majority of these huge mayflies would emerge. Dennis caught more than a dozen trout that last hour on a gray floating-nymph pattern, while Terry experienced success with the Green Weenie. In a half day's fishing the three of us caught more than 30 trout.

The Little Mahoning Creek is a ditch? Although it has a siltation problem and sparse hatches, the stream deserves a better designation. The delayed-harvest area teems with stocked trout and a few holdovers. To many area anglers the Little Mahoning Creek provides hours of fun and enjoyable fishing over a good supply of trout. If you're so fortunate as to hit the stream when the green drake appears, you're in for some top-notch fly-fishing.

YELLOW CREEK (BEDFORD COUNTY)

Access PA 36 parallels Yellow Creek from Woodbury to the lower end of Loysburg Gap. Access below that is by blacktop at the New Frontier Restaurant. PA 26 parallels the last 4 miles.

Special Regulations Delayed harvest, fly-fishing only—1.25 miles, from the mouth of Maple (Jacks) Run upstream past Red Bank Hill.

Rating ✳✳✳✳

Patterns to Match the Hatches Early Brown Stonefly (#12), Blue Quill (#18), Quill Gordon (#14), Hendrickson and Red Quill (#14), Green Caddis (#16), Grannom (#16), Sulphur Dun and Spinner (#16), Gray Fox (#14), March Brown (#12), Green Drake and Coffin Fly (#10), Light Cahill (#14), Brown Caddis (#14 and #16), Slate Drake (#12 and #14), Yellow Drake (#12), Trico (#24)

Nelson Hamel of Altoona, Carl Dodson of Martinsburg, and Bob Foor of Everett fly-fish Yellow Creek frequently. Carl owns a stretch at the lower end of the delayed-harvest area. He's one of those treasured landowners who welcomes fishermen on his stretch of the stream.

Nelson and I fished the green drake hatch on Yellow Creek in late May. The drakes hatch on Yellow in large numbers, but trout have other food on their menu this time of year. On the stream at the same time were ginger quills, sulphur duns and spinners, and some light cahills. Some trout fed on the ginger quills, while others fed on emerging green drake nymphs just under the surface. Some regular fly-fishermen on Yellow during the green drake hatch tell of catching 50 trout per day and 200 in a four-day hatch.

Green drakes disappeared from Yellow Creek in the mid-1950s. For a couple of years in the early 1980s Bob Foor collected green drakes from Cove Creek near his home and transplanted them to Yellow Creek in northern Bedford County. No one's certain how the hatch came back. Randy Buchanan of Johnstown contends that the hatch returned by 1977. Through Bob's efforts or through natural circumstances, the drake has returned to this fertile limestone stream, where it has exhibited an outstanding hatch and spinner fall the past two decades.

Carl Dodson has fly-fished over green drake hatches on Yellow Creek for years. He's seen the drake appear as far downstream as the covered bridge below the town of Yellow Creek. Carl, Len Lichvar, Randy Buchanan, and many others recommend that you stay away from the delayed-harvest water during heavy hatches because of the heavy angling pressure. During a recent green drake hatch Carl caught 27 trout below the project water—one brown measured 19 inches.

Another great fly-fishing time on Yellow occurs near the end of April. At that time you'll find blue quills, some hendricksons, and a heavy green caddis hatch on the lower end of the stream. Mid-May on Yellow Creek also presents some fine hatches. Carl Dodson says the numbers of March browns appearing the last few years around the third week in May have been phenomenal.

Several local anglers discuss strategy on Yellow Creek before the green drake hatch appears.

Even into July and August this fertile insect factory harbors decent hatches. Tricos appear every morning, and if the water temperature remains cool, you can fly-fish over rising trout for an hour each morning. Randy Buchanan says that the trico appears on the project water as early as late June and usually ends by late July. Above Waterside you'll find good trico hatches throughout August and September. Potter Creek enters Yellow Creek at Waterside. Potter holds a decent trico hatch in late summer. Some of the water on Yellow Creek above Waterside is posted, so make certain you get permission before you match the hatch. In August some anglers say that Yellow displays a white mayfly hatch on its lower half. I've heard conflicting stories about that hatch. Some anglers swear the hatch exists—others declare they've never seen the white mayfly. I've sat along the banks of Yellow Creek in the Loysburg area for hours near the end of August and I've never seen a white mayfly appear.

Even into late summer, fishing Yellow with terrestrials produces trout. Carl Dodson uses hopper imitations with yellow, green, or brown bodies.

Yellow Creek begins near Woodbury in southern Blair County. It flows south to Loysburg, where it enters Loysburg Gap, then flows east to Hopewell, where it enters the Raystown Branch of the Juniata River. Tributaries include Hickory Bottom, Potter Creek, Three Springs, Beaver Creek, and Maple Run. The state stocks parts of the last four.

There's a delayed-harvest, fly-fishing-only section on the main stem from Maple Run upstream for more than a mile. Just five years ago the Fish Commission extended the delayed-harvest area upstream a few hundred yards. Carl Dodson says that this additional section holds good nymphing water. This section accommodates a sizable number of fly-fishermen and should be extended even farther upstream. Each part of the regulated area has been named by local fly-fishermen. You'll hear names like Red Bank, School House, Junk Pile, Slate Hole, Long Hole, Scout Camp, and Molly Gordon. On any weekend during the season you'll find a half-dozen or more anglers fishing the delayed harvest. If you see too many cars and anglers in this section try some of the productive water downstream.

Yellow Creek gets its name from its coloration; it never really attains the clarity that some other limestone streams, like Spruce Creek, do. This productive water contains plenty of holdovers and streambred browns. Matching the hatch for these wily browns often requires switching patterns, since you often encounter multiple hatches and spinner falls.

Wading is tricky and hazardous in Yellow Creek. The stream contains deep pools, productive riffles, heavy pocket water, and rapids in the Loysburg Gap area. Above Loysburg, Yellow averages 20 to 40 feet wide; below, it widens out to 40 to 50 feet. Just below Woodbury the state has designated a mile as wild-trout water, but much of this section has recently been posted (see chapter 11). This area affords the open-pasture fly-fishing so typical of limestone streams, but there are many native trout below and a good canopy in most places.

Once you try this great limestone stream you too will echo its praises. Hit Yellow Creek when the green drake, March brown, or other great hatch emerges and you'll keep coming back.

COVE CREEK

Access Cove Creek flows between Evitts and Tussey Mountains south of Everett in Bedford County. You reach it by crossing the Raystown Branch of the Juniata River at Everett, and traveling through Earlston on a black-top road to the stream. PA 326 from Bedford gets you to the upper end near Rainsburg.

Rating ✳✳

Patterns to Match the Hatches Little Blue-Winged Olive Dun (#20), Blue Quill (#18), Sulphur Dun and Spinner (#16), Gray Fox (#14), Light Cahill (#14), Green Drake and Coffin Fly (#10), Dark Green Drake (#8), Slate Drake (#12 and #14)

Bob Foor lives in Everett, in Bedford County. He's a biology teacher, and his biology classes visit nearby streams to monitor water quality. Bob's students check pH, temperature, and aquatic life. His classes have adopted Cove Creek just south of Everett as one of their study streams.

Talk about an isolated valley, a beautiful limestone stream, and heavy hatches—Cove Creek has them all. Add to this healthy streambred browns and holdover trout and you have all the ingredients for an excellent trout stream. Some landowners along Cove, however, have posted their property, a problem that seems destined to get worse. If you ask permission from some landowners, they might let you fish their property. This is an example of a stream to which the state should acquire access (see chapter 11). The state stocks open areas of Cove up to the town of Rainsburg, although this limestone stream really needs no stocking, since it houses an excellent supply of streambred brown trout. Bob Foor has caught trout up to 22 inches long during the green drake hatch on Cove.

Ten years ago Bob began transporting green drake duns and coffin fly spinners from Cove Creek to Yellow Creek in an attempt to establish that species there. Four years ago the green drake became a major hatch on Yellow, maybe in part because of Bob's work.

Cove Creek exhibits true limestone characteristics, with a pH of near 8.2. The water temperature seldom rises above 70 degrees. Throughout, additional springs add cold water to the main stem. Cove ranges from 30 to 40 feet wide on its lower end. Ten miles upstream near Rainsburg, the stream narrows. It contains many deep pools and heavy, productive riffles throughout. Cove is best fly-fished when a hatch or spinner fall appears. Otherwise nymphs prove to be the proper choice. Much of the cold-spring-fed stream contains a good canopy to shade it from the sun. It does, however, flow through some open farmland.

Bob Foor and I visited Cove in late May. He wanted to show me its heavy green drake hatch. By 8:00 PM coffin flies already appeared over the water, but the big surprise for me was the density of the sulphur spinners, which appeared as a cloud over every fast section. As these clouds of spinners appeared, thousands of sulphur duns emerged. Cove exhibited its true fertility that evening—yet few trout rose. Several evenings before, a thunderstorm had raised the level of the water by more than a foot.

WILLS CREEK

Access You can reach Wills Creek at Hyndman off PA 96. A paved secondary road follows the stream to Fairhope.

Rating ✳✳

Patterns to Match the Hatches Blue Quill (#18), Quill Gordon (#14), Gray Fox (#14), Blue-Winged Olive Dun (#14), Light Cahill (#14), Green Drake and Coffin Fly (#10), Slate Drake (#12 and #14), *Pteronarcys* Stonefly (#6), Tan Caddis (#14), Sulphur Dun and Spinner (#16 and #18)

August 13, 1984, looms dark in the history of Wills Creek in Bedford and Somerset Counties. On that day the entire valley in which Wills flows flooded. The headwaters of Wills near Callimont received 6 to 8 inches of rain in two hours. As the swollen water moved downstream, it carried huge uprooted trees with it. These trees soon formed temporary dams along the narrow valley floor. When these dams burst, a 60-foot-high wall of water cascaded down the valley. Hyndman endured the brunt of the flood. Much of the town lay under several feet of raging floodwaters.

This flood destroyed aquatic life and killed the huge holdover brown trout formerly found in Wills. The flood scoured the streambed and even 15 years later the stream still suffers. Bob Bryant of Hyndman knew of a 24-inch and a 27-inch brown caught before the flood on Wills. He's heard few reports of lunkers taken since. Mayflies—once present in large numbers—returned but with much less density. As you walk up the valley floor, you can still see the scars from the flood: Huge uprooted trees line the banks for miles, and boulders larger than cars lie helter-skelter in the streambed.

Tony Stair of Hyndman, Bryan Meck, and I visited the stream several years ago to examine the water for insects. Tony lives just south of Hyndman and has fished Wills for most of his 40 years. His dad, Glenn, has fished the stream for more than 40 years. We visited the stream a mile below Fairhope.

By 8:00 PM huge *Pteronarcys dorsata* stoneflies mated in the air 100 feet above the stream. Never had I witnessed so many of these huge stoneflies egg laying at one time. In the hour just before dusk we may have seen more than a thousand of these monsters. Only on western streams have I encountered stoneflies as large as this eastern species. The western *P. californica* is closely related to this eastern stonefly, and fly-fishermen out West call it the salmon fly. Mayflies also emerged. Dozens of dark olive spinners mated and laid eggs, along with light cahills, ginger quills, slate drakes, and hundreds of sulphur spinners. Three species (*Ephemerella dorothea, E. septentrionalis,* and *E. rotunda*) emerged just at dusk. Wills Creek had returned.

Earlier that day Tony took us to one of Wills's tributaries, Brush Creek. We fished for a short time at the Pack Saddle bridge section. While we fished 100 or more green drakes emerged, along with light cahills, sulphurs, and slate drakes.

Wills Creek looks unlike any other stream in Pennsylvania. Wherever you fish on it, it reminds you of a fast-flowing western trout stream. Throughout, it's lined with huge boulders. The creek begins near Callimont at an elevation of 2,600 feet and falls 1,700 feet in 15 miles. Each rock and boulder in the water contains a covering of slime and silt, so wading in Wills is dangerous. Many areas contain cascading rapids and few sizable pools. Dry-fly fishing on the stream above Hyndman, you will encounter difficult crosscurrents. Below Hyndman the stream slows and forms deep pools. The Fish Commission doesn't stock below Hyndman, but this area would make a tremendous delayed-harvest section. Six miles below Hyndman, Wills flows into Maryland, where that state stocks the stream.

Many of Wills's tributaries carry native brook trout. Above Hyndman the state stocks Shaffers Run, Brush Creek, and Laurel Run. In Hyndman, Little Wills enters the main stem. The state stocks 6 miles of this stream. Four miles below Little Wills, Gladdens Run enters. Gladdens has a good holdover trout population. Other branches on Wills not stocked are Gooseberry Run (some mine acid), Bore Mill Run (native brook trout), and Savage or Mountain Run (native brook trout).

RAYSTOWN BRANCH, JUNIATA RIVER

Access US 220 (Business) parallels the Raystown Branch near Bedford, and PA 31 follows the river above town.

Rating ✳✳

Patterns to Match the Hatches Blue Quill (#18), Quill Gordon (#14), Black Quill (#14), Gray Fox (#14), Light Cahill (#14), Blue-Winged Olive Dun (#14), Brown Drake (#12), Slate Drake (#12 and #14), Cream Cahill (#14 and #16), Yellow Drake (#12), White Mayfly (#14)

You'll often find Bill Thomas of Bedford in Montana hunting for elk, in Quebec fly-fishing for salmon, and on the Chesapeake Bay goose hunting. When he's not on one of his excursions, you'll find him fly-fishing near his Bedford home on the Raystown Branch.

Quite often Bill fly-fishes the lower end of Raystown until early June. At that time, when he fishes the branch, he does so about one hour before dusk or near dawn. The stream warms rapidly in summer and quickly becomes a warm-water fishery populated with smallmouth bass. At this time trout seek out the cooler springs and feeder streams scattered throughout the river.

If the water temperature cooperates, fly-fishing over a trico spinner fall can prove productive on the Raystown Branch in July, August, and September. The white mayfly appears in mid-August, and you can find some late-summer fly-fishing on Raystown—that is, if the temperatures cooperate. Bob Foor of Everett also says that there's a good brown drake hatch downriver between Everett and Bedford.

Bill Thomas and his fly-fishing buddy Bill Masterson have fly-fished on the river for the past 25 years. They catch an occasional holdover on the lower end but feel the upper end holds more trout. They're both members of the Fort Bedford Chapter of Trout Unlimited. The area the two fish regularly near Bedford ranges from 80 to 100 feet wide and contains many slow pools and long, flat sections, and a few productive riffles. Below Bedford the river widens considerably. Even though trout aren't stocked this far downriver, you'll find fish. The river near the Somerset County line averages 60 to 70 feet wide, with more riffles and cooler water. The state stocks 20 miles of the Raystown Branch from Somerset County downriver to Bedford.

The Raystown Branch begins near Macdonaldton in eastern Somerset County. It picks up Breastwork Run (stocked), Three Lick Run, Spiker Brook, Shawnee Branch, Buffalo Run, and Cumberland Valley Run before it enters Bedford. Near Shawnee State Park, about 10 miles upstream from Bedford, the Raystown Branch flows through shale deposits. This area therefore gets extremely low and warms rapidly in hot dry summers.

BRUSH CREEK

Access You can reach Brush Creek from PA 96 at Hyndman, then take secondary blacktop roads to Fairhope, then to the stream. You can also reach the stream from Somerset off PA 31.

Rating ✳✳

Patterns to Match the Hatches Blue Quill (#18), Quill Gordon (#14), Sulphur Dun and Spinner (#16), Gray Fox and Ginger Quill (#12 and #14), March Brown (#12), Green Drake and Coffin Fly (#10), Light Cahill (#14), Slate Drake (#12 and #14)

Tony Stair, Bryan Meck, and I arrived at the Pack Saddle covered bridge shortly after noon. Tony lives in nearby Hyndman, and he had bragged about the beauty and inaccessibility of this high-mountain stream. Because of the limited access to Brush, Tony doubted that many anglers fished more than the couple of areas where roads crossed. At the time of day we approached I doubted that we'd see any hatches or trout rising.

Tony and Bryan fly-fished in the spectacular pool just below the bridge. Here you can see a picturesque waterfall flowing into a 10-foot-deep pool with a covered bridge in the background. The pool tailed out to 2 feet at the lower end.

All three of us were mesmerized by the waterfall and the beauty of the area. We didn't expect any hatch this early in the day. In a couple of minutes, however, some green drakes appeared in the shallow riffle just below the pool. Soon a hundred or more coffin fly spinners appeared over the water. Then slate drakes, light cahills, and sulphurs emerged with the green drakes.

Brush Creek contains some great hatches, but access is limited. The stream flows off the eastern slope of the Allegheny escarpment. Below Pack Saddle are 3 miles of heavily canopied water before you reach the next bridge at Bittners Mills. Upstream from Pack Saddle there's also limited access to this small stream, but the area is less densely forested than below.

Brush Creek begins in Somerset County where Panther and Hillegas Runs join. Several of the tributaries to Brush hold good populations of native brook trout, and you'll find holdover trout in the main stem. Brush flows south for 6 miles before it joins Wills Creek near Fairhope.

Try Brush Creek. The terrain is rugged, the scenery spectacular, and the hatches outstanding. Don't expect to park your car and take a leisurely hike to the stream; especially on its lower half, much of the creek flows through a heavily forested narrow gorge where access is difficult.

10 | Tying Patterns for Pennsylvania's Hatches

By now you know a lot about the hatches you might encounter on the streams of Pennsylvania. You know where these hatches might occur and at approximately what time of the year they appear. Go to a sporting goods store and attempt to buy some of the patterns I suggest to match these hatches, however, and you may face difficulty. Let me describe one of my early experiences trying to locate the proper fly pattern.

I started fly-fishing 50 years ago in eastern Pennsylvania. Many streams in Schuylkill and Carbon Counties, including the Upper Swatara, Lower Swatara, Bear, Lizard, and Pohopoco Creeks, saw me frequently. All of them have some hatches and good fly-fishing. The Lower Swatara near Rock contains some pale evening duns throughout the summer. Bear Creek in lower Schuylkill County was a favorite of mine. It's a small stream coming off Blue Mountain, flowing through Auburn, then into the Schuylkill River. Much of the creek is only a stone's throw from PA 895. In its headwaters it holds a good supply of small brook trout. I once found a long, slow pool on the stream 3 miles below Summit Station. Some local kids had evidently created it as a swimming hole, because it contained rocks neatly piled a foot or so high at the lower end. I passed by this dam one day and noticed several yellow stoneflies in the air, returning to the pool to lay their eggs for the next generation of Bear Creek nymphs. As I stood and stared at the insects, I saw six trout begin to feed in the impoundment. I got my fishing gear out of the car and tied on the only pattern I owned that looked anything like the bug in the air. That pattern, a Yellow Sally wet fly, proved to be the final inducement needed to encourage me to fly-fish. Trout took the pattern until it became ragged. The last half hour the Sally contained only a yellow body—no hackle or tail. The questions then became, Where did I get this fly, and where do I get another?

My total fly selection at the time amounted to no more than 20 wets and 20 drys—but that Sally had been the only light-colored fly in my box. Fifty years ago there wasn't a store within 30 miles of Bear Creek that sold flies.

I was fortunate enough to have a neighbor who tied flies. I described the Yellow Sally to him and he tied me several copies. Because of the difficulty of getting flies, and with the encouragement of this local tier, I started tying.

Those days of few fly-fishermen and even fewer fly-tiers have long passed. There are now dozens of top sporting goods stores and thousands of fly-tiers in the state, and many of them tie specified patterns. Many of the best stores, and Trout Unlimited and Federation of Fly Fishers chapters, sponsor fly-tying classes.

If you do tie, or if you're in the process of learning, you've probably acquired your fly-tying skills from several tiers. Maybe you've learned a method for tying wings from one tier, and a faster technique for tying the whip finish from another. In my case George Harvey, one of the greatest fly-fishermen in Pennsylvania, taught me the basics at a conservation camp. Adding to that initial lesson were such fly-tiers as John Perhach, Dick Mills, Barry Beck, Joe Humphreys, Greg Hoover, and others. For me the end product of all of this instruction from a wide variety of experts is my own unique method of tying. The same will happen to you. Your method will become so personal that your patterns will display a character all their own.

Let's examine tying methods for downwings or caddis patterns, for nymphs, for terrestrials. I'll look at upright patterns for many of the common mayfly hatches, spent-wing imitations to copy the spinner falls, and some of the more important wet flies. Not all the patterns I've discussed previously are described here, but I'll cover more than enough to make those trips to the Commonwealth's streams successful ones.

Some New Tying Methods

Several years ago in the great magazine *Flyfishing the West* (now called *Flyfishing*) a writer alluded to the number of new patterns and tying methods that have come in vogue lately. He grouped new patterns and methods into three categories:

1   Those new patterns that are not as good as the old standbys.
2   Those new imitations that are equal to, but not better than, the present patterns.
3   Those patterns that are truly revolutionary and are better than the present patterns.

In Group 1 the author listed the no-hackle flies, latex-bodied nymphs, and other patterns. In Group 2 he placed patterns like the Matukas and parachute dry flies. Guess what patterns he ranked in Group 3? None! I often say some patterns catch fishermen while others only catch fish. Following are some questions we should ask ourselves as fly-fishermen and tiers before we jump at every new pattern, method, or material that comes our way:

1   Is the newer method of tying a known pattern easier for me than the older one?
2   If the pattern is supposed to copy a natural insect, does the end product (the finished fly) copy the real insect more effectively than the old pattern did?
3   Is the recommended material easy to obtain?
4   Is the finished pattern relatively durable?
5   If the new pattern is a floating one, does it float well?
6   Does the new pattern catch trout? Moreover, does it produce over a wide range of waters and a good part of the season?

With the above cautions in mind let me suggest some methods that definitely make tying some of the patterns much simpler. Look, for example, at the description for tying the Deer-Head Caddis. I use the elementary concept that Keith Fulsher used to tie his famous bucktails, the Fulsher Minnows. You'll note another easy tying method that I suggest for the Poly Beetle. I tie the pattern much as its forerunner, the Crowe Beetle, was tied, but I use multipurpose polypropylene. Look at the instructions for tying the Poly Beetle. I suggest you use black poly yarn instead of the normal black deer hair used in the Crowe Beetle. Deer hair splits readily. After a few strikes on the Crowe Beetle, the deer hair often comes apart. The Poly Beetle holds up better than the Crowe, floats as well, and takes less than a minute to tie.

Emerger Patterns

At a recent autograph session in Fort Collins, Colorado, I met a fly-fisher and great fly-tier, Ray Smith. Ray teaches a fly-tying class for Rocky Mountain Sporting Goods and owner Steve Salerno. Ray asked me if I wanted to see a new tying method for emergers. I never refuse learning new methods and techniques; besides, I believe that many of the most innovative fly-tiers live in the West.

After I saw Ray's unique method of tying an emerger a light went on in my brain—what an easy technique! But would it be effective? The next morning Mike Manfredo, also of Fort Collins, and I headed for two hours of fishing on the Cache la Poudre River before my plane left for Pennsylvania.

Mike and I used a Baetis Emerger that Ray had showed us how to tie the day before. In those two short hours of fishing on the Poudre, Mike and I caught two dozen trout on those new emergers—on a morning when I saw only two trout rise. But how would this new pattern work on Pennsylvania waters?

Back in Pennsylvania the next morning I tied a half-dozen Isonychia Emergers using the same techniques Ray taught two days earlier. I weighted each pattern with three turns of .015 lead wire, tied on three black hackle tips for the tail, dubbed in a black angora body two-thirds of the way up the shank, then tied in about 30 long hackle barbules. I took these fibers or barbules from the biggest, webbiest hackles from the back of the neck—usually those that you never use. I tied the fibers in by their butts, with the tips pointing back over the body of the emerger. I cut off the butts, dubbed the front one-third of the body or the thorax with more black angora, then pulled the hackle fibers on top of the thorax, and tied them in just behind the eye. Next, I divided the tips of the barbules equally, tying one half on one side of the wing case and the other half on the other side. These barbules copied the legs of the emerger. If the legs appeared too long I cut off the excess. Dub a bit more angora on the thorax than you did on the rear two-thirds of the body. This enlarged thorax gives the impression of a dun emerging from the nymphal shuck.

I headed out to the Little Juniata River the next day to use this emerger in conjunction with the bi-cycle that I described in *Great Rivers—Great Hatches* (Stackpole, 1992). By early afternoon a fairly heavy hatch of slate drakes appeared on the surface, slowed on their takeoff by the cool late-September day. I tied a Slate Drake dry fly on my .006 tippet. I then tied a 30-inch piece of .006 tippet onto the bend of the hook of the Slate Drake. I secured the tippet with an improved clinch knot. I then tied onto the end of this extended tippet a weighted Isonychia Emerger. I prefer using Orvis Super Strong leader for this tippet. The dry fly not only catches trout but also acts as a strike indicator. During a hatch, whether trout are actively feeding on duns, or emergers, top or bottom, you're covered.

Be careful when you first attempt to cast the bi-cycle—don't forget you're casting two flies, one weighted. I used a 7- to 9-foot leader and cast upriver into a riffle where I had seen quite a few slate drakes just emerge. On the second drift my Slate Drake sank; I set the hook and landed a 12-inch brown. Several more casts into the riffle and another trout took the emerger. In two hours of fishing that afternoon I caught a dozen trout on that deadly emerger pattern. In addition I caught four trout on the strike indicator, the Slate Drake dry fly.

Tie some of the emerger patterns with a dubbed thorax the color of the dun. For example, for an Isonychia Emerger you might want to tie some with a dark gray thorax. With a Sulphur Emerger tie some of the patterns with a tan or pale yellow thorax.

Once you try this simple new method for tying emergers you too will agree how effective it is.

Tying the Terrestrials

Surprising but true: The life cycle of many ants, especially those in the genus *Lasius,* is very similar to that of the mayflies I described in chapter 2. The cycle begins with a swarming flight, mating, and death of the male. The female lives and lays her eggs. These flights or swarms of winged ants are very common in Pennsylvania toward the end of August, usually occurring in the afternoon and evening. On these late-summer days it's important to carry plenty of the winged-ant imitations in sizes 18 to 24 and with body colors ranging from black to ginger. To imitate the ant's wings use a light gray or white strip of poly yarn, and tie it downwing between the two humps of the ant. Tie the two humps in the body of the ant with black or brown poly dubbing.

Ants, as well as crickets, grasshoppers, beetles, and other terrestrials, are important to copy and use on Pennsylvania's streams, especially in July, August, and September. As often as possible use poly as wings or body material for these floating patterns. Black poly is the best yarn for the body of crickets, ants, and beetles, and an olive or pale yellow poly for the body of grasshoppers. Poly is extremely buoyant and easy to use.

Caterpillars are another important terrestrial for your summer collection of patterns. I prefer those made of cork and colored with a permanent marking pen. Test your marking pen on a piece of cylindrical cork to see the color you achieve. The pen produces a truer color with less shine than lacquer. To add legs to the terrestrial, start at the rear and palmer the hackle to the eye of the hook. Clip the top and bottom of the hackle to create a more lifelike imitation. Always carry plenty of green inchworm patterns on your summer fishing trips.

Tying the Downwings

Caddisflies appear on Pennsylvania streams throughout the entire season. An ample supply of diverse patterns copying these insects can mean the difference between a frustrating and a rewarding day. Include hackle (or legs) on some but not all of your patterns. Those with hackle, called fluttering caddis, ride fast water higher than a second type, the Deer-Head Caddis.

The usual method for imitating wings on a caddis is to tie deer hair in by the butt just behind the eye of the hook. With this method of tying, however, the hair tends to roll, so it's difficult to achieve a smooth head on the imitation. Try tying instead a Deer-Head Caddis; it is easier to tie, and the final product is a better copy of the natural. The end result resembles a smaller version of the Fulsher Minnow. To tie the Deer-Head Caddis follow these instructions:

Begin by tying in a bunch of cut deer hair, just as with the fluttering caddis. Place the deer hair so the butts are facing toward the rear (not the front) of the hook, and the hair tips extend well out past the eye of the hook. Take your tying thread and wind it securely up over the deer hair butts forward to the eye of the hook. Take a small piece of poly of the proper color, and dub it in just behind the eye. This little piece of dubbed poly becomes the chin of the caddis. Pull the tips of the deer hair back over the hook, and tie in about one-quarter of the way back from the eye. Finish off with a whip finish, lacquer the head and thread, and you have a Deer-Head Caddis. If the wings of the natural caddis you want to imitate are darker than the deer hair, use moose mane or darker deer hair.

Tying Spinner Imitations

Many female spinners die spent on the surface after laying their eggs. Others—sulphur spinners and ginger quills, for example—sometimes ride the water with their wings upright, just like the duns of the species. Conversely, male spinners of many species never get close to the water, but meet the female, mate, and die over land. Knowing beforehand a mayfly's mating behavior helps when fishing the spinner fall. Since many of the spinners ride the surface for some distance with wings upright and not spent, it's important to include some of these upright patterns in your selection. There's a bonus to using an upright pattern as a spinner—the imitation is much easier to follow on the surface than is a spent wing, especially at dusk. The upright version of the Sulphur Spinner performs well on the Delaware River during a spinner fall of the naturals.

Orvis and other top companies supply a good poly yarn for spent wings. Use this same material to tie the pattern upright, but tie the poly in as you would with calf tail and divide.

In many of my spinner patterns I include a few strands of Orvis Krystal Flash with the poly spent wings. George Harvey first recommended using this material in an article on the trico in *Fly Fisherman* magazine. Using a few strands of this material produces many more strikes.

Tying the Duns

Many new fly-tying methods and materials have come and gone since my *Meeting and Fishing the Hatches* was published several years ago. In that book I recommended using mallard quill wings to imitate the dark gray wings so common on many emerging duns. These quill sections effectively copy the wings of all blue quill species, all of the slate drakes, the quill gordon, and all of the olive duns. When you use these wings on any pattern larger than a size 18, however, they tend to twist fine leader tippets. Dun hen hackle tips shaped with a wing burner, on the other hand, are much easier to tie and don't twist the line.

In the earlier book I recommended using poly for body material as much as possible. Today there are more varieties and colors of poly than ever before. Use the synthetic material in place of the natural quill bodies, because the poly is much more durable. How many times has a Red Quill, Ginger Quill, or a Quill Gordon body unraveled after catching a few trout? This won't happen with poly. Use dark gray poly for the body of Slate Drakes, light brown for the Ginger Quill, and reddish brown for the Red Quill.

I haven't discussed comparaduns or methods for tying them. Although these patterns are extremely effective, they don't hold up as well as hackled flies. Check the comparaduns you tied last year and see how straight the wings are now.

Patterns to Match the Hatches

It happened on a fishing trip to, of all places, Silver Creek in Arizona—yes, Arizona! I spent a day fly-fishing with Virgil Bradford of Santa Fe, New Mexico, and Brian Williams of Gilbert, Arizona. The game and fish department had stocked the stream the day before and I wanted Brian to catch some trout. As we arrived on that cool April morning we saw dozens of trout rising. Remember, these trout had just been planted the day before; the very next morning they were surface-feeding on a hatch.

I handed Brian a size-20 Little Blue-Winged Olive Dun and told him to tie it onto his leader. He glanced at the pattern, commented on how unconventional it looked, and began casting to a pod of rising trout. On his first cast he had a strike and missed the trout. On his second cast he hooked a trout and lost it. On his third cast he hooked and landed a 10-inch rainbow. On the first 12 drifts with that pattern Brian had 12 strikes. How's that for success?

What pattern created all those strikes on that stream in Arizona? It looked like a conventional parachute tie without a tail, but with a body of very fine olive vernille. That vernille extended back over the bend of the hook ¼ inch.

I couldn't wait to get back to Pennsylvania to test the same tying technique for other patterns. Shortly after I arrived back I tied up some Sulphurs with this new method and headed out to test them over a hatch. I tied some of these patterns with fine yellow vernille to copy the sulphur hatch and gave a few of them to Bob Budd of Hollidaysburg. Bob tested them on his next trip and had success with them. I finally hit a hatch of sulphurs and had an opportunity to test the flies myself. They proved more successful than I would ever have imagined.

The tie is simple. In the following recipes for the hatches substitute fine vernille for the body and extend it back over the bend. I don't even add a tail. Use a match to round off the end of the body: Bring a lighted match close to the vernille, but without touching it, and the body should round off perfectly. Try this tie for some of your smaller patterns. I use it for any pattern size 16 or smaller.

Tying Wet Flies

Wet-fly patterns copying the quill gordon and other early hatches are deadly in April. One of the most memorable trips I've ever made was a day on northeastern Pennsylvania's Mehoopany Creek. No dry fly or wet fly seemed to work that day, until I switched to a Quill Gordon wet. There were a few gordons in the air, but no massive hatch. That didn't stop just about every trout in that particular pool from taking my wet fly.

Wet flies produce because they copy many emerging caddis and mayflies. They work exceptionally well in April and May and again in September and October.

The second hook number in the list of patterns at the end of this chapter refers to the wet-fly hook. Since in tying a wet fly you're tying a pattern you want to sink, use a less buoyant material than poly. Fur, wool, and some other body materials sink quickly, and they come in an assortment of colors for any wet-fly pattern. Use hen hackle for the tail and legs, and dark mallard quill sections for wings instead of the gray hackle tips suggested for many of the dry flies.

Tying Nymphs for Pennsylvania Streams

If you've looked carefully at the life cycle of aquatic insects in chapter 2, you've already noted that mayflies, caddisflies, and stoneflies live most of their life below water as nymphs or larvae. Nymphs are available as food for trout a good 90 percent of their life. It's essential, then, that you imitate nymphs on occasion. These patterns work well before and during a hatch of the naturals they represent, when the naturals move toward the surface and begin emerging. You'll note in the tying directions that I suggest angora, opossum, or just plain fur as body material. All absorb water quickly and sink rapidly. Another material, called Ultra Translucent Nymph Dubbing and sold in many of the better fly-tying stores, is excellent dubbing material for nymphs. To make nymphs less buoyant, no matter what body material you use, you might want to incorporate some weight onto the body of the nymph. Just add a piece of lead wire and wind it around the hook to get the desired sinking action.

When I use the word *wings* in the tying descriptions for nymphs I'm really referring to the insects' wing pads, and when I list *hackle* in the instructions I'm referring to the legs of the insect. Tie in the wings about halfway back on the shank of the hook. Wind the tying thread over the tip of the wing section with the shiny side of the wing up and the butt of the section pointing back toward the bend of the hook. Leave the wing pad in that position until you've completed dubbing the front end of the body and have tied in the legs or hackle. Next, take the proper soft hackle and tie it in at the same place you tied in the wing pad. Finish dubbing the front part of the body, then wind the hackle over that. Trim the top part of the hackle, bring the wing pad up over the hackle, and tie it in at the eye.

You'll note that I recommend using cree or ginger-variant hackle quite often to copy the legs of nymphs and duns. Ginger-variant hackle normally includes dark and light brown shading on the same hackle; cree contains cream, black, and brown barring. Both duplicate the multicolored legs of naturals quite well. The cream variant provides a lighter hackle than the ginger variant.

New Materials

BUGSKIN BEGINNINGS

Chuck Furimsky has owned his leather shop, Ole Man Winter, for almost 20 years. During that time he has experimented with all types and textures of leather. For example, a new machine on the market can press leather so thin that the final product feels like tissue. But the day I met him on Spruce Creek several years ago he had stepped over the boundary of sanity!

Chuck asked me to meet him on a private section of Spruce Creek and fish with him for a few hours. Just before I arrived the usually clear limestone became quickly discolored from a sudden summer storm. I expected to see Chuck in the cabin relaxing and waiting for the stream to clear. Not Chuck! No, I saw him fishing a section of the meadow a few hundred feet downstream from the cabin. Within minutes he had caught and released more than a half-dozen trout, so I walked over to where he was casting and grabbed the pattern attached to his 6X tippet. Chuck caught those temperamental Spruce Creek browns on a pattern that looked suspiciously like the San Juan Worm used on its namesake river in New Mexico—only Chuck tied his with very thin red leather. After three more trout I swallowed my pride and asked Chuck if he could give me one of those new patterns.

Since that auspicious beginning Chuck has tied patterns from the thinned leather to copy crayfish, hellgrammites, stoneflies, nymphs, and leeches. I find the crayfish to be extremely effective. He named the extremely lifelike material Bugskin. It's now available to fly-tiers across the country and throughout the world through Phil's Tackle, Box 4031, Woodland Park, CO 80866.

LARVA LACE

I have a handful of angling friends who deride any fly-fisher using synthetic materials to build his flies. Some of these refuse to even use poly to dub dry-fly bodies. I try to tell them that with the advent and onslaught of new materials they will be at a disadvantage if they don't test the new stuff. My many visits to western waters have convinced me that if I want to keep up with the anglers there, I have to keep abreast of new materials.

Recently I wrote an article for a great new regional publication, *Fly Fishing Guide,* that examined some of the new synthetics like Larva Lace. Phil Camera, who wrote the book *Fly Tying with Synthetics,* was the originator of Larva Lace. After I fished for a few days with Phil in Colorado he gave me some samples of the new material and asked me to try it. Larva Lace is a hollow plastic material that comes in a variety of colors and sizes.

The Larva Lace Phil gave me stayed in my fly-tying room for almost a year before I had the urge to try it. That urge came after Greg Hoover and I conducted an entomology course at Seven Springs. While at Laurel Hill Creek collecting insects the class saw a number of bright orange caddisfly larvae. This larva grows into the little black caddis, which appears in mid-April. Several students surmised that if this larva was so common in the stream then it behooved them to copy it.

We returned to the classroom to tie flies after our morning on the stream collecting insects. Members of this class, including Ben Furimsky and Craig Josephson, asked what pattern would copy this larva. Ben Furimsky grabbed some orange Larva Lace, slid it over the hook, and moved it back beyond the bend of the hook. He then tied in this relatively new synthetic, ribbed the Larva Lace with the tying thread, and dubbed in some tan angora at the head. The finished product look amazingly like the natural.

The beauty of these synthetics is that some effectively copy many naturals that would otherwise be difficult to copy. It's important for you to try these new materials—simply because they work and will make you a more effective fly-fisher. Larva Lace can also be obtained from Phil's Tackle, Box 4031, Woodland Park, CO 80866.

The Tying Tables

In the tables below, you'll note under most of the pattern descriptions at least two hook numbers (not sizes). The first number refers to the hook used for tying the dry fly, and the second refers to a hook preferred for the wet fly. After these hook numbers I list the preferred sizes for the patterns. When more than one hook size is listed, the pattern in question copies more than one mayfly, or the mayfly copied varies in size from stream to stream.

Each pattern listed in the tables can be tied as either a wet or a dry fly. If you plan to tie a wet-fly version, then omit poly as a body material and use angora, fur, or another less buoyant substitute. Even if you use fur or angora, you may find it necessary to add weight to a wet fly.

In almost every pattern description I suggest the body be dubbed. Dubbing, or placing small bits of poly between your fingers and actually rolling it onto prewaxed tying thread, produces a realistic, buoyant body. Many mayflies, caddisflies, and stoneflies have an underbelly that is ribbed. Use a fine, colored thread to mimic this natural ribbing.

I frequently refer to mallard flank feathers in the pattern descriptions. These are the light gray or off-white feathers, heavily barred, on the side of a mallard duck. They effectively copy the natural barring of the wings of many aquatic insects.

Poly yarn is another material used extensively in tying bodies of the patterns. It comes on a spool or card and resembles wool yarn. It's impossible to dub, but it's excellent for winding around the shank of the hook and especially well adapted for tying terrestrials. In light gray or white, poly yarn provides great wing material for spinner imitations.

The patterns listed in the following tables should copy just about all the hatches and circumstances you'll encounter on Pennsylvania's streams and rivers. When there's no hatch to match on the water and terrestrials and downwings won't work, then it's time to try an attractor. These are the first patterns I list.

Next on the tables are those patterns that copy mayflies. The first pattern listed copies the dun, the second the spinner, and the third the nymph. If a pattern copies more than one hatch, I suggest some of the species that the pattern imitates.

Following the tying descriptions for mayflies you'll find patterns for caddis dry flies, caddis larvae, and emerging caddis pupae. Next listed are some of the common patterns for stoneflies (floating) and nymphs, and finally some suggestions for patterns copying some of the state's terrestrials.

Patterns to Use When There's No Hatch to Match

Let's face it—you'll often fish Pennsylvania trout streams when there's little hatching activity. What pattern do you use then? Over the past decade or two I've experimented with the tandem on Commonwealth streams and it has proved extremely productive. I usually use an attractor pattern like the Patriot for the dry fly and a Bead Head or Green Weenie for the wet fly. This combination has proved deadly on all state streams. I tie the Patriot in sizes 12 and 14, and occasionally in size 16 to float the wet fly.

For the wet-fly half of the tandem I use a Tan Bead Head Caddis, an Olive Bead Head Caddis, a Bead Head Pheasant Tail Nymph, or the Green Weenie. I tie the Bead Head patterns in sizes 12 to 16 and the Green Weenie in a size 12. I add weight to the body of all the patterns so they sink quickly. To the size-12 and -14 Bead Heads I wrap 10 winds of .010 lead; to the size-16, 10 wraps of .005. This extra weight, in addition to the bead, gets the wet fly deep quickly. A size-12 dry fly like the Patriot that has plenty of hackle acts as a strike indicator with an attitude—trout hit the indicator and are hooked.

PATRIOT
Thread: Red
Tail: Brown hackle fibers
Body: Smolt blue Krystal Flash wound around the shank; wind some of the red thread in the middle of the shank, similar to the Royal Coachman
Wings: White impala or calf tail, divided
Hackle: Brown
Hook: Mustad 94833, sizes 10–18

BEAD HEAD PHEASANT TAIL NYMPH
Thread: Dark brown
Tail: Five or six fibers from a ring-necked pheasant tail
Body: Continue winding the pheasant tail fibers used to tie in the tail up to the bead, and tie in
Thorax: Copper bead
Hackle: Ten pheasant tail fibers
Hook: Tiemco 2457, sizes 12–16

BEAD HEAD OLIVE CADDIS
Thread: Olive
Head: Copper bead
Body: Dub with a heavy amount of dark brown opossum fur; rib with fine gold wire
Hook: Tiemco 2457, sizes 12–16

GREEN WEENIE
Body: Cut off a 5-inch piece of small or medium chartreuse chenille; form a small loop with the chenille extending out over the bend of the hook, then wrap the chenille around the shank of the hook up to the eye
Hook: Mustad 9672, size 10 or 12
Tying Notes: I include a loop as the tail of the Green Weenie. I feel this loop makes the pattern move as it drifts downstream. I often add weight to the body: 10, 15, 20, or 25 wraps of .015 lead. I then color-code the patterns. For 25 wraps I use orange thread, for 20 wraps I use chartreuse thread, and so on.

Mayfly Imitations

BLUE DUN OR LITTLE BLUE-WINGED OLIVE DUN

Copies *Baetis tricaudatus,* and other
Baetis spp.
Thread: Dark gray
Tail: Medium to dark gray hackle fibers
Body: Gray muskrat or medium gray
poly, dubbed; for the Little Blue-
Winged Olive use olive-gray poly
Wings: On smaller sizes (20) use dark
gray mallard quills; on larger sizes
use dark gray hackle tips
Hackle: Blue dun
Hook: Mustad 94840, 3906, sizes 18 and
20

RUSTY SPINNER

Thread: Dark brown
Tail: Dark grayish brown hackle fibers
Body: Grayish brown poly, dubbed and
ribbed with fine tan thread
Wings: Pale gray poly yarn, tied spent
Hook: Mustad 94840, 3906, sizes 18 and
20

NYMPH

Thread: Dark olive
Tail: Wood duck fibers, dyed dark olive
Body: Dark olive-brown opossum
Wings: Dark gray mallard quill section
Hackle: Cree or ginger variant, dyed
dark olive
Hook: 3906B, size 18

BLUE QUILL

Copies all *Paraleptophlebia* spp., and
Ephemerella deficiens
Thread: Dark gray
Tail: Medium to dark gray hackle fibers
Body: Eyed peacock herl, stripped, or
dark gray poly, dubbed
Wings: Dark gray hackle tips
Hackle: Light to medium blue dun
Hook: Mustad 94840, 3906, sizes 18 and
20

DARK BROWN SPINNER

Thread: Dark brown
Tail: Dark brown hackle fibers
Body: Dark brown poly, dubbed
Wings: Pale gray poly yarn, tied spent
Hook: Mustad 94840, 3906, sizes 18 and
20

NYMPH

Thread: Dark brown
Tail: Mallard flank feather, dyed dark
brown
Body: Dark brown angora, dubbed
Wings: One dark gray mallard quill, tied
down
Hackle: Dark gray
Hook: 3906B, sizes 16 and 18

BLUE-WINGED OLIVE DUN

Copies many *Drunella (Ephemerella)*
spp. and *Dannella (Ephemerella)* like
*cornuta, longicornus, attenuata,
cornutella, lata, simplex, walkeri,* and
others
Thread: Olive
Tail: Grayish olive hackle fibers
Body: Light to medium olive poly,
dubbed
Wings: Dark gray hackle tips
Hackle: Medium creamish olive
Hook: Mustad 94840, 3906, sizes 14–20

DARK OLIVE SPINNER

Thread: Dark olive or black
Tail: Moose mane (dark brown)
Body: Dark olive poly (almost black
with an olive cast)
Wings: Pale gray poly yarn, tied spent
Hook: Mustad 94840, 3906, sizes 14–20

NYMPH

Thread: Olive
Tail: Wood duck
Body: Dark brown angora tied over
dubbed-in olive opossum
Wings: Brown turkey
Hackle: Ginger variant, dyed olive
Hook: 3906B, sizes 14–18

QUILL GORDON

Copies species like *Epeorus pleuralis* and some *Rhithrogena* spp.
Thread: Dark gray
Tail: Dark gray hackle fibers
Body: Eyed peacock herl, stripped and lacquered
Wings: Wood duck or imitation wood duck, divided; or dark gray hackle tips
Hackle: Dark gray
Hook: Mustad 94840, 3906, size 14

RED QUILL SPINNER

Use same pattern as spinner listed under Hendrickson

NYMPH

Thread: Dark brown
Tail: Fibers from a mallard flank feather, dyed dark amber
Body: Dark brown fur or angora, mixed with a bit of lighter brown or amber
Wings: Mottled brown turkey, tied down over thorax
Hackle: Cree or ginger variant (dark and amber mixed)
Hook: 3906B, size 14

LIGHT CAHILL

Copies diverse species like *Stenonema ithaca, Stenacron interpunctatum, Heptagenia marginalis,* and many others
Thread: Cream or tan
Tail: Cream hackle fibers
Body: Cream poly, fox fur, or angora, dubbed
Wings: Mallard flank feather, dyed pale yellow, divided
Hackle: Cream
Hook: Mustad 94840, 3906, size 14

LIGHT CAHILL SPINNER

Same as dun, except omit hackle and add pale yellow poly yarn for wings; tie them spent

NYMPH

Thread: Brown
Tail: Fibers from a mallard flank feather, dyed brown
Body: Dark brown angora yarn on top and pale amber belly, dubbed
Wings: Dark brown turkey
Hackle: Dark cree
Hook: 3906B, size 12

SLATE DRAKE

Copies all *Isonychia* spp. in Pennsylvania
Thread: Black
Tail: Dark gray hackle fibers
Body: Peacock herl (not from eye), stripped; or dark gray poly, or muskrat, dubbed
Wings: Dark gray hackle tips
Hackle: One cream hackle tied in behind and one dark brown hackle tied in front
Hook: Mustad 94840, 3906, sizes 12 and 14

WHITE-GLOVED HOWDY

Thread: Dark brown or maroon
Tail: Medium gray hackle fibers
Body: Dark mahogany poly, dubbed
Wings: Pale gray poly yarn
Hook: Mustad 94840, 3906, sizes 12 and 14

NYMPH

Thread: Dark brown
Tail: Three dark brown hackles with one side cut off
Body: Very dark brown angora or opossum
Wings: Dark gray mallard quill section, tied down over thorax
Hackle: Cree, dyed pale olive
Hook: 3906B, sizes 10 and 12

SULPHUR DUN

Copies *Ephemerella rotunda, E. invaria, E. septentrionalis,* and, to a lesser degree, *E. dorothea*
Thread: Yellow
Tail: Cream hackle fibers

Body: Usually pale yellow poly with an orange (and sometimes olive-orange) cast
Wings: Pale gray hackle tips
Hackle: Cream
Hook: Mustad 94840, 3906, sizes 16 and 18

SULPHUR SPINNER

Thread: Tan
Tail: Tan deer hair
Body: Female with eggs—yellowish tan poly; female without eggs—tan poly; male—bright red hackle stem, stripped and wound around hook
Wings: Pale gray poly yarn, tied spent (also tie some upright)
Hook: Mustad 94840, 3906, sizes 16 and 18

NYMPH

Thread: Grayish brown
Tail: Brown pheasant tail fibers
Body: Brown (ground color) fur
Wings: Dark gray mallard quill section, tied down over thorax
Hackle: Cree
Hook: 3906B, sizes 14–18

HENDRICKSON AND RED QUILL

Red Quill copies the male and the Hendrickson the female of *Ephemerella subvaria* and closely related subspecies. The Red Quill also imitates many spinners like *Ephemerella subvaria*, *Epeorus pleuralis*, and the male spinner of *Ephemerella invaria* and *E. rotunda*.
Thread: Brown
Tail: Medium gray hackle fibers
Body: Red Quill—reddish brown hackle fiber stripped of its barbules and wound from the bed of the hook to the wings; Hendrickson—tan poly, dubbed
Wings: Wood duck, divided; optional on Hendrickson are gray hackle tips
Hackle: Medium gray
Hook: Mustad 94840, 3906, sizes 14 and 16

RED QUILL SPINNER

Thread: Brown
Tail: Bronze dun hackle fibers
Body: Dark tannish brown poly, dubbed and ribbed finely with tan thread
Wings: Pale gray poly yarn, tied spent
Hook: Mustad 94840, 3906, sizes 14 and 16

NYMPH

Thread: Dark brown
Tail: Fibers from a mallard flank feather, dyed brown
Body: Dark brown angora, mixed with a bit of amber
Wings: Mottled brown turkey, tied down over thorax
Hackle: Cree
Hook: 3906B, sizes 12 and 14

YELLOW DRAKE

Copies *Ephemera varia*
Thread: Yellow
Tail: Tan deer hair
Body: Pale yellow poly, dubbed
Wings: Mallard flank feather dyed pale yellow, divided
Hackle: Pale yellow with a turn or two of grizzly in front
Hook: Mustad 94840, 3906, size 12

YELLOW DRAKE SPINNER

Thread: Yellow
Tail: Dark brown deer hair
Body: Pale yellow poly, dubbed
Wings: Gray poly yarn, tied spent
Hook: Mustad 94840, 3906, size 12

NYMPH

Thread: Tan
Tail: Pale gray, trimmed
Body: Amber-colored angora or opossum
Wings: Medium to light brown turkey
Hackle: Ginger
Hook: 3906B, sizes 10 and 12

GREEN DRAKE

Copies *Ephemera guttulata*
Thread: Cream
Tail: Moose mane
Body: Cream poly, dubbed
Wings: Mallard flank dyed yellowish green, divided
Hackle: Rear—cream; front—dark brown
Hook: Mustad 94831, 3906B, sizes 8 and 10

COFFIN FLY

Thread: White
Tail: Light tan deer hair
Body: White poly, dubbed
Wings: Grayish yellow poly yarn, tied spent
Hook: Mustad 94831, 3906B, sizes 8 and 10

NYMPH

Thread: Tan
Tail: Three medium brown hackles, trimmed and tied in
Body: Pale tan angora
Wings: Dark brown turkey, tied down and over thorax
Hackle: Cree
Hook: Mustad 3906B or 9672, sizes 8–12

BROWN DRAKE

Copies *Ephemera simulans*
Thread: Dark brown
Tail: Moose mane
Body: Yellowish brown poly, dubbed
Wings: Mallard flank feather, dyed yellowish brown, divided
Hackle: Rear—cream; front—dark brown
Hook: Mustad 94831, 3906B, sizes 10 and 12

BROWN DRAKE SPINNER

Thread: Dark brown
Tail: Brown hackle fibers
Body: Yellowish brown poly, dubbed
Wings: Gray poly yarn, tied spent
Hook: Mustad 94831, 3906B, sizes 10 and 12

NYMPH

Thread: Brown
Tail: Three light brown hackles, trimmed and tied in
Body: Tan angora or opossum
Wings: Brown turkey, tied down and over thorax
Hackle: Dark cree
Hook: Mustad 3906B or 9672, sizes 10 and 12

MARCH BROWN

Copies *Stenonema vicarium*
Thread: Yellow
Tail: Dark brown hackle fibers
Body: Tan poly, dubbed and ribbed with dark brown thread
Wings: Mallard flank feather, dyed yellowish brown and divided
Hackle: One cream and one dark brown, mixed
Hook: Mustad 94840, 3906, size 12

GREAT RED SPINNER

Thread: Dark brown
Tail: Dark brown hackle fibers
Body: Dark reddish brown poly, dubbed
Wings: Pale gray poly yarn, tied spent
Hackle: Dark brown with a turn or two of pale ginger, mixed
Hook: Mustad 94840, 3906, size 12

NYMPH

Thread: Brown
Tail: Fibers from a mallard flank feather, dyed brown
Body: Cream poly, dubbed
Wings: Dark brown turkey, tied down over thorax
Hackle: Dark cree
Hook: Mustad 3906B, size 12

GRAY FOX

Copies *Stenonema fuscum* and subspecies, *S. ithaca,* and others
Thread: Cream
Tail: Tan deer hair
Body: Cream poly, dubbed
Wings: Mallard flank feather, dyed pale

yellowish tan, divided
Hackle: Cree, or one brown and one cream, mixed
Hook: Mustad 94840, 3906, sizes 12 and 14

GINGER QUILL SPINNER
Thread: Brown
Tail: Dark brown hackle fibers
Body: Eyed peacock herl, dyed tan and stripped, or grayish brown poly, ribbed with brown thread
Wings: Gray hackle tips (conventional); or pale gray poly, tied spent
Hackle: Dark ginger (conventional); or none with poly wings
Hook: Mustad 94840, 3906, sizes 12 and 14

NYMPH
Thread: Brown
Tail: Fibers from a mallard flank feather, dyed brown
Body: Brown angora yarn, tied on top over cream; tie in brown at tail, and dub in cream so that top (tergites) of body is brown and the belly (sternites) is cream
Wings: Dark brown turkey, tied down over thorax
Hackle: Dark cree
Hook: 3906B, size 12

CREAM CAHILL
Copies species like *Stenonema pulchellum* and *S. modestum*
Thread: Cream
Tail: Cream hackle fibers
Body: Very pale cream (almost white) poly, dubbed
Wings: Mallard flank feather dyed very pale yellow, divided
Hackle: Cream
Hook: Mustad 94840, 3906, sizes 14 and 16

CREAM CAHILL SPINNER
Thread: White
Tail: Pale cream hackle fibers

Body: White poly, dubbed
Wings: Pale poly yarn, tied spent
Hook: Mustad 94840, 3906, sizes 14 and 16

NYMPH
Thread: Olive-brown
Tail: Light brown hackle fibers
Body: Dub pale creamish gray on hook, then tie pale brownish olive yarn in at bend and bring over top to wing case and tie in
Wings: Dark brown turkey
Hackle: Dark olive-brown
Hook: 3906B, sizes 14 and 16

WHITE MAYFLY (DUN AND SPINNER)
Since the female dun never changes to a spinner, I've listed one pattern for both phases. Copies *Ephoron leukon* and other similar species.
Thread: White
Tail: White hackle fibers
Body: Female dun—creamish white poly, dubbed; male spinner—a couple of turns of dark reddish brown poly at rear, then white poly for rest of body, dubbed
Wings: Very pale gray hackle tips
Hackle: Cream (a turn or two of dark brown for male spinner)
Hook: Mustad 94840, 3906, sizes 14 and 16

NYMPH
Thread: Gray
Tail: Tannish gray hackle fibers
Body: Pale gray angora or opossum, dubbed heavily
Wings: Pale gray mallard quill sections
Hackle: Cream ginger
Hook: Mustad 3906B, sizes 14 and 16

CHOCOLATE DUN
Copies species like *Ephemerella needhami* (male dun) and *Eurylophella (Ephemerella) bicolor*
Thread: Brown

Tail: Medium gray
Body: Chocolate brown poly, finely ribbed with lighter brown thread
Wings: Dark gray hackle tips
Hackle: Tan
Hook: Mustad 94840, 3906, size 16

CHOCOLATE SPINNER

Thread: Dark brown
Tail: Tannish gray hackle fibers
Body: Dark rusty brown poly, dubbed
Wings: Pale gray poly yarn, tied spent
Hook: Mustad 94840, 3906, size 16

NYMPH

Thread: Brown
Tail: Light brown mallard flank feather fibers
Body: Light brown poly nymph dubbing
Wings: Dark gray mallard quill
Hackle: Brown
Hook: Mustad 3906B, size 16

OLIVE SULPHUR

Copies the female of *Ephemerella needhami*
Thread: Olive
Body: Medium olive poly, dubbed
Wings: Cream hen hackle tips
Hackle: Cream
Hook: Mustad 94833, size 16

OLIVE SULPHUR SPINNER

Thread: Dark olive
Tail: Cream
Body: Dark olive poly, dubbed
Wings: White poly yarn, tied spent
Hook: Mustad 94833, size 16

DARK GREEN DRAKE

Copies species like *Litobrancha recurvata*
Thread: Dark gray
Tail: Dark brown moose mane
Body: Very dark slate poly, dubbed and ribbed with yellow thread
Wings: Mallard flank, heavily barred and dyed dark green

Hackle: Rear—tannish brown; front—dark brown
Hook: Mustad 94833, 3906B, sizes 8 and 10

BROWN DRAKE SPINNER

Thread: Brown
Tail: Brown hackle fibers
Body: Reddish brown poly, dubbed and ribbed with yellow thread
Wings: Pale gray poly yarn, tied spent
Hackle: Dark brown
Hook: Mustad 94833, 3906B, sizes 8 and 10

NYMPH

Thread: Light brown
Tail: Three dark bronze hackles, trimmed and tied in
Body: Tan with a grayish cast angora, or opossum
Wings: Dark brown turkey
Hackle: Dark cree
Hook: Mustad 9672, sizes 8 and 10

TRICO DUN

Copies all *Tricorythodes* spp.
Thread: Pale olive
Tail: Cream hackle fibers
Body: Pale olive green poly, dubbed; male—dark brown poly
Wings: Pale gray hackle tips
Hackle: Cream
Hook: Mustad 94840, sizes 20–24

TRICO SPINNER

Thread: Dark brown
Tail: Female—short cream hackle fibers; male—long dark brown moose mane
Body: Female—rear one-third is cream poly, dubbed, and front two-thirds are dark brown poly, dubbed; male—dark brown poly, dubbed, and ribbed with a very fine light tan thread
Wings: White poly yarn, tied spent
Hook: Mustad 94840, sizes 20 to 24

NYMPH

Thread: Black
Tail: Dark brown hackle fibers
Body: Dark brownish black fur
Wings: Dark gray mallard quill section
Hackle: Dark reddish brown
Hook: Mustad 3906B, size 22

PALE EVENING DUN

Copies species like *Ephemerella dorothea, E. septentrionalis,* and many *Heptagenia* species like *H. walshi, H. aphrodite,* and others
Thread: Pale yellow
Tail: Cream hackle fibers
Body: Pale yellowish cream poly, dubbed
Wings: Pale yellow hackle tips
Hackle: Cream
Hook: Mustad 94840, 3906, sizes 16–20

PALE EVENING SPINNER

Thread: Cream
Tail: Cream hackle fibers
Body: Pale yellowish cream poly, dubbed
Wings: Pale gray poly yarn, tied spent
Hook: Mustad 94840, 3906, sizes 16–20

NYMPH

Thread: Brown
Tail: Dark brown pheasant tail fibers
Body: Dark tan Ultra Translucent Nymph Dubbing
Wings: Gray mallard quill section
Hackle: Cree
Hook: Mustad 3906B, sizes 16 and 18

PINK CAHILL

Copies female of *Epeorus vitreus;* male dun is copied with the Light Cahill, size 16
Thread: Cream
Tail: Gray hackle fibers
Body: Pinkish cream poly for female and pale yellow poly for male, dubbed
Wings: Mallard flank feather, dyed pale yellow

Hackle: Cream ginger
Hook: Mustad 94840, 3906, size 16

SALMON SPINNER

Thread: Pink
Tail: Cream ginger hackle fibers
Body: Pinkish red poly, dubbed
Wings: Pale gray poly yarn, tied spent
Hook: Mustad 94840, 3906, size 16

NYMPH

Thread: Tan
Tail: Dark brown pheasant tail fibers
Body: Dub amber on the entire shank, tie in a dark brown yarn at bend of hook, bring up and over, and tie in at spot where you tie in wings
Wings: Brown turkey section
Hackle: Several turns of ginger
Hook: Mustad 3906B, size 14

Caddis Imitations

GREEN CADDIS

Copies many members of the genus *Rhyacophila*

DEER-HEAD GREEN CADDIS

Thread: Brown
Body: Medium olive green poly with a gray cast, dubbed
Wings: Medium brown deer hair tied in with butts pointing toward bend of hook and tips extending out over eye of hook. Tie in hair securely near eye of hook, then wind thread one-quarter of the way back toward the bend. Bend deer hair back and tie in.
Hackle: If you prefer the regular fluttering caddis, you can tie as above and add a ginger hackle where you tie in the hair. Place a drop of lacquer on the thread and finished head.
Hook: Mustad 94840, 37160, sizes 14 and 16

SPOTTED SEDGE
Copies *Symphitopsyche slossanae*
Thread: Tan
Body: Grayish tan poly, dubbed
Wings: Medium brown deer hair
Hackle: Ginger
Hook: Mustad 94840, 37160, sizes 14 and 16

DARK BLUE SEDGE
Copies *Psilotreta frontalis*
Thread: Dark gray
Body: Dark gray poly, dubbed
Wings: Dark grayish brown deer hair
Hackle: Dark brownish black
Hook: Mustad 94840, 37160, size 12

GRANNOM
Copies many species of the genus *Brachycentrus*
Thread: Black
Body: Dark brownish black to black poly, dubbed
Wings: Dark brown deer hair
Hackle: Dark brown
Hook: Mustad 94840, 37160, sizes 12 and 14

LITTLE BLACK CADDIS
Copies *Chimarra atterima*
Thread: Black
Body: Black poly, dubbed
Wings: Deer hair dyed dark gray
Hackle: Dark brown
Hook: Mustad 94840, 37160, size 16

CREAM CADDIS
Copies some *Hydropsyche* spp.
Thread: Tan
Body: Creamish tan poly, dubbed
Wings: Medium brown deer hair
Hackle: Ginger
Hook: Mustad 94840, 37160, size 14

DARK BROWN CADDIS
Copies *Deplectrona modesta* and many other caddis species
Thread: Dark brown
Body: Dark brown poly

Wings: Dark brown deer hair
Hackle: Dark reddish brown
Hook: Mustad 94840, 37160, size 12

CADDIS LARVA
Thread: Appropriate color (most often dark brown or black)
Tail: Olive, green, brown, yellow, black, or tan fur dubbed and ribbed with fine wire; or use a rubber band of the appropriate color, tie in at bend of hook, and spiral to eye
Thorax: Dark brown fur, dubbed; or an ostrich herl, dyed dark brown, wound around the hook several times
Hook: Mustad 37160, sizes 12–18

EMERGING CADDIS PUPA
Thread: Same color as the body color you select
Body: Olive, green, brown, yellow, black, or tan fur or poly nymph-dubbing material
Wings: Dark mallard quill sections, shorter than normal and tied in on both sides of fly, not on top
Legs: Dark brown grouse or woodcock neck feather wound around hook two or three times
Hook: Mustad 37160, sizes 12–18

Stonefly Imitations

EARLY BROWN STONEFLY
Copies species like *Strophopteryx fasciata*

ADULT
Thread: Yellow
Tail: Short dark brown hackle fibers
Body: Dark grayish brown poly, dubbed; or peacock herl, stripped
Wings: Dark brown deer hair
Hackle: Dark brown
Hook: Mustad 94840, 3906, sizes 12 and 14

NYMPH

Thread: Brown
Tail: Brown pheasant tail fibers
Body: Reddish brown Ultra Translucent Nymph Dubbing
Wings: Brown turkey
Hackle: Brown
Hook: Mustad 3906B, size 12

LIGHT STONEFLY

Copies species like *Isoperla signata*

ADULT

Thread: Pale yellow
Tail: Short ginger hackle fibers
Body: Pale yellow poly, dubbed and ribbed with tan thread
Wings: Very light tan to cream deer hair
Hackle: Ginger
Hook: Mustad 94840, 3906, sizes 12 and 14

NYMPH

Thread: Tan
Tail: Fibers from a mallard flank feather, dyed brown
Body: Tan fox fur or nymph dubbing
Wings: Light brown turkey
Hackle: Cree
Hook: Mustad 3906B, size 12

LITTLE GREEN STONEFLY

Copies species like *Alloperla imbecilla*
Thread: Green
Tail: Short pale cream hackle fibers
Body: Medium green poly, dubbed
Wings: Pale gray hackle tips, tied down-wing
Hackle: Pale creamish green
Hook: Mustad 94840, size 16

YELLOW SALLY

Copies species like *Isoperla bilineata*
Thread: Yellow
Tail: Short cream hackle fibers
Body: Pale yellow poly, dubbed
Wings: Cream hackle tips, tied down-wing

Hackle: Cree
Hook: Mustad 94840, sizes 14 and 16

GREAT BROWN STONEFLY

Copies species similar to *Acroneuria lycorias*
Thread: Dark brown
Tail: Short dark brown hackle fibers
Body: Dark brownish gray poly, dubbed and ribbed with yellow thread
Wings: Dark gray deer hair
Hackle: Dark brown
Hook: Mustad 94840, 3906, sizes 10 and 12

NYMPH

Thread: Brown
Tail: Light brown hackle fibers
Body: Light brown fur or nymph dubbing
Wings: Brown turkey
Hackle: Light brown
Hook: Mustad 3906B, size 10

ACRONEURIA NYMPH

Copies many species like *Acroneuria arida, A. abnormis,* and *A. carolinensis*
Thread: Dark brown
Tail: Light brown hackle fibers
Body: Dark olive-brown yarn, laid over top of pale yellow dubbing fur
Wings: Dark brown turkey
Hackle: Cree
Hook: 3906B, sizes 10 and 12

GREAT STONEFLY NYMPH

Copies many species like the very common *Phasganophora capitata*
Thread: Tan
Tail: Soft ginger hackle fibers
Body: Dark cream below with darker brown on top
Wings: Mottled turkey quill
Hackle: Cree
Hook: Mustad 3906B, sizes 8 and 10

Terrestrials

POLY BEETLE

The Poly Beetle is tied exactly like the Crowe Beetle—using black poly yarn, however, rather than black deer hair. On a size-16 beetle use three strands of the yarn (about three matchsticks thick). Tie in the poly securely below the bend of the hook. If you wish, tie in a peacock herl at the bend of the hook to imitate the Japanese Beetle. Wind the tying thread up to the eye of the hook and wind the peacock. Pull the poly up over the shank of the hook and tie in securely just behind the eye. Cut off the excess poly but leave some to imitate the head. You'll really like this excellent pattern. It's simple, realistic, and takes less than a minute to tie. Tie on hook sizes 12–20.

POLY ANT

Body: Black poly, dubbed into two humps on the hook with the rear hump a bit larger than the front

Hackle: Add a black hackle after you complete the rear hump and before you start the front

KEN'S HOPPER

Body: Yellowish olive poly, dubbed heavily

Head and wings: Use deer body hair dyed yellow and tie in just behind the eye as you would with the Muddler; clip the butts also, as in the Muddler

LETORT CRICKET

Body: Black poly, heavily dubbed

Wings: Black dyed goose quill sections, tied downwing

Hackle: Deer body hair, dyed black and tied in similar to the Muddler

Some Proposals for Better Fishing on Pennsylvania Streams

Probably no other state organization in Pennsylvania has done as much good in its area of responsibility as has the Pennsylvania Fish Commission. With the remarkable foresight to classify streams in several categories, the commission, especially under the energetic guidance of its former chiefs Ralph Abele and Edward Miller and the present executive director, Peter Colangelo, has accomplished some remarkable policy changes in the past decade. Many of these moves, thought to be revolutionary at the time, have benefited fly-fishing in Pennsylvania. Especially given the Commonwealth's considerable population and development, Pennsylvania can truly boast of its fine trout fishing. With the anglers' support, however, more can be done.

Pennsylvania has a large population of fly-fishermen. In a survey conducted for the Pennsylvania Fish Commission in 1977, 10 percent of respondents indicated that they preferred to use artificial flies. That's almost 90,000 licensed fishermen using flies—in 1977. I'm certain that if a survey were conducted today the figure would be closer to 20 percent. While preparing to write this book, I had the opportunity and good fortune to fly-fish with many of the state's finest anglers. Each one of them expressed concerns about his or her local streams and the future of fly-fishing as a sport in Pennsylvania. The suggestions that follow for improving the trout fishery in our state have evolved from these interviews and from visiting more than 150 Commonwealth streams and rivers.

Lower the Daily Creel Limit

Almost every angler interviewed expressed concern with the present limit of eight trout on many streams. Almost all recommended a cutback to a four-trout-a-day creel limit immediately. Look at what effect lowering the limit would produce. First, for those who keep fish, more would go home happy. More often than not these anglers brag that they "caught their limit." More people could go home with the reduced limit. Second, the Fish Commission could spend fewer dollars rearing legal-sized trout and more on stream restoration, stream improvement, and purchasing access rights.

Streams classified as wild-trout waters can't long tolerate anglers taking a limit of eight. Look at Elk or Tea Creeks in central Pennsylvania or Oswayo Creek in the north-central part of the state. I've witnessed anglers cleaning their limit of eight on these wild-trout streams. How long will it take these native-trout waters to replace those precious trout killed?

What would happen if the limit were reduced? Let's look at an event on Caldwell Creek in northwestern Pennsylvania as an example. Jack Busch of Erie and I fly-fished for a morning on the open section on Caldwell Creek just below the delayed-harvest area. Scattered everywhere along the streambank we saw fish guts. Later in the day Jack and I experienced tremendous Hendrickson and blue quill hatches. In an hour's time, during two intense hatches, Jack and I saw two trout rise on the unregulated area. We headed upstream 2 miles to the delayed-harvest section, witnessed the same hatches, and caught over 20 rising trout. In the regulated area trout were allowed to live—at least until mid-June.

Why do many fishermen keep their limit? I've always argued that the tradition goes back to the early days of our country when our ancestors had to hunt and fish for food. Those days have long since vanished for most of us. Many anglers keep trout because they think it's the right and proper thing to do. If we can only get more people involved in fly-fishing, catch-and-release normally ensues. But how do we get more anglers involved in fly-fishing? How can we teach as many people as possible the values and long-term benefits of an avocation of fly-fishing? That's where an educational program enters the picture. Look what happened at one school.

Conduct Educational Programs

Twenty years ago Paul Hindes and Charles McKinney had an idea. Paul and Charles teach at the Baldwin High School just outside Pittsburgh and they were concerned about drug use in the schools. Together they created a club called the Baldwin Highlanders Fishing Club.

"We wanted to provide students at Baldwin High School with a recreational sport that will last them the rest of their lives," Paul said. They teach the students fly-tying, fly-fishing for trout and bass, rod building, and many other skills that will remain with the students for a lifetime. How fortunate the students are to have teachers so devoted.

Paul and Charles call their project Family Tyes, and they attempt to teach an entire value system to club members. The club doesn't devote all its time to fly-fishing, but the majority. What do they do?

The two teachers set out a series of goals they wanted to accomplish for their students. In addition to learning the techniques of fly-tying, rod building, and fly-fishing they wanted the students to appear on ESPN television and meet with businesspeople in the Pittsburgh area. Contributors and sponsors include radio stations KDKA and WSHH; television stations KDKA, WTAE, and WPXI; and dozens of other sponsors like the Pittsburgh Pirates, Foodland, Eat-n-Park, and the Equitable Gas Company.

What's in the future for the club? Paul and Charles hope to expand it to other schools in the region. Future plans call for a campsite for the club. What do they hope to accomplish with the campsite? "We want to provide the students with real-life skills," said Paul Hindes recently. The club also plans to produce several area television shows.

What would happen if every student in every school in the nation had the same opportunity to experience all the aspects of fly-fishing at such an early age? We can only wonder what the result would be.

Encourage Land Acquisition

What do Big Fill Run, Spruce Creek, Yellow Creek, Willow Run, Tipton Run, and Piney Creek have in common? They all contain sections considered class A wild-trout waters. In addition, however, since that classification some sections of all of these streams have been posted. It appears that the state's classifying these streams was an open invitation for some landowners to post their water. As soon as some landowners found out that streams running through their property would not be stocked anymore, they posted their property. In the near future much of the wild-trout and stocked waters that remain open seem destined to be posted.

The state's Fish Commission does not have the money to purchase land. Access rights should be acquired, however. Money should be appropriated to the commission by the state legislature specifically for this purpose. This action would ensure good fishing in the future, because everybody's future depends on access.

Within a few years access to many state streams will be prohibited unless we act now. Pennsylvania streams are too important—too vital—to be restricted to a handful of users.

A few years ago one area resident bought a huge chunk of stream frontage along Spring Creek in central Pennsylvania. He immediately erected an ugly fence along the entire 1-mile length of this fertile stream. For about four years this productive section was off limits to all area anglers. The owner of this section of Spring Creek eventually decided to sell it and the Fish Commission, in the true spirit of leadership, decided to take out a bond to purchase the water. Now this section of Spring Creek will be open for all to enjoy.

The Fish Commission, interested groups like Trout Unlimited, and individual anglers must do much more to ensure fishing access for future generations. One way to do this is with the formation of groups like Stream Access for All (SAFA). SAFA was formed to collect monies from anglers and interested companies and organizations for the sole purpose of purchasing land bordering streams so all can enjoy the sport. If you fly-fish streams in the state you have a moral obligation to support SAFA. You can contact SAFA at 814-237-8790.

Promote Stream Improvement

Recently I visited an experimental stream improvement site on Martins Creek in Bangor. Don Baylor and other members of the Brodhead Chapter of Trout Unlimited developed the program. Two years before, the chapter, in cooperation with the Fish Commission, conducted electrofishing surveys on two adjoining areas, each about 100 yards long. On the upper section the chapter made no stream improvement. On the lower section the chapter installed low-flow channel structures, upstream Vs, and gabion deflectors. In all, the chapter installed about 10 devices on the experimental section of Martins. Twenty months after the devices were in place, the Fish Commission again conducted electrofishing surveys in both areas. The area containing the stream devices held four times as many trout as did the unimproved area. Before the devices were installed both sections held an equal number of trout.

The Brodhead Chapter conducted another experiment—this time on its namesake stream. Brodhead Creek, devastated by floods, suffered channelization by the Corps of Engineers. This decimated the native brown trout population on the stream. After the chapter changed the habitat in a previously channelized area via stream improvement, the number of wild brown trout in the project area increased from 11 to 38.

I have seen dozens of streams in the Commonwealth that could be improved in the same manner. Travel to the East Branch of the Clarion River and look at the quality of the stream improvement devices installed above Glen Hazel. These devices fulfill a need and make almost the entire stream in that area a productive fishery. The East Branch project deserves to be a showplace.

To date much of the stream improvement in Pennsylvania has been accomplished by the Fish Commission, sportsmen's groups, Trout Unlimited chapters, Federation of Fly Fishers chapters, foundation grants, and youth groups. Streams near McConnellsburg, like Cove Creek and Spring Run, need habitat improvement devices desperately, but until recently there was no trout organization within miles. In 1992 a group of fly-fishers formed the Fulton County Chapter of Trout Unlimited. Hopefully this group will improve area streams.

The Adopt-a-Stream program instituted by the Pennsylvania Fish Commission has done much to improve habitat in many areas of the state. This worthwhile project needs the support of all anglers. If you or your organization are interested in actively contributing to stream improvement, consult the Fish Commission.

Improving trout waters is only part of stream improvement. Richard Snyder of the Fish Commission adds that working with landowners to keep livestock from the streams, diverting barnyard runoff, seeding badly eroded banks, and encouraging contour farming are also important. Without cooperation of landowners, stream improvement devices are at best a Band-Aid approach.

Continue and Expand Stocking Fingerlings

Kudos to the Pennsylvania Fish and Boat Commission for its active fingerling-stocking program. Recently it added lower Bald Eagle Creek to its list. The state also stocks fingerlings in the Little Juniata River, Youghiogheny River, Clarion River, East Branch of the Clarion River, Tulpehocken Creek, Kettle Creek (lower end), Lehigh River, LeTort Spring Run (lower end), Slippery Rock Creek, and Stonycreek River. Results from these placements in most instances have been outstanding. Ask any fisherman on the Little Juniata or the Tulpehocken what he thinks of the program. The vast majority will agree that stocking fingerlings has been successful.

More streams should be added to the list of those receiving fingerling stocked trout. Streams like Codorus Creek in York, the Allegheny River below the Kinzua Dam, Pohopoco Creek below the Beltzville Dam, and the West Branch of the Susquehanna River near Curwensville should receive experimental plantings of trout.

Encourage Studies on High-Acid Streams

Thousands of miles of potentially productive Pennsylvania trout water have been ruined by mine-acid drainage and acid rain. No longer are the experiments to combat these pollutants conducted only in the laboratory. State organizations, universities, and watershed associations now conduct viable, successful stream-site pilot programs that might eventually rehabilitate many of our presently high-acid streams. Two programs now operating are on Linn Run and Swamp Creek. All fishermen should encourage their legislators to continue these efforts.

Linn Run Acid-Rain Study

From a fisherman's perspective Linn Run, which flows through eastern Westmoreland County, stopped being a trout stream in 1959. Many of the trout housed in a cooperative nursery on the stream, and the trout stocked by the state in the preseason, died. Linn Run suffered from a high-acid environment; pH readings lower than 5 (7.0 is neutral) were common in April that year. Fish kills from preseason stockings forced the Fish Commission to delay stocking trout until May. The stockable length declined to only a few miles. The stream continued to deteriorate, and the state seriously considered taking it off the stocking list. The culprit in Linn Run's case wasn't mine-acid drainage but acid rain.

Linn Run emanates from high on the Laurel Hill escarpment. This nearly 3,000-foot mountain collects pollutants blown east, which fall as acid rain. Rainwater with a pH of near 4 enters the soil. This acid water leaches aluminum from the soil and flows into Linn Run and other nearby tributaries. Aluminum coats the gills of fish, interferes with vital body-salt regulation, and kills them.

Enter the Loyalhanna Watershed Association and Penn State University. Lysle Sherwin, executive director of the Loyalhanna Watershed Association, appealed to the university to see if it could help. In 1983 William Sharpe and David DeWalle, of Penn State's Environmental Resources Research Institute, initiated a proposal to locate well sites near Linn Run, among other goals. They hoped to locate wells near the stream that could produce water with a pH of 7 or higher. Sharpe and DeWalle asked hydrogeologist Richard Parizek to help with this phase of their project. The group located five wells. Charles Gagen, a graduate assistant with the project, coordinated and developed the experimental program. Today, from April to June, well water is pumped into Linn Run, elevating the pH of the stream during high-water, heavy-rain periods.

What has happened to Linn Run since the experiment began? The state now stocks trout again in the preseason, adds brown trout to the brook trout, and stocks an additional mile upstream of the well sites.

Linn Run is still a put-and-take trout stream, and much work remains to rehabilitate it completely. Wild trout still must depend on access to less acidic tributaries to survive year-round. The well system is currently being operated jointly by the Loyalhanna Watershed Association and Linn Run State Park, making it the only nonexperimental acid-rain-mitigation project in Pennsylvania that is continuously operated by local organizations. Through the combined efforts of the watershed association and the university, and with the financial support of the Richard King Mellon Foundation of Pittsburgh, a tremendous leap forward in acid-rain research has begun on Linn Run.

Swamp Creek Treatment Plant

The East Branch of the Clarion River resembles a human being on a life-support system. Take the patient off the machine and he suffers permanent damage or dies. Take Swamp Creek off the liming device and the East Branch Dam and the river below the dam will suffer. The Department of Environmental Resources (DER) built the Swamp Creek Treatment Plant in 1970 as part of Operation Scarlift. The drainage area of this mine-acid stream flows through sections strip-mined during and shortly after World War II. Generations to come will suffer the consequences of the devastation caused by man. Above the treatment plant Swamp Creek's pH averages 4. The water flowing out of the liming device registers a pH of nearly 9. The pH of the discharge just below the dam in the stream averages 6.5. Without the liming device the pH on the stream below would be lower and might not be able to support a great trout fishery. Swamp Creek empties into the East Branch Dam a mile below the treatment site. The East Branch flows out of the reservoir. The DER operates the device and deserves the gratitude of all fishermen and environmentalists.

The DER operates other mine-treatment plants in the state. The plant on Slippery Rock Creek near Harrisville differs from the Swamp Creek plant in that it adds a slurry to the water, while the Swamp Creek plant adds dehydrated lime. Adding slurry to the water seems to be more effective on larger streams.

Dale Eury operates the Swamp Creek Treatment Plant for the DER. Recently I spent some time at the operation. The plant consists of a lime-storage tank or silo and an automatic feeder. Two feeders add dehydrated lime to the mine acid in the stream below. There's a mixing shaft in the stream that thoroughly mixes the lime with the mine acid. Downstream from the effluent you'll see the bottom of the stream covered with an iron precipitate that is produced after the pH is elevated. This area of precipitation often runs for a mile downstream from the plant.

Without the liming device Swamp Run would carry mine acid directly into the East Branch Dam. Currently the impoundment contains a good number of bass and deep-water lake trout. Below the dam the branch holds great numbers of fingerlings, as well as stocked and holdover trout. Mayfly, caddisfly, and stonefly hatches appear on the stream throughout much of the year. Would they still appear without the treatment plant above?

Thanks to Mike Dielo, Dale Eury of the DER, and all others associated with the treatment plant, East Branch survives as a viable trout fishery. The treatment plant works. It's no longer just a pilot program, but an important alternative to mine-acid drainage in small streams.

Joining or Forming a Club

Since the first edition of *Trout Streams of Pennsylvania* was published in 1989, even more streams or sections of them have gone private. An important section of the Little Juniata River went private in 1992. What can you do to at least delay the onslaught of posted water and keep clean water that is open? Join or organize a group dedicated to the preservation of that stream. Look at an effort in north-central Pennsylvania that succeeded.

In chapter 5 I discussed the mine drainage from Babb Creek and its tributaries and the effect on aquatic life on Pine Creek below the source of pollution. Enter several organizations to combat the pollution. The Dauphin County Chapter of Trout Unlimited, the Susquehanna Chapter of Trout Unlimited, Slate Run Sportsmen, Arnot Sportsmen, the Pine Creek Preservation Association, the Pine Creek Headwaters Protective Group, the Pennsylvania Environmental Defense Foundation, the Slate Run Tackle Shop, the Army National Guard, the Pennsylvania Fish Commission, the Department of Environmental Resources, the Pennsylvania Game Commission, the Bureau of Mines, the Bureau of Forestry, and the Antrim Mining Company all banded together to attempt to solve the mine-acid problem on Babb Creek.

"It's an absolute miracle," says Bob McCullough of Williamsport every time he talks about the synergism among the organizations. "The mining company, state agencies, and sportsmen's groups all combine with one thought in mind—what can I do to help?" Appalled at the metal deposition in Pine Creek from the pollution in Babb Creek, the Pennsylvania Environmental Defense Foundation sued Antrim Mining and received a cash settlement. This money is now being used to support liming devices on some of the more polluted branches of Babb Creek. In addition the Department of Environmental Resources also sued Antrim Mining to improve the water in Wilson Run. The treatment system on the tributary now discharges effluent at a pH of 9.5 to 10, rather than 3.2 as before.

Within a couple of years anglers will see the improvement on Pine Creek because of the effort of all. Leaders in this movement were Tom Finkbiner of Slate Run Tackle; Jack Sherwood, district forester; Dean Arnold, professor, Penn State University; Robert Ross, biologist, US Fish and Wildlife Service; Paul Swanson, north-central regional supervisor, Pennsylvania Fish Commission; Joseph Schueck, hydrologist, Bureau of Mines; and Captain Chris Cleaver, Pennsylvania National Guard.

I feel certain that you believe as I do that these agencies that protect our resources need our financial support. You can contact the Pennsylvania Environmental Defense Foundation at 20 Kenwood Drive, Carlisle 17013-2111 or P.O. Box 371, Camp Hill 17001-0371.

There are many other great organizations within Pennsylvania that you as a dedicated fly-fisher can join. One of the best is the Western Pennsylvania Conservancy located in Pittsburgh. This organization, in its unique effort to preserve and protect "large-scale wildlands combining recreational, ecological, and scenic qualities," has served anglers and others interested in the outdoors throughout the western half of the state for years. Since 1932 the conservancy has preserved over 170,000 acres of choice natural lands throughout western and central Pennsylvania. A few examples of what this group has acquired include 12,000 acres in Centre County and part of a great wild-trout stream, Cherry Run; a 9.7-mile path giving anglers easy access to Oil Creek; and an abandoned railroad right-of-way obtained in 1979 along the Youghiogheny River. The conservancy continues to secure land for all to enjoy. Usually after this tremendous conservation-minded organization acquires land it sells it, at cost, to state agencies for parks, forests, or game lands. We as dedicated fly-fishers must support this worthwhile group. You can contact it at Western Pennsylvania Conservancy, 316 Fourth Avenue, Pittsburgh 15222; or call 412-288-2777.

What can you do to improve Pennsylvania streams? Become involved. If you see the need, form a group dedicated to the betterment of a stream or streams. The future of great trout fishing in the state depends on concerned anglers like you.

Appendix: Hatch Charts

Changes in Scientific Names

In the past 10 years many changes have occurred in mayfly classification. Many of these changes affect mayflies found on Pennsylvania waters. Entomologists now group both March browns *(Stenonema vicarium)* and gray foxes *(S. fuscum)* under *S. vicarium.* I have listed them separately in the chart because I see a real difference between the two former species. I must admit, however, that I seldom see a state stream or river that holds both gray foxes and March browns.

No longer do entomologists consider slate drakes—like *Isonychia bicolor, I. matilda, I. harperi,* and *I. sadleri*—as separate species. All are now lumped under *I. bicolor.* Species until recently listed as *Pseudocloeon* spp. are now grouped under *Baetis* and *Acentrella.* Many changes have occurred in genera as well. You'll note some of these below. I've reflected many of these recent changes in genus and species in the emergence charts.

CHART I Changes in Genera

Cloeon now *Procloeon*

Pseudocloeon now *Baetis* and *Acentrella*

Potomanthus now *Anthopotamanthus*

Heptagenia now *Heptagenia, Leucrocuta,* and *Nixie*

Using the Hatch Charts

Use the emergence charts in this book only as general guides. Many deviations occur in the dates listed, the times of day certain species appear, and insect coloration and size.

Column one lists the common name for the dun and the spinner of a species, with the dun listed above, the spinner below. Common names on the chart vary from region to region. Those listed are probably used most often.

The second column lists the scientific name of the mayfly, stonefly, or caddisfly species. Several hundred species of these insects are common on Pennsylvania streams and rivers; therefore it's impossible to detail all of them. Included are most of the hatches you'll meet on Pennsylvania waters.

The dates provided in column three are the average dates when the main hatch appears in central Pennsylvania. Remember, these dates vary by as much as two weeks and should be used as a guide.

The fourth column suggests the time of day at which the dun appears on the surface or the spinner fall occurs. Again, these change from day to day and year to year.

The final column suggests the best hook size to imitate the species. This too varies from stream to stream for the same species. A good rule of thumb is that most blue quills (*Paraleptophlebia* spp.) can be copied with a size-18 hook; many little blue-winged olive duns and blue duns (*Baetis* spp.) are effectively imitated with a size 20; and most sulphurs, with a size-16 hook. You'll find suggested imitations and hook sizes listed at the beginning of each stream description as well.

Notes About Chart VI

Just about every common hatch you'll ever encounter in Pennsylvania is listed in this chart, which should help you identify what hatch you've seen.

- *Season:* I've divided the hatches into early, middle, and late season. Some species—like the blue quill (*Paraleptophlebia guttata)* and the yellow drake (*Ephemera varia*)—emerge in two of the time frames.
- *Tails:* A simple way to determine which mayfly you're matching is to count the number of tails. (All mayflies have either two or three tails.) This works with most species—except the white mayfly. When the white mayfly emerges the male changes from a dun to a spinner, usually in just a few minutes. The female, however, never molts; she remains and breeds as a dun. The male spinner has two tails, and the female dun has three.
- *Coloring:* "Light coloring" and "dark coloring" refer to the back of the insect's body. For example, look at the green drake. If you examine the belly or abdomen of this mayfly you'll find a cream color but look at the back and you see a darker mayfly.

From the chart you can gather several bits of information about coloring. First, take note of the coloration of mayflies in the "early season." No mayflies appearing at this time have light backs. Why not? When mayfly duns emerge from the water they usually rest for a day or more before returning to the stream to mate and lay eggs. Where do they rest for that day or two? You'll most often find them on rocks near the stream, or on the branches of a nearby bush or tree. Normally mayflies rest on the undersides of leaves, but at this point leaves have not yet appeared. What color predominates on the rocks near shore and on the branches of nearby trees? Dark gray, of course. Over the eons, mayflies that emerged with a lighter color were easy prey for birds and other insect eaters. Those mayflies with darker backs were harder to see and so prevailed.

In the early season, then, you will want to select the darker patterns. Look also at the midseason hatches. You'll see that all the hatches that appear during the day are dark in color. This is nature's way of protecting them. This doesn't mean that all dark mayflies appear during the day; those that do, however, are usually dark. All light-colored mayflies appear near evening or at dusk.

VARIATIONS IN COLOR

Dave McMullen owns and operates the Six Springs Fly Shop in Spruce Creek. He's one of the finest fly-casters I've ever seen. Show him a narrow opening between two trees and he'll cast his dry fly delicately between them and onto the surface without getting hung up on a single branch. Dave also operates a trout hatchery in Spruce Creek and has made some keen observations there. Recently he showed me one of his findings. Dave netted three trout from a hatchery pool and placed them in a white bucket. Within minutes they had become much lighter in color. He returned the three trout to the pool and for almost 5 minutes we could tell which fish they were, because they were so much lighter than the other trout.

What does this prove? Many life forms are capable of changing color to some extent. Call it protective coloration or whatever you want, it happens. What about nymphs? Have you ever heard someone say that nymphs in one area or on one stream are lighter or darker than in another? Do you think maybe aquatic insects have the same capability?

When I prepared the manuscript for *Meeting and Fishing the Hatches* back in 1977, I sent some mayflies to Will Flowers, a skilled entomologist, to identify. There was a reddish brown mayfly, an olive one, and a cream one, all in the dun stage. The identification for all was the same—*Ephemerella inermis.* Will told me that this species, possibly more than any other, varies in color from stream to stream—and even on the same stream. Another closely related species, *E. needhami,* also varies in color tremendously. I recently experienced a hatch of the latter mayfly; the female dun had a distinct olive body with cream legs, tail, and wings. The male of this same species had a dark brown body in the dun stage.

NIGHT OR DAY EMERGERS

Mayflies listed in the following chart in bold usually emerge at night, and those in regular type usually appear during the day. Of course times vary with temperature and weather. I've seen Hendrickson hatches appear as early as 9 AM on hot April days and as late as 6 PM on others. The sulphur is another story. The first couple of days that a sulphur appears, it often does so in the afternoon. After a few days the hatch usually changes to evening, appearing just before dusk. Add drizzly, overcast weather and all kinds of things can happen. I've seen sulphurs emerge all day on inclement days in late May. Green drakes, too, will often appear earlier on overcast days and on streams with a heavy canopy.

LARGE AND SMALL

You'll see an **S** or an **L** in front of each mayfly in the chart. Hatches that can be matched with a size-14 or larger hook (14–6) have an **L** in front of them. Those matched with a size-16 or smaller hook (16–26) have an **S**. Insect sizes vary tremendously. Green drakes on Penns Creek are much larger than on many small Pennsylvania streams, for example. As another example, slate drakes have two generations each year—one appears in May and June and the second in September. The second generation—the fall one—is a size smaller than the spring generation.

OTHER FEATURES

To further help you identify these mayflies, I've added some comments that might set one mayfly off from another. Many of the references in this column are to the coloration of the mayfly, for example, if male and female duns have different colors.

CHART II The Early-Season Hatches ✳ April to Mid-May

Common Name	Scientific Name	Average Date	Time of Day	Hook Size
MAYFLIES				
Little blue-winged olive Rusty spinner	Baetis tricaudatus (B. vagans)	April 1	11 AM Afternoon	16–20
Blue quill Dark brown spinner	Paraleptophlebia adoptiva	April 18	11 AM Afternoon	18
Dark quill gordon Dark brown spinner	Ameletus ludens	April 18	Afternoon	14
Quill gordon Red quill spinner	Epeorus pleuralis	April 20	1 PM Afternoon	14
Hendrickson or red quill Red quill spinner	Ephemerella subvaria	April 21	2 PM Afternoon/early evening	14
Black quill Early brown spinner	Leptophlebia cupida	April 25	2 PM Afternoon	14
Great speckled olive dun Great speckled spinner	Siphloplecton basale	April 20	1 PM Afternoon	14
Little blue dun Rusty spinner	Acentrella carolina	May 1	Afternoon and evening Afternoon	20
Sulphur dun Sulphur spinner	Ephemerella rotunda	May 12	7 PM Evening	16
CADDISFLIES				
Little olive caddis	Hydropsyche bronta	April 10	Morning and afternoon	16
Little black caddis	Chimarra atterima	April 15	11 AM	18

Common Name	Scientific Name	Average Date	Time of Day	Hook Size
Grannom	*Brachycentrus numerosus*	April 20	Morning and afternoon	12
Cream caddis	*Psilotreta* spp.	April 25	Morning and afternoon	14
Green caddis	*Rhyacophila* spp.	May 1	Morning and afternoon	14
Dark brown caddis	*Deplectrona modesta*	May 15	Morning and afternoon	12
STONEFLIES				
Little black stonefly	*Capnia vernalis*	March 1	Morning and afternoon	16
Early brown stonefly	*Strophopteryx fasciata**	April 10	Noon	14
Great brown stonefly	*Phasganophora capitata*	April 20	Morning and afternoon	12
Light stonefly	*Isoperla signata*	May 8	Afternoon	14

*Also copies *Taeniopteryx nivalis*.

CHART III The Midseason Hatches ☀ May 15 to July 1

Common Name	Scientific Name	Average Date	Time of Day	Hook Size
MAYFLIES				
Sulphur dun	(see early-season chart)			
Gray fox	*Stenonema fuscum**	May 15	Afternoon	12–14
Ginger quill spinner			Evening	
Pale evening dun	*Ephemerella septentrionalis*	May 15	Evening	14–16
Pale evening spinner			Evening	

Common Name	Scientific Name	Average Date	Time of Day	Hook Size
Pale evening dun Pale evening spinner	*Heptagenia aphrodite*	May 18	Evening Evening	16
March brown Great red spinner	*Stenonema vicarium*	May 18	Morning and afternoon Evening	12–14
Light cahill Light cahill spinner	*Stenacron interpunctatum***	May 23	Evening Evening	14
Chocolate dun Chocolate spinner	*Ephemerella bicolor*	May 25	Late morning and early afternoon Afternoon and evening	16
Green drake Coffin fly	*Ephemera guttulata*	May 25	Evening Evening	8–12
Brown drake Brown drake spinner	*Ephemera simulans*	May 25	Evening Evening	10–12
Light cahill Ginger quill spinner	*Stenonema ithaca*	May 25	Evening Evening	14
Dark green drake Brown drake spinner	*Litobrancha recurvata*	May 25	Afternoon and evening	6–10
Slate drake White-gloved howdy	*Isonychia sadleri* and *I. bicolor*	May 25	Evening Evening	12
Cream cahill Cream cahill spinner	*Stenonema modestum*	May 25	Evening Evening	14–16
Blue-winged olive dun Dark olive spinner	*Drunella (Ephemerella) cornuta*	May 25	Late morning Evening	14
Blue-winged olive dun Olive spinner	*Drunella (Ephemerella) longicornus*	May 25	Early morning Evening	16

Common name	Scientific name	Date	Time	Hook size
Pink cahill / Salmon spinner	*Epeorus vitreus*	May 25	Evening / Evening	14–16
Gray drake	*Siphlonurus quebecensis*	May 25	Afternoon and evening	12
Gray drake	*Siphlonurus mirus*	May 25	Afternoon and evening	12
Sulphur dun / Sulphur spinner	*Ephemerella invaria*	June 1	Evening / Evening	16–18
Dark blue quill / Dark olive spinner	*Serratella (Ephemerella) deficiens*	June 1	Evening / Evening	18–20
Blue quill / Dark brown spinner (F) / Jenny spinner (M)	*Paraleptophlebia mollis*	June 3	Morning and afternoon	18
Iron blue dun / Blue quill spinner (F) / Jenny spinner (M)	*Leptophlebia johnsoni*	June 5	Late morning / Evening	16
Olive sulphur (F) / Dark brown dun (M)	*Ephemerella needhami*	June 5	Evening	16
Little blue-winged olive dun / Rusty spinner	*Baetis levitans*	June 5	Afternoon and evening / Evening	20
Little blue-winged olive dun / Dark olive spinner	*Dannella (Ephemerella) simplex*	June 15	Morning and afternoon / Evening	18–20
Blue-winged olive dun / Dark olive spinner	*Drunella (Ephemerella) lata*	June 15	Morning and afternoon / Evening	16
Light cahill / Light cahill spinner	*Leucrocuta marginalis*	June 15	Evening	14
Cream cahill / Cream cahill spinner	*Stenonema pulchellum*	June 15	Evening	14–16
Sulphur dun*** / Sulphur spinner	*Ephemerella dorothea*	June 15	Evening	18

Common Name	Scientific Name	Average Date	Time of Day	Hook Size
Yellow drake Yellow drake spinner	*Ephemera varia*	June 20	Evening	12
Blue quill Dark brown spinner	*Paraleptophlebia guttata*	June 25	Morning Morning and afternoon	18
Golden drake Golden spinner	*Anthopotamanthus distinctus*	June 25	Evening	12–14
Pale evening dun Pale evening spinner	*Heptagenia* spp.	June 25	Evening	16
CADDISFLIES				
Spotted sedge	*Symphitopsyche slossanae*	May 23	Afternoon	14
Dark blue sedge	*Psilotreta frontalis*	June 5	Evening	12
STONEFLIES				
Yellow sally	*Isoperla bilineata*	June 5	Afternoon	14
Little green stonefly	*Alloperla imbecilla*	June 5	Afternoon	16
Great stonefly	*Phasganophora capitata*	June 5	Afternoon and evening	10
Great brown stonefly	*Acroneuria lycorius*	June 15	Morning and afternoon	12

*Now grouped with *Stenonema vicarium* (March brown) by many entomologists.

**Includes *S. interpunctatum interpunctatum* and *S. interpunctatum canadense.*

***This species is often called the pale evening dun.

CHART IV The Late-Season Hatches ✳ July 1 to October

Common Name	Scientific Name	Average Date	Time of Day	Hook Size
MAYFLIES				
Pale morning dun Pale morning spinner	*Centroptilum album*	July 15	Morning	22
Little white mayfly	*Caenis* spp.	July 15	Evening	28
Trico	*Tricorythodes* spp.	July 15	Morning	24
Slate drake White-gloved howdy	*Isonychia harperi*	July 23	Evening	12–14
White mayfly	*Ephoron leukon*	August 15	Evening	14–16
Dark slate drake Dark rusty spinner	*Hexagenia atrocaudata*	August 18	Evening	8
Slate drake White-gloved howdy	*Isonychia bicolor*	August 25	Afternoon and evening	14
Little blue-winged olive Rusty spinner	*Baetis tricaudatus (B. vagans)*	September 1	Afternoon	16–20
Little blue dun Rusty spinner	*Acentrella carolina*	September 15	Afternoon	20
CADDISFLIES				
Green caddis	*Rhyacophila* spp.	July 10	Morning	14
TERRESTRIALS				
Winged ant	*Monomorium* spp.	August 25	Afternoon	18–20

CHART V Some of Pennsylvania's Major Hatches By Stream

	brown drake	green drake	little blue-winged olive	slate drake	trico	white mayfly
NORTHEAST						
Bowman Creek			x	x	x	
Brodhead Creek					x	
Delaware River	x	x	x	x	x	x
Fishing Creek (Columbia County)				x	x	
Hayes Creek		x *(upstream)*				
Lackawanna River			x		x	
Lackawaxen River						x
Lehigh River		x *(above dam)*		x		x
Mehoopany Creek				x		
Towanda Creek					x	
SOUTHEAST						
Donegal Creek					x	
Bushkill Creek					x	
Little Lehigh Creek			x		x	x

Monocacy Creek		x				
Pickering Creek			x			
Quittapahilla Creek				x		
Saucon Creek		x				
Tulpehocken Creek		x		x		
Valley Creek		x		x		
West Valley Creek		x				

NORTH-CENTRAL

Allegheny River	x				x *(Coudersport area)*	
Cedar Run		x	x		x	
Cross Fork Creek		x	x		x	
Driftwood Br., Sinnemahoning Creek			x	x		
East Fork, Sinnemahoning Creek			x	x		
Elk Creek (Lycoming County)					x	
Elk Creek (Sullivan County)		x				
First Fork, Sinnemahoning Creek		x	x	x		
Genesee Forks (Potter County)		x	x			
Grays Run (Lycoming County)		x		x		
Hammersley Run			x			
Hoagland Branch		x			x	
Kettle Creek		x	x	x		
Larrys Creek		x		x	x	

	brown drake	green drake	little blue-winged olive	slate drake	trico	white mayfly
Little Pine Creek		x	x	x		
Loyalsock Creek			x	x	x	
Lyman Run				x		
Mill Creek (Potter County)		x				
Muncy Creek				x		
Ninemile Run	x	x			x	
Oswayo Creek	x *(spotty)*	x		x	x	
Pine Creek	x	x	x	x	x	
Sinnemahoning Portage Creek	x					
Slate Run		x		x	x	
West Branch, Pine Creek		x		x		
Young Womans Creek		x				
CENTRAL						
Bald Eagle Creek (Julian)			x *[lower end]*	x		x
Bald Eagle Creek (Tyrone)			x	x		
Big Fill Run		x				
Canoe Creek		x	x			
Clover Creek			x		x	
Elk Creek (Centre County)		x	x		x	

Fishing Creek (Clinton County)		x	x	x	
Little Juniata River	x	x (spotty)	x	x	x (lower end)
Logan Branch		x (spotty)		x	
Lower Bald Eagle Creek	x (spotty)				
Penns Creek		x	x	x	x
Pine Creek (Centre County)				x	
Piney Creek		x		x	
Sixmile Run					x
Spring Creek		x		x	
Spruce Creek		x		x	x
Vanscoyoc Run					x
White Deer Creek			x		x
SOUTH-CENTRAL					
Big Cove Creek		x	x		
Big Spring Run		x		x	
Falling Spring Branch		x		x	
Green Spring Creek		x		x	
Honey Creek					x
Kishacoquillas Creek (West Branch)			x		x
LeTort Spring Run		x			
Little Tonoloway Creek			x		
Lost Creek					x

	brown drake	green drake	little blue-winged olive	slate drake	trico	white mayfly
Middle Spring Creek					X	
Willow Run		X	X			
Yellow Breeches Creek			X		X	X
NORTHWEST						
Caldwell Creek		X			X	
Clarion River			X	X		X (spotty)
Cool Spring Creek (Mercer County)	X					
East Branch, Mahoning Creek	X	X			X	
Little Sandy Creek		X				
Allegheny River below Kinzua Dam					X	
Neshannock Creek	X	X				X
North Fork, Red Bank Creek	X					
Slippery Rock Creek	X (upper end)					X
Spring Creek (Warren County)		X				
Thompson Creek	X	X			X	
Tionesta Creek	X					
West Branch, Tunungwant Creek				X		

SOUTHWEST

Brush Creek (Somerset County)		x				
Buffalo Creek	x					
Little Mahoning Creek	x					
Loyalhanna Creek	x				x	
Raystown Branch, Juniata River	x *(Everett area)*					x
Stonycreek River				x		
Yellow Creek			x	x	x	
Youghiogheny River			x	x		

CHART VI Identifying the Hatches

Key
S=small (#16 and higher)
L= large (#14 and lower)
Bold letters = emerge at evening or dusk

EARLY SEASON (MARCH TO MID-MAY)

Two Tails

DARK COLORING

S Little blue-winged olive dun—*Baetis tricaudatus*—Other *Baetis* species appear in the early season. Dun and spinner move abdomen from side to side

L Quill gordon—*Epeorus pleuralis*—Can appear as late as late June

L Dark quill gordon—*Ameletus ludens*—Usually find duns on rocks next to stream

L Speckle-winged dun—*Callibaetis skokianus*—Slow-water or lake species

L Great olive dun—*Siphloplecton basale*—Rare in Pennsylvania

Three Tails

DARK COLORING

L Hendrickson—*Ephemerella subvaria*

L Black quill—*Leptophlebia cupida*—Middle tail is somewhat shorter than outer two

S Blue quill—*Paraleptophlebia adoptiva*

MIDDLE SEASON (MID-MAY TO LATE JUNE)

Two Tails

LIGHT COLORING

L Light cahill—*Stenacron interpunctatum canadense*—Often appears most heavily around 7 PM

L Light cahill—*Epeorus vitreus*, male—Male is yellow and female has a pink body

L Light cahill—*Stenonema ithaca*

L Pink lady—*Epeorus vitreus*, female

L Cream cahill—*Stenonema modestum*—Spinner is chalky white

L   March brown (gray fox)—*Stenonema vicarium*

DARK COLORING

L   Quill gordon—*Epeorus pleuralis*—I've seen this mayfly appear in fishable numbers as late as mid-June

L   Dark green drake—*Litobrancha recurvata*—Usually appears around 2 PM; has a middle vestigial (just a trace) tail

L   Gray drake—*Siphlonurus quebecensis* and *S. mirus*, male—Spinner has black rear wing; very common in early June in northwestern Pennsylvania

L   Quill gordon—*Epeorus pleuralis*

Three Tails

LIGHT COLORING

L   Golden drake—*Anthopotamanthus distinctus*—Weak veins in wing

L   Sulphur—*Ephemerella rotunda* (and *E. invaria*)

S   Sulphur—*Ephemerella invaria*

L   Pale evening dun—*Ephemerella septentrionalis*

S   Pale evening dun—*Ephemerella dorothea*

DARK COLORING

S   Blue Quill—*Paraleptophlebia mollis* and *P. guttata*

L   Green drake— *Ephemera guttulata*—Dark on top and cream on bottom

L   Brown drake—*Ephemera simulans*

L   Blue-winged olive dun—*Drunella cornuta*

L   Blue-winged olive dun—*Drunella cornutella*—A size smaller than *D. cornuta;* appears in early to mid-June

L   Blue-winged olive dun—*Drunella lata*—Appears three weeks later than *D. cornutella*

L   Slate drake—*Isonychia bicolor*—Front legs are dark brown; rear two pairs are cream

S   Dark blue quill—*Serratella deficiens*

S   Little blue-winged olive dun—*Dannella simplex*

L   Chocolate dun—*Eurylophella bicolor*—Legs are cream

S   Olive sulphur—*Ephemerella needhami*—Legs, tail, and wings are cream; body of female dun is medium olive; body of male dun is dark brown

LATE SEASON (JULY TO LATE OCTOBER)

Two Tails

LIGHT COLORING

L   Cream cahill—*Stenonema* spp.

L   White mayfly—*Ephoron leukon,* male

DARK COLORING

L   Dark slate drake—*Hexagenia atrocaudata*—Male spinners undulate about 30 feet in the air around 7 PM

S   Little blue-winged olive dun—*Baetis tricaudatus*

Three Tails

LIGHT COLORING

L   White mayfly—*Ephoron leukon*-female

L   Yellow drake—*Ephemera varia*

S   Trico—*Tricorythodes allectus,* female

S   Little white mayfly—*Caenis* spp.

DARK COLORING

S   Trico—*Tricorythodes allectus,* male

L   Slate drake—*Isonychia bicolor*

L   Blue quill—*Paraleptophlebia guttata*

Index

A

Allegheny Highlands Trail Project, 329–330
Allegheny River, 178–180
    below Kinzua Dam, 293–295
Alliance for Acid Rain Monitoring, 331
Army Corps of Engineers, 82, 302–303

B

Bald Eagle Creek
    Julian, 204–208
    Lower, below Milesburg, 208–210
    Tyrone (BET), 210–212
Baldwin Highlanders Fishing Club, 376–377
Bead Head Olive Caddis
    patterns for, 364
Bead Head Pheasant Tail Nymph
    patterns for, 364
Bell Gap Run, 229–230
Bellwood Sportsmen's Association, 230
Big Bushkill Creek, 85–87
Big Cove Creek, 267–270
Big Fill Run, 212–213
Big Spring Run (Creek), 247–248
Binney and Smith, 103
Blacklog Creek, 270–271
Bobs Creek, 325–326
Bowman Creek, 63–66
Brandywine Creek, East Branch, 90–93
Brandywine Trout and Conservation Club (BTCC), 91–93
Brodhead Creek, 83–85
Brokenstraw Creek, 304–305
Brown Drake, 28–31
Brush Creek, 351–352

Budd, Robert
    Little Juniata River, 189–193
Buffalo Creek, 314–318
Bugskin, 361–362
Bushkill Conservancy, 103
Bushkill Creek, 102–104

C

Caddisflies
    early-season, 26–28, 388–389
    late-season, 393
    life cycle of, 21–22
    midseason, 392
    tying methods and patterns for, 357–358, 371–372
Caldwell Creek, 279–281
Camera, Phil
    Fly Tying with Synthetics, 362
Canoe Creek, 231–233
Casselman River, 328–331
Casselman Valley Watershed Association, 329
Catch and release, 376
Cedar Creek, 120
Cedar Run, 146–148
Chest Creek, 322–325
Clarion River, 297–301
    East Branch, 302–303
    West Branch, 303–304
Clarks Creek, 70–73
Classifications
    changes in, 384
Clean Streams Law of 1937, 37
Clover Creek, 221–222
Clubs, 382–383
    See also specific clubs
Codorus Creek, 257–261
Cool Spring Creek, 291
Cove Creek, 347–348
Coxes Creek, 327–328

Creeks
  access rights to, 377–378
  pollution in, 37–38
  ratings of, 16
Cross Fork Creek, 169–171

D
Davis, Bob
  Scholarship Fund, 307
Delaware River, 66–70
Delaware Water Gap National
  Recreation Area, 51
Depoe, Ken, 119–120
Donegal Creek, 119–120
Donegal Fish and Conservation
  Association, 119
Downwings
  tying methods and patterns for,
  357–358
Duns
  tying methods and patterns for,
  358–359
Dyberry Creek, 87–88

E
Eastern Pennsylvania Coalition for
  Abandoned Mine Reclamation
  (EPACAMR), 100
East Hickory Creek, 310–312
East Licking Creek, 266–267
Educational programs, 348
  Baldwin Highlanders Fishing
    Club, 376–377
  Bob Davis Scholarship Fund, 307
  Kinzua Fly Fishing Camp, 274
Elk Creek, 193–195
Elk Creek (Sullivan County),
  144–145
Emerger
  definition of, 21
  tying methods and patterns for,
  355–357
Environmental Quality Board,
  109–110

F
Falling Spring Branch, 252–256
Falling Spring Greenway, 254–256
Federation of Fly Fishers, 378

Fishing Creek, 216–220
Fishing Creek (Columbia County),
  59–63
Fishing Creek Watershed
  Association, 63
FLYbase, 131
Fly Fisherman, 43, 50, 98, 358
Flyfishing, 354
Fly Fishing Guide, 362
Fly-fishing guides
  Angling Fantasies, 224, 244, 266
  Delaware River, 66–70
  Harpster, Wayne, 225
  Six Springs Fly Shop, 193, 224
  Spruce Creek Outfitters, 193, 225
Fly Tying with Synthetics, 362
Foor, Bob, 345, 348
Forbes, Tom
  100 Trout Streams, 172
French Creek, 115–116

G
Genera
  changes in, 384
Genesee Forks, 180–181
Grays Run, 132–133
Greater Johnstown Watershed
  Association, 331
Great Rivers—Great Hatches, 356
Green Drake, 31–34
Green Spring Creek, 237–240
Green Valley Association, 109
Green Weenie
  patterns for, 364

H
Hackle
  definition of, 361
Hammersley Run (Fork), 171–172
Harvey, George
  Fly Fisherman, 358
Hatches, 22–24
  definition of, 21
  early-season, 24–26, 388–389
  identifying, 400–402
  late-season, 36–37, 393
  matching, 359–360
  mayflies, 26–36
  midseason, 389–392

new, 46–48
tying patterns for, 363–374
by stream, 394–399
Hatches II (Caucci and Nastasi), 46
Hayes Creek, 74–75
Hickory Run, 75–76
Hoagland Branch, 142–144
Honey Creek, 263–264

J

Juniata River, Raystown Branch, 350–351

K

Kettle Creek, 165–169
Kettle Creek Watershed Association, 91, 167, 169
Kinzua Creek, 305–306
Kinzua Fly Fishing Camp, 274
Kishacoquillas Creek (Kish), 261–263

L

Lackawanna Heritage Valley River, Trail and Greenway Study, 56
Lackawanna River, 52–57
Lackawaxen River, 73–74
Lafayette College, 103
Larrys Creek, 133–134
Larva Lace, 362
Laurel Hill Creek, 336–338
Laurel Run, 235–237
Lehigh River, 76–78
Leitzinger, Andrew, 201–202
LeTort Regulars, 246–247\
LeTort Spring Run, 245–247
Linn Run, 380
Linn Run State Park, 380
Little blue-winged olive dun, 38–39
Little Juniata River, 189–193
Little Lehigh Creek, 120–123
Little Lehigh Fly Fishers, 122
Little Mahoning Creek, 342–344
Little Pine Creek, 148–151
Little Sandy Creek, 291–293
Little Schuylkill Conservation Club, 100
Little Schuylkill River, 98–102
Little Tonoloway Creek, 242–244

Lloydsville Sportsmen's Association, 336
Logan Branch, 228
Lost Creek, 241–242
Loyalhanna Creek, 334–336
Loyalhanna Watershed Association, 380
Loyalsock Creek, 138–142
Lycoming Creek, 159–161
Lyman Run, 129–130

M

Mahoning Creek, East Branch, 306–308
Marinaro, Vince
Modern Dry-Fly Code, A, 41
Mayflies
brown drake, 28–31
early-season, 388
green drake, 31–34
late-season, 393
life cycle of, 19–21
little blue-winged olive dun, 38–39
midseason, 389–392
new hatches, 46–48
olive, 34–35
patterns for, 363–371
quill gordon, 35–36
slate drake, 39–40
trico, 41–43
white mayflies, 43–45
Meck, Charles
Fly Fisherman, 43, 98
Fly Fishing Guide, 362
Great Rivers—Great Hatches, 356
Meeting and Fishing the Hatches, 22, 218, 358–359
Mid-Atlantic Trout Streams, 15
Trout Streams of Pennsylvania, 50, 193, 213, 320, 382
Meeting and Fishing the Hatches, 22, 218, 358–359, 386
Mehoopany Creek, 78–79
Mid-Atlantic Fly Fishing Guide, 159
Mid-Atlantic Trout Streams, 15
Middle Spring Creek, 240–241
Mill Creek, 130–132
Modern Dry-Fly Code, A, 41

Monocacy Creek, 123–125
Monocacy Watershed Association, 125
Mowry, Russ, 5, 335
Muddy Creek, 256–257
Muddy Creek Trout Stocking Committee (MCTSC), 256–257
Mud Run, 80–81
Muncy Creek, 145–146

N

National Land Trust of Media, Pennsylvania, 247
Natural
   definition of, 21
Needham's Trout Streams, 169
Neshannock Creek, 289–291
Ninemile Run, 181–182
Nymphs
   tying methods and patterns for, 360–361

O

Octoraro Creek, 117–118
Oil Creek, 283–287
Olive bodies, 34–35
100 Trout Streams, 172
Open Land Conservancy, 109
Organizations, 382–383
   See also specific organizations
Oswayo Creek, 175–177

P

Palko, Jerry
   Scranton Times, 56
Patriot
   pattern for, 364
Patterns. See tying methods and patterns
Penns Creek, 199–204
Penn State University, 380
   Frost Museum, 197
Pennsylvania Angler, 38
Pennsylvania Department of Environmental Resources, 109, 303, 331
   Operation Scarlift, 381
Pennsylvania Environmental Defense Foundation, 153, 382

Pennsylvania Environmental Defense Fund, 72–73
Pennsylvania Fish and Boat Commission, 13–14, 91, 199, 208–210, 302–303, 329–332, 375
   Adopt-a-Stream, 88, 336, 379
   land acquisition, 377–379
Pennsylvania Outdoor Life, 52
Pennsylvania Trout, 95
Pfizer, 103
Phil's Tackle, 362
Pickering Creek, 94–96
Pine Creek, 151–158, 185–189, 283
   Little Pine Creek, 148–151
   West Branch, 158–159
Pine Creek Headwaters Protection Group (PCHPG), 153
Pine Creek Preservation Group, 153
Piney Creek, 220–221
Pohopoco Creek, 81–83
Pollution, 100, 106–110, 125, 332–334, 379
   acid rain, 325–326, 380
   mine-acid, 151–153, 302–303
   siltation, 253–254, 303

Q

Quemahoning Rod and Gun Club, 332
Quill Gordon, 35–36
Quittapahilla Creek (Quitty), 105–107

R

Raubertas, Paul, 95
Raystown Branch, Juniata River, 350–351
Red Bank Creek, North Fork, 295–297
Richard King Mellon Foundation, 380
Ridley Creek, 114–115
Rivers
   access rights, 377–378
   pollution in, 37–38
   ratings of, 16

S

Saucon Creek, 96–98

Schuylkill Headwaters, 101
Scientific names
    changes in, 384
Scranton Times, 56
Selective-harvest area, 98
Shaw Run Water Improvement
    Project, 230
Sinnemahoning Creek
    Driftwood Branch, 182–184
    East Fork, 137–138
    First Fork, 134–137
Sinnemahoning Portage Creek
    (SPC), 127–129
Sixmile Run, 226–227
Slate drake, 39–40
Slate Run, 161–165
Slate Run Sportsmen, 163
Slippery Rock Creek, 287–289
    treatment plant, 381
Somerset County Fly Fishers, 332,
    337
Somerset Rails to Trails Association,
    329–330
Southern Alleghenies Resource,
    Conservation and Development
    Program, 334
Spinner fall
    definition of, 21
Spinners
    tying methods and patterns for,
    358
Spring Creek, 195–199, 301
Spruce Creek, 222–226
Standing Stone Creek, 272
Stoneflies
    early-season, 389
    life cycle of, 21–22
    midseason, 392
    patterns for, 372–373
Stonycreek–Conemaugh River
    Improvement Project (SCRIP),
    331–334
Stonycreek River, 331–334
Stony Fork, 174–175
Stream Access for All (SAFA), 378
Streams
    access rights, 377–378
    pollution in, 37–38
    ratings of, 16

Sugar Creek, 281–283
Swamp Creek
    treatment plant, 381

T
Taylor, John
    York Dispatch, 256
Tea Creek, 265–266
Terrestrials, 45–46
    late-season, 393
    tying methods and patterns for,
    357, 374
Thompson Creek, 277–279
Tionesta Creek, 309–310
Tipton Run, 229
Tobyhanna Creek, 57–59
Toms Creek, 49–52
Towanda Creek, 79–80
Trico, 41–43
Trout Streams of Pennsylvania, 50,
    193, 213, 320, 382
Trout Unlimited, 378–379
    Allegheny Mountain Chapter,
    307–309
    Arrowhead Chapter, Armstrong
    County, 315–318
    Brodhead Chapter, 49, 84, 378
    Caldwell Creek Chapter, 281, 286
    Codorus Chapter, 260–261
    Delco Manning Chapter, 90
    Falling Spring Chapter, 254–256
    Forbes Trail Chapter, 336
    Forks of the Delaware Chapter,
    103–104
    Fulton County Chapter, 270, 379
    God's Country Chapter, 179
    Jim Zwald Chapter, 183
    Ken Sink Chapter, 344
    Monocacy Chapter, 125
    Mountain Laurel Chapter,
    331–332
    Neshannock Chapter, 291
    Oil Creek Chapter, 286, 292
    Penns Creek Chapter, 262, 264
    Tulpehocken Chapter, 114
    Valley Forge Chapter, 90, 105,
    109–110
Tulpehocken Creek, 110–114
Tunungwant Creek

East Branch, 276–277
West Branch, 273–276
Two Lick Creek, South Branch,
  319–322
Tying methods and patterns
  downwings, 357–358
  duns, 358–359
  emerger, 355–357
  new, 354–355
  new materials, 361–362
  no hatches, 364
  nymphs, 360–361
  spinners, 358
  terrestrials, 357
  wet flies, 360

U
University of Pittsburgh at
  Bradford, 273–276

V
Valley Creek, 107–110
Vanscoyoc Run, 214

W
West Chester Fish and Game, 105
Western Pennsylvania Conservancy,
  339, 383

Western Pennsylvania Fly
  Fisherman's Association, 344
West Valley Creek, 104–105
Wet flies
  tying methods and patterns for,
    360
Wheeler and Dusenberry Lumber
  Company, 310
Whistle Pigs, 138–140
White Deer Creek, 214–216
White mayflies, 43–45
Willow Run, 244–245
Wills Creek, 348–350
Wings
  definition of, 361

Y
Yellow Beeches Creek, 249–252
Yellow Creek
  Bedford County, 344–347
  Indiana County, 318–319
York Dispatch, 256
Youghiogheny River (Yough),
  338–342
Young Womans Creek, 172–174
Youth
  Bob Davis Scholarship Fund, 307
  Pennsylvania Trout, 95